I0147951

POSTCOLONIAL GLOBAL JUSTICE

Postcolonial Global Justice

SHUK YING CHAN

PRINCETON UNIVERSITY PRESS
PRINCETON & OXFORD

MIX
Paper | Supporting responsible forestry

FSC
www.fsc.org
FSC® C008955

Copyright © 2025 by Princeton University Press

Princeton University Press is committed to the protection of copyright and the intellectual property our authors entrust to us. Copyright promotes the progress and integrity of knowledge created by humans. By engaging with an authorized copy of this work, you are supporting creators and the global exchange of ideas. As this work is protected by copyright, any reproduction or distribution of it in any form for any purpose requires permission; permission requests should be sent to permissions@press.princeton.edu. Ingestion of any PUP IP for any AI purposes is strictly prohibited.

Published by Princeton University Press
41 William Street, Princeton, New Jersey 08540
99 Banbury Road, Oxford OX2 6JX

press.princeton.edu

GPSR Authorized Representative: Easy Access System Europe - Mustamäe tee 50, 10621 Tallinn, Estonia, gpsr.requests@easproject.com

All Rights Reserved

ISBN 9780691260228
ISBN (e-book) 9780691261614

British Library Cataloging-in-Publication Data is available

Editorial: Rob Tempio and Chloe Coy
Production Editorial: Sara Lerner
Jacket Design: Karl Spurzem
Production: Erin Suydam
Publicity: William Pagdatoon
Copyeditor: Leah Caldwell

Jacket Credit: Suzanne Abell, *Globe Fragile*, ceramic, 2022. Photograph by Emma Boden.

This book has been composed in Arno

Printed in the United States of America

10 9 8 7 6 5 4 3 2 1

To my mother, Ka Cheng Long 龍家蒲, who fostered my sense of justice

No, we do not want to catch up with anyone. But what we want is to walk in the company of man, every man, night and day, for all times. It is not a question of stringing the caravan out where groups are spaced so far apart they cannot see the one in front, and men who no longer recognize each other, meet less and less and talk to each other less and less.

—FRANTZ FANON, *THE WRETCHED OF THE EARTH*

There are two ways to lose oneself: walled segregation in the particular or dilution in the "universal."

—AIMÉ CÉSAIRE, *LETTER TO MAURICE THOREZ*

CONTENTS

Acknowledgments   xi

Introduction: Decolonization Unfinished:
In Search of a Just Postcolonial World Order   1

1 Foundations of a Postcolonial Global Justice:
   The Egalitarian Face of Decolonization   29

2 Postcolonial Global Justice as Social Equality   52

3 Decolonizing the Global Economy: Nkrumah, International
   Investment, and the Problem of Neocolonialism   85

4 Decolonizing Cultural Globalization: Césaire and
   the Hierarchy of Creator and Consumer   121

5 Decolonizing Global Governance: Nehru and
   the Problem of Global Democracy   158

   Conclusion   194

Notes   201
References   237
Index   259

ACKNOWLEDGMENTS

SO MUCH of writing a book is pouring oneself onto the page and into the world. My gratitude to the people who helped sustain me through this journey—intellectually, physically, and emotionally—will always remain too deep to fully capture.

This book began its life as a doctoral dissertation at Princeton University, where I was immensely fortunate to benefit from a vibrant and supportive intellectual community. My thanks first go to my terrific dissertation advisors: Charles Beitz, Anna Stilz, Desmond Jagmohan, and Lea Ypi, each of whom played an indispensable role from the development of this project at Princeton through to its final completion in London. Chuck was enthusiastic about the project from its inchoate inception and, with characteristic intellectual humility, encouraged me to point out where his generation of global justice theorists might have been wrong. I am especially grateful for his tireless efforts to help me find my voice and develop my ideas throughout the years. Annie's serious and rigorous engagement with my work reliably helped sharpen its arguments. It is in no small part due to her insightful and incisive comments that the project takes the shape it has today. Des brought to the project his enviable wealth of knowledge in all areas of political theory as well as his philosophical creativity and originality, all of which encouraged me to embark on a project that crossed traditional methodological boundaries. His support throughout personal and professional challenges has been especially crucial in the more difficult moments. Lea generously contributed to the project as an external advisor, and our many stimulating exchanges across the development of this book always left me with a new perspective on the implications of the project on broader philosophical and political questions.

I am also grateful to Alan Patten, whose support and interest in my work also contributed greatly to the shape of the project. Our intellectual collaboration on a paper that grew out of chapter 4 of this book was an especially rewarding experience that helped sharpen my views on the topic.

For their abiding friendship in graduate school and beyond, I am especially thankful for Lucia Rafanelli, Jade Ngo, Erin Miller, Dongxian Jiang, Isi Litke, Amy Hondo, Ben Hoffman, Sonny Kim, Ophelia Vedder, Ian Walling, Parkriti

xi

Paul Chacha, Olivia Chu, Kevin Villegas Rosales, Daisy Unsihuay, Po-Ta Chen, Simon Quach, Hao Yin, Riley Skeen-Gaar, Anamika Singh, Chelsea Sandridge, Susannah Shoemaker, and Thomas Wilson.

This book benefited hugely from the eighteen months I spent as a postdoctoral research fellow at Nuffield College, Oxford University, where I was given valuable time, resources, and above all a wonderfully welcoming scholarly community, all of which helped me further expand on and refine the book. My mentors, Cécile Laborde and Desmond King, offered not only enthusiastic support but also incisive and constructive feedback on the project, and they helped broaden my sense of where the book could head. As a postdoctoral researcher I could not have hoped for a better intellectual cohort and will always be grateful for the friendship I found in Temi Ogunye, Jamie Draper, Samuel Bagg, Anthony Taylor, Jacob Barrett, Eniola Soyemi, Rufaida Al Hashmi, Maxime Lepoutre, Emily Katzenstein, and Sarah Bufkin.

While at Nuffield, I also benefited hugely from the critical and constructive feedback of my manuscript workshop participants: Adom Getachew, Inés Valdez, Catherine Lu, Jeanne Morefield, and Daniel Butt. Their close and insightful engagements at the early manuscript stage helped improve it immensely.

I was fortunate to complete this book in the supportive and collegial environment of the Department of Political Science at University College London. My political theory colleagues have been nothing but warm and welcoming: Richard Bellamy, Emily McTernan, Jeff Howard, Saladin Meckled-Garcia, Adam Swift, Fergus Green, John Filling, Helen Brown Coverdale, and John Wilesmith. Richard Bellamy read and commented on drafts of chapter 5; Lauge Poulsen read and commented on drafts of chapter 3. I am also grateful for the camaraderie and friendship of Aparna Ravi and Samer Anabtawi.

For helpful conversations and valuable comments that helped advance this project over the years, I also wish to thank: Anuja Bose, Susan Brison, Joseph Chan, Samuel Chan, Emily Dyson, Paulina Ochoa Espejo, Elizabeth Fraser, Johannes Kniess, Renée Jorgensen, David Miller, Zosia Stemplowska, Annette Zimmerman, Tom Parr, Kevin Pham, Sinja Graf, David Temin, Nazmul Sultan, Claudia Perez, Arturo Chang, Elaine Yim, Johan Trovik, Adam Kern, Theophile Deslauriers, Melissa Lane, Greg Conti, Stephen Macedo, Jan Werner-Muller, Zara Goldstone, Karuna Mantena, Jennie Ikuta, Loubna El Amine, Manjeet Ramgotra, Désirée Lim, Chong-Ming Lim, Maxmilian Klinger, Rogers Smith, Elizabeth Frazer, and Joy Wang. Stefan Eich commented on drafts at various stages of the book and greatly helped its development. Jim Wilson read the manuscript from start to finish and gave immensely helpful feedback.

I would also like to thank Rob Tempio and Chloe Coy, my editors at Princeton University Press, both of whom have enthusiastically supported the book and helped shepherd it through to its completion. I also thank Gloria Leung for assistance with the endnotes and bibliography, and Leah Caldwell for co-pyediting. Finally, the final manuscript benefited hugely from the reports of two reviewers for Princeton University Press and three reviewers for Oxford University Press.

Over the years, my thinking about global politics and imperialism has been profoundly shaped by various activist groups I have been part of. For this, I am grateful to my friends and comrades at Left 21 HK, Princeton Mutual Aid, and the Lausan Collective.

Certain individuals also played important roles in the writing of this book: Sin-Ting Yung and Sebastien Kwok have been constant sources of inspiration and camaraderie. Joseph Chan and Sharifa Chan never ceased to be encouraging, and Joseph helped me grow into a political theorist from my undergraduate years. Rohini Jalan helped me stay on course as a faithful writing companion in the last few years of this project. Antonia Fried supported me during the most difficult moments in graduate school and beyond.

The debt to my family is perhaps the most difficult to put into words. I am thankful for my wonderful sisters and brother-in-law—Seara Yoshida, Kate Wilson, Tom Wilson, and Pippa Wilson—whose friendship and interest in my well-being have meant so much. My parents-in-law, Kim Sutcliffe and Colin Wilson, have been a solid rock of support for us over the years as we navigated school and health challenges, moved countries and homes, and launched our careers. My stepfather, Xiaozhong Liu, took care of problems big and small and always warmed my heart with home-cooked feasts whenever I went home.

To my brother, Kelvin Man-Lok Chan, who has cheered me on at every step and helped take care of our family so that I have had the chance to chase my dreams, I am deeply grateful for the belief that you have always had in me and my endeavors.

To my husband and most cherished partner, Hugh Wilson, who has unfailingly buttressed the foundations of my confidence with love and good humor, I owe more than I can say.

To my mother, Ka Cheng Long, I owe everything. It is because of who she is that I have been able to become anything at all. I dedicate this book to her.

POSTCOLONIAL GLOBAL JUSTICE

Introduction

DECOLONIZATION UNFINISHED:
IN SEARCH OF A JUST POSTCOLONIAL
WORLD ORDER

DECOLONIZATION IS BACK. Not that it had ever left the agenda for those living under the long shadow of colonialism or for those resisting ongoing settler colonialism. But following the wave of postcolonial state founding that spread across the world in the middle decades of the twentieth century, many in the West saw decolonization as a largely accomplished feat. For some, it had been a triumph of moral enlightenment and the beginning of the era of self-determining nation-states. For others, it was good riddance—from now on, the colonies would be responsible for their own troubles.

This story of colonialism coming to an end has become harder and harder to maintain. Not only do we live in a world marked by myriad unrectified colonial legacies, but global politics continue to feature hierarchies that resemble colonial relations. Accusations of global political domination, economic exploitation, and cultural imperialism have persisted. Across the postcolonial world, politicians and activists are re-centering the language of resisting colonialism to protest ecological destruction, linguistic and cultural decline, exploitative foreign investment and corporate land grabs, and to demand reparations and the repatriation of cultural objects.[1] Moreover, following long-standing critiques of European and American imperialism, similar charges are now made against China as a rising global hegemon.[2] The sun may have set on the British empire but not on empire itself.

Yet if empire has remained a persistent feature of global politics, it is less clear what decolonization offers as a counterpoint for reimagining global relations. After all, decolonization has not resulted in the radical transformations that many who fought for it had envisioned. The promise of the independent, self-determining, postcolonial nation-state was largely dead upon arrival into a deeply unequal and globalizing world. Today, citizens across the postcolonial world fight on two fronts—continued encroachment from transnational corporations and foreign powers on the one hand, and authoritarian regimes that seize the mantle of decolonization in service of a militant nationalism on the other.[3] At the same time, the myth of national self-determination after decolonization has allowed former colonial and neocolonial powers to wash their hands of past and ongoing exploitation and domination and to instead blame poor postcolonial governance for persistent poverty, inequality, and conflict. Moreover, across former metropoles, decolonization is increasingly synonymous with efforts to promote "diversity" and "inclusion" in cultural representation, thus becoming rather detached from the radical institutional changes that first-wave anticolonial thinkers envisioned. In short, in a world of resurgent empire, postcolonial disillusionment and long-lasting colonial legacies, what decolonization as an emancipatory vision amounts to has become rather obscured. As Olúfẹ́mi Táíwò argues in his forceful critique of decolonial politics, "The term [decolonization] has become so slippery that it no longer offers a sure handle on what success would look like in a decolonized world."[4]

This book recovers anticolonial aspirations toward equality as a resource for thinking about overcoming the neocolonial present. Engaging with the writings of four influential anticolonial thinkers and activists—Aimé Césaire, Frantz Fanon, Kwame Nkrumah, and Jawaharlal Nehru—I argue that an important theme that runs through anticolonial critique is an ideal of relating to others as equals and the rejection of hierarchy. This reading of the anticolonial tradition departs from a long-standing tendency in academic and popular discourse that treats anticolonialism as just another form of ethnocultural nationalism and therefore reduces the ambitions of decolonization to building nation-states through which postcolonial peoples can exercise collective self-determination. Instead, as I argue this book, at its most ambitious, the anticolonial tradition gives us tools to contest political, economic, and cultural hierarchies to pave the way for an egalitarian cosmopolitan world, as well as reject forms of postcolonial nationalism more concerned with policing group boundaries than realizing the equal freedom of its members. Drawing from the *egalitarian face of decolonization,* as I call it, the first part of the book develops an account of postcolonial global justice as social equality in which individuals and the groups of which they are members enjoy equal standing. Although philosophers and political theorists have traditionally articulated social equality as an ideal within shared societies, I argue that taking up an anticolonial perspective of the world compels us to see both the relevance and importance of realizing such an ideal between members of different societies. Equipped with this philosophical account of postcolonial global justice, the rest of the book then investigates objectionable hierarchies in three areas of contentious global politics and shows how they are systematically interlinked:

international investment, cultural globalization, and global governance. In each area I show that, first, anticolonial critiques that have traditionally been understood in a nationalist frame actually have deeper roots in the value of equality, and that this enables us to detach decolonial projects from the institution of the nation-state when alternative political forms are better for resisting objectionable hierarchy. Second, persistent global hierarchies that directly and indirectly perpetuate the domination and exploitation of marginalized populations justify significant reforms to international law and policy at the expense of former colonial and presently neocolonial powers. Third, the cosmopolitan tendency to celebrate global integration and universal rights must be qualified by remedial rights that specifically and disproportionately empower subordinated groups, including (but not limited to) rights to property expropriation, cultural protectionism, and counterhegemonic power-building. The aim is to develop an account of global justice that takes seriously the legacies of European colonialism and the urgency of resisting neocolonialism in global politics—in short, an account of *postcolonial* global justice.

Colonialism, Decolonization, and Global Justice

Investigating new and enduring forms of colonialism in global politics is not new. From different disciplinary angles, scholars have written prolifically on these questions. As I will discuss shortly, this book draws on their insights even as my aim of developing normative principles is one not usually shared by these critical traditions.

Among philosophers interested in global justice and international political theory, however, the question of empire and persistent global hierarchy has until recently received little attention.[5] Broadly, global justice thinking consists of trying to work out what members of different territorial groups (nations, states, societies) owe to each other as a matter of justice—how they should interact in war, what are fair terms of trade, what gives a group a claim over a piece of territory, when it might be permissible to exclude nonmembers, and so on. Global justice thinking in this broad sense has a long history and can be traced within different cultural traditions.[6] But philosophical interest in global justice largely began from a debate among Anglo-American liberals regarding whether principles of egalitarian social justice as articulated by John Rawls in the 1970s are applicable at the global level. While some argued that the same institutional or human features that demand domestic egalitarianism can also be found at the global level—such as political and economic structures that determine the distribution of advantage and disadvantage, or the mere fact of sentience—others have insisted that such talk was overblown or had misunderstood the nature of social justice.[7] This debate, taking place in the era of formal decolonization, was not merely intellectual: its primary initiator Charles Beitz was originally partly prompted by demands from postcolonial countries to argue for egalitarian reform of the international order.[8] Yet, like its domestic counterpart on social justice, the philosophical debate over global distributive justice quickly took on an ahistorical and abstract turn as competing camps grappled over the scope of democratic inclusion, the grounds for egalitarian redistribution, and the moral basis of national borders.[9]

Over time, each side ran into tricky problems now familiar to those writing about global justice. On the one side, those who argue that the demands of egalitarian justice stop at, or at least are significantly modified by, national borders risk neglecting the real-world hierarchies of domination and exploitation that continue to structure international interactions in a "postcolonial" world. John Rawls, perhaps the most prominent statist, famously attributed societies' level of wealth as largely the result of the self-determination of nations, and in particular due to "the political culture, the political virtues and civic society of the country, its members' probity and industriousness, their capacity for innovation, and much else."[10] Even more moderate statists such as David Miller who acknowledge the existence of unfair global economic arrangements tend to theorize global justice from the assumption that people belong to independent national communities.[11] This leads him to argue that a nation's culture and self-determining choices—such as models of economic development—can explain, to a significant extent, why some countries have been able to lift their citizens out of poverty while others continue to suffer.[12] The normative upshot of these statist imaginaries of the world tends to be minimalist accounts of global justice that emphasize duties of humanitarian assistance over the need for significant global redistribution, even when Western affluent states' responsibility for past injustices is sometimes acknowledged.[13] Such accounts, however, are difficult to maintain when we fully appreciate the many constraints on postcolonial countries cast by the long shadow of colonialism.

On the other side, cosmopolitans have been criticized as unwitting handmaidens of neocolonialism and global capitalism. In advancing the argument that state borders are morally arbitrary from the point of view of egalitarian justice, critics argue that cosmopolitans give too little weight to the importance of collective self-determination. Instead, cosmopolitans end up supporting global institutions that have undermined oppressed and marginalized groups' capacity to resist foreign and corporate encroachment.[14] The human rights regime, for example, and the practice of humanitarian intervention deployed to enforce such rights, have been widely criticized for enabling Western imperialist ambitions and facilitating the rise of corporate rights under international law.[15] Moreover, cosmopolitans have also been criticized for trying to extend parochial Western values to the rest of the world.[16]

Finally, both statists and cosmopolitans have focused almost exclusively on (relatively affluent) citizens in Western countries as the moral agents to whom duties of global justice are ascribed. While it is undoubtedly important to ask what the advantaged owe to the disadvantaged, reducing the question of global justice to this unidirectional relationship risks portraying the developing world as passive recipients of justice, and it neglects projects of global justice advanced by oppressed agents throughout history.[17]

The silence on race and empire in much of early global justice inquiries has been diagnosed from different angles. Broadly, most early theories of global justice were primarily developed out of a liberal framework. Yet the relationship between liberalism and imperialism is historically fraught, to say the least. As Duncan Bell notes, scholars disagree on whether the relationship is rejectionist, where imperialism is antithetical to liberalism; necessary, where imperialism is a central feature of liberal political thought; or contingent, where imperialism is not inherent to liberal commitments, but the latter have nonetheless been historically deployed to justify the former.[18] While this book is also premised on the idea that liberalism—a "complex ideology whose exemplars share family resemblances rather than any strict doctrine," as Jennifer Pitts puts it—need not inevitably end up supporting imperialist ambitions, my approach to theorizing global justice aims to be alert to and resist the tendencies of liberal political philosophy to idealize and abstract away racial oppression.[19] I return to these points in the next section.

Aside from a close association with liberalism, the general absence of race and empire in global justice theory has also been attributed to more specific factors. For example, Katrina Forrester argues that the widespread rejection of libertarianism by liberal egalitarianism in the 1960s and '70s also led the latter to turn away from questions of corrective justice, including attending to the implications of slavery and empire for contemporary distributive justice. Charles Mills points to the whiteness of analytic political philosophy as one reason for the widespread neglect of race and racism as philosophically important issues.[20] Finally, as I will discuss later, it seems likely that the long-standing Western academic reception of anticolonialism—perhaps the most significant challenge to global injustice in modern history—also played a role in occluding resources contained within anticolonial political thought for pushing theorists of global justice to take race and empire seriously.[21]

The past two decades have seen the emergence of "third wave global justice."[22] Broadly, third wave global justice theory shares several features: first, these theories tend to center the problem of domination in global politics and therefore tend to combine insights from statists and cosmopolitans. Laura Valentini, for example, argues that once we appreciate the coercive relationships that structure the global order, the value of collective self-determination *grounds* demanding principles for global distributive justice.[23] Lea Ypi argues that political associations such as the state are not always hindrances to cosmopolitan justice (and can be crucial for advancing it), and that the more minimal duties to alleviate global poverty endorsed by statists can ground cosmopolitan principles.[24] Neorepublicans such as Cécile Laborde and Miriam Ronzoni have argued that a just global order is one in which states enjoy freedom from domination.[25]

Relatedly, third wave global justice theorists have increasingly moved from abstract theorizing to home in on specific parts of the global order and the normative questions raised in areas such as migration, finance, trade, climate change, global governance, sweatshop labor, and so on.[26] This "applied turn" in global justice theory is undoubtedly an important and refreshing shift in a literature criticized for having little of relevance to say to people actually living under global injustice. By attending to specific problems as they arise in global interactions, such as domination in global finance, unfair trade deals that capital-poor countries have had to accept, or the failure of affluent states to give migrants what they are due, third wave global justice theorists have yielded important action-guiding insights for policymakers and ordinary citizens in a non-ideal world. Moreover, the concomitant rise of "practice-dependent" theorizing has enabled normative theorists to make progress on specific issues without first having to construct a comprehensive theory of global justice.[27]

Yet specificity also comes at a cost. The compartmentalized nature of third wave global justice theory has meant that we lack a critical diagnosis of the global order as a whole and therefore an understanding of how seemingly disparate instances of global injustice relate to and mutually reinforce one another. To name a few examples: How might a global racial hierarchy that places less value on the lives of nonwhite populations reinforce exploitation in supply chains? If unfair trade and investment deals exist in part because Western countries have dominated international lawmaking since the colonial era, how might these power asymmetries be addressed so that a fairer global economy or a "new global deal"[28] has a chance to come about?

In other words, with a few exceptions, the contributors to the philosophical literature on global justice have yet to grapple with the *neocolonial* nature of the global order and, more specifically, the racialized nature of a neocolonial global order.[29] Such is the broad background against which specific issues like trade and climate injustice arise. How should we characterize this background? Charles Mills calls it global white supremacy, by which he refers to "the racialised distributions of economic, political and cultural power that we have today" as a result of "the European domination of the planet for the past several hundred years."[30] Once we see the world this way, Mills argues, we appreciate that Black and Third World political thought are indispensable sources for mapping the contours of global power, as well as the need to go beyond color-blind diagnoses of global domination and inequality. Building on Mills, Olúfẹ́mi O. Táíwò describes our present global order as a *global racial empire*.[31] He argues that this global order, forged in the era of colonialism and transatlantic slavery, is one we still live with today. Global racial empire places white people at the top, but it can also capture a shifting global political landscape where predominantly nonwhite countries like China are becoming increasingly powerful and problematic in their dealings in Southeast Asia and Africa.[32] From an international law perspective, TWAIL (Third World Approaches to International Law) scholar B. S. Chimni argues that the existing network of international institutions constitute a "global imperial state" whose function is "to realize the interests of transnational capital and powerful states in the international system to the disadvantage of third world states and peoples."[33] This conception captures the overlapping importance of race and class in reinforcing the subjection of disadvantaged populations and is able to make sense of the existence of postcolonial capitalist elites. Central to all three descriptions is the idea that the world is constituted by a set of mutually reinforcing racialized hierarchies that perpetuate the subjugation of some populations for the benefit of others. This is the international system I call neocolonial: where political domination is backed by racial hierarchy to facilitate economic exploitation.

Grappling with neocolonialism opens important avenues of investigation for theorists of global justice. First, it enables us to analyze the systematicity of global injustice: identifying where global problems overlap and how they reinforce each other. Like colonialism, which developed into a full-blown international system, neocolonialism is constituted by a set of interlocking power relations in global governance, economic exchange, and cultural and knowledge production. As a result of the systematic nature of neocolonialism, the harms faced by racialized and marginalized postcolonial groups are compounded. Therefore, solutions to global injustice also need to empower them along multiple dimensions. In other words, zooming out to a critical diagnosis of the world order as neocolonial encourages us to think of global justice as a program—indeed, as worldmaking[34]—where different aspects of an oppressive system need to be accounted for and resisted simultaneously. Without a systematic diagnosis of global injustice, practice-dependent or area-specific theorizing risks generating principles of justice that take for granted deeper background inequalities.[35] Adopting this comprehensive approach, however, need not mean sacrificing concrete problem-based normative theorizing. As I show throughout the book, we can grapple with specific areas of global politics while also appreciating how a common problem, that of racialized hierarchy, ties them together.

Relatedly, it pushes us to go beyond attending to the material, structural basis of global injustice and engage with what Glen Coulthard, drawing from Fanon, has called the "subjective, psycho-affective" basis of colonial oppression, by which he refers to the human attitudes and dispositions cultivated to reproduce colonial relations.[36] These attitudes and dispositions are cultivated in both colonial subjects and colonizers. For the former, an internalized sense of what Aimé Césaire calls an "inferiority complex"[37] gradually takes hold; for the latter, a distorted set of beliefs regarding the world and racialized others, or what Mills calls white ignorance—"a pervasively deforming outlook"[38] causally linked to white people's situation within a racialized social system— becomes entrenched. These dispositions are produced by and help prop up oppressive political and economic structures. They are also fostered in a global culture dominated by Western epistemic production and appropriation. Hence anticolonial thinkers often argue that resisting colonialism is not only a matter of resisting political and economic structures, but also, as Césaire puts it, a matter of soul-making through cultural production, or, as Fanon similarly argues, the making of a new human through practices that restore self-respect.[39] Yet, like early work in global justice, recent work has also largely been silent on issues of race and racialization, self-respect, and unequal status. Nor have third wave theorists attended to inequality and domination in global cultural and knowledge circulation. And yet, unequal power in global cultural and knowledge production may itself be a site of global injustice as well as contain important implications for agents' abilities to make progress in other areas of global justice.

Third, if the denial of equal agency (as I will argue) was central to colonial oppression, tackling the neocolonial nature of global injustice cautions us to center the agency of the subjugated in theorizing solutions and transitions to global justice. With a few recent exceptions, however, neither early nor third wave global justice theory has said much on the roles of the dominated or subjugated in resisting global injustice and bringing about global justice and what these groups might be entitled to do for these ends.[40] Throughout the book, I defend institutional changes and extrainstitutional practices whose aims are to resist neocolonial investment, cultural imperialism, and global political domination.

This book develops an account of global justice that foregrounds questions of empire, race, and hierarchy in a neocolonial global order. In doing so, we will draw on insights from disciplines beyond political theory. Critical scholars of international relations and international law, for example, have shown how legal principles that were developed and evolved in European colonial encounters serve the interests of colonizing powers, and how contemporary international law has inherited features that continue to constrain and undermine postcolonial sovereignty. The contributions of TWAIL scholars have been particularly valuable in shedding light on how international practices and norms such as the human rights regime, international development, the idea of good governance, and so on have been used by corporations and hegemonic states to erode the rights of individuals and their capital-poor states.[41] Second, work in postcolonial studies has historically taken the lead in interrogating the legacies of colonialism in cultural and social discourse, literary work, and knowledge production.[42] Following thinkers such as Fanon, Foucault, and Gramsci, postcolonial theorists such as Edward Said have exposed and deconstructed the workings of power in shaping dominant frames of references and perceptions of the foreign "other," and questioned how subaltern agency might be uneasily recovered or forever erased.[43] Finally and more recently, renewed interest in the concept of racial capitalism has led to an outpour of scholarship in sociology, history, and critical theory on the nexus between racialization and capital accumulation. Building on the work of Cedric Robinson, Eric Williams, and Walter Rodney, these scholars argue that the historical development and contemporary operation of global capitalism cannot be understood without considering the role of race and racialization in creating nonwhite bodies for ownership, exploitation, disposal, and removal.[44]

This book learns from these critical traditions where they are relevant for diagnosing our neocolonial present, but our focus is ultimately different. In their emphasis on critique, these traditions do not usually take developing a normative account of postcolonial justice as their primary or explicit aim. This book is an effort to do just that. Our central question is: What values ought to animate a just postcolonial world order? I draw on anticolonial thought to develop *one* answer to this question: the elimination of global hierarchy and the realization of global social equality.

In developing this view, the book brings together two literatures that have largely remained separate: anticolonial political thought and contemporary global justice theory. While recent work by historians and political theorists such as Frederick Cooper, Gary Wilder, Adom Getachew, and others has begun to recover anticolonial internationalist and federative projects that have important normative implications for thinking about global justice, these works do not develop a full-blown account of global justice for thinking about contemporary global politics.[45] In contrast, I employ what I call historically inflected normative theorizing, which treats specific historical actors as interlocutors in developing normative principles for the present.[46] Bridging normative and critical traditions is not without complications, as I discuss in more detail in the next section. And yet the potential payoffs are significant. Anticolonial thinkers struggled against one of the greatest forms of global injustice in modern history, and their situated perspectives are indispensable for understanding the different interlocking dimensions of global injustice as well as what resistance might look like. What's more, anticolonial thinkers were not only engaged in situated critique, but also offered visions of a just postcolonial world that lies beneath the critique. Focusing exclusively on recovering critique risks missing subaltern resources to construct alternative norms of justice to those dominant in the neocolonial present.

By bringing together the anticolonial political tradition with normative analysis, this book takes up recent calls for an "insurgent" or a "postcolonial" cosmopolitanism as a fresh way of theorizing global justice.[47] As Catherine Lu, one of the few global justice theorists who has grappled directly with the colonial origins of the modern international order in their work, states, "The project of constructing a just global order is inseparable from the project of decolonizing contemporary international order."[48] My aim is to approach long-standing questions in global justice by critically engaging with the perspectives of those who theorized and resisted one of the most significant forms of global injustice in modern history—in other words, to take up a postcolonial perspective on global justice. Rather than signifying the end of colonialism, as Stuart Hall puts it, "*postcolonial* means after the epoch when imperial power was exercised by direct colonization, but it also means an era when everything still takes place in the slipstream of colonialism and hence bears the inscription of the disturbances that colonization set in motion."[49] To think about questions of global justice without keeping these disturbances in view is therefore to ignore the very epoch in which we live.

Global Justice from a Postcolonial Perspective

Once we start seeing global justice as a project in decolonization, we begin to see that the issue of neocolonial hierarchy touches upon many, if not all, aspects of global social life, and dismantling them or preventing their formation is not at all straightforward. One reason for this is that sustained interactions between unevenly situated agents are always at risk of becoming entrenched hierarchies of domination and exploitation, a risk made even more heightened at the global level due to the lack of a world state. Another reason is that history casts a long shadow.[50] Colonial legacies such as structural poverty, economic dependency, global ideologies of white supremacy, and so on remain largely unaddressed, and it is not difficult to see how these intertwine with many topics of concern in global politics.

Centering these issues in theorizing global politics means approaching questions of global justice from a postcolonial perspective. Here, I follow Leela Gandhi's definition of postcolonialism as "a theoretical resistance to the mystifying amnesia of the colonial aftermath."[51] As a mode of public intellectual inquiry, postcolonialism is committed to the "task of revisiting, remembering and, crucially, interrogating the colonial past."[52] This interrogation is not only an exercise in understanding how the colonizer maintained—and maintains—his power (although that is important), but also a study into how the colonized opened up spaces of resistance. In Gyan Prakash's words, postcolonialism needs also "to fully recognize another history of agency and knowledge alive in the dead weight of the colonial past."[53] Understood this way, a postcolonial perspective signifies both a refusal to forget the imperial histories that made the world today, and an insistence on grappling with the hierarchies that remain by drawing from an archive developed by the oppressed. Specifically, in developing an account of global justice, taking up a postcolonial perspective entails at least two methodological commitments. First, *to take a fully decolonized world as a normative aspiration*. This invites the further question of what a decolonized world is, and this book attempts to provide *part* of an answer by investigating what values ought to inform global relations. Without getting into that here, the thought is that a postcolonial perspective focuses on dismantling the kinds of unjust structures and relations that constituted colonialism. It necessitates, therefore, charting a different path from the "historical amnesia" that has underpinned much of Anglo-American analytic global justice theory.[54] In thinking about what global justice demands, someone committed to a postcolonial perspective would take this to be a central aim of her view.

Second, in both critical diagnosis and normative prescription, *a postcolonial perspective is informed by the thinking of those who have lived through and struggled against colonial oppression*. Instead of a view from nowhere, a postcolonial perspective on global justice is derived from situated knowledge. There are at least two reasons why this is important. First, as feminist standpoint epistemologists have argued, members of oppressed groups plausibly acquire valuable insight into situations of oppression and marginalization through their lived experience, and their reflections on the causes of and solutions to injustice ought to be accorded some special weight.[55] Second, an important part of decolonization *is* to recover and recenter the agency of the colonized and to deprovincialize marginalized perspectives while provincializing dominant ones. By engaging seriously with the former's political thought, the moral imperative to decolonize is built into the exercise of theorizing global justice.

However, insofar as the resulting normative view primarily aims to be action-guiding, committing to a postcolonial perspective cannot mean simply taking onboard everything that is recovered from anticolonial actors. These texts were written in a different context and for a different time, and it would be a mistake to think they can be straightforwardly transposed to the present. More importantly, anyone thinking about norms of justice has a responsibility to defend views that are valuable and attractive, and not only because great historical figures held them. While it is important to accord special weight to the views of those writing from situations of oppression, this does not mean uncritical acceptance. Insisting on uncritical acceptance would not signify respect for these thinkers as equal interlocuters with whom one can reasonably disagree, and instead treats them as objects beyond the pale of critique, and at worst amounts to a kind of patronization or fetishization. Equally problematic is the other end of the extreme, where the theorist imposes and channels her own preconceived normative commitments through the voices of these thinkers, without allowing their views to challenge and alter hers, and failing to take seriously where they may genuinely part company.

Hence this exercise in historically inflected normative theorizing is far from straightforward and, in addition to the two pitfalls above, there is at least one more challenge that needs to be grappled with: insofar as the selected thinkers are not primarily philosophers, but activists, politicians, and revolutionaries, recovering their normative commitments requires paying attention to the different registers in which they wrote and the different audiences they had in mind.

In the book, I attempt to develop a view of global justice for the present by engaging with a set of anticolonial thinkers who struggled against colonialism at the height of the decolonization movements of the twentieth century. My hope is to avoid the pitfalls above by thinking of the exercise as a dialectic between reconstruction and normative query. Through close readings of the key writings of these thinkers, I extract what I judge to be the most morally defensible and appealing set of anticolonial commitments, and I supplement these with my own arguments to form a single, distinct view of global justice. The resulting view, I hope, is recognizably guided by the core values and aspirations of these thinkers, but at the same time cannot be simply ascribed to any one thinker as a view that they actually held.

This attempt to excavate and build a normative theory from anticolonial thought raises some important questions. Specifically, there are at least three points of apparent methodological tensions between the anticolonial tradition and the normative analytic tradition. Roughly, we might call these (1) moral theory vs. political critique; (2) individualism vs. collectivism; and (3) universalism vs. particularism. Insofar as particular methods can lead to different focuses, result in blind spots, bring on certain assumptions, and so on, methodological tensions can have substantive implications. Anyone attempting to excavate normative theory from critical thought will, therefore, need to grapple with them. While I do not pretend to fully resolve all the tensions here, the following discussion attends to each in an effort to persuade skeptics that a project bridging anticolonial thought with normative theory offers a valuable approach to political theory and need not be a nonstarter.

Moral Theory vs. Political Critique?

Much of normative theory uses the language and reference points drawn from moral philosophy. For example, what justice demands is often couched in the language of claim-rights and duties, and critiques of injustice are commonly expressed in terms such as moral wrongness. This can seem deeply at odds with the anticolonial archive, the majority of which consists not of academic papers debating principles of morality, but manifestos, autobiographies, pamphlets, speeches, and critiques aimed at instigating political change. The worry here is not primarily of genre, however, as the latter can, with careful interpretive effort, be fruitfully read as political philosophy. Rather, the worry is that reconstructing the political philosophy of anticolonial activists with the normative analytic method reduces the former's political projects to moral suasion.

To assuage this worry, we should first avoid assuming that anticolonial thinkers were not engaging in moral discourse (i.e., making moral judgments and moral claims) simply because they were also political actors.[56] In their painstaking efforts to detail the injustices and human misery wrought by colonial rule, thinker-activists could not take for granted their various audiences' (including fellow colonial subjects) rejection of colonialism. Instead, like any other political movement responding to moments of crises, anticolonial thinkers were engaged in live debates with their contemporaries of different stripes on what a meaningful alternative to the status quo should amount to. What *was* wrong with the colonial situation? And could it be overcome with reformist solutions? Or did the problem of colonialism require, indeed demand, "shatter[ing] the colonial structures in definitive fashion," as Césaire put it?[57] If so, what would that entail as a matter of concrete policy and practice? Did it mean the redistribution of land and capital? Did it mean democratizing the colony? And for whom would the projects and imperative of decolonization be? In other words, who are the postcolonial demos, the India that Nehru set out to "discover"?[58] Why ought the boundaries of the postcolonial collective self-determination be drawn in this particular way? And so on.

Beneath each thinkers' responses to these questions lie their understandings of what was objectionable about colonialism as a mode of political governance and set of social-economic arrangements, and, correspondingly, what demands ought to be pressed against their oppressors *and* each other long after the colonizers had gone. These are *moral* claims insofar as they invoke ideas of right and wrong, fairness and unfairness, and not merely considerations of who has power and how to most effectively get it. To be sure, it is not always straightforward to read these moral arguments from an anticolonial text. That, indeed, is the interpretive challenge of drawing from a critical tradition to construct normative theory, a challenge taken up in this book. But like any other challenges in textual interpretation, our focus should be on discerning how differences in interpretation result in substantively different normative theories rather than on denying the possibility of excavating from critical texts any normative theory altogether.

What is clear, however, is that discerning the moral claims is only the first step; the second is to attend to the political practices needed to bring about change. This brings us to a second point: constructing normative theory need not and ought not imply that political change happens through getting moral principles right. For example, as we criticize the contemporary investment regime as an instance of racialized exploitation and explore what an investment regime consistent with the aims of decolonization might look like, we should also consider the obvious fact that none of these changes will happen without political contestation. Thus, unlike earlier waves of global justice theory, questions of political agency and how to build it are just as important to a theory of postcolonial global justice that emerges from sustained engagement with anticolonial political thought.

Individualism vs. Collectivism

Normative theory often relies on an individualist framework that can come into tension with the group-based nature of colonial oppression and the collective rights that are arguably needed for resisting it. In *Not Enough*, Samuel Moyn criticizes early theorists of global justice such as Peter Singer, Onora O'Neill, Charles Beitz, and Henry Shue for their "ethical individualism." The focus on individuals as the moral agents to whom global justice (whatever its content) is owed, Moyn argues, betrayed the "collectivist claims of third-world nationalism" encapsulated in decolonial projects such as the New International Economic Order. He traces this as at least one of the reasons why global justice theory became deradicalized. The deeper worry here is that bridging anticolonial thought with normative theory will result in an objectionable form of deradicalization when the focus becomes shifted to individuals as the units of moral and political analysis.

To better understand and grapple with this concern, let us zoom in on the different forms of individualism at play here. Following Charles Mills, we can draw a distinction between normative individualism and individualist ontology.[59] Add to this a third kind of individualism: what we might call political individualism. Normative individualism is the idea that *individuals*, and not social collectives, are the locus of value. In other words, social collectives do not have independent moral value over and above individuals. Their value derives from whatever value they might have for individuals. On the other hand, individualist ontology (or ontological individualism) denies that individuals are largely socially molded, constrained, and positioned, and instead understands individuals as decontextualized, rational beings whose characters, beliefs, and behavior are independent of the social reality that shapes them. Finally, political individualism emphasizes individual rights and individual empowerment over group rights and group empowerment.

The first observation from this disaggregation is that endorsing normative individualism need not entail also endorsing ontological and political individualism. We can hold that membership in social collectives such as nations or racial groups is an important constitutive feature of individual subjectivities (hence denying ontological individualism), without also thinking that the former have independent moral value beyond their value for individuals such that when the interests of the two come into apparent conflict, the group ought to take precedent over the individual.[60] Likewise, we can hold that political empowerment for individuals (say, in the form of human rights, for example) is an inadequate response to the problem of a neocolonial world order, and that collective empowerment of some form is instead essential for contesting neocolonial exploitation, cultural imperialism, and global political disenfranchisement. Yet that need not commit us to the further thought that national sovereignty has independent moral significance even when it is deployed against the very individuals in whose name it is exercised.[61]

Whether normative individualism is in tension with specific anticolonial thinkers' views will depend on how we interpret those views. To take an example where these might collide, consider Léopold Senghor's and Aimé Césaire's arguments for universal suffrage based not on "one person, one vote," but rather, as Kevin Duong put it, the "corporate, collective voice that centuries of colonialism had repressed: the voice of Black folk."[62] At times, some of these arguments—and certainly Senghor more so than Césaire—seem to be motivated by the claim that there is an African collective subject with a "voice" whose moral significance is independent of the individuals who make up that subject. This is certainly in tension with normative individualism. At other times, however, their resistance against merely enfranchising individuals *within French imperial institutions* can be seen as a rejection of *political* individualism. Here, the worry is that political rights for individual African colonial subjects would mean drowning out their voice vis-à-vis other Europeans and other non-European subjects.[63] This reading of the demand for collective enfranchisement is perfectly compatible with the idea that the freedom and well-being of individual persons are ultimately what matter, even if the route to securing these is inevitably collective.

Parsing out the three kinds of individualism enables us to bring back the importance of collectives into theorizing global politics, while *also* taking seriously the problem of ruling elites seizing the mantle of anticolonialism to dominate their own citizens. Accordingly, the account of postcolonial global justice defended in this book endorses normative individualism. Specifically, I argue that nations do not have independent moral standing over and above individuals—that the moral value of the nation is dependent on its potential to contribute to individuals' emancipation, which is itself a historically contingent fact that can change in different contexts. As we shall see in chapter 1, in the historical struggle against colonialism, the nation *was* instrumentally important, and yet, as the later chapters seek to demonstrate, we can no longer rely exclusively—or even primarily—on the nation-state to further the project of decolonization today. This understanding of the value of nations and nationalism is compatible with and indeed inspired by our four anticolonial thinkers' qualified endorsements of nationalism, their openness to internationalism, their critiques of national elites who work within and for colonial and neocolonial regimes, and finally, their incessant warnings that rule by co-nationals ought not be conflated with full and genuine decolonization.

However, nothing in the account developed in this book implies or necessitates ontological and political individualism; on the contrary, the account explicitly rejects both. Adopting a relational or social understanding of equality, for example, is important precisely because *relations*, i.e., the social, matter in constituting the individual's freedom and subjectivity. This insight echoes Fanon's analysis of the colonial situation and the ways in which the colonizer creates the colonized, which I will draw on in chapter 2 to develop an account of relational or social equality. Moreover, chapters 3–5 each defend a different kind of group-based empowerment for overcoming neocolonial exploitation, cultural imperialism, and global disenfranchisement. Each of these strategies is drawn from a different thinker's insights: Nkrumah's argument for political unity against "the last stage of imperialism"; Césaire's diagnosis of cultural imperialism as creating a hierarchy of agency between racialized collectives; and finally, Nehru's early attempts at alliance-building between social movements across the world.

Universalism vs. Particularism

Normative theorists often make moral claims whose scope is implicitly understood as universal. At its crudest, critics complain, normative theory gives off the impression that its goal is to develop an ideal of justice from abstract reasoning and apply it across time and space with little or insufficient regard for either the specific situation from which said ideal emerged or the particularities of the contexts to which it is applied. This invites a worry about universalism that can be further broken down into two versions. In one version of the worry, call it the historicity problem, normative theory ignores histories of how the world got to where it is and thus often arrives at universal ideals of undifferentiated justice that are premature at best and concealing oppression at worst.[64] As Sundhya Pahuja argues in her critique of normative global justice theory, "Although [the] claim to universality is asserted as a virtue which carries the promise of inclusion and universal access to moral rights, when combined with power, it has the effect of dominating those who are included within it."[65] In a second version, call it the totalizing problem, normative theory's claim to universalism is also a claim to epistemic authority over others: that a theory of justice developed in dominant societies can be applied straightforwardly to other contexts. As Jeanne Morefield argues, in assuming that abstract moral principles are "universally germane and entirely modular" for the rest of the world, normative theory risks neglecting or dismissing "alternative ethical responses" to injustice, responses that have been developed from subjects of past and ongoing colonialism themselves.[66]

We should be careful to avoid either mistake as we develop an account of postcolonial global justice. Ultimately, all ideas are particular in the sense that they come from somewhere with certain motivations, for certain people, performing certain social and political functions. We should indeed be suspicious of normative theory that tries to disguise this by portraying itself as somehow above the social and political fray. And yet we should also avoid making the opposite assumption: that responses to injustice developed by oppressed actors in particular contexts cannot also have universal content. It bears remembering that these actors often see their struggle against tyranny as not only for their immediate group but for "the whole world."[67] To borrow from Césaire, in developing a different kind of normative theory that draws from the resources of the oppressed, the trick is to neither get trapped by "walled segregation in the particular" or end up in "dilution in the 'universal.'"[68]

The anticolonial thinkers considered in this book provide resources for developing such an account. While they seldom explicitly laid out a systematic normative vision for what a decolonized world looks like, I contend that we can find glimpses of that world in their critiques of colonial domination, exploitation, and racial hierarchy: that is, a world in which relations between societies and between groups are structured to enable freedom, nonalienation, and robust self-respect. Put together, these glimpses of equality allow us to generate an account of postcolonial global justice that has critical implications for existing global political, economic, and cultural relations and that points to certain directions of necessary change and action that remain sensitive to history, context, and circumstances of power. In this sense, postcolonial global justice as social equality aims to be what Serene Khader calls a non-ideal universalism—a universalism whose content is defined by opposition to injustice (in this case, objectionable hierarchies) in a non-ideal world, rather than a universalism that idealizes away the histories and complexities of unequal power in making claim on the rest of the world.[69] Following Gary Wilder, anticolonial thinkers can also make normative claims that, although perhaps short of universal, are applicable beyond their own immediate situation.[70] As Wilder puts it, "What is the analytic and political cost of assigning to Europe such categories or experience as self-determination, emancipation, equality, justice, and freedom, let alone abstraction, humanity, or universality? Why confirm the story that Europe has long told about itself?"[71] Moral and ethical claims are not the exclusive province of Europe, and it is this assumption that underlies our exercise.

The methodology used in this book can therefore be understood as an attempt to pursue what Adom Getachew calls another kind of universalism, which starts from specific problems that political actors face and reconstructs the political ideas that come out of their responses to those problems.[72] To take an example, in chapter 3 we will start from the specific problem of economic dependence that postcolonial societies faced upon independence, and then turn to how Nkrumah responded to this problem both in terms of critical diagnosis and also in terms of the normative values that underpin his diagnosis. From there, we bring this to bear on the contemporary investment regime, which is a problem not only for the postcolonial Global South but also a problem for citizens everywhere who want to pursue domestic social equality but are prevented from doing so by corporate empowerments. In this sense, Nkrumah offers us an account of neocolonial exploitation that is universal but also particular.

Still, avoiding the trap of a totalizing universalism also means acknowledging and having in one's view important qualifications to the resulting account of justice. To illustrate this point, this book focuses on anticolonial thought produced in former overseas colonies, or, to employ a common distinction, extraction colonies as opposed to settler colonies.[73] Our account of global justice will primarily focus on the international order that structures interactions between groups that are no longer subjects of the same state. To be sure, we should not draw too strong a distinction between postcolonial global justice for citizens of postcolonial states and subjects of ongoing settler colonialism, if only because Indigenous peoples' struggles also exist in the postcolonial Global South, and their campaigns often aim to push postcolonial governments along the unfinished path of decolonization. Moreover, Indigenous peoples have campaigned to reform an international order that only recognizes states and corporations as legal entities.[74] As such, there are overlapping concerns between Third World anticolonial thought and Indigenous political thought that are worth noting. First, both traditions complicate the distinction between the global and domestic, or the external and the internal, which global justice theory has tended to rely on. As Robert Nichols argues, the struggles of Indigenous peoples in countries like the United States show that focusing only on justice between North and South countries while treating countries as internally homogenous units is deeply inadequate.[75] On the other hand, as we will see, Third World anticolonial thinkers also saw a close connection between global and domestic justice, in many cases arguing that one cannot fully decolonize the colony without also decolonizing the international order as the latter places significant constraints on domestic transformative projects. In this sense, Indigenous and Third World anticolonial thought both challenge the distinction of the global versus the domestic.

Second, and relatedly, both traditions prompt global justice theory to question the place of the nation-state in a just postcolonial world order. As Catherine Lu argues, Indigenous peoples' struggles in cross-border situations like the US-Canada border demonstrate that a decolonial cosmopolitanism ought not construe territorial states as the exclusive or even primary agents of global justice, as the institution of the nation-state is often the very object of anticolonial struggle.[76] In Lu's words, "Ultimately, the quest for global justice may entail truly revolutionary structural transformations of world order that involve pluralizing the agents that can have political standing in domestic, international, and transnational institutions and structures."[77] As I hope to show in the following chapters, Third World anticolonial thinkers were also less committed to the institution of the nation-state than we commonly think. Grounded in the need to overcome objectionable hierarchy as it is, my egalitarian account of postcolonial global justice empowers nonstate collectives and endorses the devolution of sovereignty in ways that promote social equality.

Finally, there are shared strategies of resistance that Indigenous peoples and postcolonial societies have adopted, such as asserting collective rights over land and natural resources and demanding the equal freedom to develop and sustain one's culture.[78] In defending a right to popular appropriation or a right to cultural protectionism, this book defends claims that Indigenous activists and thinkers have also advanced.

Notwithstanding these commonalities, there are obvious and undeniable differences between colonial oppression in extraction colonies and settler colonies. For one, as Nichols and other theorists of racial capitalism have pointed out, racialization in the former consisted mainly of creating nonwhite bodies for coerced labor. For the latter, the interest in land meant that racialization took the form of portraying Indigenous peoples as "outdated savages" to pave way for genocide rather than exploitation.[79] Moreover, as Jodi Byrd and Michael Rothberg (and others since then) have pointed out, while there are commonalities between the postcolonial project of contesting neocolonialism and the project of indigeneity in challenging ongoing colonialism, there are also tensions between the two that should not be erased.[80] As such, one can expect that an account of postcolonial global justice that draws primarily from Third World anticolonial thought will be different from one that emerges from close engagement with Indigenous political thought. The latter is undoubtedly an important and urgent project, but not one that I can engage in here.[81] Therefore, I do not claim that this is *the* postcolonial view of global justice, but merely that this is *one* view that someone taking up a postcolonial perspective may plausibly come up with. To claim that this is *the* postcolonial view of global justice would be to commit a version of what Serene Khader calls "justice monism"—the idea that justice can only be realized through one particular set of social or political forms.[82] This book will attempt to persuade the reader that postcolonial global justice as social equality is a normatively attractive view for our present and has critical purchase across settler colonial and neocolonial contexts. Yet depending on the selection of thinkers and one's own normative precommitments, one could construct very different and potentially competing views using the same method I employ here, i.e., historically inflected normative theorizing.

Decolonization beyond the Nation-State

As discussed above, despite global justice theory's origins in the decolonial moment, questions of empire and race have so far been largely neglected. The long-standing reception of anticolonial political thought in the broader Western academy would seem at least partly responsible for its neglect as a source for global justice thinking. Up until recently, anticolonial thinkers (and the movements they represented) have been narrowly received as nationalists. As I discuss in chapter 1, Cold War politics combined with Eurocentric frameworks of engaging with the Third World meant that Anglo-American political science tended to neglect or dismiss radical egalitarian and socialist currents within anticolonial movements and instead reduce them to ethnocultural nationalism, or what Isaiah Berlin infamously called "pagan self-assertion."[83] Following this trend, the few global justice theorists who make reference to anticolonial movements in their work have tended to treat them as synonymous with demands for national self-determination, with little else to say about the global order beyond that.[84]

Recent work in the history of political thought and empire has begun to correct this narrative by recovering anticolonial projects that do not easily fit into or cannot be subsumed under the framework of nationalism. At the end of World War II, as empires became increasingly untenable, anticolonial politicians, intellectuals, and activists saw an opening in which dramatic reforms to the world order could be made. This period of "anticolonial worldmaking" raised questions beyond how colonies might attain national independence.[85] For anticolonial leaders and thinkers, this historic moment also represented a chance to reshape global and political structures. Kwame Nkrumah urged for the creation of an "all-union government" to unite Africa, as well as transnational organizations of solidarity with Asian and Latin American peoples, to guard against neocolonialism.[86] Jawaharlal Nehru advocated for the creation of a "World Union" in which nation-states would devolve their sovereignty and collective issues would be resolved democratically instead of resorting to war.[87] Anticolonial activists and thinkers thus looked beyond the nation-state for sites of solidarity and developed what Inés Valdez has called a "political craft" in fostering new political subjectivities to resist global injustice.[88] As Frederick Cooper reminds us, the nation-state was not a predetermined end.[89] Anticolonial resistance comprised a diverse political spectrum, and an exclusive focus on nationalism obscures other questions that were important to anticolonial actors at the time and remain relevant for us in a neocolonial world today.

The recent recovery of anticolonial internationalism poses two related questions important for a theory of postcolonial global justice. First, at a theoretical or philosophical level, how might we understand anticolonial nationalist and internationalist commitments as compatible (if, in fact, they are)? While Adom Getachew and others have compellingly traced what Michele Louro calls a "blend of internationalism and nationalism"[90] in anticolonial thought, in practice these often proved contradictory. To be sure, the failure of anticolonial internationalism can hardly be attributed solely or even primarily to a theoretical or practical tension between internationalism and nationalism. Historical circumstance—most obviously an increasingly bipolar world hostile to multilateralism under the Cold War—is important for understanding the constraints and pressures on anticolonial worldmaking in the '60s and '70s. But it is hard to say there was no tension at all. Analyzing debates over a federal Africa, for example, Getachew shows that anticolonial leaders such as Nnamdi Azikiwe were concerned about the loss of national autonomy that a strong African federal state implied and therefore resistant to Kwame Nkrumah's proposals of continental political and economic integration.[91]

Second, and even more pressing for the normative purposes of this book, in theorizing global justice for the neocolonial present, what is the place of the nation-state? Is the nation-state compatible with a postcolonial cosmopolitanism that takes individuals as ultimate units of moral concern?

This book contributes to ongoing efforts to broaden academic and popular imaginations of anticolonialism and decolonization. By focusing on egalitarian themes within anticolonial writings, I put forth a reading of anticolonial critique that emphasizes social hierarchy as a central injustice of colonial oppression and (relational) equality as a guiding value in decolonization. My analysis suggests that we can understand anticolonial internationalism and nationalism better by shifting our attention to the more fundamental value of equality. That is, anticolonial projects at different levels can be understood as different ways of resisting colonial and neocolonial hierarchy. While some of these projects were emancipatory in specific historical circumstances, they can also be detrimental to the broader goal of attaining relations of equality in other contexts, especially in an age of disillusionment with many postcolonial states.

This suggests an account of postcolonial global justice that endorses certain constraints on national sovereignty by empowering other kinds of subnational and transnational groups, while also recognizing that global institutions are more often than not instruments of the powerful. In the book, as we analyze neocolonial hierarchies in different domains of global politics, one of my underlying contentions is that we can abandon the notion that empowering the nation-state is always the best instrument for securing equality and freedom without also abandoning arguments for collective rights that serve as bulwarks against neocolonial exploitation and domination. Ultimately, as I suggest in chapter 5 and in the concluding chapter, postcolonial global justice relies on building credible threats to power from organized groups and citizenries everywhere.

Anticolonial Thinkers

In developing an account of postcolonial global justice, we will engage primarily with the writings of Nehru, Nkrumah, Césaire, and Fanon. These thinkers are undoubtedly some of the most influential intellectuals and politicians in their time (and beyond). While they in no way exhaust the diverse currents of twentieth-century Third World anticolonial thought, we can nonetheless say they have a certain degree of representativeness. Geographically, the four are dispersed throughout the imperial world: Nehru in British Asia, Nkrumah in British Africa, and Césaire and Fanon in the French Antilles (and, for Fanon, also French Algeria). They also had different versions of the institutional vehicle through which decolonization would occur. While Césaire spent much of his political career advocating for departmentalization within France rather than national independence, seeing that as an important way to make claims on the wealth accumulated in the metropole, the other three focused more on state- and nation-building for overcoming the legacies of colonial oppression. Moreover, they opted for different strategies of resistance. Nkrumah, inspired by Gandhi, endorsed nonviolent "positive action" campaigns such as strikes.[92] On the other hand, Fanon famously supported violent resistance against the French in Algeria.[93]

Despite these differences, they also had similarities. Most obviously, all four share socialist leanings and were at one time or another involved in Marxist and socialist politics. Relatedly, as I aim to show, they shared an egalitarian critique of hierarchy that remains undertheorized. Finally, for the purposes of this book, each thinker's writings help illuminate a different dimension of decolonization that will prove to be important for our systematic account of postcolonial global justice. Fanon provides the clearest exposition of social inequality, and we will engage closely with his writings in outlining our philosophical account in chapter 2. Nkrumah is, of course, a pioneer in theorizing neocolonial economic relations, and his work is important for our analysis of international investment. As a poet and leader of the anticolonial cultural movement Negritude, Césaire's reflections on cultural imperialism are valuable for thinking about the objectionable dynamics at play in global cultural exchange today. Perhaps the least well known among the four for his political thought, Nehru's transnational activism and writings on global governance provide an important vantage point into the problem of global democracy.

As mentioned previously, Third World anticolonial thinkers encompassed a wide political spectrum, and this book makes no claim on capturing the whole of this tradition. At least two strains of anticolonial thought are not included in my selection: first, anti-state and antimodernist views. Gandhi is an exemplar of this strain of anticolonial thought. Arguing that colonialism was inherently rooted in European civilization and industrialization, Gandhi criticized the modernist developmental projects of the postcolonial state and instead advocated for self-sufficient village economies that relied on traditional methods of production.[94] By contrast, although the thinkers discussed in this book also condemned capitalistic European modernity and argued that postcolonial Asia and Africa should not simply "imitate Europe,"[95] as Fanon puts it, they also thought that some form of industrialization was needed to secure freedom for both the postcolonial state and its citizens. As we shall see, all four thinkers advocated for a blending of European and Indigenous practices, and none saw decolonization as the straightforward rejection of the West. Also excluded from my selection are communist revolutionary views, as exemplified by figures like Mao Zedong, who advocated for a sweeping (and often violent) uprooting of society from top to bottom.[96] Instead, the three thinkers I draw from in chapters 3 through 5 for looking at transitions to postcolonial global justice in specific topic areas—Nkrumah, Césaire, and Nehru—tended to favor what André Gorz calls nonreformist reforms.[97] Put simply, these are political and economic reforms that pave the way for more radical change in the long run instead of either working within the broader status quo of global and domestic capitalism or trying to do away with existing frameworks in one fell swoop. As Steven Metz states, even as Nkrumah began to advocate more openly for revolution to achieve socialism after the 1966 coup that deposed him, he was "much closer to a reformist than a revolutionary" for most of his political life, and certainly as prime minister of Ghana.[98] Occupying this complex and nuanced middle ground meant that criticism would and did come from multiple sides for these thinker-leaders, especially for Nehru and Nkrumah, who became leaders of government and therefore practitioners of their own political theory. Yet I submit that this search for a so-called third way amid significant political and practical constraints is also what makes them helpful and relevant for thinking about transitions toward a just world order in our deeply non-ideal world.

Looking Ahead: Postcolonial Global Justice as Social Equality

This book defends a view of postcolonial global justice as social equality. This view is developed in conjunction with a particular reading of the anticolonial tradition. Chapter 1 engages primarily with the key writings of Jawaharlal Nehru, Kwame Nkrumah, Frantz Fanon, and Aimé Césaire. There is a long-standing tendency to read these thinkers as nationalists, and their struggle for decolonization as a struggle for independent nation-states. Moving away from this standard reading, I argue that an important set of themes within anticolonial thought can be theorized as a critique of relations of inequality, and decolonization understood as the construction of egalitarian global and domestic relations. By recovering equality as a central value within the anticolonial tradition, I call our attention to the *egalitarian face of decolonization*, which suggests interaction on terms of relational equality as an ideal of postcolonial global justice. In this view, the nation-state was primarily a historically contingent instrument to achieve equality rather than an end in itself.

It should not surprise us that the value of equality, understood relationally, can be found within the anticolonial tradition. Since the publication of Elizabeth Anderson's 1999 essay "What's the Point of Equality?" there have been attempts among contemporary egalitarians to turn away from increasingly abstract debates about distributive equality to political and social movements that have demanded equality throughout history.[99] These social or relational egalitarians take inspiration from antiracist, feminist, and left-wing movements to theorize what it means to be equal.[100] Though the specific implications differ, a common thread that runs through accounts of social equality is the idea that the point of equality is to stand in relations of nondomination, mutual respect, and reciprocity with others, rather than having equal amounts of the morally relevant currency.

At the same time, social egalitarians have focused almost exclusively on theorizing social inequality within societies. While Anderson has pointed in her recent work on social equality to its possible global applicability, others such as Thomas Scanlon and Niko Kolodny have either argued that certain kinds of inequality are not (as) morally salient outside of shared societies, or said little on the topic altogether.[101] One oft-cited reason for thinking that social inequality is irrelevant at the global level is that unequal status (often seen as the quintessential example of social inequality, if not social inequality itself) is only objectionable if persons are situated in a social context in which status signifiers and norms are shared.[102] At the global level, it is often said, this condition does not obtain.

Yet once we take seriously our thinkers' critique of interlocking colonial hierarchies from chapter 1, it becomes apparent that the legacies of empire are not only economic or political but also cultural and discursive.[103] Most obviously, empire and transatlantic slavery gave birth to a global racial ideology that continues to operate not only in former metropoles but, crucially, in the postcolonial Global South today.[104] In chapter 2, I question prevailing domestic articulations of social equality and argue that the shared social contexts and institutions inherited from empire give us reason to think that relational inequalities that are objectionable within societies are also objectionable at the global level. Drawing on Fanon's analysis of the colonial situation, I analyze three kinds of global racialized hierarchies—of political authority, esteem, and moral standing—and show how they are both objectionable in themselves, as well as objectionable as constraints on citizens' capacity to pursue domestic social equality. Postcolonial global justice as social equality, I argue, requires that persons across the world enjoy *equal status as authoritative social agents whose interests are owed equal concern.* This account, though expressed in analytic terms, is designed to encapsulate the normative core of the egalitarian face of decolonization recovered from our four anticolonial thinkers. And yet it is a distinctive view of postcolonial justice built for the present age of neocolonial world order. The view, I contend, has important implications for what those historically denied social equality can justifiably press against dominant actors, including former colonizing powers, transnational corporations, and their own governments.

These implications are fleshed out in the rest of the book. I bring postcolonial global justice as social equality to bear on three areas of global politics that remain understudied in the global justice literature: international investment, patterns of cultural globalization, and political justice in trade governance. In each, I engage more closely with the political thought of a specific thinker to investigate the distinctive manifestations of global social inequality, and the remedial (collective) rights and reforms each area calls for.

Despite their ambitions for decolonization, anticolonial leaders, upon attaining formal independence, were immediately faced with the paradox of depending on external capital for realizing that very agenda. As former colonies faced increasing encroachment from foreign corporations and capital-exporting states, Nkrumah developed an account of neocolonialism that became widely influential across the Third World. While much attention has been given to Nkrumah's account of neocolonialism as foreign infringement, in chapter 3 I draw attention to parts of his critique that emphasize neocolonialism as (racial) exploitation.[105] In this reading, neocolonialism is primarily an effort to impose onto vulnerable states an economic model that advantages the neo-imperialist state and international capitalists at the expense of vulnerable states' abilities to escape persistent vulnerability. I argue that neocolonialism as (racialized) exploitation remains an important framework for understanding contemporary global economic relations. Through an extended analysis of contemporary international investment law, this chapter shows how disadvantaged groups in postcolonial (and often even Global North) countries are constrained by the terms of investment from pushing for measures that rectify structural inequalities, even as those same terms enable investors to pursue self-enrichment. Emphasizing neocolonialism as exploitation rather than merely foreign interference suggests that responses to neocolonial economic relations are insufficient if they only aim to strengthen the postcolonial state against the predations of foreign powers. Instead, I argue that responses should also aim to constrain the postcolonial state (and foreign investors) to a practice of international investment that facilitates rather than hinders the pursuit of decolonization as egalitarian transformation.

Yet, as Nkrumah presciently reminded us, neocolonial exploitation does not only work through international treaties. Its operations cannot be fully understood without an analysis of global cultural production and dissemination. Chapter 4 turns to the question of cultural decolonization by focusing on the global trade in cultural goods. Engaging with Césaire's critique of cultural imperialism, I argue that decolonizing cultural globalization can be understood as a project in overcoming a global racial hierarchy inherited from colonial discourses of civilization. Historically oppressed groups should be empowered to engage in cultural production so as to reclaim their equal status as value-makers. To this end, I argue for reforms to the global communications infrastructure along the lines first proposed by the anticolonial project of the New World Information and Communication Order (NWICO). These reforms would oblige dominant culture-exporting countries to engage in tech transfer and contribute to funds that support postcolonial cultural and knowledge production, as well as prioritize the import and distribution of cultural goods from peripheral countries. On the other hand, I also defend a remedial right to cultural protectionism for postcolonial societies so long as participation in global communications remains deeply unequal. Importantly, this defense of cultural protectionist rights is grounded on egalitarian rather than nationalist commitments.

If the previous two chapters addressed two aspects of substantive change that postcolonial global justice as social equality demands—i.e., economic and cultural empowerment through a nonexploitative investment regime and a democratized global communications regime—chapter 5 addresses the question of decision-making at the global level through the case of undemocratic trade governance. As such, it also indirectly considers the question of how the substantive reforms that I have argued for (as well as other kinds of just decolonial ends) might be pursued. A persistent criticism of contemporary proposals for global democracy claims that a functioning democracy requires a shared solidarity. Skeptics argue that it is both undesirable and impossible to build a cosmopolitan solidarity because of global cultural pluralism. Turning to Nehru's writings and speeches on internationalism, this chapter suggests a different approach to global democracy, one that neither forecloses its possibility nor denies the importance of solidarity. While Nehru is often regarded as India's foremost anticolonial nationalist, lesser known is his lifelong support for what he called a "democratic world union." But for Nehru, the primary obstacle to global solidarity was not cultural pluralism but persistent subordination of historically oppressed populations within a global political hierarchy. The primary challenge of building global democracy was cultivating an internationalist outlook among the very agents who had good reason to retreat from global political integration and cooperation. Nehru's response was to foster transnational solidarity in the very process of contesting subordination.

Drawing from these ideas, I argue for a recharacterization of the problem of global democracy: from vertical deficit in democratic control between individual citizens and global institutions, to horizontal deficit in political equality between groups. This shift enables us to see more clearly that resisting political marginalization ought to be the first task of the global democrat. Instead of settling for modest reforms of accountability that skeptics of global democracy tend to propose, or aiming for idealistic proposals of world parliament, I argue that the path to global democracy depends on creating counterhegemonic power for marginalized states as well as nonstate actors, and on cultivating a transnational solidarity in the practice of resistance.

Many postcolonial regimes ultimately took an authoritarian and neocolonial turn. As anticolonial thinkers had feared, the social revolution was often betrayed once national independence was attained. Moreover, as new global hegemons gradually form, the moral and political dilemmas of engaging in cross-border anticolonial resistance remain as urgent today as they did in the time of our four thinkers. The book concludes by anticipating future work on the ethics of political action at the global level. In resisting injustice, especially where revolutionary practices might be called for, a key question that anticolonial thinkers grappled with was how political agents might avoid creating new hierarchies that enable domination and exploitation. Was it possible for anticolonial practices of resistance to lead to a decolonized world after all?

Before answering those questions, however, we need to know what decolonization as a normative vision amounts to. This book argues that decolonization ought to be understood as an egalitarian transformation that aims to construct global and domestic relations governed by respect, solidarity, and reciprocity. If the historical moment for realizing this vision was once open and then closed, perhaps we might see the gaps again once we reimagine this ambitious political project of living in the company of one another.

1

Foundations of a Postcolonial Global Justice

THE EGALITARIAN FACE OF DECOLONIZATION

THIS CHAPTER argues that an important dimension of anticolonial thought can be understood as a form of egalitarianism. By anticolonial thought, I refer to a body of thought that grew out of responding to European colonialism and served as the theoretical foundation for the politics of decolonization in the twentieth century. To be sure, anticolonial thinkers, even in an era of eased global communication and travel, by no means formed a cohesive cohort. Across South Asia, the Middle East, Francophone and Anglophone Africa, the Caribbean and West Indies, the colonial realities in which anticolonial thinkers wrote and theorized often differed significantly. Nonetheless, the anticolonial thinkers and political leaders I discuss here—Kwame Nkrumah, Aimé Césaire, Frantz Fanon, Jawaharlal Nehru—all came into direct or indirect contact with one another, often in European metropoles or the United States, where they traveled or studied. They read and influenced one another's work, followed and learned from the development of each other's anticolonial struggles, and organized numerous international conferences and anticolonial groups together.[1] Moreover, these thinkers shared overlapping core concerns regarding relations and structures of inequality. In discussing their work together, I focus only on elucidating these shared concerns regarding inequality, and I do not mean to dismiss other important differences or pretend to attend to all the complexity of each thinker.

There is a long-standing tendency in Western scholarship to read anticolonial thinkers as nationalists, and anticolonial movements as groups sharing an identity contending for a right to form independently governed territorial units.[2] The dominant view is that colonized subjects imagined themselves to be distinct nations entitled to self-determination and on that basis demanded freedom from alien rule.[3] Statist global justice theorists, in turn, have invoked nationalist interpretations of anticolonialism in defending national self-determination as a central premise of a just world order.[4]

In a prominent study of anticolonial movements published in 1960, for example, Rupert Emerson portrays the "rejection of colonialism" as "the universally demonstrated unwillingness of peoples, as they come to an awareness of themselves in the modern world, to tolerate being run by aliens or to continue subordinate to a foreign state."[5] Seen as the aspiration to attain national self-determination, he criticizes anticolonialism for mistaking rule by co-ethnics with genuine liberation. Emerson, referring to Kwame Nkrumah, writes,

> In a logic detached from the record of recent history there is no necessary reason why people should passionately prefer to be governed by what they regard as their own kind rather than to allow an efficient corps of alien administrators to manage their affairs for them. Yet nationalists the world over have revolted against alien domination and, in occasional bursts of frankness, have stated their case in such classic phrases as that they would rather be governed like hell by themselves than well by their imperial rulers. Nkrumah's Convention People's Party in the Gold Coast took as its motto: "We prefer self-government with danger to servitude in tranquility."[6]

Yet, in a speech delivered by Nkrumah in 1953 to the Gold Coast (now Ghana) legislative assembly on the motion for independence, shortly after quoting the party motto that Emerson cites above, Nkrumah states,

> I want to emphasize, Mr. Speaker, *that self-government is not an end in itself* [italics original]. It is a means to an end, to the building of the good life to the benefit of all, regardless of tribe, creed, color or station in life. . . . The self-government which we demand, therefore, is the means by which we shall create the climate in which our people can develop their attributes and express their potentialities to the full.[7]

Here, Nkrumah's claim that self-government is *a means to an end* already hints at a much more expansive decolonial agenda than Emerson's notion that self-government was the exclusive goal of anticolonial struggle.

The exclusive focus on anticolonialism as nationalism has occluded our understanding of anticolonial thinkers' far-ranging critiques of imperialism. As I argue below, significant aspects of anticolonial thought are best theorized as a form of egalitarianism that takes relations of equality as a central value. Indeed, anticolonial nationalism—the construction of a nation and the demand for institutionalizing its self-determination—itself formed part of a broader mandate to critique and transform relations of inequality to make freedom possible in a decolonized world. Seen in this light, these thinkers' relationship to the nation-state is less straightforward and their commitment to self-determination as a *nation* is more qualified than has usually been realized, a point that has important implications for thinking about global justice today. Specifically, by untangling the broader aspirations of decolonization from nationalism, we can question the idea that *national* self-determination is an independent value in tension with egalitarian projects that require weakening the rights of the nation-state. On this reconstruction, rather than a straightforward defense of self-determination within the nation-state, anticolonialism as a normative orientation can entail a strategic valuation of the nation-state where it is potent for contesting imperialism, along with a clear-eyed view of its limits and an openness to alternative forms of global political agency.

From the outset, there are at least two reasons to doubt that the standard narrative fully captures anticolonial thought. First, recent historical work on anticolonial thought and anticolonial movements has emphasized the historical contingency of the nation-state as the primary institutional vehicle of decolonization. For many anticolonial thinkers, these historians argue, failed attempts to transform empire into republic or federation were precursors to demands for national independence.[8]

Second, throughout their writings, anticolonial thinkers were deeply concerned about the threat of neocolonialism, and the dangers that the illusion of national self-determination posed to postcolonial societies. To resist these dangers, many anticolonial thinkers reached for transnational and internationalist solutions that would require weakening postcolonial states' national sovereignty.[9] Their openness to these political experiments demonstrates an acute awareness of the nation-state's limits as a vehicle for decolonization. Reading anticolonial demands as exclusively demands for national self-determination implies that anticolonial thinkers were politically naive about the global and domestic structures of inequality that persisted beyond formal decolonization, when their writings evince precisely the contrary.

How might we explain the tendency to subsume anticolonialism under nationalism? Karuna Mantena argues that this is both because formal decolonization ended up in the proliferation of nation-states and also because of a longstanding tendency in Western scholarship to apply European frameworks to the rest of the world.[10] Decolonization, seen in this light, was the process of the non-West gradually attaining the prerequisites for a European model of independent nationhood.[11] In another influential analysis of anticolonialism, John Plamenatz states, "Democracy and freedom are European ideals. . . . To the extent that peoples of Asia and Africa subject to European rule demand independence for the sake of democracy and freedom, they can be said to be claiming against the West the right to imitate the West."[12] Ironically, the idea that decolonization consists of colonized subjects becoming ready for European models of national self-governance fits perfectly the narrative of the civilizing mission.

Moreover, two major geopolitical developments across the second half of the twentieth century came to shape and ultimately narrow decolonial agendas. First, decolonization occurred within the struggle for dominance between two new global hegemons, the United States and the USSR. As Jessica Chapman and others have argued, Cold War politics distorted the decolonial agendas of many newly independent postcolonies that quickly found themselves entangled in the proxy conflicts of superpowers.[13] Threatened with foreign subversion—a fear made exceptionally real by the US-assisted assassination of anticolonial leader Patrice Lumumba—and grappling with the formidable task of constructing a unified polity out of the ruins of colonial divisions, postcolonial leaders placed an increasing emphasis on defending the political sovereignty and territorial integrity of the nation-state.[14] Securing national sovereignty appeared more and more like an end in itself.

As the Cold War came to a close with the fall of the Soviet Union and the ascendance of Reagan-Thatcherism, the general sense of revolutionary possibility and radical political and economic experimentation that defined much of the twentieth century also began to shift. While anticolonial leaders such as Nehru had already by that time broken with an earlier enthrallment with the Soviet Union, the fact that another source of political support and economic aid existed as an alternative to capitalism had created space for postcolonial governments to engage in the kind of ambitious state-led industrialization and redistributions promised in the anticolonial struggle.[15] With the Soviet Union disintegrating into economic and political chaos, however, structural adjustment programs came to fill the void, placing further constraints on fledgling postcolonies' ability to continue to pursue a more expansive decolonial agenda.[16]

In recovering the normative horizon of decolonization, then, it becomes all the more important to return to the writings of anticolonial thinkers at the threshold of imperial breakdown, when anticolonial critique was far-ranging and decolonization seen as an opportunity to remake a world structured by hierarchy. Even in later writings, as in Nkrumah's *Neocolonialism*, I hope to show (in chapter 3), a closer reading suggests that a deeper concern with (relations of) inequality often drove the defense of national self-determination.

Yet even when the egalitarian aspirations of decolonization have been picked up, these aspirations have sometimes been interpreted as and reduced to demands for a hollow kind of equal status. Isaiah Berlin's famous critique of anticolonial movements in his essay "Two Concepts of Liberty" is a good case in point. In the essay, Berlin characterizes anticolonial struggles as a search for status in which colonial subjects "prefer to be bullied and misgoverned by some member of [their] own race or social class, by whom [they are], nevertheless, recognized as a man and a rival—that is an equal—to being well and tolerantly treated by someone from some higher and remoter group."[17]

These anticolonial demands, for Berlin, led to "illiberal conclusions" by conflating freedom with equality.[18] The implication here is that anticolonial struggles for equality trades substance for rather empty forms of recognition or respect from co-nationals. "It is this desire for reciprocal recognition," Berlin states, "that causes a member of some newly liberated Asian or African state to complain less when he is rudely treated by members of his own race or nation, than when he was governed by some cautious, just, gentle, well-meaning administrator from the outside."[19]

As I show in this chapter and across the rest of the book, this narrow interpretation of anticolonial demands for equality is deeply mistaken. Against a backdrop of centuries of racial domination and exploitation, anticolonial thinkers indeed demanded a postcolonial world in which the "darker peoples of the world" would enjoy equal status to whites. Yet this equal status required radical and substantive changes to the political, economic, and social *relations* that underpin agents' treatment of and attitudes toward one another. Without dismantling the hierarchies that defined colonial rule and global imperialism, domination and exploitation would only reemerge in new manifestations.

In what follows, then, I recast these thinkers as egalitarians whose nationalism grew out of a particular historical juncture. It should perhaps not come as a surprise that many anticolonial thinkers had broader and more radical egalitarian aspirations that went beyond national self-determination; after all, with the exception of Fanon, whose relationship with Marxism is much debated,[20] these anticolonial thinkers were self-declared Marxists and socialists at one point or another.[21] Shifting our focus to the egalitarian dimension of anticolonial thought, I reconstruct these thinkers' broader critique of colonial injustice as structural inequality, and their radical visions of *decolonization as egalitarian transformation*. Attending to the egalitarian dimension of anticolonial thought not only enriches our understanding of a multifaceted tradition, but also, as I develop in the rest of the book, provides plausible and appropriate resources for thinking about global justice today.

Anticolonial Critique: An Egalitarian Reconstruction

An anticolonial view roughly comprises two parts: first, a critique of colonialism that illustrates its central wrong-making features and, therefore, the moral basis of claims to decolonization; and second, a normative vision of what decolonization entails. Implicit in both parts of these views is a response to a deeper question about the composition of the colonized group and its flip side, the question of who ought to constitute the postcolonial demos.

In a nutshell, I shall argue that many anticolonial claims can be understood as claims against the relations of inequality that shaped the colonial encounter and went on to form the backbone of colonial society. In this view, colonial rule is illegitimate because it is grounded on a set of objectionable hierarchies on which I shall elaborate shortly.[22] As relations of inequality became entrenched, groups that were hitherto disparate gradually become aware of their shared subordination. Collective resistance against this shared predicament, requiring mutual trust and great sacrifice, organically gives rise to a shared identity, which serves as a valuable resource for the struggle. But the moral claim against colonialism is not dependent on showing that colonizers and subjects have come to bear different identities, or even that they were different throughout history. Rather, it is a claim against the relational inequality that created politically salient identities in the first place. The group for which decolonization is a right is thus constituted by its unequal position within the colonial social structure and global imperial network. Alienation between colonizers and the colonized is less a result of difference in identity, and more fundamentally a result of inequality. Decolonization, in this view, is an egalitarian movement aimed at reforming social relations at the global and domestic levels. Let us now turn to these themes in the texts.

Egalitarian Critique: Colonialism as Structural Inequality

Anticolonial thinkers often characterize colonialism as a form of institutionalized power grounded on a racialized hierarchy between groups.[23] Colonizers set up political, economic, and social institutions and practices that grant a host of formal and informal privileges to colonial officials, settlers, and Indigenous collaborators on the one hand, and exploit, repress, and stigmatize the rest of the population on the other.

Let us take a closer look at three kinds of inequality that are said to characterize colonialism. First, colonial political rule is essentially, as Nkrumah states in *Africa Must Unite*, "the undemocratic rule of a majority by a minority."[24] While colonial settlers enjoyed civil freedoms and political rights, including the right to vote, "barriers of race" prevented granting equal political rights to colonial subjects.[25]

Moreover, colonizers create or reinforce local political hierarchies to help them maintain order.[26] The Indian princes, whose political power greatly troubled Nehru, are a good example. These were, on Nehru's description, "autocracies" based on "an almost complete denial of civil liberties," often coupled with "completely feudal" economies that left people in poverty.[27] Unpopular with the people, the Indian princes "would not have survived," Nehru argues, if it were not for the fact that "the whole of India . . . is under one dominant power which protects them."[28] The autocratic princes suppress demands for democratic institutions "with the aid of the British power."[29] In short, the colonial order depends on political hierarchies between unaccountable rulers and disenfranchised subjects.

Accompanying political inequality is economic inequality. Here, the concern is broader than foreign theft and plunder of resources. Instead, colonial economics was a process of primitive accumulation by capitalists who happen to be foreign in origin. This process fundamentally changed systems of economic production and property ownership.[30]

Nehru details this process at length. British colonialists in India, he states, break up communal forms of land ownership and artisanal practices, creating a dispossessed peasantry and an urban proletariat.[31] Land and resources became privately owned, and colonial settlers as well as Indigenous leaders became the "new landowning class."[32] Villagers are "deprived of all control over the land and its produce," Nehru laments, and the "chief interest and concern of [the] community now became the private property of the newly created landowner."[33] Importantly, this landowning class was seldom British.[34] Instead, the British preferred to receive revenues collected by Indigenous landowners, and thus purposely created a social class whose interests would be identified with the empire.[35]

Like most of his contemporaries with socialist aspirations, Nehru did not advocate for a revival of village economies.[36] To his mind, although they were cooperative and more egalitarian in character, they were also limited in their productive capacity to meet the needs of the population.[37] But colonial capitalism was categorically worse. Nehru argues that the deeply unequal capitalist system that replaced Indigenous economies left millions impoverished and at the brink of starvation.[38]

Similarly, in *Discourse on Colonialism*, Césaire argues that a central injustice of colonialism was to have imposed on the colony an economic model— capitalism—that entails the *thingification* of all things: from the natural world, which is treated as a resource to be conquered, to the "indigenous man," who is turned into "an instrument of production."[39] Colonial capitalism, he argues, brought to light "the value of our old societies"—societies that, Césaire asserts, "were communal societies, never societies of the many for the few."[40] Lamenting the destruction of what he calls "*anti-capitalist*" (italics original) societies, he argues for a "systematic defense of the societies destroyed by imperialism."[41] Rather than understanding Césaire to be advocating for a return to precolonial society—which he adamantly denies in the sentences that follow—we can understand him to be leveraging an image (however embellished) of an alternative mode of egalitarian economic production and ownership to critique European colonialism and its hollow promises of progress. If colonialism *just is* the forcible extension of an extractive, "proletarianizing" capitalism to the rest of the world, there was no reason for the colonized to remain enthralled with European civilization.[42]

Not only did the colonial economics of dispossession, privatization, and exploitation lead to significant domestic economic inequalities within the colony and changes in social relations, but it also created great inequalities of capital and wealth at the global level. Colonizers did more than fail to develop colonies—they underdeveloped them so as to eliminate competition with the metropole.[43] Nehru argues, for example, that the British deliberately prevented major industries, such as a shipping industry, to develop in India.[44] Whatever infrastructure was allowed—such as railways—was set up only to enable the imperial network of resource extraction that enriched the metropole.[45] Colonies are turned into cash crop plantations, and they enter the world market as "colonial and agricultural appendages" of European empires.[46]

This laid the foundation for global inequality upon colonies obtaining independence. Nkrumah, describing postcolonial Ghana, a country "whose output of cocoa is the largest in the world" and yet had "not a single chocolate factory,"[47] argues that single-crop agricultural economies lock former colonies into the most unprofitable position within the global division of labor.[48] As long as former colonies remain dependent on former colonial powers for capital, technology, and knowledge transfers, the latter can "perpetuate colonialism while at the same time talking about 'freedom.'"[49]

The third component of colonial structural inequality is an ideology of racial hierarchy. As Nehru states, "The whole ideology of [colonial] rule was that of the *herrenvolk* and the master race, and the structure of government was based upon it."[50] Ideologies of racial superiority and inferiority shaped and justified unequal patterns of rights and privileges, legitimizing the colonial enterprise itself. The darker peoples of the world were told that white colonizers "had a god-given right to govern [them] and keep [them] in subjection."[51] Their cultures are deemed barbaric and backward, and they are seen as passively dependent on the genius of the white man.

This racist colonial discourse originated and supported some of the worst economic atrocities of colonial rule. Nkrumah, citing Eric Williams's *Capitalism and Slavery*, argues that, "the myth of 'color' inferiority" supported "the subsequent rape of our continent with its despoliation and continuing exploitation under the advanced forms of colonialism and imperialism."[52] But this ideology did not come out of nowhere. As Nkrumah writes, "It was not that a nasty-minded bunch of men awoke simultaneously one morning in England, France, Belgium, Germany, Portugal, or in any of the other colonial countries, and decided that it would be a good thing to jump into Africa and grind the people's noses in the dust."[53] Rather, Nkrumah argues, European capitalism had reached a stage where the need for raw materials, markets, and security against competing capitalist powers prompted European powers to "evolve the means, their colonial policies, to satisfy the ends, the exploitation of the subject territories for the aggrandizement of the metropolitan countries."[54] From the Scramble for Africa and the transatlantic slave trade before that arose a "special denigration of Africans."[55] "Colonialism and its attitudes," Nkrumah writes, "die hard."[56]

An important consequence of living under deeply racist institutions and norms is that many colonial subjects gradually develop what Césaire calls an "inferiority complex"—distorted beliefs about the equality of the racialized group to which they are ascribed.[57] They come to believe that their values, practices, and ways of life are inferior and that they must become European to be equal to others. For many anticolonial thinkers, overcoming this "psychological wound of cultural inferiority," as Adom Getachew and Karuna Mantena put it, was the first and perhaps most crucial step toward decolonization.[58] As I discuss in the next section and develop further in chapter 4, for Césaire (and his anticolonial contemporaries such as Léopold Senghor), cultural production was an important way to combat and address the long-term consequences of colonial racial hierarchies. Cultural decolonization, Césaire argues, was important not so much because of a need to return to precolonial cultures, but because the act of creating is an act of reclaiming one's equal status as history-makers.[59]

To sum up, anticolonial thinkers characterized colonialism as a form of political domination backed by racial hierarchy for the purpose of economic exploitation. Within this deeply unequal and oppressive colonial structure, then, two forces contribute to the formation of the colonized nation.

First, alienation inevitably develops between oppressors and oppressed, and second, collective resistance brings about a shared identity. Rather than existing all along, the colonized "nation" is better understood as growing organically out of individuals' gradual awareness of their situation vis-à-vis those atop the colonial hierarchy, and a subsequent identification with each other's common purpose—resisting the colonial structure that placed them together at the bottom of the pyramid.

Let me elaborate on both points. First, these thinkers grappled with the question of how the colonized population might be understood as a cohesive and distinctive subject from European settlers and colonizers. They traced the emergence of the colonized nation to the particular hierarchical relations that constitute colonial rule, relations that inevitably alienated, divided, and set apart locals from settlers.

One of the most explicit reflections on this question is Nehru's *Discovery of India*. Throughout *Discovery*, Nehru emphasizes that India was and had always been deeply diverse, and that it was "absurd and presumptuous" to talk of "an impulse . . . underlying the growth of Indian civilization."[60] He chronicles the

many episodes of different "races" arriving at what was later British India, starting with the "coming of the Aryans" to the Indus Valley, which he describes as
"the first great cultural synthesis and fusion" that "grew the Indian races and
the basic Indian culture."[61] This emphasis on newcomers and reciprocal
integration, on "foreign influences [that] poured in . . . and were absorbed" is
repeated throughout the book.[62] After surveying thousands of years of history,
Nehru concludes,

> The discovery of India—what have I discovered? Today she is four hundred
> million separate individual men and women, each differing from the other,
> each living in a private universe of thought and feeling . . . India is a geo-
> graphical and economic entity, a cultural unity amidst diversity, a bundle
> of contradictions held together by strong but invisible threads.[63]

In other words, in theorizing India as a collective subject, Nehru emphasizes the themes of difference and synthesis, diversity amid unity. What "has
kept [India] vital and going through these long ages," he argues, was its inhab-
itants' "tender humanity" and "a varied and tolerant culture."[64] For Nehru,
what defined India was not a particular racial identity or ethnicity, but a social
milieu that enabled foreigners to integrate and allowed diverse religions and
cultures to flourish through mutual influence. On the introduction of Islam in
medieval times, a momentous development for Hindus, for example, Nehru
describes that India "[absorbed] the foreign element . . . herself changing
somewhat in the process."[65]

British India, however, was a different story. "British rule in India," Nehru
states, "was an entirely novel phenomenon . . . not comparable with any other
invasion or political or economic change."[66] Rather than integrating with the
local population, the British deliberately "maintain [their] prestige by keeping
aloof, exclusive, apart from Indians, living in a superior world of [their] own."[67]
In other words, the British purposely set up rigid social hierarchies to maintain
a racialized distinction between whites and nonwhites. "Previously," Nehru
goes on, "races had merged into one another, or at least fitted into an organically
interdependent structure." Under British colonialism, however, "racialism became the acknowledged creed . . . intensified by the fact that the dominant
race had both political and economic power."[68]

Therefore, the British could not become part of India because they had
chosen the path of subjugation. The result was that, instead of the cultural
unity amid diversity that was India's defining feature, in colonial India "there
were two worlds: the world of British officials and the world of India's millions,
and there was nothing in common between them except a common dislike for
each other."[69] This, then, is what distinguishes the colonial situation from previous encounters with the foreign—that is, relations of inequality that mark

out one group as inferior to another. On this diagnosis, for Nehru, founding an independent Indian republic was, as Manjeet Ramgotra puts it, "the means through which to gain political and social freedom as well as equal standing between individual citizens and between equal states."[70]

Along similar lines, throughout his work Césaire states that civilizations are necessarily composed of a continuous mixing of foreign and indigenous, new and old. "[It] is a good thing to place different civilizations in contact with each other . . . it is an excellent thing to blend different worlds," he writes in the *Discourse*, for a civilization that "withdraws into itself" becomes stagnant and "atrophies."[71] For cultures and civilizations, Césaire claims, "exchange is oxygen." The specific content of a culture, on his view, is necessarily unfixed and evolving.[72]

And yet, Césaire asks, "has colonization really placed civilizations into contact? . . . I answer *no*."[73] Instead, he argues that, "between colonizer and colonized," there can be "no human contact" but only "relations of domination and submission."[74] As he puts it vividly, the "colonizing man" is turned into "a classroom monitor, an army sergeant, a prison guard, a slave driver, and the indigenous man into an instrument of production."[75] In other words, cultural exchange and synthesis are predicated on the equal freedom of all participants to give and receive in turn. Within the context of colonialism, where one group is subordinated to another, deeply unequal relations prevent the emergence of a new culture. As Césaire states in "Culture and Colonialism," if Africans all over the world shared an original culture prior to transatlantic slavery and diaspora, they had also come to share a "horizontal solidarity," that is, "a solidarity created for us by the colonial, semi-colonial or para-colonial situation imposed upon us."[76] The continued subordination of one group to another halted what would otherwise have been a natural process of exchange and integration with the populations that the African diaspora now lived among.[77]

Instead, common subjection demands collective action, and this consolidates an emerging identity among colonial subjects. We can turn to Fanon for a poignant analysis of this process. In French Algeria, Fanon writes, colonialism "[stirred] up these men and women . . . regrouped them beneath a single sign."[78] Prior to the Algerian War, Fanon argues, different families, tribal groups, and villages had not formed a coherent unit, and many had a history of conflict. But colonialism changed that: it forced groups with diverse interests to view themselves as part of one collective, indeed to see themselves as "equally victims of the same tyranny, simultaneously identifying a single enemy . . . founding in suffering a spiritual community which constitutes the most solid bastion of the Algerian Revolution."[79] This is what he calls the first stage of the revolution, in which the "problem is clear-cut: The foreigners must leave. Let us build a common front against the oppressor and let us reinforce it with armed struggle." The people come together in "a state of genuine collective ecstasy," and former rivals "decide to wipe the slate clean and forget the past."[80] This, Fanon states, is where "national unity begins," when "everybody is hunting the enemy, everybody is taking a stand."[81] The colonized nation is "made."

Emphasizing the egalitarian aspects of anticolonial critique, it becomes clear how anticolonial thinkers might hold that colonial subjects form a cohesive political collective entitled to decolonization, even as this collective is internally diverse in many ways. The moral basis of the political collective is common subjection to an enduring set of colonial hierarchies. Furthermore, attending to analyses of colonial injustice as structural inequality also requires us to rethink these thinkers' support for national sovereignty as less a commitment to the nation as an independently valuable entity, and more as a political strategy to resist objectionable hierarchies at a particular historical juncture.

This is demonstrated in anticolonial experiments with different kinds of proposals short of national independence to reform the political, economic, and racial hierarchies described above. Some argued for republican federation with the metropole, others for departmentalization on the basis of equality; some argued for comprehensive economic planning, others for expanded labor rights. However, persistent opposition from European metropoles led anticolonial thinkers to conclude that, first, obtaining national sovereignty was the only way to implement political and economic reforms, and second, that national independence was an important way to compel white Europeans to regard them as moral equals.

First, reforming the political and economic structure within empire proved impossible.[82] Colonial rule, grounded on the hierarchies elucidated above, was inherently in tension with the kind of egalitarian relations that anticolonial thinkers sought. In British India, for example, Nehru argues that political equality could not be realized because the British could only tolerate "[a] kind of tame and subservient democracy."[83] To that end, the British would only allow incremental political reform "compatible with the structure and values and vested interests they had built up."[84] Any real democracy in India, he argues, was "incompatible with the British and political economic structure," and "conflict between the two was inevitable."[85] Colonial rule thus proved to be a "steel framework" that constrained what Nehru saw as growing demands for democratic reform among the people.[86]

Economic reform was similarly opposed. Like many of his anticolonial contemporaries with socialist aspirations, Nehru believed that addressing widening socioeconomic inequality required the democratic control of the means of production, and collective ownership of land and resources.[87] In late 1938 he headed a National Planning Committee, composed of representatives of diverse sectors within society, to draft a plan for the future. Their plan, Nehru describes, was fundamentally socialist. Its central aim was "limiting the acquisitive factor in society" and "planning for the benefit of the common man."[88] These efforts were met with strong opposition from the British Raj, and before the committee's work was finished, Nehru was imprisoned.

Writing from prison, Nehru argues that any such plan could only be implemented under a "free national government" responsive to the people's interests and able to make "fundamental changes in social and economic structure."[89] Under the British Raj, economic plans that conflicted with colonial interests and the colonial social structure would be blocked. Thereafter, for Nehru and his anticolonial colleagues, "the attainment of national freedom and the elimination of foreign control became an essential pre-requisite for planning."[90]

Within the French empire, Césaire encountered similar resistance to economic reform. Starting his career as an advocate for the French Antilles to become a department of France, Césaire argued that the social welfare and labor rights that applied in metropolitan France should be extended equally to the Antilles and that "there should not be two capitalisms: a metropolitan capitalism that is opposed and limited, and an overseas capitalism that is tolerated."[91] In a 1953 parliamentary speech, Césaire argued that colonial subjects "only demanded one thing, but an essential thing," which was "a new contractual status founded on nondiscrimination and equal rights between local populations and French citizens living in metropolitan France."[92] Yet these proposals to remake empire into republic were repeatedly opposed and delayed.

The French empire's refusal to undertake egalitarian reforms eventually led Césaire to give up on departmentalization and to instead advocate for autonomy. Lambasting French opposition, Césaire warned the metropole that, "when, under the flag of assimilation and the pretext of standardization, you will have piled up injustice upon injustice, when it will be evident that instead of a true assimilation, you intend to only offer them a caricature, a parody of assimilation . . . you will have caused to be born among these men a . . . national feeling."[93] Unequal rights, economic rights among them, would deepen alienation among the marginalized.

In short, anticolonial thinkers found that political domination and economic exploitation could not be addressed without first obtaining the rights and powers of an independent nation-state. As Nkrumah explains, the reasoning behind the Convention People's Party's infamous slogan ("Seek ye first the political kingdom") was that "without political independence none of our plans for social and economic development could be put into effect."[94]

Second, the exercise of self-government *itself* constituted a challenge to the core of colonial racism. As a central premise of the colonial project, the idea that Africans and Asians were incapable of solving problems and "making history" justified their subordination to the white man, and the ideology of racial hierarchy was deeply entrenched in colonial society. In societies where, as Fanon describes, colonial subjects are "turned . . . into an animal" and spoken of in "zoological terms," the anticolonial demand of racial equality was unlikely to be achieved without the racialized population first breaking away to form their own political unit.[95]

Self-governance as an independent nation-state, then, acted as a *public display* of the equality of the "darker peoples." As the prime minister of the first Black African colony to obtain independent statehood in sub-Saharan Africa, for example, Nkrumah felt the weight of the world's judgmental gaze. In an address to the Gold Coast Legislative Assembly, he states, "We shall soon become masters of our own country and for that reason a very great responsibility rests upon us all. We must show the world that Africans can give a lead in justice, tolerance, liberty, individual freedom and in social progress."[96] On the day Ghana became formally independent, Nkrumah declared, "Today, from now on, there is a new African in the world and that new African is ready to fight his own battle and show that after all the black man is capable of managing his own affairs."[97]

Therefore, prompted by the persistent domination, exploitation, and racial stigmatization of the colonized population, anticolonial thinkers concluded that national sovereignty was an essential first step to decolonization.

Yet they were also acutely aware of the limits of nationalism. A shared identity enables reconciliation of insignificant differences in the anticolonial struggle, but it can also mask over other differences in ways that hinder the egalitarian projects of decolonization.

Indeed, shortly after describing the formation of national identity, Fanon argues that the simple colonial dichotomy of "black versus white" or "Arab versus European" can easily slip into a "sterile formalism."[98] The colonial dichotomy is sterile as it fails to track a more complex reality in which "some blacks can be whiter than whites" and where "a national flag or independence does not automatically result in certain segments of the population giving up their privileges and their interests."[99] Almost as soon as the colonized nation is formed through collective struggle, then, Fanon argues that nationalism must be "deepened" by "a social and political consciousness" of this reality and transformed into a "humanism" that makes *human* emancipation the final end, rather than the emancipation of the nation. Otherwise, he warns, "nationalism . . . leads to a dead end."[100]

The dead end was in part due to indigenous elites who had occupied important roles in the colonial order and who would now come to rule in the postcolony. Contra interpretations (such as Emerson's and Berlin's) that take the central anticolonial demand to be rule by co-nationals, it is not uncommon to find in anticolonial writings critiques of and warnings against conflating rule by co-nationals with emancipation.[101] Fanon, for example, famously warned those who had just fought off their colonial oppressors against losing their vigilance toward the "national bourgeoisie" who would form the postcolonial ruling elite. This elite class, bent on maintaining the same colonial structures that would enable them to enrich themselves at the expense of the people, would put forth a popular leader who, "incapable of offering the people anything of substance," instead "pacifies" the people with old tales of "battles waged" and "victories won" from the anticolonial struggle.[102] Meanwhile, the postcolonial bourgeoisie would stage a "transfer into indigenous hands of privileges inherited from the colonial period."[103] Thus the relationship between equality, freedom, and rule by co-nationals is construed as far more nuanced.

Similar criticism of nationalism and the nation-state are echoed among Nehru and Césaire.[104] In resisting colonial rule, having tried other alternatives and failed, anticolonial thinkers concluded that there was no other way for colonial subjects to break from the political, economic, and racial hierarchies that were part and parcel of colonialism, unless these subjects formed a separate nation-state. At the time same, these thinkers worried that an excessive focus on nationalism would undercut broader decolonial aims. As Nehru put it in *The Discovery*, the anticolonial movement must always beware of falling into a "narrow nationalism" in which the only politics is a "single-track and negative" politics of opposing alien rule. This fosters "complexes and prejudices and phobias . . . and darken the mind," and gradually, "mental idols of the group and the community take shape, and slogans and set phrases take the place of inquiry into real problems."[105]

Therefore, anticolonial thinkers also turned to transnational and internationalist solutions to overcome the limits of the nation-state. Nkrumah, for example, argued for an African political federation equipped with central planning powers that could engage in the "total mobilization of the continent's resources" for economic development.[106] Nehru envisioned the eventual attainment of a democratically governed "World Union," in which "narrow nationalism" would gave way to the spirit of "one world," and issues common to humanity would be collectively decided upon.[107] As we will see in the next section, these thinkers endorsed forms of transnational integration that would significantly weaken and constrain the sovereign rights of the postcolonial nation, and they sometimes even articulated an ideal of a future cosmopolitan world in which cultural groups across the world would form a common political union and solve the world's collective problems together as equals.

To sum up, the critique of colonialism expounded here focuses centrally on relations of inequality arising from the colonial encounter and that became embedded in the structure of colonial society. These relations gave birth to groups that, by virtue of the oppression they shared, came to see themselves as fundamentally different from their oppressors. Through collective political action, individuals from previously different religious and ethnic backgrounds came to identify with one another as members of a common political entity. To the extent that the colonized nation as a political construct served an important function in resisting colonial oppression, anticolonial thinkers embraced it. At the same time, they cautioned against conflating national liberation with genuine emancipation.

Decolonization as Egalitarian Transformation

In the opening pages of *The Wretched of the Earth*, Fanon states, "Decolonization is truly the creation of new men."[108] At its most ambitious and expansive formulation, decolonization was viewed as a radical restructuring of relations between groups.[109] This radical restructuring, for Fanon and others, would engender a new kind of humanity, one in which interdependence would no longer be occasion for domination and exploitation, but governed by what Nehru calls "the spirit of the age," which, to his mind, "demands equality."[110] Without relations of equality, freedom from domination would always remain a distant dream.

This vision of decolonization demanded at least three broad categories of egalitarian reform. First, decolonization requires democratization.[111] Colonial political hierarchies were to be rejected in favor of political empowerment for ordinary citizens. Nkrumah, for example, argues that the first step to legitimate government, especially in "communities of mixed races and creeds" such as the colony, is to "give every adult, irrespective of race and creed, the right to vote."[112] Eradicating the legacy of colonial hierarchies depended on it, as he argues: "When each citizen thereby enjoys equality of status with all others, barriers of race and color will disappear, and the people will mix freely together and will work for the common good."[113] To this end, he argues that the postcolonial constitution in Ghana must be based on "the principle that all citizens of Ghana are equal and are all entitled to the same rights."[114] This included European settlers who had made their homes in Ghana. Nkrumah emphasizes that they should be accorded equal rights on the condition that, unlike colonialism, "the rights of the 3 percent" are no longer privileged over the other "97 percent."[115]

Not only does decolonization require democratic reform within the colony, but it also requires democratic reforms to (what is called today) global governance. While anticolonial thinkers condemned European imperial powers for exclusionary and unilateral international lawmaking, they also argued that strengthening global governance was important for avoiding future wars as well as addressing collective action problems—such as redistribution of capital and technology—that inevitably arise in pursuing the goals of decolonization. But in order to play these roles, global governance had to be radically reformed. Groups previously excluded from collective decision-making needed to be equally represented. States would contribute to the federation with the aim of resolving conflict in a multilateral rather than bilateral or unilateral fashion; disarmament of standing national armies would be the ultimate goal.

Nehru, for example, was a vocal advocate of a democratic, egalitarian, and inclusive "World Federation," which he proposed as the antithesis of the League of Nations or the British Commonwealth.[116] He criticized these, as well as the United Nations' veto system, as continuations of the global rule of the few.[117] As we will see in chapter 5, Nehru believed that internationalism—which he found deeply appealing—would only be attainable if global relations were made democratic and egalitarian. Political decolonization, therefore, demanded far more than independent nation-statehood for former colonies. As Nehru puts it, "The old type of complete national independence was doomed, and there must be a new era of world co-operation." Yet for postcolonial India to willingly "limit [its] independence," Nehru makes clear, this would have to be on egalitarian terms where other powers also agree to limit their sovereignty.[118]

Second, in terms of economic decolonization, anticolonial thinkers argued that global economic exploitation must be replaced with deliberate measures to empower postcolonial states to develop and diversify their economies. Unfair terms of trade and investment, which colonies had been forced to accept, continued to lock postcolonial states in cycles of asymmetric dependence on others. These colonial economic relations, anticolonial thinkers argued, must be reformed to empower former colonies to produce more than primary commodities and cash crops, and to compensate for decades and, in some cases, centuries of global exploitation.

To this end, foreign investment must be subject to policies developed by a democratically elected government that serves the interests of the people, rather than multinational corporations and capital-rich states. For Nkrumah, some key policies include knowledge and technology transfer, which would enable Ghana's citizens to "take over management, direction and technical posts at all levels."[119] If Ghana was able to "build up [a] body of knowledge, techniques and skills," he argues, aside escaping from global exploitation, this would also "make us more self-confident and self-sufficient."[120] Developing local industry, then, is not only important for decreasing reliance on capital-rich countries, but also an important way for formerly oppressed groups to reclaim their self-respect.

Fanon also demanded investment and technology transfers, but as a form of reparation. Arguing that Europe's wealth was built on the backs of the enslaved and the colonized, he states that the "underdeveloped regions must receive generous investment and technical aid," but crucially, "not . . . with gratitude" for it is a "just reparation."[121] Europe had grown rich through enslaving Africans and exploiting the labor and resources of African and Asian colonies. "European opulence," Fanon states, "was built on the backs of slaves . . . and owes its very existence to the soil and subsoil of the underdeveloped world."[122] Hence, Fanon claims, "the wealth of the imperialist nations is also our wealth."[123] The Third World must receive "generous investments and technical aid" not as a matter of charity but of justice.[124] Full decolonization, Fanon states, means that "*they* [i.e., former colonial powers] *must pay up* [italics original]."[125]

Anticolonial thinkers had no illusions that capital-rich countries would simply relinquish their advantages in the global economy. Instead, as Nkrumah argues, only through a "struggle" with the "external forces" that have a "vested interest" in keeping former colonies in a state of economic dependence will compel a transition to economic decolonization.[126] To that end, he advocates for an African union that would be powerful enough to "force the developed world to pay it a fair price for its cash crops."[127] Moreover, building on the "spirit of Bandung," he argues that Africans must form transnational alliances with similarly situated groups, including strengthening Afro-Asian solidarity and "[seeking] the adherence on an increasingly formal basis of our Latin American brothers."[128]

Within the domestic economy, decolonization often meant replacing colonial capitalism with a more egalitarian economic system. "[The] capitalist way of life," Fanon argues, "is incapable of allowing us to achieve our national and universal project [of decolonization]."[129] Socialism was often the preferred alternative.[130] Yet many of these thinkers also came to reject Soviet-style socialism, which, in Fanon's words, requires extraordinary "self-sacrifice" by exhausting the labor of "men and women, young and old" for the sake of the country. "We must not," Fanon states, ask the people to "Work to death, but let your country get rich!"[131] As Léopold Senghor—Césaire's longtime friend and ally—critiqued, Soviet communism was yet another form of totalitarian oppression.[132] Instead, anticolonial thinkers developed alternative forms of socialism that emphasized popular and democratic control of the economy.[133]

Importantly, economic decolonization at the domestic and global levels are seen as closely linked. Without fairer terms of global economic interaction, postcolonial states would be constrained by rules of trade and investment that prohibit or penalize domestic policies deemed antithetical to free trade.[134] Likewise, economic decolonization depended on political decolonization. Without a more egalitarian and democratic form of global governance, international law would remain biased in favor of powerful multinational corporations and their states.[135]

Third, decolonization extends beyond democratization and economic empowerment to undoing colonial racial ideology and its pernicious effects by reclaiming racialized persons' status as "history-making" agents.[136] To this end, anticolonial thinkers thought of cultural production as an important way to challenge the myth that nonwhites were less capable of creating value and contributing to the human good.

In a speech titled "Man of Culture and His Responsibilities," for example, Césaire argues that colonialism creates "a hierarchy of *creator and consumer.*"[137] In this racist ideology, the colonizer is "the creator of cultural values . . . and the consumer is the colonized."[138] This belief underlies the colonizer's posture as the bearer of civilization and modernity. But once the *colonized* starts to write, make art, and produce knowledge, cultural production "converts the colonized from *consumer* into a *creator.*"[139] The colonial lie is thereby exposed, and the result is a challenge to the heart of colonial racial ideology: "Even inside the colonial system itself," Césaire argues, "[cultural production] restores historic initiative to those whom it has been the mission of the colonial system to deprive of all historic initiative."[140] Moreover, while indigenous cultural production unsettles the colonizer, it is "reassuring, in the true sense of the word, to the colonized," because it "counterbalances the inferiority complex which it is the mission of all colonization to instill into the colonized."[141]

To this end, Césaire explicitly stresses that he is not advocating for a return to past traditions.[142] Instead, Césaire emphasizes the political import of cultural production by members of historically oppressed groups. By mixing European and African cultural elements to create new syntheses, Césaire argues, African artists and writers are demonstrating that African cultures *can* serve as valuable sources for modernity and that Africans *are* capable of innovation and creativity.[143] In other words, indigenous cultural production is important not because the postcolonial demos necessarily identifies with precolonial cultures, but because it is a way to contest the ideology of racial inferiority and assert one's equality.

Therefore, Césaire's call for returning to "native tradition" can be read as a call for former colonial subjects to destigmatize their culture and appropriate its elements without shame, just as they should reappropriate European culture for their own creative use.[144] In doing so, postcolonial citizens would be able to regain a sense of self-respect and see themselves as equal producers of value, rather than passive consumers of the innovations of the white West.

These three aspects of decolonization—political, economic, and sociocultural—were central to these thinkers' vision of a genuinely postcolonial world. As we have seen, each aspect was connected to an element in these thinkers' diagnosis of the structural injustice of colonialism. Together, they would affect the transformation of hierarchical imperial relations into relations of equality. Furthermore, these thinkers believed that achieving decolonization was morally and politically urgent not only for the formerly colonized world, but also for European powers and new hegemons such as the United States. Peaceful coexistence and freedom depended on attaining global relations of equality, without which new hierarchies resembling colonialism would only reappear, with different faces and different names, but as relations of domination and exploitation all the same.[145]

This vision of decolonization contrasts with the view that attaining nation-statehood was the primary end. Instead, as I have argued, the drive for national independence was motivated by a larger vision of egalitarian transformation. Furthermore, to varying degrees, anticolonial thinkers imagined that decolonization would enable humanity to eventually transcend nation-states and found a new kind of internationalism—one that consists of greater global integration on equal terms. Before concluding, let us briefly examine this anticolonial imagination of a postcolonial cosmopolitan world.

In *The Discovery*, Nehru argues that colonialism hinders the emergence of internationalism.[146] A consistent advocate of an ideal of "One World" under democratic global government, Nehru nonetheless points out that when a group of people is systemically dominated and exploited by another, it is inevitable that the former will focus on fighting the latter. "Internationalism," he writes, "can indeed only develop in a free country," because "all the thought and energy of a subject country are directed towards the achievement of its own freedom."[147] Once oppressive relations are fully eradicated, however, Nehru argues that internationalism is both inevitable and morally desirable. Toward the end of the book, outlining his vision for a decolonized India in which democracy, socialism, and racial equality have been attained, Nehru states:

> Such a development in India . . . would help in the realization of that one world towards which we are inevitably being driven, even though our passions delude us and our minds fail to understand it. The Indian people, freed from the terrible sense of oppression and frustration, will grow in stature again and lose their narrow nationalism and exclusiveness. Proud of their Indian heritage, they will open their minds and hearts to other peoples and other nations, and become citizens of this wide and fascinating world, marching onwards with others in that ancient quest in which their forefathers were the pioneers.[148]

In other words, on the basis of equality, Nehru believes that a new kind of global citizenship, within a democratic global "Federal Union," would be politically possible and morally appealing.[149] Importantly, global citizenship does not mean abandoning the world's diverse cultures. Instead, Nehru imagines a form of global political integration that is compatible with distinct and open cultural groups interacting and learning from one another as equals.[150] As he states, "Real internationalism is not something in the air without roots or anchorage. It has to grow out of national cultures and can only flourish today on a basis of freedom and equality. . . . Thus we shall remain true Indians and Asiatics, and become at the same time good internationalists and world citizens."[151]

Fanon paints a similar vision in the concluding chapter of *The Wretched*. The tragedy of European colonialism, Fanon argues, was that it cut off dialogue between different parts of humanity, so that Europe became stuck in a "permanent dialogue with oneself"—a "narcissist" whose self-imposed isolation as the oppressor of others made Europeans "immeasurably sickened."[152] The task of Third World decolonization, Fanon argues, is to help Europe and humanity in general break through this "stasis" and to "resolve the problems to which Europe has not been able to find the answers."[153] The central "question of mankind" that Europe tried to solve and failed so miserably, for Fanon, is the perennial question of how diverse human beings can live together in reciprocal dialogue and work together to create new possibilities.[154] This, he states, is "the question of the cerebral mass of all humanity, whose connections must be increased, whose channels must be diversified and whose messages must be re-humanized."[155]

The key to answering this question lies in relations of equality. Fanon concludes,

> What we want to do is to go forward all the time, night and day, in the company of Man, in the company of all men. The caravan should not be stretched out, for in that case each line will hardly see those who precede it; and men who no longer recognize each other meet less and less together, and talk to each other less and less. . . . For Europe, for ourselves, and for humanity, comrades, we must turn over a new leaf, we must work out new concepts, and try to set afoot a new man.[156]

Instead of some staying ahead and others forced to trail behind—a snapshot of human social relations under European colonialism—people must walk together in each other's company to be able to "talk" and work out new solutions to age-old questions.

To be sure, all this remains highly abstract. Anticolonial thinkers, standing at the threshold of the first stage of decolonization, could not know exactly what new kinds of global political and social life would be possible when, if ever, decolonization as egalitarian transformation is achieved. As I argue in the rest of the book, we have also not traveled very far from that threshold.

But my point here is that the egalitarian resources within anticolonial thought analyzed in this chapter offer little reason to think that a postcolonial cosmopolitanism—in which the rights of the nation-state are subject to the broader imperative for global and domestic egalitarian transformation—is necessarily in tension with anticolonial values. The question, instead, is whether it can be done without producing new hierarchies or entrenching old ones. Liberal cosmopolitanism under formal empire in the past, or neoliberal capitalism in the present, is clearly antithetical to anticolonial thinkers' vision of a just postcolonial world. This leaves us with the urgent task of constructing a vision of a just postcolonial world order inspired by these anticolonial aspirations, to inform the kinds of changes to contemporary global relations that might move us closer to realizing the egalitarian face of decolonization.

Toward a Postcolonial Global Justice

Most anticolonial aspirations were never realized. Strong opposition from the United States, Western Europe, and increasingly authoritarian postcolonial regimes eventually put a premature end to decolonization as a historical moment. Since the 1980s, global integration on the basis of free market capitalism has been the dominant trend. Trade and investment agreements significantly constrain postcolonial states' capacity to pursue egalitarian forms of economic development; global governance continues to exclude effective participation from citizens of marginalized countries; and cultural globalization remains largely one-sided as many postcolonial states continue to lack the resources and capital to develop robust cultural industries. Moreover, as authoritarian postcolonial states like China become increasingly dominant, anticolonial thinkers' fears that new hegemons may arise as long as global hierarchies remain appear to be vindicated. In theorizing global justice for today, we should hold clear the distinction between what modest gains anticolonial thinkers could realistically achieve, and what ambitious ends they had hoped to attain. We ought not confuse constraints on the oppressed with their aspirations.

I have argued that much of anticolonial critique can be understood as a form of egalitarianism that takes relations of equality as a central value. Focusing on anticolonialism as nationalism captures some aspects of anticolonial thought, but it can also end up oversimplifying its claims. Anticolonial thinkers theorized the nation in response to the alienation and resistance produced by colonial rule. But many did not imagine the nation as a stable or prepolitical entity, nor did they hold that difference in identity was the fundamental moral objection against colonial rule. Instead, they tended to see nations as emerging from the experience of common oppression and collective resistance, and they challenged the structures of inequality that alienated individuals from one another in the first place. Moreover, these thinkers did not categorically hold that political sovereignty for the nation was a necessary feature of a just postcolonial world. On the contrary, they were open to forms of transnational integration that could better reform global relations of domination and exploitation, and at times even imagined a postcolonial future of democratic global political integration. Focusing on the egalitarian dimension of anticolonial thought not only broadens our understanding of the anticolonial tradition, but also offers us important resources with which to theorize global justice today. The next chapter takes up these resources and develops an account of postcolonial global justice as social equality.

2

Postcolonial Global Justice
as Social Equality

IN THE previous chapter, I argued that a distinct concern of equality runs through anticolonial thinkers' analyses of colonial injustice in the political, economic, and cultural spheres. The egalitarian face of decolonization, as I called it, amounted to attempts to dismantle colonial hierarchy and attain relations of equality at both the global and domestic levels. This raises several important questions: First, what do relations of equality consist of? Second, why should we think that this form of equality—traditionally articulated by philosophers as an ideal *within* societies—is also a relevant ideal at the global level? Relatedly, who is the agent for whom global social equality is a valuable ideal?

In this chapter, I sketch out in a systematic fashion an account of postcolonial global justice as social equality. This account takes the egalitarian critique of colonialism recovered from the previous chapter and reconstructs it for the neocolonial present. While it is useful here to give a succinct statement of the core normative argument underlying the book, it is worth emphasizing that the account grows out of, and indeed previews, arguments to come in the next three chapters, where we take a closer look at concrete problem-areas in contemporary global politics, as well as our anticolonial thinkers' theoretical interventions in each. It may be helpful, then, to think of the next three chapters as filling in the details that this broad and at times telegraphic sketch inevitably lacks.

The first two sections draw from Fanon's analysis of objectionable colonial relations to characterize relational or social equality as an ideal in which individuals stand in relations governed by robust dispositions of mutual respect, reciprocity, and solidarity. Such relations are valuable, I argue, because they enable individuals to experience freedom, maintain self-respect, and enjoy nonalienation with one another. Moreover, although social equality is valuable for *individuals*, social equality between individuals will often demand *group or collective empowerment*. As we will see, this raises some questions regarding the relationship between groups and individuals that become even trickier when transposed to a global scale.

While most relational and social egalitarians have theorized social equality and inequality within societies, I argue that it is a mistake to neglect the importance of such relations at the global level.[1] Global hierarchies between states and other socially salient groups, I argue, are objectionable both for their direct and indirect effects on individuals. In the third section, titled "Global Hierarchies and Global Social Equality," I put forth an account of three kinds of global hierarchies—in political power (especially authority), esteem, and moral standing. Together, these hierarchies create an objectionable form of *unequal global status* between individuals in majority nonwhite, capital-poor postcolonial societies and individuals in majority white, affluent neocolonial societies. Social equality at the global level, I argue, requires that individuals across the world enjoy equal political authority, equal recognition as social agents, and equal consideration of interests. In practice, I suggest, fulfilling these demands will require empowering collectives such as the state and organized nonstate actors.

Anticolonial Equality

Recent egalitarians have argued that we can distinguish between two ways of viewing equality: distributive equality, which is concerned with the distribution of goods (whether that consists of income, opportunities, capabilities, etc.), and relational equality, which is concerned with the kind of relations between agents: whether they are dominating, exploitative, humiliating, stigmatizing, and so on.[2] While critiques of inequality from a distributive view tend to focus on whether agents have equal amounts of the currency of egalitarian justice and the bases on which unequal amounts can be justifiable, critiques from a relational view tend to focus on whether agents interact with mutual respect and reciprocity. Distributions of the relevant currency, in this view, are important insofar as they constitute or cause objectionable forms of relations between agents. To take a simple example, say that wealth is the appropriate currency. Distributive equality asks on what moral basis (such as maximal benefits to the worst-off, desert, individual responsibility, and so on) unequal distributions of wealth can be justifiable; absent such a basis, an equal distribution is a demand of equality. On the other hand, a relational view of equality asks what distributions of wealth would undermine the possibility of agents interacting as equals and see those deviations from equal distribution as objectionable.[3] In evaluating whether equality has been attained, the relational view focuses on the structure of relations between agents instead of the comparative amount of relevant goods they have.

In the previous chapter, we saw that anticolonial thinkers critiqued the structural inequality that defined much of colonialism. Hierarchies—organized along the lines of race and culture—were central features of colonial governance, enabling one group to dominate, stigmatize, and exploit the other. Colonial subjects had little to no say in the laws and policies under which they lived; bodily features and ways of life marked them out as barbaric and backward; their labor was forced and/or unfairly compensated for; and their basic rights disregarded. These deeply unjust relations resulted in vast material inequality between the two.

In response, as we also saw, anticolonial thinkers conceived of decolonization as a radical restructuring of relations between groups. In place of political domination, anticolonial thinkers argued for democratic equality. In place of economic exploitation, anticolonial thinkers advocated for fair terms of economic interdependence. And in place of racial hierarchy, anticolonial thinkers argued for resisting internalized notions of inferiority, partly by reclaiming agency as value-makers in cultural production. This critique of colonialism was generally concerned with unequal *relations* (of domination, exploitation, stigmatization, and alienation), which are enabled and constituted by unequal distributions, but nonetheless distinct from it.

Consider Fanon's analysis of the colonial situation. "The colonial world," Fanon states, "is a compartmentalized world . . . a world divided in two."[4] On the one hand there is the colonialist's sector, "a sector of lights and paved roads, where the trash cans constantly overflow . . . a sated, sluggish sector . . . permanently full of good things."[5] On the other hand there is the "native" sector, in which people are "born anywhere, anyhow . . . die anywhere, from anything . . . a famished sector, hungry for bread, meat, shoes, coal, and light."[6] The relationship between these two sectors is one of domination and exploitation. While "the two confront each other . . . one of them is superfluous."[7] The colonialists depend on colonized subjects to prop up their opulent standards of living. Moreover, this relationship extends globally beyond the colony. The colonized subject, Fanon writes, "fuels as best he can the spiral [of 'domination, exploitation and looting'] which moves seamlessly from the shores of the colony to the palaces and docks of the metropolis."[8]

The colonial situation, therefore, creates "two species"—the colonialist and the colonized. These categories are relational: one exists only with the other.[9] Neither can realize their humanity, because the oppressor-oppressed relation between them means they are "locked in a battle," and both live in "a constant denial of man."[10] Against this, Fanon argues, decolonization must bring about "a new humanity" by reforming these relations. In both the opening and closing pages of *Wretched*, Fanon describes decolonization as "the creation of new men."[11] Echoing the call in his earlier work (*Black Skin, White Masks*) for a "genuine communication to be born," Fanon concludes that "what we want is to walk in the company of man, every man, night and day, for all times," instead of groups being "so far apart they cannot see the one in front," and "men . . . no longer recognize each other."[12] Decolonization, in this view, is primarily a project in creating a new kind of relations between agents. Rather than demanding an equal distribution of the relevant goods, the (egalitarian) anticolonial demand is better understood as a demand for agents to interact and relate as equals. While equal distributions of certain goods may be constitutive of such relations, they are not exhaustive, as will become clear in the next section.

When applied to questions of global justice, a relational approach to equality has two important advantages. First, it gets around a problem that some contemporary global egalitarians who have generally focused on distributive equality face: namely, either defending the existence of a global equivalent of the domestic social structure, or rejecting the relevance of national or institutional membership in determining the scope of justice. Even in the absence of a global basic structure, we might think, agents are already situated in a host of complex relations with one another, and these relations, whether thick or thin, can be objectionable.[13] Laura Valentini, for example, argues that insofar as coercion is prevalent in global politics, that alone is sufficient to ground a robust theory of global distributive justice.[14] Along similar lines, Cécile Laborde and Miriam Ronzoni argue that citizens cannot be fully free unless their states are free from domination, and this calls for significant reforms to patterns of wealth and resources in the international order.[15] Freedom from coercion and domination are *relational* concerns that have distributive implications.

Aside from domination and coercion, other morally significant harms also come into view when we examine the nature of global relations through a postcolonial perspective.[16] Alienation, involving a problematic separation between two entities, is one—as we will see from Fanon below, when agents stand in certain kinds of hierarchies, they experience alienation from one another. Injuries to one's self-respect is another. While some relational harms may be rectified by global redistributions of resources or wealth, others may require different kinds of measures and reforms to the terms of global interaction. In other words, if we focus on whether and how objectionable hierarchies have persisted beyond formal decolonization, there might be more straightforward ways to see why justice may demand more robust and diverse duties at the global level than commonly recognized.

A second advantage of the relational approach to egalitarianism is that, from the outset, it disarms a popular defense of empire and, similarly, a defense of contemporary international relations that look like empire. The defense goes something like this: for all its flaws, colonial rule was needed to lift its subjects out of absolute poverty and jumpstart a modern, industrial economy.[17] Jobs and opportunities need to be created, resources extracted, wealth generated. Violations of basic rights are objectionable in themselves, but unequal distributions of goods are not, at least not until a threshold of sufficiency has been met. We might call this the threshold defense.

One response is to contest the claim that colonialism in fact created these economic benefits at all; as Walter Rodney points out, European colonialism is more aptly described as a process of *underdevelopment*.[18] The relational approach to equality, however, gets around the threshold defense altogether. Relational equality can be practiced and institutionalized between agents before any particular currency of distributive justice surpasses a sufficient threshold. What is required for relational equality is that whatever amount there is, it is distributed in ways that do not undermine the possibility of interacting as equals. Therefore, regardless of what economic benefits are wrought by colonial governance, the hierarchies that formed the backbone of the enterprise are objectionable nonetheless. Even if objectionable hierarchies are the only way through which *essential* economic development can be obtained—a highly dubious premise considered here only for the sake of argument—on the relational view, we can and should still register an important moral remainder.[19] This means that, if economic development (whatever that entails) could be conducted in ways that are compatible with maintaining a society of equals, relational equality demands that that be pursued instead.[20]

The idea that economic development should be conducted in ways compatible with social equality is expressed in many anticolonial thinkers' rejection of the capitalist model of development imposed by European colonialists. Fanon, for example, calls on newly independent states to reject "a caricature of society where a privileged few hold the reins of political and economic power without a thought for the nation as a whole."[21] Instead, as we saw in chapter 1, Fanon argues for a "third way" that is neither Western capitalism nor Soviet socialism. Discussing the way forward for newly liberated colonies, Fanon points to the United States, whose rapid economic growth was built on deeply unjust racial hierarchies, as a warning for the Third World. "Two centuries ago," he writes, "a former European colony took it into its head to catch up with Europe. It has been so successful that the United States of America has become a monster where the flaws, sickness, and inhumanity of Europe have reached frightening proportions. Comrades, have we nothing else to do but create a third Europe?"[22]

It appears, then, that the relational focus of anticolonial critiques of colonial inequality is valuable for thinking about global justice. This approach to the question of global equality helps us gain some ground vis-à-vis those who are unconvinced by the demands of global distributive equality after the breakup of empire, or even before that. But we have not yet explored what it would mean to endorse relational or social equality as an ideal of postcolonial global justice.[23] In the next section, I discuss the ideal of social equality and the problem of objectionable social hierarchies. In the third section, "Global Hierarchies and Global Social Equality," I fill in the requirements of this ideal at the global scale and defend its moral significance.

The Ideal of Social Equality

What does it mean to relate to others as social equals? Let us start with a vignette of its antithesis: Fanon's portrait of the relationship between colonial subjects and colonialist doctors.

As a psychiatrist trained in France who worked for years in the flagship Blida-Joinville psychiatric hospital in Algeria, Fanon was intimately familiar with the colonial politics of European medicine and science. In an essay on "Medicine and Colonialism," Fanon states, "With medicine we come to one of the most tragic features of the colonial situation."[24] Analyzing doctor-patient relations in the colony, Fanon argues that the racial hierarchies of domination and exploitation inherent in the colonial situation "[standardize] relations" between people such that there can be no relationships *outside* of the dynamics of colonial hierarchies.[25] To the colonized, Fanon writes, "the French medical service in Algeria could not be separated from French colonialism in Algeria."[26] Since French authorities point to the hospitals they have built in Algeria to demonstrate the supposed benevolence of colonial rule, it is difficult for the colonized to accept what is "in all objectivity . . . a good thing" without experiencing a deep sense of humiliation.[27] Moreover, Fanon argues, accepting that things associated with the colonizer can sometimes still be objectively good has political consequences beyond subjective humiliation. When, "in certain periods of calm," the colonial subject "frankly recognizes what is positive in the dominator's action," the "colonizer perverts his meaning and translates, 'Don't leave, for what would we do without you?'"[28]

Within this context, Fanon's story of an Algerian father's struggle regarding whether to take his sick son to a European doctor is a particularly sharp analysis of what it means to stand in social relations of inferiority and superiority. Fanon writes from the father's perspective,

> [If] I find myself literally insulted and told I am a savage . . . because I have made scratches on the forehead of my son who has been complaining of a headache for three days; if I tell this insulter he is right and I admit that I was wrong to make the scratches which custom has taught me to do—if I do all these things I am acting, from a strictly rational point of view, in a positive way. For, as a matter of fact, my son has meningitis and it really has

to be treated as a meningitis ought to be treated. But the colonial constellation is such that what should be the brotherly and tender insistence of one who wants only to help me is interpreted as a manifestation of the conqueror's arrogance and desire to humiliate.[29]

In this scene, Fanon shows how interactions between individuals standing in deeply unequal social relations play out. First, when something that is objectively good—in this case, knowledge about how to treat his son's illness—is associated with those marked superior along an objectionable social hierarchy, individuals who are marked inferior cannot endorse the good without injury to their self-respect. Social inequality thus presents constant threats to the self-respect of those placed at the bottom. Second, even as the Algerian father tries to give the European doctor the benefit of the doubt by characterizing him as "want[ing] only to help," the doctor fails to escape the socializing effects of standing atop the colonial social hierarchy and expresses his "brotherly and tender insistence" through the language of racial inferiority ("told I am a savage [for following custom]"). As a result, the Algerian father is deeply mistrustful of the European doctor and struggles with whether he should go back. Thus, individuals standing in deeply unequal social relations are unable to express or experience the good of solidarity. They are alienated from each other. Lastly, the interaction between the two is mediated through a racist worldview that expresses deep disrespect toward Algerians as moral equals. The Algerian father registers this "insult" to his dignity.

From this analysis, we can understand social equality as denoting the opposite kind of social relations: relations regulated by dispositions and attitudes of mutual respect, reciprocity, and solidarity.[30] First, by mutual respect, I mean that persons recognize each other as appropriate objects of consideration in their moral and practical deliberations, to be given the weight that is appropriate to the other's status as moral equals.[31] More specifically, individuals accept an obligation to justify their actions by principles acceptable to others, who similarly accept such an obligation.[32] To ensure that one's actions are based on principles acceptable to others is to respect them as moral equals.

Second, individuals stand in relations of reciprocity when their contributions to a joint venture are fairly returned or compensated for. I mean to use "joint venture" in a very broad way, including personal relationships such as friendship and romantic partnerships, but also economic enterprises and systems of production in general. Individuals who stand in relations of reciprocity are confident that their friends will return their kindness and generosity, their partners will reciprocate their love and care, and their fellow co-participants in a productive venture will reciprocate their contributions fairly. They don't feel cheated, and they are not made to routinely advance others' interests at their own expenses.

Third, by relations of solidarity, I mean that individuals facing vulnerability are reasonably confident that they can rely on others' assistance and support instead of being taken advantage of. Solidarity can arise from one or multiple bases—shared interests or vulnerability, goodwill, a shared sense of justice, love, compassion, and so on.[33] The more bases that ground solidarity, the more confident individuals can be that a disposition to support pursuits of valuable ends robustly governs their relations with others. As mortal beings with complex needs and finite capacities, vulnerability is an inevitable and universal fact of human existence, even if it comes at different degrees and in different forms for individuals. Solidarity is a valuable social response to this fact.

These dispositions and attitudes may broadly overlap—for example, perhaps a part of regarding others as appropriate and weighty objects of consideration is to not take advantage of their vulnerability. Not much depends on these dispositions remaining analytically and practically separate. It suffices for my purposes that we can see these kinds of relations as valuable and (as I discuss shortly) essential for the basic goods of freedom, nonalienation, and robust self-respect. The further and primary question of the chapter is why such relations are also required at the global level.

Moreover, the emphasis on what we can expect individuals to be *reasonably confident* about is important. On the one hand, individuals must not be duped into believing that relations of respect, reciprocity, and solidarity obtain when in fact they don't. Hence their confidence must be reasonable. On the other hand, the fact that people are disposed to interact with one another on these terms must be generally known to them. Otherwise, individuals cannot formulate plans around this fact and will not be able to fully experience the values of social equality (to which I will turn shortly). Taken together, these points suggest that, although social egalitarian relations centrally consist of individuals having the right kinds of dispositions and attitudes, this is insufficient. There needs to be *objective evidence* in the world (such as institutional arrangements, social practices and norms, patterns of social behavior) that individuals can point to in support of their confidence that such relations obtain, and for others to come to similar conclusions.[34] In other words, an essential feature of a society of equals consists of institutions that constitute relational equality. The further question for a social egalitarian is *which* institutions need to do so.

Furthermore, if egalitarian relations are to be considered as stable and reliable descriptions of the social world, around which individuals can align expectations and formulate plans, these relations must hold robustly across time and situations. One-off acts of solidarity in an otherwise hostile and exploitative world, for example, hardly matter for individual freedom, self-respect, and flourishing as nonalienation and, in any case, cannot be described as a form of "relation."[35] For attitudes and dispositions to be robust, however, social practices and institutions must not hinder their development and maintenance. As Waheed Hussain recently argued, institutions that "pit people against each other"—such as a competitive economy in which access to basic goods like healthcare are conditional on winning employment—encourage a "mutual disregard" among citizens.[36] Aside from institutions that constitute relations of social equality, then, a society of equals also requires institutions that promote rather than undermine egalitarian dispositions.

Social egalitarian relations are valuable for multiple reasons. First, such relations are intimately bound up with freedom. When we know that we can rely on others to regulate their interactions with us on the bases of respect, reciprocity, and solidarity, we experience freedom from domination. We can formulate plans with the reasonable expectation that others will not arbitrarily interfere with us. We need not subscribe, consciously or subconsciously, to principles of action that give disproportionate weight to others' wills.

Some critics of the republican notion of freedom as nondomination have questioned whether the institutional empowerment of individuals is sufficient to guard against arbitrary interference.[37] If someone capable of interfering with one's plans decides to do so, the critique goes, they can still do so, as long as their disposition changes. And as long as we know that, it seems that we are, in some sense, dominated. Social egalitarian relations present noninstitutional reasons why we can be reasonably confident that others will not intervene arbitrarily. If we know and see that others generally respect us as sources of weighty moral claims, treat us fairly, and come to our assistance in times of need, this gives us a justified sense of security with which to proceed in our lives. Of course, as mentioned previously, social egalitarian relations need to be undergirded by particular kinds of institutions, without which the mere resoluteness of individual wills to treat others as equals would hardly be sufficient for individuals to experience freedom. But social egalitarian relations are not exhausted by patterns of institutional arrangements. They consist of patterns of social behavior that are encouraged and buttressed by equality-expressing and equality-promoting institutions and practices (about which I will say more later). When we stand in such relations, we come as close to experiencing freedom as is possible for interdependent beings.

Second, social egalitarian relations are an essential basis for maintaining robust self-respect. As social beings, our self-perception is vulnerable to the perception of others. When individuals are persistently treated by others as inferiors, and subjected to institutions and practices that express a judgment of inferiority about them, it can become hard for individuals to maintain their self-respect and a sense of self-worth.[38] As a result, individuals' beliefs about themselves become distorted, and this "inferiority complex," as anticolonial thinkers call it, poses an obstacle for resistance against oppression and for individuals' pursuit of their own plans.[39] On the other hand, social egalitarian relations provide a firm, "objective" basis on which subjective beliefs of self-worth can be underpinned, thus generating a robust sense of self-respect that enables individuals to safeguard what is owed to them, as well as formulate and pursue life plans that they value.

Third, social egalitarian relations enable individuals to experience other relational goods that are constitutive of well-being. As we saw from Fanon, objectionable social hierarchies pit individuals and groups against one another and alienate individuals from one another. By contrast, when social relations are structured in ways that express and promote respect, reciprocity, and solidarity, it becomes possible to experience a host of relational goods that constitutes individual well-being, such as trust, love, compassion, and care. Commenting on the Algerian father's distrust of the European doctor, Fanon states, "In a noncolonial society, the attitude of a sick man in the presence of a medical practitioner is one of confidence. The patient trusts the doctor; he puts himself in his hands. He yields his body to him."[40] Here, as in throughout his writings, Fanon characterizes the ability to trust and share one's vulnerability with others as a valuable state for individuals as social beings.

With this brief sketch of the ideal of social equality, let us now turn to real-world social relations. Hierarchies of all kinds prevail in social life. By hierarchies, I mean unequal distributions of goods (where "goods" are broadly defined) that are durable and group-based.[41] These unequal distributions are reproduced by institutions and practices (thus durable) and, over time, they create sets of people who share similar expectations (thus group-based). In other words, hierarchies are uneven patterns of sets of expectations attached to the different social positions in which individuals find themselves.[42] While some hierarchies are unobjectionable, and compatible with social equality, others sit in deep tension with the ideal.

Consider three kinds of hierarchies commonly found in most societies.[43] First, some agents routinely enjoy more power than others in some domains: they can get others to do what they would otherwise not do. Steven Lukes's well-known analysis of power makes a further disaggregation between three dimensions of power: compelling behavioral change, controlling the agenda, and shaping agents' perception of their own interests.[44] Hierarchies of power can be compatible with social equality, if certain conditions—what Niko Kolodny calls "tempering factors"—obtain.[45] Without trying to give an exhaustive list here, the general consideration is what makes unequal power compatible with the kind of social relations we have reason to value. Consider a specific kind of power hierarchy—that of authority, whereby some have the power to command the obedience of others. For hierarchies of authority to be compatible with reciprocity, for example, unequal distributions of decision-making power would have to realize some important good from the point of view of those with less decision-making power; otherwise, it would be unfair to ask individuals to accept this inequality. Furthermore, there must be some way for those with less authority to hold those at the top accountable so that this inequality does not threaten their freedom. This requires, at a minimum, that there be some reliable way for those below to remove those above should the latter abuse their power. Going back to Fanon's example, doctors are generally accorded greater authority on handling matters of health. But this would not normally pose threats to patients' self-respect, or make them less free, if the point of unequal authority in this respect is to benefit them and, importantly, they have the power to ensure this. Even so, if most experts persistently come from certain social groups, this hierarchy may produce or reinforce notions that some groups are not fit to be experts. This may pose a threat to the latter's self-respect as well as undermine their chances of interacting with others as equals. So for hierarchies of authority to be compatible with social equality, positions along the hierarchy also need to be fairly open to all. Finally, even with these features in place, given the risks of power abuse, it seems reasonable to prefer an egalitarian alternative to a social hierarchy wherever the former is just or almost as likely to attain a similar level of good. This suggests that justified hierarchies of authority are also those for which an egalitarian alternative does more-than-marginally worse.

The hierarchies of authority that rightly concern us lack these features to offset potential threats to social egalitarian relations. When the French Second Republic extended democratic rights to the colonies, for example, French (male) settlers acquired the right to elect political representatives to the metropolitan National Assembly, while indigenous Muslim Algerians were excluded from such rights.[46] In other words, the settler population wielded political authority over the indigenous population on matters that pertained to both. There is no reason to think that this arrangement was for the benefit of the latter, or that this was the only way in which such benefits (if any at all) could be attained. Moreover, the indigenous population lacked effective means to hold the military government accountable for abuses of power. Furthermore, the racialized and religious nature of the hierarchy expresses the demeaning idea that North African Muslims are inherently less capable of coming to valuable judgments than Europeans. Lastly, legal institutions far from exhaust the ways in which objectionable hierarchies of authority are produced or perpetuated. Beyond formal inequality of authority, social and cultural norms that give French settlers greater de facto authority over indigenous Algerians also created an inferior social status for the latter.

A second type of hierarchy consists of unequal distributions of esteem. Esteem picks out certain individuals as fitting objects of positive appraisal.[47] If esteem is accorded for reasons that others can reasonably accept, and does not spill over to other domains of life, higher esteem for some need not undermine the equal social status of others. Yet when some groups persistently attract greater esteem for the wrong reasons, it would be unreasonable to ask others to accept this. Moreover, as unjustified esteem spills over to multiple domains of life, the esteemed group effectively enjoys an unjustifiable higher social standing, which affects how others are expected to relate to them. This undermines the common interests that usually ground relations of solidarity. It also has corrupting effects on higher status-holders who come to believe they are deserving of superior treatment. Furthermore, while some groups are unjustifiably accorded positive appraisal, others can be unjustifiably accorded the opposite: stigma. Members of these groups are portrayed and seen as fitting objects of fear, disgust, contempt, and/or hatred. Stigma undermines equal social standing as individuals come to see the stigmatized group as inappropriate agents with whom they ought to engage on bases of mutual respect, reciprocity, and solidarity.

Consider the deep stigma attached to nonwhite peoples in the colonial context. While white Europeans were esteemed in various social domains, colonial subjects were represented as corrupt, malevolent, poisonous and depraved.[48] In extreme manifestations, Fanon states, "the colonist speaks of the colonized [in] zoological terms."[49] Quoting General Charles de Gaulle, Fanon writes that colonial subjects are stripped of their individuality and referred to as "yellow multitudes."[50] As I will argue later, the same objectionable hierarchies of positive and negative esteem exist at the global level and beyond formal colonialism.

A third type of hierarchy consists of unequal consideration by agents and/or institutions that otherwise owe agents equal concern. A type of institution commonly accepted as a bearer of a duty of equal concern is the state.[51] But, as I will elaborate later, states need not be the only type of institution that owes agents equal concern. Rule-based schemes that rely on participants' endorsement and willing cooperation are only reciprocal if the terms reflect equal consideration of participants' equally important interests. Otherwise, participants rightly feel that they are unfairly treated; that their contributions and cooperation are not reciprocated. Furthermore, failing to consider agents' interests equally *just* is a failure to accord sufficient weight to moral agents and therefore constitutes disrespect of their status. Such institutions—and individuals' explicit or implicit support of them—convey the idea that some individuals lack equal standing. Lastly, when institutions pit participants against each other, such that some gain at the expense of sacrifices to others' basic interests, this undermines the bases of solidarity.

These three kinds of hierarchies often reinforce each other. Consider that those with less power to influence political processes—thus wielding less than an equal share of political authority—also tend to be in a weaker position to bargain for fair terms of cooperation. In this way, domination exposes individuals to a higher risk of exploitation. And persistent domination and exploitation often lead to, and are buttressed by, the development of stigma attached to dominated and exploited groups.

We might conceptualize standing below others in an objectionable hierarchy as having an *unequal status*. James Wilson argues that we can understand status as a set of expectations about how one will be treated by others.[52] Those who unjustifiably lack an equal share of political authority, for example, have an inferior political status. They are treated as less authoritative, and their perspectives are counted for less in collective decision-making. Those whose interests are unjustifiably not given equal consideration have an inferior moral status. Their interests are seen as less morally significant to others'. When individuals are subjected to all three kinds of objectionable hierarchies, we might say they possess an inferior *social* status.

With this account of objectionable hierarchy and unequal status, let us now turn to their global manifestations. Relational and social egalitarians have seldom theorized objectionable forms of social inequality beyond shared societies.[53] Elizabeth Anderson, for example, puts forth an account of social equality in which individuals are entitled to the capabilities necessary for functioning as an equal citizen in a democratic state.[54] Niko Kolodny's recent account of social hierarchy and equality focuses also on justifying the democratic state.[55] Moreover, while neorepublicans have begun to look at how domination occurs between states at the global level, they have exclusively focused on the first kind of hierarchy (of authority).[56] Lastly, some advocates of social equality like David Miller have argued that hierarchies of esteem/status are objectionable only when agents already share a set of social norms and a common way of life.[57]

Yet there is reason to think that all three kinds of hierarchies exist at the global level, and objectionably so, such that it is appropriate to say that individuals in postcolonial societies generally possess an *inferior global social status* to individuals in the Global North. If this is true, then we need an account of global social equality. Extending existing accounts of social equality, I contend that global social equality requires that individuals across the world enjoy equal political authority, equal recognition, and equal standing.

From the outset, thinking about social equality at the global level runs into an important problem, which will recur in different forms throughout our examination of the different aspects of global social equality.[58] That is, while equal status is valuable *for individuals*, attaining equal status at the global level requires empowering intermediaries in the form of groups or collectives. And yet the logic that justifies empowering group agents, such as states, as an indirect way to realize equal status for individuals is not straightforward. Benefits secured by collective rights are not necessarily equally distributed across members. And individual members do not always identify with or feel particularly attached to the group. We might call this the individual-group problem.

As we will see, the specific configuration of the individual-group problem will vary depending on which aspect of global social equality we are concerned with, and thus my response in each case will also vary accordingly. Still, for the sake of clarity it may be helpful to foreground some general thoughts on the problem. Put simply, there are two reasons why an account of global social equality grounded on normative individualism should nonetheless include the empowerment of states and nonstate groups. First, the equal (or unequal) status of socially salient groups has implications for the status of their individual members. As an inevitable part of social life, individuals are ascribed group membership by others with whom they interact directly or indirectly. As such, how a group is perceived and treated can deeply affect its members' interests, whether they identify with the group or not. Socially salient groups are those groups that have, by convention, come to play important roles in social life, "guiding how we perceive and judge others and how we are perceived and judged," as Linda Alcoff puts it.[59] While familiar groups include race, ethnicity, and gender, in a world structured around nation-states, as I argue below, state membership or nationality (which is often bound up with race and ethnicity) has also been made a socially salient identity.

Second, as I argued in the introduction to this book, endorsing normative individualism need not entail rejecting political collectivism. The anticolonial thinkers in this book show us that group or collective rights are an essential basis of power for marginalized or subordinated individuals in a deeply unequal world. To affect change and to safeguard their interests, individuals need to be organized as group agents that can act on their behalf. This is true at the domestic level, but arguably even truer at the far greater scale of the global level. When properly constituted and empowered, states (or collective entities that resemble states, with jurisdictional authority and powers of enforcement) are one such kind of agent at the global level. As I argue across the next chapters, states can be powerful instruments for individuals to push back against capitalist exploitation, political domination, and cultural imperialism. Yet precisely because collective rights can fail to translate into equal benefits for individuals, attaining egalitarian relations between individuals also requires reforming a state-centric world order to make space for a plurality of global agents.

Global Hierarchies and Global Social Equality

Global Hierarchies of Political Power

Since formal decolonization, postcolonial states have enjoyed formal equality to other states under international law. Yet any observer of contemporary global politics will quickly conclude that some states enjoy significantly more de facto influence over the terms of global interaction than others. States that can exercise power over others are enabled by (i) global institutions that routinely accord them greater decision-making power, and (ii) relations of asymmetric dependence. These are the bases of global hierarchies of power.

It is no secret that global political and economic institutions routinely accord greater decision-making power to states such as the United States, the UK, and China. To give a few well-known examples, members of the United Nations Security Council have veto power over the far more democratic General Assembly. The IMF determines vote shares based on financial contributions of each state, thus marginalizing representation for capital-poor countries.[60] The WTO, which we will examine more closely in chapter 5, has historically been dominated by powerful states in shaping the terms of global trade.[61]

Relations of asymmetric dependence, on the other hand, are less straightforward, and analyzing these kinds of relations as well as the possibility of resisting them preoccupied many anticolonial thinkers—most notably Nkrumah, who wrote an entire treatise on it. The next chapter takes a closer look at his account of neocolonialism. Here, I merely provide an abstract account of asymmetric dependence: a state, we might say, is *economically* dependent on x if its citizens lack reasonably uncostly alternatives to gaining access to important economic resources (e.g., capital, basic necessities). A state is *politically* dependent on x if citizens lack reasonably uncostly alternatives to gaining protection against political violence, invasion or conquest.[62] To be sure, interdependence is an unavoidable fact of globalized social life. But interdependence can be compatible with agents enjoying equal authority, if agents are reciprocally dependent on each other such that neither can disregard the will of the other, at least not without significant costs. On the other hand, when dependence is asymmetric to the extent that x can disregard y's will without significant cost to itself, we might say that y is under the power of x.

Many low-income countries are dependent on industrialized countries and transnational corporations for capital, whether in the form of loans, aid, or investment. Capital-rich industrialized countries, in turn, need cheap labor and primary commodities from low-income countries, but dependence remains largely asymmetrical for two reasons. First, with exceptions like OPEC, low-income countries are generally not organized into effective blocs that can inflict costs significant enough to constrain the power of industrialized countries. Rather, they often compete with one another for capital, and industrialized countries can pit them against each other by "shopping around" for better terms of interaction.[63] Second, many low-income countries lack alternatives to selling primary commodities, and thus lack bargaining power, as their economies are highly vulnerable to fluctuations in international market prices of just a few commodities.[64] As commodity prices go into general decline, these countries' economies become even more dependent on loans and aid from capital-rich countries.[65]

As a result, capital-rich states and powerful transnational corporations can routinely exercise power over capital-poor states. The former can compel the latter to adopt or avoid particular courses of action, but they also need not explicitly do so. Given their asymmetric dependence, capital-poor countries have reason to act in ways that avoid incurring the wrath of the powerful, whether this means ensuring that their domestic and foreign policy is compatible with their interests or acquiescing to schemes of global cooperation that disproportionately advantage the latter, and so on.

Unequal power of the kinds described above lack the important "tempering factors"[66] that can offset threats to social equality. As discussed, unequal decision-making power needs to be justified by reasons acceptable to those at the lower end of the hierarchy. From the point of view of citizens in low-income countries, however, the fact that a state like China or the United States can routinely tell their governments what to do is hardly justified by some important benefit that this arrangement realizes for them. Instead, these states wield authority over their government *just because* they have more wealth and resources. Furthermore, to avoid an intolerable threat to freedom, those at the lower end of a hierarchy of authority need to be able to hold accountable those at the top of the hierarchy. But very little accountability exists at the global level, especially against powerful actors. Individuals can boycott transnational corporations, protest against states that compel their governments to go to war or to cede territory, for example, but the deep imbalance of power and the fact that there is no direct way to impose costs on these actors means that global actors are generally shielded from accountability from those over whom they wield significant power.

This suggests that global hierarchies of power are objectionable for two distinct kinds of reasons. The first consist of these hierarchies' direct effects on individuals. Consider how unaccountable global hierarchies of authority undermine freedom from domination. Individuals' plans are always subject to revision, so to speak, by the wills of global actors over whom they have no meaningful control. At the individual level, one's life plans may be drastically upended if a foreign government, sometimes backed by other powerful states, can annex the jurisdiction under which one lives.[67] At the collective level, democratically determined outcomes are not the final say on a policy issue if transnational corporations can threaten to withdraw enough capital to significantly set back a country's economy.[68] Being under the threat of arbitrary or uncontrolled interference, as neorepublicans have argued, is itself a form of unfreedom.[69]

Another direct effect of global hierarchies of power is that they constitute disrespect of individuals' equal status. This is especially apparent in the hierarchies of authority that structure many global institutions. When, for no good reason acceptable to the less powerful, global institutions accord some agents greater authority to make decisions on matters that pertain to all, the former can rightly see in this arrangement a failure to recognize their equal status as moral agents whose views on common issues ought to matter. Unlike the public health expert, whose greater authority on a restricted matter only affirms and reflects the expert's greater competence in a specific set of issues, the political power wielded by superpowers in global institutions is much more comprehensive. It would be false to claim that individuals represented by these states, or the government officials of these states, have superior competence in all things that pertain to global political and economic interactions. But such a conclusion is hard to avoid for those reflecting upon these hierarchical global political and economic institutions.

We might pause here and question whether the purported connection between respect and political equality is in fact culturally or historically contingent. Perhaps for people living in societies without a strong democratic tradition or history of democratic governance, political inequality lacks the same moral significance. The supposed connection between individuals' interest in recognition and the structure of political institutions may just be an extrapolation from a specific set of societies, namely Western liberal democracies.

Yet whatever people may think of the significance of political equality within their states, as a matter of fact, there does seem to be an important difference when some nation-states are persistently able to exercise authority over others. One reason may be that nationality has become a social identity functionally akin to other kinds of politically salient social identities. Social identities such as race and ethnicity are social constructions that play an important role in shaping social interaction partly by ascribing certain attributes to particular persons. Thus, it is reasonable for someone to care about how their ascribed identity group is perceived, because it has an indirect and potentially significant impact on their lives. Nationality has arguably come to perform a similar social role. Although it is technically merely a legal status, people associated with a certain nationality are assumed to have certain characteristics, traits, values, and so on. While these essentialist assumptions are often both objectionable and factually wrong, to deny that they exist in shaping people's interactions would be untenable. Nor must these assumptions be quite strong to have an impact on how individuals are treated or perceived. Someone could think that the traits associated with nationality x are mutable with effort, and still operate on the general presumption that members of nationality x will, all else equal, possess those traits. Because of this, it makes sense for people to care about the kinds of assumptions attached to their national identity, and to interpret their states' global status as partly indicative of what those assumptions are.

In the domestic case, this is clear: it would be reasonable for an African American citizen to think that exclusion of African American rights groups from a civil rights conference, for example, says something about how others view *her* as a Black person, even if those groups were not internally democratic. Likewise, it would also be reasonable for a Vietnamese citizen to take unequal inclusion of Vietnam in an important global governance institution as saying something about how others view her as a Vietnamese person, even if the state of Vietnam was not internally democratic. In other words, insofar as nationality has an important social function in mediating how people are perceived and treated, individuals are not mistaken when they care about how global political inequality expresses a judgment about their nation-states. This sort of judgment is made even more salient *in context*: when we consider the long history of unilateral global governance by imperialist powers, it does not seem at all implausible that persistent patterns of unequal authority at the global level are experienced as an insult to people's status as moral equals. This point is made clear by Nehru's critique of global political domination, which chapter 5 will consider in more detail.

A second kind of reason that makes global hierarchies of power objectionable consists of their *indirect* effects on individuals in less powerful countries. Put simply, global actors can constrain domestic actors' capacity to create and foster a society of equals. The next chapter illustrates this point by taking international investment treaties as a case study. Here, the broader point is that agents atop global hierarchies of authority are far from impartial. Instead, they have specific sets of interests: profit-making and wealth accumulation for transnational corporations and investors, and for powerful states, continued geopolitical influence, national security, and profit for their citizens' corporations.[70] When these actors are enabled (by undemocratic global institutions and relations of asymmetric dependence) to exercise authority over others, they predictably pursue these interests. Yet these interests routinely conflict with the interests of citizens from less powerful countries to address domestic social inequality. By compelling disadvantaged states to accept trade deals that prohibit strategies important for economic diversification, for example, superpowers and their corporations reap large profits while making it difficult for low-income countries to escape commodity dependence, thus decreasing the latter's economic capacity to address domestic inequality. Superpowers and transnational corporations can also pressure disadvantaged states to adopt domestic policies that help pursue their interests at the expense of rectifying domestic social inequality, such as weaker labor protections, weaker capital controls, lower tariffs, and privatization. Finally, these agents can prop up domestic elites who benefit from their patronage and who can help pursue the former's interests.[71] Formal colonialism, as we saw in the previous chapter, thrived on promoting internal hierarchies among the colonized to incentivize collaboration. Observing a similar danger in newly independent states, Fanon warned that the postcolonial bourgeoisie may act as "conveyor belts" for foreign companies, delivering to them the postcolony's resources and allowing them to continue exploiting the people.[72] While these corrupt governments are propped up by interested foreign agents, democratically elected leaders committed to a postcolonial agenda of egalitarian transformation are targeted in foreign-assisted coups. In short, political equality within societies is also undermined when some domestic agents enjoy disproportionate influence over collective governance by virtue of foreign patronage.

Despite formal equality between states at the global level, then, powerful states and transnational corporations routinely enjoy greater influence over the terms of global interaction. Inequalities in global political power, including hierarchies of authority inscribed in global institutional arrangements, undermine individual freedom and constitute disrespect of individuals' equal status as agents whose judgments on common issues ought to matter. They are also objectionable because partially interested agents reliably constrain states and their citizens' capacities to build a society of equals. To the extent that building a society of equals comprised an important commitment in decolonization, hierarchies of global political authority continue to undermine this transformative project.

Toward Equalizing Global Political Power

If my analysis above is right, then we have reason to favor patterns of global political power and authority that affirm individuals' equal status and which enable individuals to ensure that their interests are considered equally in global decisions. Taken together, these demand significant changes to the bases of global unequal political authority, which, recall, consist of undemocratic decision-making within global governance institutions and relations of asymmetric (political and economic) dependence.

This has several implications, which I can only gesture toward here. First, the need to rectify global power hierarchies lends support to principles of redistribution that put downward pressure on economic inequality between states. Not unlike domestic economic inequality, which needs to be kept in check to secure fair political procedures, equal political authority between states requires significant limits on global economic inequality. Moreover, states should have access to a sufficient level of resources so that most of their citizens' basic needs can be taken care of, without having to routinely rely on the goodwill of others. To be sure, complete self-sufficiency is impossible. But access to the resources needed to meet most citizens' basic needs would still seem important, and practically achievable. Otherwise, it is hard to avoid being under the power of others. This lends further support to the thought that global redistribution of wealth, including capital and technology, is essential for attaining global social equality. More broadly, the global distribution of rights over resources and wealth ought to be structured in such a way that agents are no longer asymmetrically dependent. Instead, dependence becomes reciprocal when each agent cannot neglect another's will without significant cost to themselves. Finally, even before (and indeed, as a means to attaining) radical changes to the economic basis of global political injustice, some measure of reciprocal dependence may be attainable if states at the lower end of global hierarchies are able to form coalitions and alliances, much like workers forming unions to resist their employers' immense power over them. Indeed, this was the central insight driving anticolonial projects of federation and Third World solidarity.[73] In chapter 5, I argue that democratizing global governance depends on institutional and extra-institutional power-building among persistently marginalized populations, including counterhegemonic interstate associations and transnational social movements.

Yet even if political authority between states becomes more equal, this does not always translate into greater political equality between *individuals*. Recall Fanon's worry of postcolonial regimes that betray the promise of democracy.[74] Consider contemporary China: a former semicolony, China is now set to become a superpower rivaling traditional hegemons like the United States and the UK. Other states—even traditional hegemons—are becoming increasingly dependent on China, as it is the world's soon-to-be largest economy. It would seem, then, that China has acquired a share of global political authority comparable to, if not soon to be greater than, traditional Western hegemons. But this does not immediately translate into greater global political authority for individuals within China. On the contrary, the authoritarian and illiberal nature of the Chinese political regime means that citizens' wills, for the most part, are not effectively represented by the state's authority at the global level. Not only do Chinese citizens lack equal political authority, they are also denied the freedoms to make themselves heard through other means, such as freedom of speech and of assembly. Global political authority wielded by the Chinese state fails to represent authority wielded by its citizens. Moreover, this problem of disconnect exists not only under postcolonial authoritarian regimes, where it may be most severe, but also in countries like the United States, where historically disadvantaged and marginalized groups such as African Americans continue to struggle to obtain fair and equal political representation and where significant economic inequality has undermined equal access to the means of political influence for low-income groups and the working class. In general, insofar as substantive political equality does not obtain within states, we should be skeptical that reforming international relations will suffice for realizing the ideal of global social equality. Unable to hold global actors accountable through holding their own state accountable, disadvantaged groups within dominant states remain dominated.

In other words, we run into the first manifestation of what I called the individual-group problem for an account of global social equality: insofar as social equality is valuable because it constitutes and contributes to *individual persons'* freedom and well-being, we ought not lose sight of this even as transposing the ideal to the global level will often mean addressing hierarchies between collectives such as states. We can only face up to this problem, I think, by recognizing that the same reasons for valuing global political equality between states also give us reason to endorse the empowerment of persistently marginalized groups *over and above their states*. The latter, I will argue in chapter 5, can be just as important for democratizing global politics.[75]

Global Hierarchies of Esteem

A second kind of hierarchy, recall, is that of esteem. As mentioned, some relational/social egalitarians, such as Miller and Scanlon, are skeptical that this sort of objectionable inequality can exist beyond a society with shared norms of esteem. Yet I will now argue that there are at least two kinds of objectionable global hierarchies of esteem.

First, most apparently, empire gave rise to a global hierarchy of esteem in which some racialized groups are seen and represented as inferior and others as superior.[76] As an ideology to justify slavery and colonialism, this hierarchy of status did not disappear with formal decolonization and the decline of scientific racism.[77] Instead, implicit representations of nonwhite peoples as objects of fear, contempt, and tutelage have persisted in international politics, the media, and academic scholarship.[78] These representations help justify the idea that some racialized groups are incapable of solving their own problems and instead need guidance and intervention from competent others.[79]

A second kind of global hierarchy of esteem is less straightforwardly apparent, but, as we will see, reinforces the first. This is stigmatization that results from global economic inequality. Within the domestic context, social egalitarians have argued that economic inequality can lead to stigmatization when citizens who fail to meet a society's consumption and living standards are marked as ineligible for certain opportunities and associational goods.[80] On this argument, economic inequality translates into objectionable status inequality when there are shared norms of living and consumption standards.[81] But we should not draw from this the conclusion that inequality *between states* cannot generate objectionable hierarchies of esteem. In a globalized world, individuals see how others live halfway across the world. With the development of mass and online media, it is difficult to maintain that individuals are, as Charles Beitz puts it, "either unaware of or indifferent to the standards of living found in other societies."[82]

Yet someone committed to the domestic scope of social equality might ask, even if individuals are aware of wildly varying standards of living across the world, why should they not simply be *indifferent*? Consider what Rawls calls "non-comparing associations" within societies, which enable individuals to maintain their self-respect in face of (otherwise justifiable) economic inequality.[83] If such associations work within societies, it seems like they would work even better at the global level. States may act as "non-comparing associations" within which individuals' social status is evaluated based on domestic norms, standards of consumption, and ways of living. So long as individuals meet domestic standards, the objection goes, their equal social status seems secure. In other words, it should matter less how the distant foreigner lives than how one's neighbor lives.

The objection is weakened once we shift our focus back to a postcolonial perspective. A central wrong of colonialism and imperialism—as we explore further in chapter 4—is that some cultures and ways of life were stigmatized while others were elevated and forcibly imposed. After (formal) colonialism, Western culture (values, norms, practices, way of life) has retained a hegemonic status as the United States and former European colonial powers have enjoyed greater political and economic capacity to promote their cultures across the world. At the same time, non-Western values, practices, and ways of life continue to be represented (by media, politicians, international organizations, and academics) as lesser or problematic in some way. Therefore, even if alternative standards of social esteem still exist across the world, *these very standards* have become stigmatized.

To bring out our intuitions, allow me a highly stylized hypothetical for a moment:

> Take two societies, A, which is affluent, and B, which is less affluent. In society A, wearing jeans is a sign of prestige.[84] Not owning jeans is considered an undignified anomaly. In society B, no such prestige is accorded to jeans. Instead, linen clothing is the norm. Now, jeans-selling companies in A want to reach the market of society B. They target members of society B with aggressive advertising campaigns, selling jeans as modern, urban, and hip, while presenting loose clothing as rural and out of step with the times. Scholars and practitioners of development develop indicators of modernization that include how many in a given society possess jeans.
>
> Over time, many members of B feel that their lack of jeans is undignified. When members of B argue that economic inequality between A and B makes it hard for B to attain the same standards of acceptable dress and avoid

shame (which would, in a domestic setting, register as an important harm of economic inequality), A replies: you belong to a different culture with a different standard, so just abide by that standard and don't feel ashamed.[85]

The intuition brought home by this hypothetical scenario is that the differing standards objection fails to consider the hegemonic status of certain cultures and the fact that interested agents actively export them to the rest of the world. At least two points seem clear: (1) A is not in a position to demand that B now disregard a standard that A helped impose onto B; (2) it is unreasonable for us to expect B to be indifferent to the standards of A.

Since formal decolonization, Western-centric civilizational standards have not disappeared; rather, they have remanifested in subtler forms. Consider modernization theory. Modernization theory was a major school of thought in political science and economics in the United States in the 1950s and '60s. As a response to European colonies becoming formally independent, and spurred by Cold War competition to beat the Soviets to these regions ripe for geopolitical influence, the school's main proponents—such as Walt Rostow— had a huge influence on US foreign policy in that period.[86] According to the theory, societies' level of development is defined by the extent to which they import the Western model of society, culture, and political economy. Typical features included cosmopolitanism, mobility of goods and people, conquest of the environment, secularism, a complex division of labor, and mass consumption.[87] In Rupert Emerson's words, "What makes 'modernization' modern is the ability to live, to think, to produce, to organize, in substantially the same fashion as the Western countries whose imperial hold has now been almost totally broken."[88] Societies that lacked these features were "traditional," and explanations for the lack of economic growth can be traced back to these traditional values, practices, and ways of life. Once traditional ways of thinking and living were abolished, and "modern" values imposed, postcolonial peoples would be better for it.

Although the crudest forms of modernization theory fell out of fashion by the mid-1970s, its core premises—that development and progress are linear and measurable against an existing standard that is exemplified by the West— retain considerable influence over political and academic discourses surrounding development.[89] While it is beyond our scope here to survey these, the broader point is that a shared (because unilaterally imposed and/or diffused) standard of what counts as acceptable and dignified ways of living does exist globally, such that it is reasonable to expect individuals whose way of life fails to meet that standard to feel stigmatized.

This does not mean we should, as a matter of fact, accept that there should always be a shared global standard. There are two ways that we might respond to a global hierarchy of esteem: one is to acknowledge that a shared cultural standard exists and to support redistribution of wealth partly so that individuals can meet the shared standards of dignified living. A second response would be to empower citizens of postcolonial societies to rebuild cultural norms and ways of life that their members endorse and value. This second response has some advantages that the former lacks: first, we may have independent reasons to critique the consumption-driven conception of the good life that has become so prevalent across the world; second, it is valuable for individuals to live under cultural standards that they had a role in creating; and finally, there is value in individuals exercising what I call "social agency" and being recognized as equal social agents. I will return to this point shortly.

Importantly, these two kinds of global hierarchies of esteem—between racialized groups, and stigma that stems from economic inequality—tend to overlap in mutually reinforcing ways. Because the world's wealthiest individuals tend to be individuals coded white, and most of the world's poorest tend to be racialized as people of color, economic inequality between these groups makes it even more likely that the latter are seen to exemplify all manner of negative traits and qualities. This thus leads to a vicious cycle, where one axis of stigma reinforces the other.

If such hierarchies of esteem are objectionable, it is not only because they foster beliefs of inferiority and erode individuals' self-respect. Within the domestic context, for example, Scanlon argues that even if individuals do not experience feelings of shame and humiliation, stigma remains because individuals become marked as ineligible for or excluded from important opportunities (i.e., jobs, better education) and associational goods (i.e., friendships, club and team memberships) for no good reason.[90] Can anything like that be true at the global level?

While Scanlon focuses on thicker associational goods like friendships, there are more fundamental goods from which individuals marked as inferior can be excluded. One such associational good is what we might call epistemic equality.[91] Epistemic equality is a relational or associational good—at the minimum, there is a speaker (in the broad sense of "speech") and there is a hearer. Individuals not seen as epistemic equals have their testimonies, perspectives, and judgments disregarded or discounted for no good reason other than their perceived inferiority. Epistemic equality is a "fundamental" good in the sense that prior to enjoying other kinds of associational goods like friendship, agents must regard each other as epistemic equals (it is hard to imagine a friend who never takes one's views seriously). Furthermore, relations between agents do not have to be very thick for epistemic equality to matter. Consider an encounter between a black Nigerian NGO worker (call her X) with a white American INGO worker (call her Y). X needs to get Y to understand that the INGO's plans have neglected some important fact about the area, and many people would consequently be harmed. It is crucial, then, for Y to take seriously what X is saying—to give it a fair hearing. Global hierarchies of social esteem interfere with this when, given X's (racial and/or economic) status, Y fails to do so.

Emma Crewe and Elizabeth Harrison's ethnographical account of international development contains many examples of this kind.[92] For instance, in the 1990s, the United Nations Food and Agriculture Organization partnered up with the local Department of Fisheries in Luapula, Zambia, to administer the international development program "Aquaculture for Local Community" (ALCOM) with the aim of building up the local fishing industry. However, Crewe and Harrison's study shows that the international ALCOM workers often disregarded the recommendations and perspectives of the local department. While the latter believed that rehabilitating two government fish-farms and developing commercial fish-farming should be a priority, the former wanted to focus on developing fish-farming activities of small-scale, self-provisioning farmers, as they were allegedly more appropriate subjects for development assistance. Crewe and Harrison describe the perspective of one local provincial fisheries development officer (PFDO):

> He had held his post for many years. Among the nine PFDOs in the country, he believed his position to be relatively important, because of the significance of fisheries overall. He was a native of Luapula and felt he had a good understanding of the problems of the province. In Mansa, he was widely known as "the Big Fish." . . . While he had years of experience, creating an understandable belief that he should be accorded respect and status, he was forced to live in poor housing, with no transport or visible evidence of his position. The ALCOM workers were half his age, white, and newly arrived in Zambia. However, they were paid international salaries, which enabled them to live in comfortable housing and have personal vehicles in addition to the project vehicle. . . . At [ALCOM's] program headquarters in Harare, people complained about the local bureaucracy: "That X [the local officer]—he's a disaster. The whole department in Mansa does nothing. How can we be expected to get anything done ourselves?"[93]

Moreover, Crewe and Harrison recorded some common statements that workers in international development agencies use to portray local workers with whom they are partners: "They are not ready to take charge yet," "they couldn't organize a picnic let alone a development project," "they could not manage without us," and "they're so lazy because they don't really care."[94] These attitudes express a deep disrespect toward the local Zambian officials and a dismissal of their expertise.

If we understand social egalitarian relations as relations of respect, reciprocity, and solidarity, it is not difficult to see how stigmatization of racialized groups and/or low-income populations across the world undermine such relations. Such stigma constitutes disrespect toward these individuals, justifies their unfair treatment, and marks them out as unsuitable allies and undeserving of assistance in times of need.

Toward Global Equal Recognition

Following from this, a second constitutive element of global social equality, I propose, is equal recognition of individuals as social agents. In a nutshell, to be a social agent is to have the capacity to create value for others.

This idea of social agency, as I use it here, comes from two ways of thinking about the idea of historical agency. The theme of historical agency runs through much of the anticolonial tradition, as colonial subjects' supposed lack thereof was a common justification for European colonialism.[95] One (familiar) way of conceptualizing historical agency is to think of history as teleological and to see those groups and individuals that move history toward its final telos (however defined) as historical agents.[96] History's telos, whatever it is, is purportedly valuable. To be a historical agent is, in a sense, to be a value-maker.

A second way to think about historical agency decouples value-making from teleology. In this view, historical agency denotes the capacity to solve common problems that humanity faces.[97] Some finer-grained capacities include: the capacity to reflect on the world and identify problems, to innovate, and to act upon those innovations to solve a problem. Problems need not be defined along one comprehensive view of the good. They can be issues that most individuals would see as obstacles to pursuing their own conceptions of the good. Moreover, solving them need not move humanity toward some grander end. They could just improve lives in morally important ways. A medical researcher, for example, displays historical agency by contributing to research that cures diseases. An artist displays historical agency by enriching our understanding of some social or human condition. A construction worker gets around some technical problem in building a bridge. A caregiver figures out how to fulfill a specific person's needs.[98] And so on. Problems can be big or small. In other words, this non-teleological notion of historical agency is better thought of as "making a (valuable) mark on history"[99] rather than "bringing history to its ultimate end." It is thus better termed *social* agency. In principle, all human beings have social agency, even if not all are allowed or enabled to exercise it to the fullest extent.

By virtue of their capacities to solve problems and, therefore, create value (broadly defined), persons are owed recognition as social agents. The failure to accord equal recognition of this fundamental kind constitutes some of the most objectionable status hierarchies discussed above. In particular, central to racial hierarchies of status is the recognition of some groups as contributors to the human good and others as passive receivers of the former's genius. While the former are seen as proper objects of esteem, the latter are marked as inferior. The products of their critical engagement with the world are not seen as equally valuable; their cultures, systems of knowledge, and innovations are seen as belonging to the past and useless for the present/future. To flip Césaire's statement around, these agents are removed from the stage of history.[100]

In contrast, individuals express recognition of others' social agency when they regard each other's capacity for critical engagement and innovation as possible sources of value. The fact that someone possesses these capacities, which are recognized as having the potential to generate value for others, is taken as a *pro tanto* reason to refrain from undermining their ability to exercise those capacities. Acts that undermine persons' ability to exercise their social agency might come in the form of intervention, as in cultural destruction and forced assimilation, or in longer-term processes such as stigmatization, like the kind discussed in *Jeans*. When certain groups are persistently seen and presented as lacking in social agency, restoring recognition to them as equal social agents may demand going beyond the negative duty of non-hindrance and instead require active promotion of the social and institutional conditions that empower their social agency.[101] Securing these conditions not only constitutes recognition of individuals' potential to create value but also instrumentally addresses the failure of recognition as stigmatized groups are empowered to engage in value-making on their own initiative.

What might equal recognition of social agency mean at the global level? In evaluating whether global recognition of social agency has been attained, it is important to look beyond global institutional arrangements to the political and cultural discourses surrounding global interaction. For example, as we saw in the case of modernization theory, the discourse surrounding international development has been criticized for portraying non-Western cultures as obstacles to modernity. The ways in which individuals are represented in these domains impact the extent to which they can relate to others as global social equals. If we are concerned about status hierarchies and equal recognition, then extra-institutional social phenomena are just as important for global justice as social equality. In chapter 4, I discuss how objectionable status hierarchies stemming from a lack of equal recognition of individuals and groups as social agents are reproduced by persistent inequalities in global cultural production and dissemination. I argue that postcolonial global justice as global social equality requires measures that aim at democratizing global communications.

Global Hierarchies of Standing

Now let us turn to hierarchies of standing. Recall that hierarchies of standing are those in which some agents' interests are given greater weight by institutions that otherwise owe everyone equal concern. Like hierarchies of esteem, however, it can be hard to see what a global hierarchy of standing means, because there is no obvious agent that owes equal consideration to everyone across the world. This argument is developed by Scanlon, who argues that the duty of equal concern is unlikely to obtain at the global level, given that there is no equivalent of a single political agent that has an obligation to provide equal access to goods.[102] In this view, when the United States negotiates a trade deal with Mexico, the US government has no obligation to consider the interests of Mexicans and Americans equally. Since equal concern is only owed to one's citizens, the United States only needs to ensure that the trade deal does not unjustifiably benefit some Americans more than others.

Short of a single global political agent, however, there are global institutions whose rules regulate the provision of benefits that states and their citizens collectively create. These institutions also have formal and informal power to sanction noncompliance with those rules. Together, these institutions significantly impact many domains of life. Take the WTO, for example, which regulates much of the global economy. The WTO comprises a set of legal agreements to which states' domestic laws are expected to conform, a system of committees and councils, a consensus-based practice of decision-making and a voting procedure, and, importantly, a dispute settlement mechanism that hands down verdicts and penalties to offenders of the institution's rules. To be sure, the WTO is not as coercive as the state. Moreover, exit options for its members, though drastically costly, are not as nonexistent as they are for citizens who cannot emigrate without another coercive state's consent. Still, insofar as withdrawing from a global institution like the WTO would significantly undermine a state's ability to provide for its citizens the basic goods and conditions needed for reasonably decent lives, participation cannot be seen as fully optional. Furthermore, as we will see in the case of international investment, against a background of significant economic inequality, we have reason to be skeptical of the moral significance of states' consent in legitimizing the terms of global cooperation.

Participants within global institutions of this nature, I think, owe each other equal concern. To see this, let us briefly revisit the domestic case. As mentioned, Scanlon argues that governments are the bearers of a duty of equal concern. One way to ground this duty is to say that governments are coercive, and coercion cannot be justified if some individuals or groups persistently and unfairly lose out on public goods.[103] This justification, when applied at the global level, invites the question of whether global institutions are equally coercive. Yet this doesn't get at the whole story. Governments do not redistribute manna from heaven; they redistribute from some individuals to others. Thus the duty of equal concern that a government has toward its citizens is better thought of as grounded on something more fundamental: a duty of equal concern that we owe one another and that we entrust the government as the collective agent entrusted to discharge. In this view, individuals rely on one another's cooperation with the rules of the basic structure to achieve their own ends. They "enlist" each other's will, so to speak.[104] Yet if individuals are to treat one another as moral equals, they can't reasonably ask their co-citizens to comply with rules that persistently neglect or reduce the latter's interests, especially when access to essential goods depends on continued participation in the scheme. At a minimum, individuals have a duty to make sure that the rules under which they pursue their own ends display equal concern for others' interests in pursuing *their* ends. Put differently, absent reasons justifiable to all, individuals relying on each other's cooperation cannot reasonably ask others to accept that their interests matter less.

Going back to the global economy and the WTO, states—and the citizens they represent—are the participants of a scheme in which each depends on the other's wills to achieve their own ends. They do this when expecting one another to bide by, say, WTO rules (among others). When the terms of cooperation are such that parties' equally important interests are not considered equally, interdependence in the global economy becomes exploitation: some are enabled (by the rules) to take unfair advantage of others. For example, if American farmers are allowed to dump subsidized corn onto Mexico while Mexican farmers are not allowed similar subsidies, then the latter's interests in making a livelihood have not been given equal weight.[105] Or if pharmaceuticals are allowed to reap profits from royalties while individuals in low-income countries suffer huge costs to their health due to unaffordable drugs, the latter's interests in life have not been accorded the weight that they should.[106] In chapter 3, I argue that global economic arrangements are neocolonial insofar as they enable capital-rich agents to take advantage of capital-poor agents while undermining the latter's capacity to escape their position of disadvantage.

The global hierarchies of standing that I've described are in direct tension with relations of social equality. Recall that one aspect of social egalitarian relations is that parties interact with reciprocity. Each is reasonably confident that their contributions to a joint venture will be fairly compensated or returned, and no one feels cheated. Yet, under global hierarchies of standing, many individuals across the world see that their interests matter less than others', not for reasons they can accept, but because others are simply more powerful. It would be reasonable, then, for these individuals to feel that they are persistently being taken advantage of and not treated with the due respect owed to a moral equal. Moreover, leaving such relations, if it is an option, does little to mitigate that one is not being treated as an equal by others—indeed, one leaves *because* one has not been treated as an equal, and leaving does not in itself restore recognition of one's equality.

Furthermore, global hierarchies of standing have distributive implications. When rules systematically advantage some agents' interests over others, those advantaged will accrue more goods and resources over time. Thus, another reason why such hierarchies are problematic is that they lead to unfair shares of compensation for one's contributions in a rule-based network of interdependence. Lastly, when some individuals' important interests are persistently neglected, the scheme gradually loses legitimacy. It is hard to see why individuals should be expected to bide by a scheme that fails to treat them as having equal moral worth. Insofar as noncompliance remains significantly costlier than continued compliance, the scheme, for those at the bottom, appears more and more as a necessary evil than a joint venture for mutual good. Hierarchies of standing thus seem objectionable for that reason, too.

Toward Global Equal Standing

A third requirement of global social equality, then, is equal standing. Individuals enjoy equal standing when their comparatively weighty interests are considered equally by the rules of institutions and practices of which they are participants.

To start, individuals have interests of varying weight. They have a set of *basic* interests regardless of their particular conceptions of the good. Some basic interests include freedom from domination, not being stigmatized as inferior, fair compensation for contributions to cooperative schemes, enjoying a decent standard of living, not being alienated from others with whom they could otherwise pursue valuable relationships, and so on. Basic interests are not only weighty; they are qualitatively different, as their realization is a prerequisite for pursuing other kinds of interests. Beyond basic interests, individuals have further interests in pursuing and realizing their conceptions of the good, that is, what they take to be valuable for themselves and/or others.

Within a rule-based network of interdependence where individuals must enlist one another's will in pursuing their own ends, terms of interaction need to be set collectively, as discussed under equal authority. In setting these terms, each person has a legitimate demand for her comparatively weighty interests to be regarded as equally weighty. This means that, first, the terms of interaction ought to make it possible for everyone to fulfill their basic interests. Assuming it is possible for everyone to enjoy nondomination, for example, the terms of cooperation should not be structured such that some individuals are free from domination while others are not. Where individuals' basic interests cannot all be met at once, equal standing demands putting in place some fair procedure.[107] No one's interests should be arbitrarily accorded more weight than others. Second, less weighty interests should not be allowed to override basic interests. Say that I have an interest in making profit, and you have an interest in a decent standard of living; should these interests come into conflict, our terms of interaction should not allow me to make money at the expense of your ability to live decently. Otherwise, our terms of interaction would fail to treat you as an equal whose basic interests are less important than my nonbasic interests.

In short, when the rules of global institutions are such that participants' comparatively important interests are given equal weight, they enjoy equal standing. This constitutes relations of reciprocity and mutual respect and encourages dispositions of solidarity in times of need.

When domestic institutions fulfill the requirements of equal concern, states can be appropriate proxies for equal standing at the global level. In other words, global institutions and practices can take equal consideration of states' interests as a proxy for equal consideration of individuals' interests. States have interests in securing the conditions that enable their citizens to pursue reasonably decent lives, and global institutions ought to accord equal consideration to these interests.

On the other hand, when states persistently fail to give equal concern to their own citizens, the groups that are disadvantaged become relevant proxies for evaluating whether individuals enjoy equal standing. As in the case of political inequality at the domestic level, remedial measures that go over and above the state may be needed. For example, as I argue in chapter 3, disadvantaged groups in low-income countries ought to be empowered under international law to exert greater control not only over transnational corporations, but also their own states, should the latter fail to give their interests equal consideration to those who benefit from deals with transnational corporations.

Conclusion

We have, once again, come a long way; let me recap what has been said in this chapter. First, drawing from Fanon's analysis of human relations in the colonial situation, I characterized its opposite—social egalitarian relations—as relations primarily governed by robust dispositions of mutual respect, reciprocity, and solidarity. I argued that these relations are valuable because they enable individuals to experience freedom, nonalienation, and maintain self-respect. When individuals are subjected to objectionable social hierarchies, I argued, they are dominated, alienated from one another, and unable to robustly maintain a sense of self-respect and self-worth.

With this account of social equality, I challenged the exclusively domestic focus prevalent among theorists of social and relational equality by arguing that hierarchies of authority, esteem, and standing exist in global political and social life. These hierarchies are objectionable because they constitute disrespect toward individuals across the world. They are also objectionable because they create obstacles for individuals to develop and maintain social egalitarian relations with fellow cohabitants of the world, as well as fellow citizens in their immediate societies. Subjection to these global hierarchies amounts to having an inferior global social status.

Against this picture, I have argued that individuals ought to enjoy equal global political authority, equal recognition as social agents, and equal standing in the moral and practical deliberations of others with whom they are engaged in global cooperative schemes, which should be reflected in the terms of those schemes. In other words, global social equality requires that individuals are treated *as equally authoritative social agents whose interests deserve equal consideration.* Moreover, I argued that we should attend to the potential disconnect between sovereign equality for states and global social equality for individuals. Global social equality is only fully realized, I argued, if states are also internally organized in ways that enable their citizens to relate to each other as equals. Likewise, domestic social equality is unsustainable if individuals are subject to objectionable global hierarchies. Thus, the close connection that anticolonial thinkers observed between domestic justice and global justice, between decolonizing the colony and decolonizing the world, is an important insight for a theory of postcolonial global justice.

Finally, one might question whether the normative individualism underlying this account of postcolonial global justice as social equality is compatible with the stress a thinker like Fanon has tended to place on collectives such as the nation. While I addressed a general version of this concern in the introduction, it is worth saying something more specific here about Fanon, whose thinking informs the normative core of the postcolonial ideal sketched in this chapter. Put simply, I do not think the normative individualism in the ideal and Fanon's emphasis on collective empowerment are necessarily contradictory. As I have argued so far, we should distinguish between the idea that collectives have a moral standing of their own, and the idea that collectives lack such standing over and above their members while remaining politically important and strategically useful. That we must impute the former to Fanon is questionable. Writing about the early stages of the Algerian Revolution, for example, Fanon argues that the colonized intellectual comes to realize that the European values of individualism ("the idea of a society of individuals where each person shuts himself up in his own subjectivity, and whose only wealth is individual thought") are barriers to the struggle for freedom.[108] But it is important to note that Fanon's critique is aimed at individualism construed as moral egoism—"the motto 'look out for yourself,'" as he puts it—rather than the idea that individuals are the fundamental units of moral concern. He argues that, in the revolution, the colonized intellectual learns that "the interests of one will be the interests of all, for in concrete fact *everyone* will be discovered by the troops, *everyone* will be massacred—or *everyone* will be saved."[109] The idea that common oppression creates a common destiny is compatible with the thought that each *individual* has to be emancipated before genuine collective emancipation is fully achieved. Finally, as we saw in the previous chapter, Fanon's preoccupation with genuine emancipation for differently situated groups within Algerian society suggests that he does not see emancipation for the nation and for its individual members as equivalent—in fact, quite the opposite.[110]

Now that our account of postcolonial global justice as social equality is laid out in systematic fashion, the subsequent chapters will discuss three different areas of global politics. In each, I discuss the distinctive set of concerns raised by specific manifestations and configurations of one or more of the objectionable hierarchies surveyed in this chapter, as well as consider principles for guiding reforms in that area. We start with Nkrumah, international investment, and the problem of neocolonialism in the world economy.

3

Decolonizing the Global Economy

NKRUMAH, INTERNATIONAL INVESTMENT,
AND THE PROBLEM OF NEOCOLONIALISM

IN 2006, Evo Morales was elected as president of Bolivia on a platform of regaining greater control over the management and extraction of the country's natural resources. Shortly after, his government nationalized the oil and gas industries by ordering foreign companies to relinquish control of the oil fields, channel future hydrocarbon sales through the state-owned energy company, and renegotiate existing contracts with the government or leave the country.[1] Promising to repay foreign investors' original investments, the Morales administration touted two aims: first, to fairly redistribute profits made from natural resources through dramatic increases in public investment and social spending; second, to industrialize and diversify the economy and enable Bolivia to become an exporter of value-added goods (such as liquefied natural gas) rather than merely natural resources.[2] While the former was designed to address domestic social inequality, the latter would enable Bolivia to narrow the gap of global inequality. In the following years, however, multinational corporations filed lawsuits against the state of Bolivia, alleging violations of bilateral investment treaties with their countries and demanding far more than what the Bolivian government had offered.[3] Settlements for most cases were reached, with Bolivia agreeing to pay upward of a billion dollars in compensation.[4]

In 2003, the South African government passed the Black Economic Empowerment Act to address the economic legacies of racial injustice. The act regulated the amount of Black ownership in a range of industries, including mining and petroleum. Among its objectives, the act lists "[promoting] the achievement of the constitutional right to equality" by increasing "meaningful participation in the economy by black people" as its goals.[5] To this end, it required firms in designated industries to restructure their ownership so as to conform to certain targets.[6] Foresti, a Luxembourg firm, and a group of Italian investors, sued South Africa under the Italy-South Africa and Luxembourg-South Africa bilateral investment treaties, arguing that the act amounted to expropriation. In the end, a confidential settlement was reached.[7]

These cases exemplify two Global South countries—each with different histories of colonialism—attempting to overcome long-standing global and domestic inequalities by enacting fundamental reforms to the structure of the economy. As we saw in chapter 1, in its most ambitious formulation, decolonization was a pursuit in (relational) equality, a prerequisite for substantive freedom. Anticolonial thinkers rejected the structural hierarchies that constituted colonial governance and global society. They fought for a postcolonial future that replaced racial domination and exploitation with relations of equality. To do this, many believed it was important to pursue a "third way" between European capitalism and Soviet socialism: an economic development that fit the specific circumstances of the postcolony and, importantly, rectified the deep divisions and inequalities that colonial rule had left behind.

Yet even before the end of formal decolonization, anticolonial leaders already warned of the dawn of a new exploitation and domination, which would, in Kwame Nkrumah's words, "perpetuate colonialism while at the same time talking about 'freedom.'"[8] Observing that formal independence would not in itself realize genuine self-determination, anticolonial thinkers worried that the postcolony would be prevented from pursuing the expansive decolonial agenda they had fought for. Decades and centuries of colonial exploitation had left newly independent states impoverished and local economies destroyed. To overcome this predicament, the postcolony needed significant investment. Thus anticolonial leaders were presented with a paradox: without reparations forthcoming, the postcolony depended on foreign capital and technology for the decolonial agenda, and yet this dependency would constrain how much, if at all, that agenda could be achieved. Already in the 1950s Global North jurists were circulating drafts of foreign investment conventions that gave multinational companies special protections, including the right to appeal to international tribunals and circumvent domestic courts.[9]

Anticolonial leaders responded to this paradox with attempts to tame foreign capital by asserting economic sovereignty in international law. Unlike the era of formal colonialism, if foreign governments and capitalists wanted to invest in newly independent states, they would now have to bide by "a national plan" drawn up by the postcolonial government representing the interests of the people, as Nkrumah put it.[10] This pushback culminated in several high-profile campaigns of international legal activism. In 1962, postcolonial countries successfully passed in the UN General Assembly Resolution 1803 on Permanent Sovereignty over Natural Resources, which required foreign investors engaged in a dispute with the host state to exhaust domestic remedies before international arbitration could be called upon.[11] Yet the legal status of the resolution quickly came under attack and has since remained largely sidelined in international law. In another attempt to transform the legal infrastructure of the global economy, postcolonial countries put forth the Charter of the Economic Rights and Duties of States (CERDS) as part of the New International Economic Order (NIEO). The NIEO was a set of demands for global economic reforms to address the economic legacies of colonial exploitation.[12] The most controversial part of CERDS was Article 2, which asserted the sovereign rights of newly independent states over their territory and natural resources and allowed for states to expropriate foreign property on their territory with compensation in accordance to *domestic* law.[13] Both CERDS and NIEO were fiercely opposed by countries in the Global North, which pushed back with bilateral trade and investment deals that undermined the anticolonial attempt to establish a new kind of global economic order.[14] With the rise of Reaganism and Thatcherism toward the end of the twentieth century, proposals to shape the global economic order in a fairer direction were gradually buried.[15]

Charges of a neocolonial world economy persist today. Global finance, foreign investment, and aid and loans are often seen as undermining state sovereignty. In this chapter, I turn back to the widely influential account of neocolonialism developed by Kwame Nkrumah. While much attention has been given to Nkrumah's account of neocolonialism as foreign infringement, I draw attention to parts of his critique that emphasize neocolonialism as exploitation.[16] In this reading, neocolonialism is primarily an effort to impose onto vulnerable states an economic model that works to the advantage of the neoimperialist state and international capitalists. In this sense, it is similar in aim to formal colonialism although different in form. As Nkrumah writes, neocolonialism was an attempt to "sweeten the well-known aims of rapidly disintegrating political [i.e., formal] colonialism: the maintenance of less developed areas of the world as the providers of cheap raw materials, spheres of investment, and markets for expensive finished goods and services."[17] In this view, the central problem of neocolonialism was not only that postcolonial sovereignty was infringed upon, but more specifically, that the postcolony's ability to pursue alternative forms of economic development to the benefit of postcolonial citizens was undermined by state and corporate actors taking advantage of its economic vulnerability.

For Nkrumah, as for many Third World anticolonial leaders, some form of socialist planning was essential for overcoming the economic legacies of colonialism.[18] But socialist planning required that mass-based parties like the Convention People's Party retain control over domestic and foreign capital. This control was threatened by the terms of economic interaction offered by capital-rich countries and multinational corporations on which the former colony depended. Through a range of seemingly innocuous measures that Nkrumah analyzes in painstaking detail, such as aid, investment, loans, and currency monopoly, neoimperialist states ensnare the neocolony into a web of contractual relations that undermine the latter's ability to regulate the economy while enriching themselves. The result of neocolonial exploitation is that postcolonial citizens are unable to gain political control over the means of production to realize the radically egalitarian aspirations of decolonization.

Much of this diagnosis remains crucial for understanding how contemporary global economic relations reproduce domestic and global inequalities. Through an extended analysis of contemporary international investment law, this chapter shows how disadvantaged groups in postcolonial (and sometimes even Global North) countries are constrained by the terms of investment from pursuing measures that rectify structural inequalities, even as those same terms enable a global investor class to pursue self-enrichment. Emphasizing neocolonialism as exploitation rather than merely foreign interference better captures the border-crossing nature of capital empowerments. As we will see in the case of international investment, the line between domestic and foreign capital is blurred when the former can strategically incorporate as the latter and receive the same protections and privileges over the state. Relatedly, neocolonialism as exploitation suggests that responses to neocolonial economic relations are insufficient if they only aim to strengthen the postcolonial state against the predations of foreign powers. Instead, I argue that responses should aim to develop a practice of international investment that prioritizes the pursuit of global and domestic social equality.

In the first section, titled "Talking about Freedom," I reconstruct Nkrumah's account of neocolonialism. As one of the earliest systematic studies of global inequality that challenged the mainstream wisdom of modernization theories of development, Nkrumah's theory of neocolonialism went on to influence what is commonly known as "dependency theory."[19] However, although dependency theory was a prominent approach to understanding economic underdevelopment in the 1960s and '70s, many of its major tenets have subsequently been challenged and discredited.[20] Critics argue that the North-South dichotomy assumes far too much homogeneity within both; that contra the claims of an "ever increasing wealth gap" between the North and South, global inequality has decreased; and that dependency theorists' recommendation for lower- and middle-income countries to delink from the global economy were deeply misguided. While some of these criticisms of dependency theory are also applicable to Nkrumah's claims, a closer reading of his account of neocolonialism reveals that there is more nuance than these criticisms imply.[21] In particular, I argue that we can understand neocolonialism as a specific form of group-based exploitation, where neocolonial agents take advantage of the neocolony's asymmetric dependency to enrich themselves at the expense of the latter's ability to escape that dependency. Understanding neocolonialism in this way helps avoid certain pitfalls of dependency theory.

In the second section, titled "International Investment as Neocolonial Exploitation," I analyze the international investment regime to show how neocolonial exploitation plays out. The investment regime, I argue, enriches investors (and their home countries) while imposing costly (and sometimes prohibitive) constraints on host states' ability to pursue economic policies required for rectifying social inequality. The key to seeing this is recognizing who is empowered by the terms of global economic interaction: transnational capitalists whose primary interest is to maximize profit. I argue that this leads to the investment regime reliably hindering the pursuit of equality. The accumulative effect of neocolonial economic relations is that objectionable global and domestic hierarchies become entrenched, thus persistently subjecting the non-capital-owning class, especially within capital-poor states, to the harms of inequality.

In the third section, titled "Decolonizing International Investment," I argue for an investment regime that prioritizes the egalitarian aims of decolonization. Such a regime would go beyond restrengthening national sovereignty but instead constrain both the state and investor by empowering the non-capital-owning class—such as working-class citizens and Indigenous peoples—to exercise greater control over foreign investment. Moreover, until such a regime is in place, I suggest that citizens in host states can justifiably press their governments to refuse to comply with investment arbitration when doing so would undermine or penalize the pursuit of social equality. Citizens of postcolonial capital-poor countries have an important interest in securing the conditions required for global and domestic social equality, which far outweighs foreign investors' interests in self-enrichment. To refuse compliance and to act as if a fairer investment regime has already arrived is to engage in *regime-shifting from below*.

Yet resisting neocolonialism and fighting to reform the terms of the global economy requires coordination among postcolonial capital-poor countries and their disadvantaged populations.[22] I take up this question in chapter 5, when we turn to the question of counterhegemonic power-building in democratizing global governance. In this chapter, our main question is instead: Insofar as organized political actors can fight for change, what new terms of global economic interaction can they legitimately demand? This chapter suggests one answer to this broad question: an investment regime that enables decolonization as the pursuit of equality.

Talking about Freedom: Neocolonialism

As Nkrumah suggests in the quote in the prior section, for anticolonial thinkers, the end of formal colonialism did not spell the end of objectionable global hierarchies. Instead, as we saw in the previous chapter, global hierarchies of authority, esteem/status, and standing are prevalent in global politics. These hierarchies, objectionable in themselves, interact with one another. States and foreign corporations wield unaccountable and unjustifiable authority over low-income states. They exercise this authority in ways that take unfair advantage of the latter, through extracting benefits or setting up institutions and practices that give their own interests disproportionate weight. Hierarchies of esteem/status serve as ideological justifications for both.

For Nkrumah, the phenomenon described previously is aptly called "neocolonialism." First officially used in the 1961 All-African People's Conference in Cairo, the term was later incorporated into the preamble of the Organization for African Unity Charter in 1963.[23] Both organizing efforts had been spearheaded by Nkrumah, whose central concern in his 1961 book *Neocolonialism* was to characterize forms of global relations that bore structural similarity to, and often (though not necessarily) historical continuity with, formal colonialism. Upon publication, the book stirred huge controversy in the Global North, and the United States—a main target of Nkrumah's analysis—promptly withdrew $25 million in aid to Ghana.[24]

Influenced by Lenin's account of imperialism, Nkrumah argues in *Neocolonialism* that the "essence" of neocolonialism is that "the State . . . is in theory, independent and has all the outward trappings of international sovereignty," but "in reality its economic system and thus its political policy is directed from outside."[25] In other words, neocolonialism refers to a state of affairs in which a state is unable to exercise sovereignty and its citizens unable to exercise self-determination. As Nkrumah states, "A State in the grip of neocolonialism is not a master of its own destiny."[26]

In Nkrumah's account, the root cause of neocolonialism is the *asymmetric economic dependence* between capital-poor countries—many of whom were newly independent colonies—and capital-rich states, many of whom were former colonial powers. Decades and sometimes centuries of colonial exploitation had left postcolonial countries impoverished and underdeveloped. As Nkrumah recalled years later in *Africa Must Unite*, at the point of independence from the British empire, Ghana "made not a pin, not a handkerchief, not a match" and had no industries "except those extracting gold and diamonds."[27] Instead, Nkrumah lamented, Ghanaians lived in slums and suffered from illiteracy, disease, and malnutrition. There were few roads and railways, and Ghana's trade relations with the outside world remained largely relations with European powers. As a result, Nkrumah states, "we were reliant upon the outside world, and more particularly upon the United Kingdom, for practically everything we used in our daily life."[28] The economic legacy of colonialism had set the postcolony up for failure, unless they chose the path of least resistance—continued dependence on capital-rich states. Nkrumah writes,

As things are, most of our new States, alarmed at the prospect of the harsh world of poverty, disease, ignorance and lack of financial and technical resources into which they are thrust from the womb of colonialism, are reluctant to cut the cord that holds them to the imperialist mother. Their hesitancy is fostered by the sugared water of aid, which is the stop-gap between avid hunger and the hoped-for greater nourishment that never comes. As a result, we find that imperialism, having quickly adopted its outlook to the loss of direct political control, has retained and extended its economic grip (and thereby its political compulsion) by the artfulness of neo-colonialist insinuation.[29]

In other words, newly independent states quickly find themselves caught up in offers of aid and investment from capital-rich states and private actors such as transnational corporations. But the terms of these offers allow the latter to shape the former's economic policies to cater to their own interests, and the promise of "greater nourishment" never comes, thus trapping the capital-poor country in a cycle of economic vulnerability and dependence.

Nkrumah points to three kinds of agents that together perpetrate what he calls neocolonialism. Together, these agents pursue and enable profit maximization at the expense of the postcolonial masses. First, Nkrumah argues that the primary agents of neocolonialism consist not of states, but a transnational "consortium of financial interests."[30] This comprises multinational corporations and the banks that finance them. This "consortium" occupies a middle ground between state power and private power. While corporations lobby governments to secure favorable protections for their assets and investments abroad, Nkrumah argues that they are also "quite capable of acting on their own and forcing those imperial countries in which they have a dominant interest to follow their lead."[31] In other words, Nkrumah understands transnational corporations as corporate agents with a distinct set of interests and the capacity to act to pursue them. Their goal of profit-making should not be subsumed under the political interests of their governments, although the two are often aligned. It is because they might come apart that Nkrumah states that "neo-colonial control may be exercised by a consortium of financial interests which are not specifically identifiable with any particular State."[32] These international capitalists control "financial empires" that are worth more than some smaller states' total revenues.[33] They see in the waves of formal decolonization the threat of "a major blow" to their continued exploitation of Third World economies and thus orchestrate a "brazen onslaught"[34] upon newly independent states by "push[ing] their interests in the parliaments and governments of the world."[35]

The second class of neocolonial agents consists of the governments of capital-rich states. Benefiting financially and politically from the support of wealthy capitalists, state officials use their political leverage to negotiate trade deals and investment treaties that secure economic advantages for the former. Thus business and government work in tandem to benefit each other by extracting advantages abroad. Their relationship, Nkrumah argues, echoes relationships between capitalist ventures and states in the era of formal colonialism. Drawing an analogy between leaders of capital-rich countries' relations to transnational capitalists, and the British colonial government's relation to the East India Company, Nkrumah argues that political leaders are complicit in the "wholesale plunder" of other countries. Despite politicians' "many just and humane sentiments," they are "modified or nullified by a demand for money."[36] In other words, governments of capital-rich countries are "partners-in-crime" with transnational capitalists, so to speak; it is in both groups' interest to exploit capital-poor countries.

Yet Nkrumah stresses that neocolonialism is not only driven by transnational capitalists and their home governments but, crucially, also the governments of capital-poor countries. The ruling class of postcolonial countries often acts as collaborators or facilitators. In some regimes, political leaders are propped up by foreign powers; in others, ruling elites supported by domestic capitalists benefit from partnerships with transnational corporations. Nkrumah writes, "The rulers of neo-colonial States derive their authority to govern, not from the will of the people, but from the support which they obtain from their neo-colonial masters."[37] Even for political leaders who genuinely want to act in their citizens' interests, they are generally constrained by the lack of reasonable alternatives and must defer to the interests and wills of those who can threaten to withdraw capital. In other words, the connection between the masses and those who hold the instruments of the postcolonial state is severed. The latter have "little interest" in "strengthening the bargaining power of their workers employed by expatriate firms" or "taking any step . . . to challenge the colonial pattern of commerce and industry."[38] Instead, the organs of the postcolonial state are employed to suppress their own citizens when they protest land grabs, poor working conditions and low wages, the high cost of basic utilities, pollution, and so on. "[The] governments of new States," Nkrumah writes, "are seen in the role of policemen for the banking and industrial consortia bent upon continuing the old imperialist pattern in Western-African relationships."[39]

Moreover, the neocolony appears to consent to the foreign trade, investment, and aid that further entrench its dependency. This illusion of self-determination gives neocolonial relations a veneer of legitimacy that formal colonialism no longer enjoys. This "new scramble for Africa," Nkrumah argues, was carried out "under the guise of aid, and with the consent and even the welcome of young, inexperienced States."[40] It is this veneer of legitimacy that makes neocolonialism "the worst form of imperialism" to Nkrumah. Under "old-fashioned colonialism," he argues, the colonizers that were formally responsible for governing the colony at least had to answer to their constituents back at home to "justify . . . actions it was taking abroad."[41] The self-proclaimed bearers of the white man's burden had to show how their actions and policies were discharging that burden. Under neocolonialism, by contrast, neocolonial agents appear to have little to answer for—interactions between states are consensual, and domestic woes can be ascribed to domestic governance. Thus, Nkrumah argues, "for those who practice [neocolonialism], it means power without responsibility and for those who suffer from it, it means exploitation without redress."[42]

On Nkrumah's account, then, capital-rich states and transnational corporations take advantage of the economic dependence of postcolonial capital-poor states to offer terms of economic interaction that prioritize the former's interest in profit maximization and political control. Domestic ruling elites facilitate this by suppressing local resistance, whether because they personally benefit from foreign patronage or because the neocolony will incur significant costs for failing to protect the interests of transnational corporations. While this analysis may seem overblown, we will see later from the case of contemporary international investment that it is in fact not far from reality.

As a result of these constraints, the promise of postcolonial democracy could not be fulfilled. Faced with unresponsive political leaders and unaccountable foreign powers and corporations, citizens in the postcolony are unable to exercise democratic control over their economy and thus unable to adopt the kinds of social and economic policies that benefit them. In particular, for Nkrumah, these were social and economic policies that made up an alternative economic model that he called "African socialism."

The idea of African socialism sparked much debate among Afro-anticolonial thinkers at the time.[43] Léopold Sédar Senghor, the first president of Senegal and one of the most influential theorists of African socialism, had published a book titled *On African Socialism* in 1962, in which he posits a controversial distinction between African and European ways of being. Africans, he writes, acquire knowledge primarily through intuition and lived experience, while Europeans acquire knowledge through analytic reasoning.[44] He argues for an economic system that would synthesize European values with "Afro-cultural values." Senghor argues that postcolonial states' lack of genuine self-determination made this difficult, if not impossible, to pursue.[45]

Like his counterpart in Senegal, Nkrumah thought that genuine decolonization could only be attained through an "African socialism" that was a superior alternative to Western capitalism and Soviet communism. Unlike Senghor, however, Nkrumah saw African socialism not as socialism embedded in what he thought was a mystifying notion of Africans' way of being. Referring to Senghor in a 1967 speech titled "African Socialism Revisited," Nkrumah states, "It is clear that socialism cannot be founded on this kind of metaphysics of knowledge."[46]

Instead, for Nkrumah, African socialism consists of integrating the ideals that underlie African communalism with the means of scientific socialism. This appeal to African "traditional values" served more as a political strategy than an assertion of historical fact. As Steven Metz argues, even as Nkrumah "sought to foster a particular image of pre-colonial Africa which emphasized an 'attitude towards man which can only be described, in its social manifestations, as being socialist,'" he also argued against a "return to pre-colonial African society."[47] For Nkrumah, Metz states, the "true value" of traditional Africa was its political potential as a "motivational myth" when suitably reconstructed by a class vanguard such as himself and his party.[48]

What are these values? The "traditional African society," Nkrumah states, "was founded on principles of egalitarianism," although in reality it had major "shortcomings."[49] The "humanist impulse" of African communalism was nonetheless a worthy ideal, one that, as Nkrumah puts it, "continues to urge us towards our all-African socialist reconstruction."[50] He elaborates on this ideal:

> We postulate each man to be an end in itself, not merely a means; and we accept the necessity of guaranteeing each man equal opportunities for his development . . . Any meaningful humanism must begin from egalitarianism and must lead to objectively chosen policies for safeguarding and sustaining egalitarianism. Hence, socialism.[51]

In other words, socialism, "according to which the major means of production and distribution ought to be socialized," was to Nkrumah's mind the most appropriate economic model for realizing the egalitarian values underlying African communalism. Socializing the major means of production and distribution is needed "if exploitation of the many by the few is to be prevented; if, that is to say, egalitarianism in the economy is to be protected."[52] Its opposite, laissez-faire capitalism, inevitably creates "class cleavages" and "economic disparities" that lead to "political inequalities." Nkrumah concludes that "socialism, therefore, can be, and is, the defense of the principles of communalism in a modern setting."[53]

To Nkrumah, neocolonialism is the most significant obstacle to realizing socialism in postcolonial Africa. Despite the "obvious advantages of socialist development" for societies that are "evolving out of a colonialist domination," neocolonial powers are "decided that the new States shall develop along the capitalist path" and continue to serve as "the source of [these powers'] super profits."[54] In other words, neocolonial agents have a "vested interest" to ensure that neocolonies remain "underdeveloped."[55] Foreign capital, he writes, is "used for the exploitation rather than for the development of the less developed parts of the world."[56] As a result, "investment under neo-colonialism increases rather than decreases the gap between the rich and the poor countries of the world."[57]

In short, Nkrumah characterizes postcolonial relations between states and between states and transnational corporations as a new form of colonialism, in which economically powerful parties undermine the postcolony's ability to adopt alternative economic models from the one that enriches them. Postcolonial and low-income countries are unable to pursue economic development that is compatible with egalitarian aspirations of decolonization, whether it is addressing domestic inequalities or diversifying their economies. Instead, capital-poor countries are consigned to be the primary commodities exporters of the world while international capitalists and capital-exporting states enrich themselves.

In the next section, I analyze the case of international investment and argue that the general shape of Nkrumah's account—that the terms of global economic interaction, negotiated by capital-exporting states, enable transnational capitalists to undermine the ability of citizens in capital-receiving states to pursue social equality—remains highly relevant. But before that, let us survey some of the common criticisms of dependency theory that also seem applicable to Nkrumah's account.

First, Nkrumah's analysis of the global economy, as with much of dependency theory, seems to rely on a rigid dichotomy of the Global North versus the Global South and treats each as internally homogenous.[58] This is to a certain extent true—after all, Nkrumah's main point of reference was Ghana and other newly independent countries in Third World, which were deeply unequal to the Global North in his time. Yet such a dichotomy fails to capture the heterogeneity that exists across both. The transnational capitalist class no longer draws exclusively from the Global North but increasingly includes the elite of the Global South. At the same time, ordinary citizens in affluent societies like the United States are also unable to exercise democratic control over their economy, as policymaking is increasingly driven by the extremely rich. To use the language of dependency theorists, peripheries exist within cores and cores within peripheries. As such, an exclusive focus on state-level analysis seems woefully inadequate to capture problematic relations of economic dependency and the loss of political control over capital.

Yet although Nkrumah often writes in terms of the state, he also makes various distinctions between the capital-owning class and the working class within states. For one, he thought that neocolonialism emerged out of a need to "[transfer] the conflict between the rich and poor from the national to the international stage."[59] In this view, the postwar welfare state was a class compromise to redistribute gains from the continued exploitation of the Third World.[60] Therefore, Nkrumah argues, the end of neocolonialism would also reinvigorate labor movements in the North and transnational capitalists would "come face to face with their own working class in their own countries."[61] In this sense, the exploitation of the working class in the affluent countries was tied to the exploitation of their counterparts in less affluent countries.[62] Both suffer from the dominance of transnational corporations and the political elites who support them, but the former were unwilling or unable to recognize this as long as they were allowed to share in the gains of trade—a compromise that fell apart after Nkrumah's time. As I argue in the next section, the international investment regime is precisely a case where transnational capitalists are empowered to undermine the pursuit of egalitarian objectives everywhere, including in affluent countries like the United States.

Moreover, as we saw above, Nkrumah did not treat the postcolonial state as internally homogenous—on the contrary, he critiqued the failures of domestic governments in aligning with citizens to resist neocolonial exploitation. If Nkrumah often wrote in terms of the state, it is because he saw the state as an important instrument of planning when wielded by the right agents—not postcolonial domestic capitalists or ruling elites detached from the people, but mass-based parties that represented the interests of workers, farmers, and "the so-called little man."[63] Although his main concern was relations of dependency between capital-rich states and former colonies, this analysis does not preclude and in fact was sensitive to other units of analysis such as class. As I argue below, reforms to the investment regime are insufficient if they fail to take into account the heterogeneity that Nkrumah was sensitive to and merely empower the state without attention to the possibility of domestic neocolonial capture.

Relatedly, relying on a dichotomy between homogenous actors risks attributing uniform intentions to each. Throughout *Neocolonialism*, Nkrumah seems to ascribe conspiratorial intentions to transnational corporations and capital-rich states, as if they work to keep large swaths of the world's population in poverty, ready to be exploited. As he states, "The economic object of neo-colonialism is to keep those standards depressed in the interest of the developed countries."[64] Such sweeping claims about diverse actors' agendas are difficult to maintain. But they are also not needed for his broader argument regarding exploitation to get off the ground. Indeed, in other moments, Nkrumah is rather clear on the irrelevance of actors' intentions. Discussing President Truman's declaration of a "war" on global poverty, he states, "Nothing is gained by assuming that those who express such views are insincere."[65] Those who express the desire to "help" the Third World may be well intentioned, but

the need to subsidize their welfare states without redistributing from the domestic rich, as well to fund their "ever-growing" arms race, meant that the
interests of Third World populations would inevitably be sacrificed.[66] Capitalism, Nkrumah concludes, always provides strong incentives for agents to come
down on the side of exploitation.[67] As I argue in the next section, if we see
agents as embedded in broader economic structures that confer incentives and
disincentives to act in certain ways, we need not subscribe to claims about a
conspiracy on the part of transnational capitalists and capital-rich countries
to keep the rest of the world oppressed, to think that some agents are "invested" in terms of economic interactions that predictably disadvantage the
already disadvantaged.

Third, dependency theorists often make the claim that economic growth
for peripheral countries is near-impossible, or that the center grows richer *at
the expense of* the periphery such that inequality between the two necessarily
widens. As we saw above, Nkrumah also seems to make such claims. But this
claim has not held up against empirical scrutiny. On the contrary, a global
"middle class" has grown relative to the global poor.[68] To be sure, this trend is
mostly due to the rise of just China and India, and they have arguably employed the kinds of developmental strategies that have precisely been unavail-
able to postcolonial countries with less bargaining power.[69] Still, it is hard to
deny that some economic growth *has* been possible for so-called peripheral
countries. Like claims about intent, I suggest that rejecting the claim of ever-
growing global inequality is compatible with holding that capital-poor countries are constrained in various ways by global economic arrangements when
attempting to escape their disadvantaged position within the global division
of labor, and that this is unjust.

Lastly, and perhaps most importantly, dependency theory has been criticized for putting postcolonial capital-poor countries on the mistaken track of
attempting to delink from the global economy. The developmental economic
policies that came out of the dependency tradition, such as imports substitu-
tion, turned out to be largely unsuccessful. More broadly, it is hard to see how
delinking might be a feasible or even desirable goal today.

Against neocolonialism, however, Nkrumah's solution was not to reject
foreign capital altogether. He emphasizes multiple times that "the struggle
against neo-colonialism is not aimed at excluding the capital of the developed
world from operating in less developed countries."[70] Instead, "it is aimed at
preventing the financial power of the developed countries being used in such
a way as to impoverish the less developed."[71]

In this sense, Nkrumah differed from the anticolonial economists who
came after him in their proposals to delink from the global economy.[72] Rather
than delinking, his solution was twofold: first, postcolonial citizens must

regain control over how foreign capital is used and how the fruits of economic growth are distributed by actively participating in grassroots and party politics. As discussed previously, Nkrumah was a fierce critic of rulers of neocolonial states who respond to the will and interests of neocolonial masters instead of the people. So, the solution to neocolonialism was not just strengthening the postcolonial state but also empowering the people through political education and organization. Nkrumah argues that grassroots organizations like the All-African trade union federation, the pan-African youth movement, as well as "women, journalists, farmers," are the ones who "make, maintain or break revolutions" by ensuring that "liberatory forces are in power" and guarding against neocolonial governments.[73]

Second, Nkrumah believed that neocolonialism was possible because many postcolonial states were too small in scale to have any meaningful bargaining power on their own. As he puts it, they "lack the financial strength to force the developed countries to accept their primary products at a fair price."[74] Therefore, a second and essential part of the solution was to build a regional market and political union across the African continent on the one hand, and form closer ties with other similarly situated postcolonial states in Latin America and Asia—the "spirit of Bandung," as he puts it—on the other.[75] A prominent pan-African thinker throughout his life, Nkrumah advocated for an African Federation that at times closely resembled a unified African state. The proposal ultimately failed, partly due to other anticolonial leaders' concerns about losing their autonomy in a continent-wide federal state.[76] The broader point is that, in the face of vulnerability, Nkrumah's solution was not to retreat from economic cooperation with more powerful actors, but to strengthen one's position by banding with other similarly situated actors.

Bringing together the threads of Nkrumah's analysis, we can conceptualize neocolonialism as a specific form of group-based exploitation.[77] In this view, neocolonialism occurs when (i) group y is asymmetrically dependent on group x, and (ii) x offers y terms of cooperation that enrich x while undermining y's ability to escape its position of disadvantage. While group y's initial disadvantaged position may or may not have been (partly or wholly) x's doing, y's subsequent position of disadvantage—where y continues to be asymmetrically dependent on x (or other third parties)—is partly or wholly a result of the terms of cooperation in x's offer. This persistent dependency allows x, or other third parties, to continue exercising power over y.

Two clarifications are in order. First, y may derive benefits from interacting with x but nonetheless remain objectionably dependent on x and/or others. Thus neocolonial exploitation does not necessarily entail that the exploited party gains nothing—indeed, it would be difficult to explain why states agree to such offers if that were the case. Nkrumah's analysis was precisely aimed at exposing the dark side of neocolonial economic relations beyond their immediate benefits. As we will see in the case of international investment, host states may benefit from foreign investment but nonetheless remain constrained from escaping its disadvantaged position within the global economy.

Second, although I use y and x for simplicity above, when analyzing real cases, we must further differentiate within these groups. As Nkrumah's analysis suggests, whatever benefits wrought from exploitative terms of economic cooperation are unevenly distributed within group y, such that some agents—such as the postcolonial ruling elite and/or domestic capitalists—are more willing to accept exploitative offers than others, such as the grassroots. In reality, then, we might sometimes say that advantaged members of y and x collaborate to construct terms of economic interaction that enrich both, at the expense of disadvantaged members of y's ability to escape their position of disadvantage.

To put the point more sharply, consider Nicholas Vrousalis's triadic conception of what he calls structural domination.[78] Structural domination, in this view, involves dominators, the dominated, and regulators. Regulators "impart structure" on the dominating relationship by stabilizing the positions of the dominated and the dominator and providing assurance that each complies with the rules that reproduce these positions.[79] Capitalism, in Vrousalis's analysis, is a form of structural domination in which capitalists' domination of workers is made possible by the state and market norms that enforce the existence of private property in the means of production, thereby stabilizing the position of the capitalist and wage laborer.[80]

We can think of something similar as happening in neocolonial exploitation. Capital-rich states and terms of trade and investment (call these the neocolonial regulators) enable the transnational capitalist class to exercise power over the non-capital-owning class in capital-poor *and* capital-rich states by enforcing the global existence of private property in means of production. In the case of international investment, as we will see, neocolonial regulators *enlist* capital-poor states to *also* act as a regulator for neocolonial exploitation—to enforce the property rights of foreign investors *at the expense of* their own citizens' capacity to escape (global and domestic) social inequality. Moreover, in neocolonial exploitation, some regulators are also dominators and exploiters themselves—capital-rich states benefit from gains in geopolitical power whenever other states remain asymmetrically dependent on them. And, even more obviously, government officials can themselves be invested in the profit-maximization of transnational corporations whose interests they help promote. Recall Nkrumah's condemnation of the East India Company and the English government.

So far, we've only discussed (in fairly abstract terms) what neocolonial exploitation looks like. But what exactly is *wrong* with it? More precisely, in making an offer to interact with y, why does x have a duty to help y escape their position of disadvantage? After all, x could choose not to make any offers at all—to not interact with y, which would predictably leave y (which is asymmetrically dependent on x) even worse off. To be sure, if y's disadvantage was x's doing in the first place, it is easy to see why this x's offer is wrong. For example, if x is a former colonizing power and y a postcolony, x's duty of reparative justice toward y plausibly includes offering terms of economic interaction that correct for y's disadvantaged position.

But Nkrumah's account of neocolonialism is broader in scope and is meant to capture objectionable economic relations between states without a previous history of colonialism. We can flesh out the wrong of neocolonial exploitation here by revisiting the value of social equality discussed in the previous chapter. Recall that relations of equality are valuable because they enable individuals to experience freedom, maintain robust self-respect, and enjoy nonalienation from one another. Individuals, therefore, have a fundamental interest in social equality. Recall also that relations of equality are partly constituted by reciprocity, where agents' participation in joint ventures (or schemes that require their cooperation) are fairly compensated for, and none is required to routinely advance the interests of another at their own expense. At a minimum, the terms of joint ventures ought to reflect equal concern for agents' equally important interests. Now, insofar as group y's initial position of disadvantage exposes them to domination and other kinds of objectionable treatment from others, (members of) y's interests in escaping that position are extremely weighty, as they amount to an interest in escaping an inferior status. By any reasonable comparison, (members of) x's interests in self-enrichment are less significant. And so, when x offers terms of economic interaction by which they enrich themselves while undermining y's ability to escape their disadvantaged position, this is a failure in reciprocity. The terms offered reflect the idea that members of y matter less (or don't matter at all). To be sure, x can choose to not interact with y. But insofar as they opt to do so, the terms of their arrangement should be compared not to a baseline of no offer, but a moralized baseline whereby x's enlisting of y's will into a joint venture is compatible with y enjoying an equal status to x (which, again, is partly constituted by the idea that y and x's equally significant interests matter equally).

Finally, the fact that y *consents* to x's offer does not in itself make it acceptable. After all, x can make an offer to their own advantage and expect acceptance precisely due to y's initial position of disadvantage. As we will see in the case of investment, states routinely consent to international arrangements against a background of inequality. The greater the asymmetric dependence between parties, the less relevant consent is for evaluating the moral status of an arrangement.

To sum up briefly, neocolonialism can be understood as a kind of exploitation in which some agents take advantage of others' dependency to offer terms of interaction that enrich themselves at the expense of the latter's capacity to escape their position of disadvantage. The result is that the latter's dependency becomes entrenched and this exposes them to further harms that come with being unable to relate to others as equals. This account captures Nkrumah's claim that the neocolony's capacity to pursue alternative and more egalitarian forms of economic development is undermined by terms of aid, loans, trade, and investment that enrich capital-rich countries and international capitalists.

But defending this rather abstract account as an accurate characterization of global economic relations today requires application to a real-world case. In the rest of the chapter, I illustrate how neocolonialism as exploitation plays out in the contemporary global economic order with a critical analysis of international investment as it has been practiced since the end of formal colonialism. The key insight from Nkrumah's analysis that I suggest we take on is that the current rules of the global economy place undue constraints on citizens' capacity to pursue social equality. Based on this analysis, I argue for an investment regime that takes redressing inequality as a priority—in other words, an investment regime that facilitates rather than undermines the egalitarian aspirations of decolonization.

International Investment as Neocolonial Exploitation

My analysis focuses on international investment for three reasons. First, international investment law has origins in the history of imperial expansion.[81] As TWAIL scholars Ciaran Cross and Christian Schliemann-Radbruch note, European investment from the seventeenth to nineteenth centuries mainly took the form of corporations such as the British and Dutch East India trading companies, with European states backing these companies to secure favorable treatment.[82] The contemporary investment treaty regime,[83] which emerged with the first bilateral investment treaty signed between Germany and Pakistan in 1959, in turn evolved as part of the so-called Global North's response to decolonization. As former colonies became independent, and waves of nationalization spread across the Third World, a host of reforms to the global economy were designed specifically to curtail demands for social justice. In particular, to counter postcolonial states' nationalization of natural resources and foreign assets, foreign investors were accorded the right to sue states in international tribunals.[84] These reforms were often justified with racist arguments that closely resembled colonial discourse. "Wild men bent upon revenge" were said to be expropriating Dutch assets in postcolonial Indonesia, and Hermann Joseph Abs's so-called Capitalist Magna Carta—whose content laid the groundwork for international investment law today—was presented as reestablishing the rule of law against the "law of the jungle" in the Third World.[85] The "externalization" of investment regulation, as international investment law expert M. Sornarajah puts it, marked a significant departure from the Calvo doctrine, under which the jurisdiction over foreign investment lies with the host country and foreign investors do not enjoy additional rights beyond those secured by domestic law.[86] Examining the investment regime that has resulted since then seems apt if we want to evaluate the extent to which a charge of neocolonialism is appropriate.

Second, international investment makes up a significant part of the world economy, and yet, unlike trade, the regime that governs it has received little philosophical treatment within the global justice literature.[87] Since 1990, foreign direct investment, or FDI, has grown steadily by 7.6 percent ($50 billion) a year, and for lower- and middle-income countries, foreign direct investment has become the greatest source of external capital.[88] It seems important to examine the more unique issues raised by this significant aspect of the world economy.

Third, many key features of investment treaties—such as the principles of most favored nation and national treatment, which I'll discuss soon—are also found in trade agreements, and vice versa. As Pierre Kohler and Francis Cripps state, there is increasing "blurring" of investment and trade agreements, as it is now common to include investment provisions and private dispute settlement mechanisms in "mega" regional free trade agreements.[89] At least some of my analysis here, then, is applicable to other parts of the global economy.

To start, recall the two cases that this chapter opened with—Bolivia's and South Africa's entanglements with international investment law. These cases are the tip of an iceberg of controversies related to the economic and political leverage that investment treaties afford to powerful, private actors. Bolivia and South Africa's predicaments are not unique among societies attempting to decolonize by nationalizing key economic sectors and redistributing resources across historically advantaged and disadvantaged groups.[90]

In the following, I highlight four core features of the regime that are relevant for our analysis:

(i) *Bilateralism.* Unlike trade agreements, investment treaties are generally bilateral rather than multilateral affairs. Thus, the expansiveness of protections given to investors often varies depending on power dynamics between the two signatories. For example, Todd Allee and Clint Peinhardt found that the power and preferences of the capital-exporting country (as measured by GDP, the presence of multinational corporations, and a right-wing government) was the most significant determiner of the expansiveness of investment protection provisions in a given treaty.[91] Furthermore, Beth Simmons found that host states accept stronger constraints on their sovereignty when they are in a weaker bargaining position (for example, when there is slow economic growth).[92]

(ii) Vagueness of treaty provisions. The terms of investment treaties, like any treaty, are subject to parties' contestation. But investment treaties tend to be excessively vague. For example, the term "investment" itself is controversial: the term has expanded from tangible property to include intellectual property and the administrative rights necessary for business operations.[93] This means that state regulatory acts such as compulsory licensing and denial of operation permits can be construed as "indirect" expropriation of an investment, exposing states to litigation.[94] Another ambiguous provision is the guarantee of "fair and equitable treatment" to foreign investors. International tribunals have interpreted this as realizing foreign investors' legitimate expectations.[95] For example, in the case of *Tecmed v. Mexico*, despite acknowledging that Tecmed's landfill operations had breached local environmental regulations, the tribunal found that the Mexican government had failed to uphold Tecmed's expectations of having its operating license renewed, thus violating "fair and equitable treatment" standards.[96]

(iii) Strong investor protections. Under investment treaties, investors are generally guaranteed a host of protections, most notably: (i) national treatment, under which foreign investment is to be given equal treatment to domestic business, thereby prohibiting requirements such as the use of local content and labor, skills, and technology transfer; (ii) fair and equitable treatment, as mentioned; (iii) most-favored-nation, which guarantees that advantages given to another state are also conferred to parties to the investment treaty. This allows investors to utilize favorable provisions in the host country's treaties with other states and, combined with the practice of jurisdiction shopping,[97] opens up a host of venues for investors to sue[98] states; (iv) full protection and security, a clause evolved to include the controversially broad notion of guaranteeing "conditions of stability" for investment.[99] This clause effectively puts pressure on host states to crack down on labor unrest and other forms of protest deemed threatening to investors' property interests.[100]

These protections are not only granted to foreigners. In what is known as "treaty shopping," a state's own capitalists can strategically incorporate abroad to utilize the protections and privileges offered by a bilateral investment treaty that their own state has signed with the state in which they have incorporated. Due to complex corporate structures that are seldom transparent and therefore difficult for a state to track, host states end up having to assume that the investor protections in the treaty signed are "owed to every State and every company."[101]

Lastly, since the cost of litigation is not prohibitive for major multinational corporations, and the benefits of winning and/or obtaining more expansive interpretations of investment protections are significant, there is incentive for some investors to "try their luck" in arbitration.[102] Furthermore, there is an increasing trend of third-party for-profit funding for investment settlement disputes, which increases capacity and incentive for investors to file suits against host states.[103]

(iv) Investor-state arbitration. Investment treaties empower investors to sue states without obtaining approval from their home states.[104] Investors can bypass domestic courts in the host state and bring their case to an international tribunal composed of three private arbitrators, at least one of whom the investor has a right to appoint. The majority of respondents in investment dispute cases are lower- and middle-income countries, with Argentina being the most sued state (60 cases as of 2018), and US investors having filed the most cases (174 as of 2018).[105] Between 1987 and 2018, tribunals decided in favor of investors in 60 percent of cases.[106] According to a 2016 study, companies with more than $1 billion in annual revenue, and individuals with over $100 million in net wealth, are the major beneficiaries of awards, accounting for roughly 94.5 percent of the aggregate compensation.[107] Awards are enforced by the domestic courts of the host country, to be regarded as the decision of the highest court of the land, as stipulated in the New York and Washington conventions.[108] Nonpayment could result in the state's property being seized elsewhere in the world.[109]

From this brief overview, one might criticize the investment regime for its lack of transparency and accountability and its potential for corruption, and many critics have done so.[110] In the rest of the section, I argue that the investment regime both constitutes and entrenches objectionable hierarchies by disempowering capital-poor countries in their pursuit of social equality.

We can start by identifying a broad range of economic policies as instrumental to or constitutive of social equality and call these egalitarian economic policies. As I argued in chapter 2, we can understand relations of social equality as relations in which agents govern their interactions with one another with robust and publicly known dispositions of respect, solidarity, and reciprocity. Such relations are essential if individuals are to enjoy freedom from domination, a robust sense of self-respect, and nonalienation. The antithesis of such relations are hierarchies in which some agents unjustifiably enjoy greater authority, moral standing, and/or social status than others. Moreover, for such relations to be robust, I argued that they must be embedded in and promoted by the political, economic, and sociocultural arrangements under which we live—in other words, agents cannot merely rely on others having the right kinds of egalitarian attitudes at some point in time. By egalitarian economic policies, then, I mean a broad range of regulatory and policy options that rectify or prevent objectionable inequality between agents, even when the policy is not justified only or primarily by egalitarian reasons. Without being exhaustive, we can identify at least four such kinds of economic policies:

(i) *Redistributive policies.* To prevent wealth disparities from becoming or creating objectionable hierarchies, it seems fairly uncontroversial that a society of equals would require at least a heavily redistributive economic system.[111] Redistributive policies that put downward pressure on economic inequality are important for preventing problems such as corrupt governance, class domination, and stigmatization of the poor.[112]

(ii) *Democratic control of key sectors.* Second, certain sectors need to be protected from private ownership to prevent an unaccountable minority from wielding too much power over the rest of the population. This may include essentials such as water and energy but also natural resources that constitute a country's main source of revenue. The extent to which private ownership is incompatible with social equality will depend in part on how effective it is for the state to regulate private capital, which tends to find ways to escape political control. For our purposes, it suffices to say that the state may sometimes or often need to directly or indirectly expropriate property (through eminent domain, nationalization, compulsory purchases, and/or socialization) to address capitalist domination and exploitation.[113]

(iii) *Rectifying historic injustices.* Third, building a society of equals requires addressing historic injustice. Policies such as redistributing land for historically oppressed and/or dispossessed groups, reparations such as payments to victims or their descendants, and/or targeted community investment are important to this end.[114] These policies are not only instrumental to dismantling objectionable hierarchies between groups, but they can also be seen as constitutive of social equality insofar as they express recognition that the historical treatment of these groups were wrongful violations of equal status.

(iv) *Empowering structurally disadvantaged groups.* Relatedly, it is also important to have forward-looking policies that aim to transform power relations between unequally positioned groups. For example, feminists have argued for policies such as socialized childcare and elderly care as important for empowering women.[115] Similarly, it may be impossible for workers to enjoy freedom from domination without an economy predominantly made up of workers' cooperatives as opposed to the traditional hierarchical corporation.[116]

Again, this list of "egalitarian economic policies" is not meant to be exhaustive, nor does it preclude more radical accounts. Nkrumah, as we saw, thought that postcolonial Africa would not be able to overcome the oppressive legacies of colonialism without some form of socialism. In his view, capitalism was inherently expansionist (and therefore imperialist) and required persistent subjugation of the majority of the world's population as cheap or reserve labor. But unlike other anticolonial communists of his time who pursued sweeping social and economic revolutions (such as Mao Zedong in China), Nkrumah argued that the path to socialism in postcolonial Ghana was through reform.[117]

Whether social equality is compatible with capitalism is a large topic that I cannot settle here, although there are good reasons to believe it is not. In particular, if contemporary theorists of racial capitalism and their anticolonial precursors (such as Nkrumah) are correct that capitalism creates and functions through status hierarchies (such as racial hierarchy), then it is hard to see how global and domestic social equality could be attained within a capitalist political economy.[118] Other contemporary thinkers—from liberal egalitarians to neo-Marxists—have also argued that social equality is not compatible with capitalism, although they differ on the limits of the market, the role of centralized economic planning, and the specific modes of property ownership.[119] My more limited claim here is that dismantling objectionable hierarchies and building a society of equals requires at least economic policies that move away from capitalism and toward some form of social democracy. As I argue shortly, this already has critical implications for the investment regime.

The discussion so far has been focused on economic policies that are important for rectifying domestic social inequality. At the global level, without a world state, what we might call egalitarian policy is less clear. Still, it is possible to identify a range of policies that rectify or prevent objectionable hierarchies between states. For example, insofar as economic inequality is a driver of hierarchies of authority that allow some states to dominate others, policies that ameliorate the wide economic gap between states can be considered egalitarian. There is obviously no global scheme of redistribution, and it is hard to see how anything like it could be attainable in the foreseeable future. Instead, policies aimed at fostering economic diversification and escaping commodity dependence may be seen as one (though not the only) kind of egalitarian policy at the global level.[120] A country is commodity-dependent when its commodity exports account for more than 60 percent of its total merchandise exports in value terms. According to UNCTAD, nine more economies became dependent on commodity exports between 2010 and 2015. In total, around two-thirds of all 135 lower- and middle-income countries are commodity dependent. Commodity dependence puts countries at a significant disadvantage, as their economies are tied to the value of natural resources and foodstuff, whose prices are volatile and tend to decrease in the long term. Commodity dependence thus renders countries highly vulnerable and economically dependent on others for aid, investment, and loans.

Specific strategies to overcome commodity dependence will vary across countries' circumstances, but generally speaking, some policies that have proven to be effective include: subsidies for domestic industries, imposing requirements on foreign investors' transfer of knowledge and technology, maintaining strict capital control, and so on. These strategies all have in common what Nkrumah argued for—*political control over domestic and foreign capital.* They have helped countries like China escape from a disadvantaged position in the global division of labor, lessening economic dependency and narrowing the economic gap between countries in the Global South and North.[121]

Now that we have a clearer sense of what global and domestic egalitarian economic policies might consist of, let us turn back to the international investment regime. Investment treaties, as we saw, empower a class of agents—namely, investors (including individuals and transnational corporations). These agents' economic interests are reliably opposed to egalitarian policies. By *reliable*, I do not mean that economic interests exhaust the interests agents have, or that agents always act in the rational pursuit of their economic interests. I mean that, by virtue of one's position within a specific economic system, an agent has objective interests that come apart from subjective preferences and behavior, such that we can safely assume that a sufficient number of agents so positioned will act to pursue those interests.

Within an economic system driven by capital accumulation, the investor's primary interest is to maximize returns on their investment. To this end, investors generally have a strong interest in economic policies that are precisely the opposite of egalitarian policies, such as weakening labor regulations, prohibitions against requirements for technology transfer, and, whenever it is more efficient to import foreign workers and use foreign parts in production, prohibitions against local content requirements. Similarly, they have an interest in the host state maintaining minimum levels of taxation and a strong regime of private property rights.[122] It is no coincidence that investment treaties have been used to push back against these policies.[123]

One might argue that the interests of investors and citizens overlap at least in *some* areas. After all, to do business, investors need social stability, personal security, and rule of law. There are two responses: first, we can grant that these basic interests overlap while still finding it problematic that policies realizing more robust ideals of social justice—such as social equality—are heavily, sometimes prohibitively, penalized. Why should citizens have to settle for minimal justice so that an already advantaged minority can gain even more? Second, we can question the extent to which the two groups' basic interests overlap *substantively*. For investors, the relevant kind of social stability requires the elimination of strikes and other forms of labor unrest, yet for workers, the right to strike is essential leverage against capital owners. Likewise, personal security for workers has proven to be irrelevant to capital owners when profit can be maximized by compelling workers to work dangerously long hours and in poor conditions. Lastly, as some commentators have argued, the suite of protections given to foreign investors—whereby privately appointed international tribunals can compel public domestic courts to reverse decisions—undermines the rule of law and yet is precisely in the interests of investors as a class.[124]

Recall the cases of Bolivia and South Africa. In both cases, investors sued states when the latter's new policies threatened to negatively affect their economic interests. Those policies, however, were important for rectifying domestic and global inequality. In the case of Bolivia, decades of conditional loans from the IMF had resulted in little economic progress.[125] The nationalization of key sectors, like the oil and gas industry, on the other hand, played a crucial role in the country's dramatic economic transformation since 2006, which, even by the IMF's own account, has largely been successful.[126] This new wealth became the basis for a host of public investments and social welfare programs.[127] Nationalizing natural resources industries was also important for Bolivia to become an exporter of processed goods, a far more valuable position within the global economy. In the case of South Africa, a policy aimed at addressing domestic inequality as a result of historical injustice was penalized when investors sued and received a confidential settlement.

Nor is this phenomenon limited to lower- and middle-income countries. Transnational corporations also make use of investment treaties to constrain what citizens and/or disadvantaged groups in affluent societies can press for. The Keystone XL Pipeline in the United States is a good example. In face of widespread resistance from Native Americans and environmental activists against the pipeline's infringement on Indigenous land and the risk of water contamination, the US government halted the project. Soon after, TransCanada Corporation filed a $15 billion lawsuit against the United States by invoking investor protection provisions in NAFTA.[128] In a separate case, investors sued the United States for measures designed to protect Native American lands, arguing that this effectively expropriated its mining rights.[129] In these cases, demands for egalitarian policies such as respecting the land rights of Indigenous peoples were put at risk by an investment regime that empowers investors. In these ways, the investment regime hinders states' capacity to secure and protect disadvantaged groups' interests, not only in the Global South, but even in the richest countries. More generally, as Fabio Morosini and Michelle Badin argue, investment treaties have allowed investors to challenge a wide range of policies crucial for basic interests and addressing historic and social inequality, such as policies aimed at realizing rights to water, health, and medicine; the protection of cultural sites and Indigenous rights; and so on.[130]

In short, by empowering investors to impose costly constraints on states' policy space, the investment regime hinders disadvantaged groups and their governments' capacity to pursue economic policies that dismantle objectionable hierarchies.[131] In some cases, the costs are so high for the host state that the threat of litigation is not merely a constraint but a deterrence to law- and policymaking. As such, the investment regime is a prime example of how the terms of the contemporary global economy can enrich a minority while undermining postcolonial citizens and marginalized groups' capacities to escape the harms of domestic and global social inequality.[132]

One might object here that domestic inequality is not only a result of global economic arrangements like investment treaties. Domestic factors such as corruption also matter.[133] In arguing that the investment regime harms individuals in disadvantaged parts of the world, I seem to have committed "explanatory cosmopolitanism," i.e., one-sidedly attributing domestic ills to global causes.[134] But my argument need not deny domestic causes of inequality. Indeed, it does precisely the opposite. In my view, global institutions like the investment regime hinder the redress of domestic inequality by allowing investors to constrain citizens' self-determination. Even if citizens push for reforms that address domestic causes of inequality, they are nonetheless at risk of being heavily penalized by investors, whose interests may be undermined by those reforms. Similarly, political leaders that benefit from a more deregulated economy can cite "our hands are tied" to rebuff domestic pressures for egalitarian policies. Even if they wanted to act in their citizens' interests, they still face the problem of potentially having to generously compensate corporations. In other words, the investment regime is a classic case of how global and domestic institutions can interact to compound the harm(s) faced by disadvantaged individuals.

Still, a critic might ask, did states not sign on to investment treaties knowing their terms? In doing so, states consented to how their future actions would be constrained. So even if the investment regime imposes constraints on egalitarian policy, it seems that it does so only because the host state agreed to it. As such, a defender of the investment regime might argue, what gives the latter a legitimate complaint against self-imposed constraints?

In response, given the vagueness of treaty provisions that lend themselves to interpretations by tribunals in the ways discussed above, and the lack of existing arbitrations that states could look to at the time of signing, we can hardly say that states were able to give informed consent.[135] In the case of South Africa, officials signed on to the first bilateral investment treaty at a time when there was scant information regarding the implications of these broad treaty provisions.[136] Moreover, the more fundamental problem is the deeply unequal background conditions in which states contract with one another.[137] Nkrumah's observation that states that appear outwardly independent may nonetheless be unable to exercise self-determination is instructive here. As he pointed out, the root cause of neocolonialism is asymmetric dependence. Postcolonial capital-poor countries depend on foreign capital and technology for their economic development and therefore have strong incentive to accept the terms offered by capital-rich states. Against a background of prejudice against Third World governance, these states also have reason to do what appears needed to signal that they are governed by the rule of law—in this case, signing on to investment treaties that remove from them the power to settle future disputes. Moreover, unequal background conditions also play out in subtler ways than mere desperation for investment. As Lauge Poulsen's work shows, state officials in capital-poor countries often lack the resources and access to legal expertise in international investment law to fully scrutinize the risks of investment treaties.[138] Under these conditions, states' consent ought not be accorded the same moral significance as it should be under more equal background conditions.

Moreover, Nkrumah also cautioned against an uncritical acceptance of state consent as a legitimizing force for global relations, because the state could be captured by neocolonial collaborators who benefit from foreign and/or capitalist patronage, instead of representing the interests and wills of the masses. Consider the protests against increasing Chinese investment in various parts of the Global South in recent years. In 2018, Vietnamese citizens protested the establishment of special economic zones that would lease land to Chinese foreign investors for ninety-nine years.[139] In Kazakhstan, citizens protested against a costly infrastructure deal with China.[140] These protests illustrate the inadequacy of state consent to economic deals when those states neglect the wills of those they claim to represent.

Finally, it may appear strange to think that the investment regime *undermines* postcolonial citizens' capacity to overcome social inequality. After all, foreign investment is at least an important part of a country's economic growth, which is presumably needed for addressing poverty and other kinds of social deprivation. Insofar as the investment regime facilitates foreign investment that would otherwise not be available to the host country, in what sense does the regime subject individuals to the harms of inequality?

This objection conflates absolute deprivations with the harms of relational inequality. Even if we grant that investment treaties bring in foreign investment that leads to economic growth and alleviation of the worst forms of deprivations, this does not by itself secure a more egalitarian society. As discussed above, a range of domestic egalitarian economic policies are needed to redistribute wealth, address long-standing structural inequalities, and prevent a minority from amassing too much economic power. Moreover, I also argued that developmental strategies that help countries escape commodity and asymmetric dependence are an important part of dismantling objectionable global relations. But these are precisely the policies that can threaten the investor's profits and that, under the current terms of the investment regime, can invite litigation. Thus we might say that the investment regime hinders the pursuit of equality, even as it might bring in some economic benefits.

More broadly, when evaluating the fairness of a sociopolitical arrangement, we should not only compare the status quo with the counterfactual of no arrangement at all.[141] Instead, we should compare the status quo with the counterfactual of an alternative, fairer regime along the lines that postcolonial countries fought for from the outset—one that does not prioritize foreign investors' interests in profit-making and instead enables the host state to exercise greater control over the terms of operations, such as imposing obligations of technology transfer. Insofar as a fairer alternative is practically feasible, there is no reason why a moral assessment of the existing regime should not draw upon it. Compared to *that* alternative, we can say that the current regime *does* undermine postcolonial countries' ability to rectify social inequality because it empowers the wrong kinds of agents.

To sum up this section, the international investment regime is a form of neocolonial exploitation insofar as it enriches investors at the expense of host states' capacity to enact the kinds of economic policies that would enable them to escape objectionable global and domestic hierarchies. This exposes the agents at the bottom of these hierarchies to continued domination and other harms of inequality discussed in the previous chapter.

It is worth noting that the investment regime is not an isolated phenomenon of the global economy. Consider the following cases, which are commonly associated with the charge of neocolonialism.

- *Structural adjustment loans*: The IMF, led primarily by Western capital-rich countries, offers loans to capital-poor countries under a set of conditions, including privatization of a range of key industries and sectors, allowing transnational corporations to access and privatize basic services such as water and other utilities. Structural adjustment loans have been criticized for exacerbating poverty, in part because they prevent states from departing from a strict program of austerity.[142]
- *Debt traps*: A capital-rich state such as China offers a capital-poor state such as Sri Lanka high-interest financing to develop infrastructure, under the condition that, should the latter be unable to repay the loan (which is arguably predictable given the interest rate), China will then acquire ownership over a key commercial and military port.[143] Sri

Lanka is compelled to accept terms of financing that entrench a relationship of domination between China and Sri Lankan citizens, who have lost political control of a strategic asset that matters to their security and economic welfare.

- *International intellectual property law*: Under the TRIPS agreement, aside from highly exceptional circumstances, countries are required to enforce intellectual property rights even when this comes at the expense of technology and knowledge transfers that can help diversify their economies and/or protect their citizens from harms such as a public health crisis.[144]

Much more needs to be said about each case, but insofar as these are also instances of capital-rich countries and corporate lobbyists taking advantage of capital-poor countries' economic dependency to offer and benefit from rules that are disempowering, we might say that these aspects of global economic arrangements are also neocolonial.

Decolonizing International Investment

So far, I have argued that the international investment regime can be understood as an instance of neocolonialism insofar as it undermines disadvantaged countries' capacity to address social inequality at the domestic and global levels. If transforming objectionable hierarchy into relations of equality was a central aim of decolonization, postcolonial societies have not been able to realize the full aspirations of the decolonial agenda.

In this section, I argue for an investment regime that prioritizes host states' ability to address domestic and global inequality over investors' interests in profit maximization. Postcolonial global justice as social equality ought to be a regulative ideal of the practice of investment rather than something that must be made compatible with private capital accumulation. Regulating the investment regime along these lines demands a host of "nonreformist reforms," that is, procedural and substantive changes whose goals are to shift power from investors to citizens. Furthermore, until an investment regime compatible with the egalitarian aims of decolonization is in place, I suggest that host countries (and their citizens) can justifiably refuse to comply with investment arbitration outcomes where the latter penalize policies or legislation aimed at rectifying social inequality.

To start, a regulative ideal places a constraint on the terms of an institution or a practice by according greater weight to considerations that align with, help realize, or are constitutive of the ideal. For example, if providing a good education is the regulating ideal of a university, then in considering how to cut costs to the university's budget, the aim of providing a good education should figure prominently in deciding what costs should be cut—perhaps cutting high-level administrators' salaries before eliminating teaching staff, for example. A regulating ideal is not, however, a trump card.[145] It would be objectionable to pursue it at all costs, especially if at the expense of individuals' basic rights. Instead, a regulative ideal gives us reason to prioritize or confer greater weight to certain considerations over others.

In the previous two chapters, I argued that decolonization can be understood as an attempt to transform a world of domestic and global hierarchies into relations of equality. I interpreted this vision of equality as an ideal of social equality, and I argued that such an ideal is relevant not only within societies but across borders. Global social equality enables individuals to enjoy freedom from domination, maintain a robust sense of self-respect, and experience nonalienation from one another.

As we saw in the previous section, egalitarian economic policies are a crucial part of transforming power relations and can also in themselves constitute egalitarian treatment. Therefore, an investment regime regulated by the ideal of social equality would entail investment rules that allow and protect host states' claims to enact such policies. This requires both procedural and substantive changes to the current regime with the aim of empowering postcolonial citizens to exercise political control over foreign capital.

This is distinct from the state-centric reforms that many Global South governments and legal scholars have advocated for.[146] To be sure, state-centric reforms are necessary and can make substantial progress toward removing disproportionate empowerments for foreign investors. For example, as a response to public outrage over the challenge to the Black Economic Empowerment Act, the South African government dispensed with investor-state dispute settlement altogether.[147] In 2015, the South African government passed the Protection of Investment Bill, which requires investors to exhaust remedies through domestic courts before proceeding to state-to-state arbitration if necessary. Similarly, India has removed international tribunals' jurisdiction over legal issues that have been settled in final by a judicial authority of the state, making it harder for international arbitration to overturn domestic rulings.[148] Brazil has established negotiations between the investing company and government representatives as a mandatory step before triggering state-to-state dispute settlement.[149] Furthermore, to increase states' regulatory space, countries have also started to narrow the range of state actions liable to litigation and compensation. For example, South Africa's new investment protection bill eliminated indirect expropriation—regulatory acts that inadvertently significantly diminish the value of an investment—as a compensable offense.[150] Moreover, to rebalance power between investors and states, as well as to increase transparency and procedural regularity in dispute settlement, some commentators have proposed a multilateral international investment court, and there have been proposals within the EU for such a court.[151]

These initiatives, aimed at reimposing domestic law on foreign investment, are part of a long history of postcolonial states attempting to tame foreign capital to their ends. Undoubtedly, empowering the postcolonial state vis-à-vis foreign investors is an important part of any program to decolonize the practice of international investment. Without these reforms, as we have seen in the case of Bolivia and South Africa, governments are constrained from and/or penalized for pursuing egalitarian policies even when they are committed to doing so. But it would be a mistake to consider a state-centric practice of international investment as adequately reformed to meet the egalitarian aims of decolonization. As we have seen throughout the chapter and in Nkrumah's analysis of neocolonialism, the agents wielding postcolonial sovereignty can come apart from the agents representing the interests and wills of the masses. Postcolonial governments are not necessarily responsive to the interests of workers, Indigenous peoples, and other disadvantaged social groups. M. Sornarajah argues, for example, that the proliferation of bilateral investment treaties in the 1990s is partly a result of many postcolonial regimes embracing neoliberal free-market principles.[152] These governments will not necessarily make use of the legal powers available to them to regulate foreign investment in ways that promote social equality.

In other words, an investment regime that prioritizes the egalitarian aims of decolonization should not only bolster the rights of the state versus foreign investors, but also offer tools that empower nonstate actors to exercise control over foreign capital and their own governments. *These* reforms are "nonreformist" in their focus on shifting power from one class of agents to another, thus staging a "modification of relations of power"[153] that can pave way for more ambitious changes to the global economy in the long run.

To be sure, legal tools are only as powerful as the agents that can utilize them. In chapter 5, I consider the broader question of building political power at the global level. Here, I only focus on how international investment law can provide tools of empowerment for these groups so that if and when they are suitably organized and mobilized, the investment regime can serve as an important site (among others) of political contestation from below.

Procedural Reforms

The first and most basic (yet crucial) form of legal empowerment is standing under international law. Under the current investment regime, the only nonstate actors that have a private right to action are foreign investors.[154] Other nonstate actors such as Indigenous peoples and workers' unions do not have similar legal standing to hold foreign investors or their own states accountable in international courts, unless the latter commits egregious human rights violations. This is not to say that these groups have not found alternative ways of doing so—indeed there is long history of nonstate actors attempting to bring cases against multinational corporations in their home states, usually by utilizing tort law.[155] But establishing that a home country has jurisdiction over the actions of its investors abroad tends to be extremely difficult and consists of half, if not more, of the battle.[156] Corporations will often employ legal strategies such as registering in a third country to avoid such lawsuits.

Standing for nonstate actors to take legal action would allow them to monitor and directly hold investors accountable to a set of obligations centered on the pursuit of equality (about which I will say more shortly). If an international investment court was established, for example, instead of only allowing state-investor or state-state dispute settlement, it might allow nonstate actors to file class action lawsuits against foreign investors over and above their own state.

Substantive Reforms

A second form of legal empowerment consists of a host of substantive rights and obligations that can be incorporated into investment law and invoked by citizens and marginalized populations against investors and/or their own states wherever necessary. While a plethora of such reforms have been suggested by commentators, these proposals have mostly focused on imposing stricter sustainability and environmental protection rights for host states and duties for investors.[157] The argument advanced in this chapter suggests that it is important to complement these with rights and duties surrounding the aim of rectifying social inequality. The general proposal is to re-order the priority of competing goals within the practice of investment—specifically, subsuming investors' profit-making under the far weightier need to address objectionable social inequalities. Prioritizing the latter means ruling out and/or significantly weakening investment protections that have been used to undermine the kinds of egalitarian economic policies discussed in the previous section. For example, this lends support to removing prohibitions against imposing requirements on investors to contribute to the host state's developmental strategies, such as engage in technology and knowledge transfer, and to utilize local content (i.e., hire local labor and source supplies from local businesses). As we saw above, these developmental strategies are important for diversifying the economy and reducing long-term asymmetric economic dependency.

Subsuming investors' interests under the imperative to address social inequality also requires imposing significant qualifications on investment protection. Here, the South African model can serve as a starting point. Due to its constitutional commitment to undoing the legacies of apartheid, South Africa's new approach to international investment explicitly qualifies foreign investors' rights with reference to the need to overcome social inequalities. For example, where expropriation has occurred, the amount (if any) of compensation owed must take into account considerations such as South Africa's "commitment to land reform and access to land on equitable basis."[158] Likewise, the principle of national treatment (according to which foreign investors enjoy the same rights and protections as domestic businesses) has also been qualified by exempting "any law or measure the purpose of which is to achieve equality or to preserve cultural heritage."[159]

More ambitiously, the moral imperative to rectify social inequality could expand what is known as the "public interest" clause in investment law, so that addressing social inequality constitutes a legitimate public interest. Currently, the public interest clause tends to be interpreted narrowly to mean matters in public health, safety, and environmental protection. Yet it is hard to see why rectifying social inequality should not count as public interest—in fact, insofar as relations of equality are important for other fundamental goods such as freedom from domination and exploitation, attaining it would seem to be of paramount public interest. Expanding "public interest" this way would have radical implications. Under current investment treaties, expropriation of foreign investment is prohibited unless it is shown to be in the interest of the public, narrowly understood. On a reformed regime, however, expropriation could be justifiable if it is done to correct for egregious inequalities. In the South African case, for example, even if the Black Economic Empowerment Act amounted to expropriation of foreign assets, it could still be justifiable and South African citizens should not have had to pay a penalty for it. To be sure, whether an instance of expropriation is *all things considered* justifiable depends on other factors, too: such as the manner in which it is conducted, how expropriation compares to other feasible policy options, and so on.[160] While I cannot flesh out a full account of justifiable expropriation here, the point is that the "public interest" exception to a general prohibition against expropriation could in principle be expanded to include postcolonial citizens' interest in social equality.

Finally, a reformed investment regime should also allow citizens to demand their states to revoke protections to investors whose businesses fail to contribute to sustainable and egalitarian development, and to pursue litigation in an investment court to recover damages to the environment, for example, or demand compensation for workers whose rights are violated.

To sum up briefly, an investment regime that enables rather than hinders addressing inequality would strengthen state and popular sovereignty over foreign capital, enable the former to ensure that investment contributes to rather than hinders a country's ability to escape asymmetric economic dependency, and place a strong egalitarian constraint on the terms of investment protection. The result would be an investment regime that empowers postcolonial citizens to decide on the allocation of capital to meet genuine needs, rather than a regime that prioritizes profit maximization for a few.

Regime Shifting from Below

Yet a significantly reformed investment regime will not come about without contestation. And some of these reforms could happen on paper without real change: legal tools could still be deployed in a manner that is biased against capital-poor countries. The "public interest" clause, for example, is broadly defined on paper as regulatory activities that affect the interest of the public. Yet in practice it has often been interpreted inconsistently. When the Argentinian government appealed to the public interest to justify emergency measures such as freezing utility price hikes during the debt crisis, for example, international tribunals were unmoved.[161] Yet when European and US governments took expropriatory measures in the banking sector as a response to the 2008 financial crisis, these were seen as uncompensable regulatory practices needed to prevent further damage to the public interest.[162]

To resist neocolonial exploitation and push for a fair investment regime, I submit that citizens are justified in refusing compliance with the existing regime, for example, by demanding that their governments refuse to pay awards made by investor-state dispute settlement (ISDS) arbitration panels. As we have seen, the current terms of international investment are exploitative as they wrongly enable investors to maximize self-enrichment at the expense of the host state's ability to overcome economic dependency and address internal social inequality. By refusing to pay what is in effect a penalty on pursuing egalitarian objectives, citizens refuse to be exploited. The message is clear: your capital is only desirable insofar as it actually contributes to our economic empowerment rather than perpetuate our disadvantage.[163]

More broadly, if suitably coordinated, host states could actively build an alternative practice of international investment by acting as if a nonexploitative regime is already in place. Instead of waiting for changes in rules to allow for egalitarian economic policies to be free from sanction, host states could pursue these policies and refuse to pay the penalty if investors sue and arbitration panels rule against them. In doing so, host states would be engaging in "regime-shifting" from below—i.e., acting in such a way that the accumulative result is a collective shift toward a different set of rules.[164] As we will see in chapter 5, regime-shifting has often been employed by dominant actors to circumvent more egalitarian and democratic global institutions such as the

UN General Assembly. There is no reason why less powerful actors should not employ the same strategy for a more just regime.

One might worry that defending noncompliance with investment law ends up licensing states to do whatever they wish, including allowing ruling elites to expropriate for their own gain rather than the benefit of the people. Yet the goal of developing a nonexploitative practice of foreign investment also places principled limits on host states' disobedience of the current regime. If states expropriate foreign assets just for the domestic ruling class's self-enrichment and not in pursuit of egalitarian objectives, this would not move toward the kind of regime defended so far and would not be justifiable in my view. My account thus offers normative resources for postcolonial citizens to condemn their states when they abuse a moral permit to disobey the law for their own gain. The account also points to the need for states engaging in regime-shifting to develop and voluntarily bind themselves to a public set of rules and standards—for example, the alternative terms for investment defended above—with the aim of making these the de facto new terms for governing foreign investment. For counterhegemonic legal entrepreneurship only works if agents are willing to act in accordance to a different set of norms and rules, rather than arbitrarily. This alternative set of rules and standards would specify, for example, when investors may or may not expect to be compensated for expropriation; what an expanded definition of public interest that includes the need to rectify global and domestic social inequality entails; what domestic grievance procedures might be available for disputes; and so on. Instead of emphasizing the mere restrengthening of state sovereignty against foreign infringement, as many legal critics of the investment regime have done, the account of decolonizing international investment developed here centers the value of equality and therefore offers no justification for exercises of state sovereignty that contravene it.

A more pressing worry is the possibility of capital flight. If these reforms go ahead, the worry goes, and the practice of investment prioritizes the rectification of social inequality over profit-making, surely investors would no longer be incentivized to invest in lower- and middle-income countries. Insofar as foreign investment is important to a country's economic development, this would seem to result in dire consequences for its citizens.

This is a genuine dilemma. Yet we need not overly despair. As Bonnitcha, Poulsen, and Waibel argue, existing evidence on the importance of BITs for bringing in foreign direct investment are at best mixed, and results also vary depending on a host of factors such as the type of sector that needs investment, the type of political regime in the host state, and so on. In face of these complexities, to assume that making progressive changes to the investment regime would necessarily result in massive capital flight would be too simplistic.[165]

More importantly, whether a reformed investment regime would result in massive capital flight depends on how much political unity there is among host states endorsing these reforms. If host states compete in a race to the bottom, investors will continue to hold leverage over them. If, on the other hand, they are willing to hold steadfast to investment rules that enable greater political control over capital and policies designed to make good on the egalitarian promise of decolonization, investors will find it much harder to circumvent the new rules. In this sense, Nkrumah was right about the solution to resisting neocolonialism: that it depended on united action among similarly situated postcolonial states. And, it seems, he was also right that *that* depends on politically aware and organized citizens demanding their governments to reject exploitative economic terms that undermine economic self-determination and perpetuate inequality.

Conclusion

Yet we live in a deeply divided world where political unity—even among similarly situated agents—is not easy to build or sustain. The powerful can undermine the solidarity of the oppressed in numerous ways, including offering bilateral deals to undermine efforts to establish multilateral institutions within which capital-poor states—forming the world's majority—have a significantly better chance to demand terms of economic interaction that prioritize their agendas. Looking back to the rise and fall of PSNR, CERDS, and the NIEO, this divide-and-conquer playbook has largely succeeded in forging a global economic order that prioritizes powerful agents' self-enrichment over others' ability to live and relate as equals. It bears noting that China—having avoided many of these disadvantageous investment terms due to its market size—has now become a major exporter of capital and is pushing traditional bilateral investment treaties with other countries in the Global South that contain investor-state dispute settlement provisions.[166]

Still, even at times when prospects of a united pushback from capital-poor states remain dim, it remains important to recognize how and why the practice of international investment, as it is today, is problematic and amounts to a form of neocolonialism. As I have argued in this chapter, neocolonialism can be understood as a form of exploitation, in which powerful agents take advantage of vulnerable agents' asymmetric dependency to offer terms of interaction that enrich themselves at the expense of the latter's ability to escape disadvantage. The current investment regime is a result of these offers. By granting investors' a suite of protections designed to insulate the interest in profit-making from the demands of social equality, the regime benefits the powerful while undermining the decolonial agenda to dismantle domestic and global hierarchies. In place of this, I argued for an investment regime that takes social equality as a regulative ideal.

In face of neocolonial exploitation, political contestation rather than moral suasion is needed. As Nkrumah noted, "The developing world will not be developed out of the good will or generosity of the developed world."[167] A key part of decolonizing international investment, then, is for disadvantaged actors to form counterhegemonic transnational alliances to exert power in shaping the global economy and global governance more broadly. I shall discuss this in more detail in chapter 5, where I will argue that nonstate actors can be just as, if not more, well placed to contest objectionable global hierarchies. This marks a departure from Nkrumah's emphasis on state-to-state alliances, but as I suggest, it tracks his (and other anticolonial thinkers such as Fanon's) concern that postcolonial states can often also be an obstacle to emancipation and an agent of neocolonialism.

But before that, we turn to a different part of the global order. One reason why neocolonial exploitation is so difficult to overcome is because these hierarchies are not merely maintained by the threat of military action or economic collapse. Instead, as Nkrumah pointed out, neocolonial exploitation is buttressed and legitimized through the production and global dissemination of culture.[168] On films, Nkrumah writes, "One has only to listen to the cheers of an African audience as Hollywood's heroes slaughter red Indians or Asiatics to understand the effectiveness of this weapon. For, in the developing continents, where the colonialist heritage has left a vast majority still illiterate, even the smallest child gets the message contained in the blood and thunder stories emanating from California."[169] Here, Nkrumah suggests that political solidarity among subjects of colonial oppression is undermined by racist cultural representations produced in the neocolonial metropole.

This leads us to the broader question of cultural decolonization, and our second site of inquiry. In the next chapter, we examine the persistent charge of cultural imperialism in contemporary cultural globalization by turning to Aimé Césaire, an influential anticolonial leader who was also a renowned poet and playwright. Thinking with his critique of cultural imperialism, we will consider cultural decolonization as another essential component of postcolonial global justice as social equality, and what that might amount to.

4

Decolonizing Cultural Globalization

CÉSAIRE AND THE HIERARCHY
OF CREATOR AND CONSUMER

IN 1980, a UNESCO commission comprising representatives from sixteen countries, mostly from the developing and/or postcolonial world, published a report named after the president of the commission, a former member of the Irish Republican Army (IRA) and later Nobel Peace Prize laureate Sean MacBride.[1] The MacBride report, titled *Many Voices, One World*, was the result of a coordinated initiative to decolonize and democratize global communication.[2] This initiative had begun with UNESCO's groundbreaking "Mass Media Declaration," adopted in 1978.[3] The MacBride report marked the first major international study of inequalities in global communication, focusing primarily on news media and cultural goods. The report argued for a "New World Information and Communication Order" (NWICO).[4] Seen as the social and cultural complementary to the New International Economic Order (NIEO), the NWICO consisted of a set of policy recommendations that aimed to create a more egalitarian and participatory model of communication *between* and *within* states.[5] As MacBride described years later, the goal of the NWICO was that "everyone would be both '*producer* and *consumer* of communication'" (italics mine).[6]

From 1977 until the early 1980s, postcolonial developing states pushed for the NWICO through UNESCO and the UN General Assembly, setting up the International Program for the Development of Communication (IPDC) to facilitate international technical cooperation and communications developmental assistance and passing resolutions that made the NWICO an accepted item on the global political agenda. In the heyday of decolonization, reforming global communication in its informational and cultural forms was a crucial part of the struggle against "colonialism, neo-colonialism, foreign occupation and all forms of racial discrimination and oppression," as the "Mass Media Declaration" stated.[7]

The principles and reforms of the NWICO, however, were strongly opposed by the Reagan administration, backed by conservative US-led groups such as the World Press Freedom Committee, the Heritage Foundation, and the International Federation of Publishers, which saw the NWICO as a threat to the commercial interests of US media and cultural industries.[8] They condemned the NWICO as an affront to the principles of freedom of speech, information, and press. Postcolonial countries' policy recommendations were portrayed as plans for Soviet-friendly authoritarian states to "control and to regulate the distribution of news and ideas."[9] Weeks after the Non-Aligned Movement held its first media conference in New Delhi to promote the NWICO, the "great media debate" finally culminated in the United States withdrawing from UNESCO in 1984.[10] Following this fallout, funding for the IPDC remained scarce, and numerous developing countries' attempts to implement domestic policies conducive to the goals of the NWICO failed after similar campaigns from lobbying groups linked with the US-based Inter-American Association of the Press.[11] From the late 1980s onward, as the WTO became the main global institution for governing international communications, the deregulation and privatization of media and cultural sectors also became the prevailing norm.[12]

Since then, concerns about cultural imperialism have persisted. With the rapid development of communications technologies that can easily deliver foreign cultural influences across the border, countries with weaker domestic capacities to produce and disseminate cultural goods such as films, music, literature, and so on, continue to express concerns about threats to their domestic cultures.[13] Nor is foreign cultural influence limited to these more conventional goods. Much of knowledge production, for example, appears to be centered in Global North academies and diffuse from English-language journals to the rest of the world.[14] In other words, a pattern of asymmetric cultural production and dissemination has persisted beyond formal colonialism. Historically advantaged groups (citizens of capital-rich, majority-white states) have continued to act as the global cultural producer, innovator, and disseminator, while historically disadvantaged actors (citizens of postcolonial, capital-poor, and majority nonwhite states) appear to be primarily on the receiving end, at most supplying raw materials and traditional knowledge for the former's creativity.

This global pattern of asymmetric cultural flows is qualified by two observations. First, counterhegemonic cultural flows undeniably exist. In many cases, however, these cultural flows are facilitated by precisely the kinds of cultural protectionism defended in this chapter and which are prohibited under the current trade regime. Second, much of counterhegemonic cultural flows are often not captured in the "official record"—i.e., not occurring in the formal economy and, more importantly, not registering in public memory or historical narrative. As I discuss later, the practices of white appropriation and whitewashing have tended to erase the role of historically oppressed and racialized populations in contributing to global cultural and knowledge production, thus worsening the perception of a global division of creative labor. Yet from the point of view of postcolonial global justice as social equality, I will argue, a *perceived* division of creative labor can be just as problematic.

Even as the question of global cultural production and circulation has been extensively discussed in the fields of postcolonial, media, and communication studies, it remains largely absent in global justice debates.[15] Instead, global justice theorists have either rather optimistically assumed that cultural globalization would eventually lead to a progressive cosmopolitan identity, or else said little on the topic altogether. On the other hand, philosophical debates over multiculturalism have mostly happened within the context of the liberal state.[16] Conclusions from that debate, however, cannot apply straightforwardly to the global context. For example, while there is extensive debate on whether the state's obligation to treat citizens equally prohibits or requires cultural accommodations, there is no obviously equivalent global institution to which similar obligations might apply.[17] Yet in the age of cultural globalization, if there is no defensible case for countries to protect domestic culture(s), the goal of multiculturalist policies—to protect domestic minority cultures—will be difficult to meet. Both minority and majority cultures could be under threat. Moreover, while liberal nationalists who argue that states ought to preserve valuable forms of national culture come closest to discussing cultural protectionism, they have not grappled more directly with foreign cultural influence via the flow of cultural goods, which has traditionally been the main concern of critics of cultural imperialism. Instead, liberal nationalists' focus has been defending cultural change as a legitimate concern in thinking about migration flows.[18] Whatever one may think of cultural change via migration, the flow of cultural goods invites a different set of considerations such that the liberal nationalist position on one cannot simply be transposed onto the other.

And yet there are well-known problems associated with talk of cultural imperialism and cultural decolonization. One common worry is that it leads to ideas of recovering an authentic culture—that is, either a culture untouched by the European colonial encounter or produced by someone who is "authentically" African, Asian, and so on.[19] Many problems plague this way of approaching cultural decolonization. It is essentializing to suggest that we can discern what an "authentic" culture is by someone's social identity.[20] Disputes over whether a certain practice or set of ideas counts as indigenous or non-Western, in this critique, can bleed into disputes about who is authentically indigenous or non-Western (as an example of the messiness of drawing such distinctions, note that many of the most prominent Third World anticolonial thinkers—including those considered in this book—whose political thought became the basis for postcolonial theory were educated in the metropole). And in the wake of the mutual influence that colonizers and colonial subjects had in shaping each other's societies over decades and sometimes centuries of imperial entanglement, an emphasis on retrieving an "uncontaminated" indigenous culture relies on, in Olúfẹ́mi Táíwò's words, "gross representations of objective processes and events."[21] As Adom Getachew and Karuna Mantena put it, the colonial encounter and conscription into modernity[22] meant that non-Western thinkers were "always . . . simultaneously insiders and outsiders" of Western political traditions.[23] Moreover, contemporary efforts to retrieve past practices are also fraught with contradiction. As Rajeev Bhargava admits, even as he advocates for the revival of neglected epistemic traditions to address the "epistemic injustice" of colonialism, "There is a sense in which there is no going back to pure indigenous cultures because every rediscovery is at least partly a reinvention . . . every revival of tradition has turned out to be its reinvention."[24]

These points testify to the fact that culture is inherently dynamic, heterogeneous, and constantly evolving, thus casting doubt on calls for cultural decolonization understood as cultural retrieval. As Kwame Anthony Appiah has argued, "Cultural purity is an oxymoron."[25] Even more disturbingly, talk of authentic national cultures can easily lend itself to insidious policing by the state and/or dominant groups. The Chinese and Indian governments, for example, have attempted to enforce state-sanctioned visions of Han Chinese and Hindu national cultures by repressing religious and ethnic minorities.

This chapter articulates a different way of understanding the charge of cultural imperialism that does not rely on appealing to the authenticity or intrinsic value of a particular form of national culture. Drawing from Aimé Césaire's political thought on culture and colonialism, I argue that we can understand cultural decolonization as the restoration of what I call equal social agency. Social agency is a set of capacities that enable human beings to contribute to the good.[26] Historically, a group's supposed lack of equal social agency has been used to justify their oppression. Over time, a hierarchy of social agency has become a core feature of a global racial ideology that remains very much alive today. Persistent patterns of real and perceived asymmetries in global cultural flows, I argue, reproduce this ideology and therefore undermine moving toward postcolonial global justice as social equality.

This diagnosis of cultural imperialism keeps with a central theme of this book, which has been to shift our focus from nationalist readings of anticolonial critique to a broader understanding of anticolonial demands as demands for relations of equality. As I argued in chapter 1, while nationalism was an important part of the struggle against colonialism, it did not exhaust the contours of anticolonial imaginations for a postcolonial world. Rather, decolonization was also imagined as a fundamental restructuring of social relations between groups—that is, the dismantling of hierarchies that constituted colonialism to make way for egalitarian relations. As in the previous chapter on neocolonial international investment, I aim to show that this egalitarian reading of anticolonial critique allows us to detach the moral underpinnings of decolonization from defenses of nationalism. Instead, concerned with objectionable hierarchies of social agency as it is, the account of cultural decolonization suggested in this chapter makes as many demands on the postcolonial nation-state as it does on dominant states and existing global institutions.

Relatedly, critics of the cultural imperialism framework within media and communication studies have challenged the idea of North-South cultural imperialism in several important ways. They point to the role of the active consumer in localizing the global; challenge the assumption that there is a homogenous national culture promoted abroad via cultural goods and, correspondingly, that there is a homogenous national culture to be defended against Western influence; and point to the increasing importance of regional South-South cultural transmission.[27] My aim in this chapter is not to propose a new model of cultural imperialism. Instead, taking into account these critiques, I argue that we can still identify an important injustice in real and perceived patterns of asymmetric cultural flows between Global North countries and postcolonial Global South countries.

In the following, I first reconstruct Césaire's critique of cultural imperialism and his views on the role of cultural production in decolonization. In the second section, titled Cultural Globalization and Its Discontents," with these perspectives in mind, I turn to contemporary cultural globalization. I argue that real and perceived persistent asymmetric cultural flows between Western and non-Western postcolonial societies can reinforce objectionable hierarchies in two ways: first and more familiarly, through problematic cultural representations of disadvantaged and marginalized populations; second and less obviously, asymmetric cultural flows can reinforce ideas of inferior social agency, which have historically been ascribed to these societies.

Considering all this, in the section titled "Decolonizing Cultural Globalization" I argue that we can think of decolonizing cultural globalization as a project in restoring historically oppressed groups' status as equal social agents. This entails efforts along two dimensions: first, empowering members of these groups to exercise social agency in the cultural sphere, and second, recovering the roles that they have already played in creating what we know to be valuable today. Together, these efforts require demanding egalitarian reforms to the infrastructure of global (and domestic) communications. At the same time, I argue that postcolonial and developing countries have a remedial right to cultural protectionism so long as participation in global communications remains deeply unequal. This right is grounded not in the value of a particular kind of culture, but on individuals' fundamental interest to stand as equals to others. Finally, in the conclusion, I conclude by considering what it means to view the broader project of cultural decolonization as a project in restoring historically oppressed groups' status as equal social agents.

Global cultural production and transmission are broad phenomenon that can occur within the formal economy but also via migration and other forms of cross-border mobility. For reasons of scope, it will be impossible to include in my analysis all the different cases of cultural transmission. Throughout the chapter, my main reference will be the case of cultural goods such as music, literature, film, and visual arts, and I also make occasional reference to informational and knowledge goods such as scientific research. But this should not be taken to mean that the transmission of culture exclusively takes these forms. Insofar as the global transmission of highly valued forms of culture today often occurs in the form of cultural goods, I submit that it is important to analyze why it might be objectionable when some societies (and groups within those societies) are disproportionally and persistently prevented from taking up the role of global cultural producer, innovator, and disseminator, and to be recognized for it.

Culture and Colonialism

Culture and Cultural Goods

Let us start with the concept of culture and cultural goods. Césaire defines culture broadly: as "the whole corpus of material and spiritual values created by society in the course of its history," including all manner of things: "elements as diverse as technics and political institutions, things as fundamental as language or as fleeting as fashion, the arts as well as science or religion."[28]

How should we understand this almost all-encompassing view of culture? We can think of culture as consisting of, first, the practices, beliefs, and norms that a group develops when they share what Alan Patten calls "formative conditions."[29] These conditions may include a shared geographical environment, history (including shared experiences of oppression, for example), political and economic systems, and so on. Individuals develop practices and systems of norms and beliefs as a response to life under a particular set of formative conditions. As Césaire puts it, culture is a "fund of wisdom" that comprises "a whole intellectual equipment" that members of a group draw upon in their daily life.[30] His conception of culture, then, need not be understood in essentialist terms: rather than identifying any particular content, it instead captures the accumulative result of a group's actions and creativity. This sets Césaire apart from his close friend and fellow cofounder of the Negritude movement, Léopold Senghor, whose conception of culture tended to appeal to a Black racial essence.[31] Already in the 1930s, Césaire, as Jane Hiddleston details in her biography of him, argued against such appeals to a "black substance," seeing it as an uncritical reversal of European racial hierarchy rather than a radical rejection of racialism.[32]

From this broad conception of culture, then, we can think of cultural *goods* as human attempts to communicate within a specific format. Cultural goods can include aesthetic and expressive goods such as literature, film, music, visual arts, and so on, but also informational and intellectual goods such as newspapers and academic/scientific research. What they have in common is that they embody the ideas, meaning, and knowledge that human beings communicate with one another as a necessary part of social life.[33] While news media conveys information about significant happenings, and scientific research communicates findings about the natural and physical worlds, artistic goods tend to draw on the shared practices, beliefs, and norms—i.e., the culture—of a group that shares a set of formative conditions. Cultural goods are a significant (though not only) way through which cultural transmission occurs, either between members of the group (e.g., intergenerationally) or toward outsiders of the group. This can happen via commodification—when cultural goods are sold and bought on the market; or outside of the formal economy—for example, when publicly funded institutions put on exhibitions, festivals, and so on.

Two Problems with Cultural Imperialism

With this broad understanding of culture and cultural goods, let us now turn to Césaire's critique. In his speech "Culture and Colonisation," Césaire famously argued that colonialism "kills the creative power of [the] people."[34] "Wherever colonialism has existed," he states, "whole peoples have been deprived of their culture, deprived of all culture."[35]

Let us unpack this charge. For Césaire, different social and economic systems give rise to different kinds of culture.[36] By replacing indigenous institutions and practices with European institutions, colonizers also destroy Indigenous culture in the process.[37] As he states, "When the English destroy the state organization of the Ashantis in the Gold Coast, they deal a blow to Ashanti culture."[38]

The thrust of Césaire's critique, however, is not about cultural change per se. As he argues, living cultures are dynamic and inevitably consist of a mix of indigenous and foreign elements.[39] We saw in chapter 1 that Césaire adamantly stresses that he has never advocated for a "return to the past," and that "to culture, exchange is oxygen," without which any culture would wither away. Instead, Césaire draws a distinction between borrowing and taking from foreign culture out of one's self-perceived need, and having it imposed onto one. Césaire argues that borrowing from foreign cultures out of "an interior state of mind that *calls* for it" enables "what was external [to become] internal."[40] The freedom to decide whether and to what extent to adopt elements from foreign culture enables individuals to assimilate those elements in a way that does not disrupt the continuity of their culture as they see it—it enables them to retain what Césaire calls "cultural harmony," a state in which "heterogeneity is lived internally as homogeneity."[41] Under colonialism, however, individuals are forced to take up foreign cultural elements even when these do not serve their purposes. As Césaire decries, "Foreign elements are dumped on [the colonized's] soil, but remain foreign . . . White man's things! White man's manners! Things existing alongside the native but over which the native has no power."[42]

In this critique, colonialism hinders what we might call appropriative agency—the power, as the philosopher of alienation Rahel Jaeggi puts it, to "actively work through and independently assimilate" external objects rather than "passively" accepting them.[43] The free exercise of appropriative agency is important for overcoming alienation when confronted with the foreign and the unfamiliar. By contrast, forced to adopt the colonizer's culture, colonial subjects experience what Césaire calls "cultural anarchy."[44] This, according to Césaire, is a situation in which different cultural elements are "juxtaposed but not harmonized."[45] French colonial education, for example, taught students the history of Europe and France rather than their own history.[46] This knowledge, however, is not generally useful for students, whose society and environment were shaped by different historical factors. On the one hand, colonizers created an artificial situation in which students had to master a European curriculum to gain access to better opportunities and higher status. On the other hand, students living under European colonialism experience a very different reality. We might say that students' knowledge of Europe and students' lived experiences are "juxtaposed," in that there is a stark division between the two, and the former is of little use for the latter.[47] This results in a pervasive sense of alienation among the colonized.

For Césaire, this sense of alienation can be ameliorated by anticolonial writers and artists' efforts to create a cultural synthesis out of the foreign and the familiar. Before we turn to his analysis of the political power of cultural production, however, let us turn to a second, egalitarian critique that Césaire puts forth. In a nutshell, Césaire argues that colonial rule sets up a "hierarchy of *creator* and *consumer*," whereby "the creator of cultural values . . . is the colonizer. And the consumer is the colonized."[48] Taking up this critique makes it clear that the question of who can produce and disseminate cultural goods in relation to others is central to addressing the injustice of cultural imperialism.

In this critique, the destruction of indigenous cultures and the imposition of the colonizer's culture gives concrete reinforcement to the myth that some groups—namely, non-European, nonwhite peoples—are incapable of producing anything valuable enough to be called culture, and instead can only consume or at best react to and appropriate the genius of others. According to this familiar myth, colonized societies could produce only primitive cultures, and cultural progress requires the imposition of European culture. As Césaire puts it, *time* itself is divided "in reference to colonization."[49] Essentially, he argues, "everything before colonization is prehistory. And *history* only begins with colonization."[50] Under colonialism, existing forms of cultural production are devalued: "African science, African philosophy, African history, all that becomes *folklore*, that is to say debased literature, philosophy and science, just as art itself becomes primitive art."[51]

This perceived hierarchy of creator and consumer exerts real power: on the one hand, it provides justification for perpetuating political domination and economic exploitation. On the other, it cultivates what Césaire calls an "inferiority complex" among colonial subjects, whose environment is saturated with reminders of European cultural dominance—European languages, art, literature, and music. "Colonisation," Césaire argues, "raises doubts regarding the concepts on which the colonized could build or rebuild their world."[52] Colonized peoples come to believe that their own culture, having been stigmatized across decades and even centuries as "primitive," is unworthy as a source of value for the future. Thus colonialism undermines what Glen Coulthard, writing in the context of settler colonialism, calls "collective self-recognition."[53] Instead, the colonized come to believe that they must turn to European ideas and practices to progress. As Getachew and Mantena put it, drawing from Fanon and Gandhi, the "psychological wound of cultural inferiority" was often "expressed via an enthrallment to the West and the desire to emulate its values and institutions."[54]

But indigenous elites from the rural and urban middle classes who try to do just that risk being co-opted by the colonizers, which further undermines the potential of unified political resistance. As we saw in chapter 1, indigenous elites were granted political and economic privileges in return for maintaining the colonial order. These inequalities foster alienation between Indigenous elites and the people, who nonetheless share a relation of subjection to the colonizers. Aside from economic inequality and political hierarchy, a hierarchy of cultures also works in a similar way. Internalizing this hierarchy, indigenous elites make every effort to assimilate into the colonizer's culture, and, as a class, they consider themselves different and superior to the colonial population. Rather than supporting the struggle against colonial oppression, these indigenous elites are invested in its continuation. Negritude, the well-known anticolonial cultural movement spearheaded by Césaire and his colleague Léopold Senghor, was precisely an attempt to reverse this trend by pushing elites— including Césaire himself—to affirm the value of African cultures.[55]

In short, in this second critique, colonialism sets up a hierarchy of consumers and producers of culture, which denies that colonial subjects have equal capacities to produce value. This reinforces the colonial myth of racial inferiority that helps legitimize and strengthen colonial rule.

The Political Import of Cultural Production

Against this racial hierarchy, cultural production plays an important role in pushing toward decolonization. Let us now turn to Césaire's analysis of the political import of cultural production.

Speaking at the International Congress of Black Writers and Artists, an annual gathering of anticolonial cultural producers that Césaire helped organize, he argues that colonized artists and writers, as comparatively privileged elites among the colonized, have a responsibility to make use of their relative freedom and access to resources to make art as a form of anticolonial resistance. This did not preclude appropriating elements of the oppressor's culture. For inspiration, he tells his audience to "look at the Black novel . . . at Black poetry."[56] Due to transatlantic slavery and colonialism, the materials that African and African American literatures draw upon were often "disparate and heterogeneous": a mixture of different cultures. Nonetheless, Césaire argues, these works were exemplars of writers and artists "restoring order to the cultural chaos."[57] In these works, Césaire states, "everything has been recast, everything has been transcended, everything is dominated and reconstructed."[58] Consider Césaire's own literary work. Written in French, Césaire draws on European religions, symbols, and historical events, but these elements from the colonizer's culture are assembled in ways that express condemnation of colonial and racial oppression that Césaire and his fellow colonial subjects face.[59] In this sense, to appropriate "foreign [cultural] elements" is to "bend them to my uses"; to repurpose them for one's needs and in one's interests.[60] Exercising agency in this way—insisting, as Edward Said puts it, on "a right to see the community's history whole, coherent, integrally"[61] by *reclaiming* the elements of the oppressor's culture for one's purposes—helps colonial subjects overcome subjective alienation. As Césaire describes in an interview at the 1967 Cultural Congress of Havana, "while using as a point of departure the elements that French literature gave me . . . I have always striven to create a new language . . . I wanted to create an Antillean French, a black French."[62]

Furthermore, Césaire believed that the colonial racial hierarchy can be upended by indigenous cultural production. Cultural production, he argues, "precisely because it is creation," "disturbs . . . the colonial hierarchy" as it "converts the colonized *consumer* into a *creator*."[63] Césaire emphasizes cultural production as an example of "the great power of the act."[64] At the core of colonial oppression, Césaire states, is "the negation of the act, the negation of creation."[65] Colonial subjects are seen as unable to create, and they are denied the freedom and resources to do so. As a form of creative activity, then, cultural production challenges colonialism at its ideological core. Cultural production, Césaire argues, "restores historic initiative to those whom it has been the mission of the colonial system to deprive" and contests the myth of racial inferiority.[66] When members of the colonized population—such as Césaire and his colleagues—produce culture, the argument goes, this undermines the colonial lie that colonial subjects are inferior agents and therefore ought to be put under European tutelage.

Restoring this sense of self-confidence is not only important for individuals' well-being, it also has important political implications. A major task of decolonization, for many anticolonial thinkers, was to cultivate independent agents who would resist colonial oppression and, importantly, remain assertive and vigilant as democratic citizens of a postcolonial state.[67] Decades of subjection to colonial hierarchy, these thinkers argue, had fostered in individuals the habits and dispositions of submission to authority.[68] Turning the promise of colonialism on its head, Césaire argues that "colonialism cannot be a school for independence" as it stifles agency and fosters beliefs of inferiority, thus undermining the very qualities that independent agents possess.[69]

These habits and dispositions of low self-respect and passivity had to be overcome in order to build a genuinely *post*colonial society, in which individuals remain guardians of freedom and equality in face of threats of neocolonialism from foreign states, multinational corporations, and their own new government. As such, cultivating the habits and dispositions needed for democratic citizenship was seen as a crucial part of decolonization.[70]

Cultural production, for Césaire, plays a crucial role in cultivating democratic citizenship. For genuine decolonization to take place, Césaire argues that former colonial subjects must rid themselves of inferiority complexes and regain the self-confidence of an independent citizen. Cultural production "counterbalances the inferiority complex" by demonstrating concretely to colonial subjects that individuals *like them* are equally capable of producing value.[71] In doing so, Césaire states, artists and writers are "engineers of the soul . . . [and]

in the last resort, *inventors of the soul*."[72] In this sense, their craft is also soul craft for the oppressed. Writers and artists give birth to a culture that, in Said's words, "organizes and sustains communal memory . . . reinhabits the landscape using restored ways of life, heroes, heroines, and exploits . . . formulates expressions and emotions of pride as well as defiance, which in turn form the backbone of the principal national independence parties."[73]

However, to perform the work of overcoming the inferiority complex and restoring self-respect for the colonized, not just any kind of cultural production will do. In particular, for Césaire, top-down, elite-driven cultural production is self-defeating. Even in the early days of the Negritude movement, Césaire was uncomfortable with and critical of the elitism he saw in *Revue du monde noir*, the first journal established by Paulette Nardal and others to celebrate Black culture.[74] The journal's explicit aim of creating a transnational Black intellectual elite departed from his more radical vision for the role of cultural producers.[75] Addressing his fellow anticolonial artists and writers in 1956, Césaire argues against conjuring up an "*a priori* . . . plan of future native culture" but instead beckons them to connect with the people and their reality.[76] One way to understand this is that for cultural production to act as a conduit for restoring self-respect, cultural producers must not be detached from the people. Their art must reflect on people's everyday reality, engage critically with their needs, demands, and perspectives, in order for individuals to see *their own* agency reflected in these cultural goods. Since colonial oppression was the most important reality that the people faced at the time, Césaire argues that the responsibility of a "man of culture" is to "[embody] our efforts in the efforts of the colonized peoples for liberation."[77] The artist and the writer, Césaire states, should connect their cultural production to the budding "national sentiment" among the oppressed masses and "convert" this sentiment into a "ripening of popular consciousness."[78] Without being rooted in the experiences and perspectives of the people, cultural production results in goods that are as irrelevant and alien as the colonizer's. In other words, the indigenous elite would end up reproducing a cultural hierarchy not dissimilar to that under European colonialism. As we will see, these points bear important implications later for the role of the postcolonial state in cultural protectionism.

Thus Césaire has what we might call a democratic view of cultural production—democratic in at least two ways. First, culture is not the province of the elite. Rather, the everyday reality of the masses is, and ought to be, the stuff of culture. Second, cultural production serves a democratic function by helping to cultivate self-respect in oppressed agents and foster an active and engaged citizenry for postcolonial democracy.

We should not, however, interpret Césaire's democratic view of cultural production as a kind of "moral populism" in which the people's values and beliefs are necessarily worthy of preservation. The role of the writer and the artist is not simply to parrot in their art whatever values happen to be prevalent among the masses. Rather, Césaire saw cultural producers as also playing the important role of the social critic in critiquing a group's values and practices and shaping them in progressive ways. The "second duty" of the "man of culture," he argues, is to "pave the way for good decolonization."[79] "Good decolonization," as opposed to "imperfectly decolonized nations," goes beyond changing the composition of the ruling class. It consists of structural change— as Césaire puts it, the duty of "good decolonization" is a duty "to shatter the colonial structures in definitive fashion."[80] The responsibility of cultural producers is therefore not only to take the masses' everyday reality and struggles and incorporate it into their art, but in doing so, also communicate their own critical reflections on social and political issues.

To sum up this section, for Césaire, colonialism prevents its subjects from freely engaging in creative activity, appropriating both the foreign and the familiar to create culture for their own purposes. Instead, colonial subjects were forced to adopt one and abandon the other. We can call this the critique from appropriative agency. At the same time, in destroying indigenous cultures and elevating European culture, colonialism establishes a racialized cultural hierarchy in which the colonized are seen as incapable or inferior producers of value. We can call this the critique from equality. Cultural imperialism under colonialism, in this analysis, results in the dual problems of alienation and internalized inferiority.

Against this, Césaire argues that cultural production plays an important role in the process and aftermath of decolonization. Cultural production of the kind described above challenges the colonial racial hierarchy, fosters self-respect and helps overcome divisions among colonial subjects.

In the next section, I turn to discuss problems in contemporary cultural globalization. While many features of cultural globalization today are different from the colonial context in which Césaire theorized, I argue that his central ideas regarding the relationship between cultural production, racial hierarchy, and the political import of cultural production are still highly relevant. In particular, I will argue that the critique from equality is especially important in a world where cultural production and exchange remains deeply unequal.

Cultural Globalization and Its Discontents

Since the end of formal colonialism in many parts of the world, forced cultural assimilation is no longer the main source of cultural degradation for most postcolonial societies. Having obtained formal independence, postcolonial societies are no longer coercively prohibited from reviving and using their own languages and developing their own cultural goods such as literature, film, music, and visual arts.

At first glance, then, it is unclear why cultural globalization through economic exchange should trouble us. After all, as some contemporary cosmopolitans have held, the development of a global cultural identity is just a result of increasing and irreversible economic and political interdependence.[81] Cultural globalization may even be a positive development for global justice, David Held and Anthony McGrew argue, insofar as it helps individuals become a "citizen of the world" with a sense of "global belonging" that "transcends loyalties to the nation-state."[82] Lastly, cultural protectionism seems to be self-defeating. As Jeremy Waldron puts it in response to proponents of minority cultural rights within the domestic context,

> Cultures live and grow, change and sometimes wither away; they amalgamate with other cultures, or they adapt themselves . . . To preserve or protect it, or some favored version of it, artificially, in the face of that change, is precisely to cripple the mechanisms of adaptation and compromise (from warfare to commerce to amalgamation) with which all societies confront the outside world.[83]

Such views, however, neglect the fact that cultural globalization has largely occurred in a *one-sided* manner and the moral implications of this trend within the context of a legacy of colonial racism. Furthermore, the case for cultural protectionism need not be grounded in a claim to preserve a particular form of culture. Instead, as I argue in the rest of the chapter, cultural protectionism can be justified on an important interest that individuals have in relating to one another as equals.

Let us start by looking at some instances of persistent inequality in global cultural production and dissemination.

Imbalances in the Global Flow of Cultural Goods

Until relatively recently, the flow of cultural goods between "developed" and "developing" countries has been deeply imbalanced.[84] In 2002, for example, developing countries still accounted for less than 1 percent of global exports of cultural goods.[85] The UK was the biggest exporter of cultural goods with $8.5 billion, while the United States followed closely with $7.6 billion.[86] While this trend has been tempered by a certain degree of "contra-flows" in recent years, this is mostly due to the rise of China and to a lesser but still significant extent, India, as global exporters of cultural goods.[87] Including China and India, cultural exports from *all* developing countries surpassed developed countries for the first time only in 2014, with developing countries accounting for 53 percent of the global export of cultural goods.[88] Excluding China and India, however, developing countries account for only 26.5 percent of the global export of cultural goods of the same year (with 23.3 percent of music goods, 32 percent of arts goods, and only 18.3 percent of publishing goods), a number that only moved up to 30 percent in 2019.[89] Moreover, according to a 2013 UNESCO report, Central Asia and Eastern Europe accounted only for 2.7 percent of the world's cultural exports, while Arab states, the Pacific, sub-Saharan Africa, and the Caribbean played an even more "marginal role," with their share of cultural exports totaling less than 1 percent, despite making up around 20 percent of the world's population.[90] The so-called least developed countries, which comprise forty-six countries and roughly 12 percent of the world's population, had by 2022 only reached a 0.5 percent share of the world's cultural exports.[91] Additionally, given the difficulty in estimating cultural goods that are "imported" by individual citizens via digital platforms such as Netflix and HBO, it is likely that the percentage of cultural exports from Western developed countries—from which these digital platforms tend to originate—is higher. A 2022 UNESCO estimate put developed countries' global share of digital cultural exports (including film and music streaming) at an overwhelming 95 percent.[92] As communications scholar Tanner Mirrlees puts it, the United States "basically dominates the global digital platform market."[93] In recent years, the United States has continued to push for liberalization of countries' regulations surrounding on-demand video streaming platforms.[94]

These imbalances are not limited to cultural goods such as films, music, literature, and media; they also encompass knowledge production and dissemination. As an illustration, consider a recent finding regarding inequalities in research on economic development: according to this study, just 16 percent of 24,894 articles published in twenty top development journals between 1990 and 2019 were from authors in the Global South, while 73 percent were from those in the Global North, and 11 percent were North-South collaborations.[95] This was the case even when the majority of the research was focused on the Global South. Similarly, climate science research has also seen a stark North-South divide, with more than 85 percent of authors of relevant publications (out of more than ninety thousand) in the period from 2000–14 based in Global North countries. As climate researchers write in a *Nature* perspective, "Northern domination of science globally relevant to climate change policy and practice" threatens to undermine "bottom-up global agreements and nationally appropriate actions to address the climate crisis."[96]

These patterns ultimately trace back to persistent inequalities in capital and therefore leverage, which constrain postcolonial societies' ability to invest in domestic cultural production and to disseminate the cultural goods and knowledge produced. Let us take the film industry as an example. The US film industry has developed an extensive international distribution system by which American films are marketed in foreign markets through distribution cartels like United International Pictures, which represent major Hollywood studios such as Paramount, Universal, and MGM/UA.[97] US media conglomerates also invest and acquire non-US media firms and engage in "cross-border production" in which US firms tend to retain control of creative decision-making and copyrights while specific tasks for production are outsourced to non-US media firms and their cultural workers. Licensing agreements, whereby US media content is sold to non-US firms at a reduced cost, also incentivize non-US firms to buy US content from Hollywood studios rather than produce new content.[98] Furthermore, the US government—lobbied by the Motion Pictures Association of America—leverages its power over other states to secure terms of trade that favor the export of US films.[99]

To be sure, cultural production does not only take the forms of commodified goods and published research. Taking a broader view of cultural flows outside of these formal economies easily demonstrates that influences routinely happen in the other direction—to use the language of dependency theory, there are cultural flows from the "periphery" to the "center," or from the "periphery-within-center" to the rest of the world. Think of the pervasive global influence that African American culture has had on musical styles, fashion, cuisines, and so on, for example. Or consider the fact that many scientific innovations (especially in medicine and climate research) are built on traditional knowledge developed by Indigenous peoples in the Global South. Despite these counterhegemonic cultural flows, however, marginalized producers do not tend to get formal or public recognition for their creative labor. In the era of formal colonialism, colonized peoples' practices and ideas hugely influenced the metropole, and yet those influences have been largely erased from public memory; in the era of neocolonialism, similar dynamics are at play.

Specifically, there are at least two ways in which the role of historically oppressed groups as cultural producers is often erased. The first consists of dominant groups appropriating practices and ideas developed by marginalized groups. This phenomenon is found across music, fashion, cuisines, art, and so on, but it is perhaps most concerning in pharmaceutical and biotechnology, where instances of appropriation have been called biopiracy, i.e., "the unauthorized commercial use of biological resources and/or associated traditional knowledge, or the patenting of spurious inventions based on such knowledge, without compensation."[100] To take an example, in 2009 a French research institute patented a new anti-malaria drug without giving credit to the Indigenous peoples of French Guiana, whom they had interviewed to discover the relevant plant.[101] A full appraisal of cultural and knowledge appropriation is not possible here, but the critical point for our purposes is that in these

instances, the (usually white) appropriator occupies the visible role of the innovator.[102] Importantly, appropriation is compatible with the appropriator
from a dominant group crediting the marginalized group for providing the
"inspiration" for the innovation in question. Indeed, some forms of cultural
appropriation *depend* on advertising their supposed "exotic" origins for commercial value—think of the French designer Isabel Marant appropriating a
pattern unique to the Purepecha community of Mexico, claiming that she was
"[paying] tribute" to the community despite their protests against it.[103] But
mere acknowledgment does not undermine the broader dynamic where the
dominant group continues to act as the creative innovator while the marginalized group supplies "traditional" material to be modernized.

A related but distinct way in which the role of historically oppressed groups
is erased might be called *whitewashing*. In the film industry, whitewashing refers to casting white people in roles that were written for people of color, usually leading to demeaning portrayals of the latter. More broadly, we can take
whitewashing to denote the outright erasure of the contributions of historically oppressed groups from public memory and historical narrative. Think of
the history of American music from country to rock-and-roll, for example.
These cultural forms have been dominated by white artists and traditionally
been seen as white Americans' creations. Only recently have there been renewed efforts to recover and document the significant and foundational contributions made by African Americans in developing these musical genres.[104]
Or think of the many deep and long-lasting influences that the colonies had
on metropolitan culture that are only now being recovered by the new imperial
history movement.[105] Moreover, whitewashing can also be seen in former
colonial powers' historical narratives about themselves. Until recently, for
example, the role of troops from the empire in defending Britain in World
War II—a historical episode that has become central to contemporary British
national identity—has largely been erased.[106] Similarly, the Haitian Revolution and the founding of the Republic of Haiti, a pivotal episode in French
history, has largely been ignored in France's national history curriculum.[107]

To sum up this section, patterns of deeply asymmetric cultural flows have
persisted beyond formal colonialism. Although citizens of postcolonial societies are, for the most part, no longer coerced into adopting foreign languages,
practices, and ways of life, capital-rich and majority-white societies continue
to disproportionately produce and export their cultural goods to the rest of the
world. Furthermore, counterhegemonic cultural flows are often made invisible by
the dynamics of appropriation and whitewashing. In both real and perceived
senses, then, cultural globalization has remained a largely one-sided affair.

In the rest of the chapter, I focus on exploring how global inequality in
cultural production and dissemination reinforces a racialized hierarchy of

creator and consumer, thus contributing to the stabilization of neocolonial global hierarchies. To be sure, there are other reasons why these patterns are problematic. For example, when the majority of scientific research is carried out in a few dominant Global North countries, one worry is that the questions asked and the concepts and solutions developed will be irrelevant to or unsuited for understanding and solving problems faced by the rest of the world. As Getachew and Mantena argue, another important legacy of European epistemic domination is the "analytic failures" in understanding colonized (and postcolonial) societies when Eurocentric concepts are stretched too far.[108] To borrow the language of philosophers of epistemic injustice, we might think of this as a problem of hermeneutical injustice—where the oppressed lack epistemic resources to understand their experiences on their own terms.[109]

The view developed below focuses on the effects of global inequality in cultural production and dissemination on *relations between groups*. But rather than displacing these other concerns regarding cultural/epistemic hegemony, I seek to complement them by drawing out their implications for global social equality. As we will see, one implication (not often highlighted in the kind of critique above) is that citizens of postcolonial societies have an important interest not only in opportunities to engage in cultural and knowledge production, but also in acting as cultural and knowledge disseminators. Finally, the view of cultural decolonization I defend in the section titled "Decolonizing Cultural Globalization: Restoring Social Agency," which emphasizes the *restoration of equal social agency*, has implications for addressing the hermeneutical injustice wrought by European epistemic domination. Empowering postcolonial citizens to act as social agents in the cultural sphere entails creating space for the kinds of knowledge production that Getachew and Mantena argue for— "conceptual innovation" and "conceptual reanimation," where new concepts are generated out of the postcolonial experience and existing concepts reformulated/retheorized as a result of their encounters with the postcolonial.[110]

Cultural Imperialism and the Repression/Erasure of Social Agency

A common response to the accusation of Western cultural imperialism is that individuals in non-Western societies are not simply passive consumers.[111] Instead, they are active appropriators of Western cultural goods. With globalization has also come "glocalization"—think of local variations of the English language, fast food, and Hollywood filmmaking. Worrying about Western cultural flows seems to deny that citizens in postcolonial societies can respond in critical and creative ways.

Recall the two critiques derived from Césaire above. The "glocalization" argument goes *some* way to responding to the first critique—that colonialism denies individuals the freedom to exercise appropriative agency. Free from formal colonialism, even as resources are often inadequate, individuals are still undoubtedly freer to engage with foreign cultural elements in their desired manner: to integrate and localize these elements as they see fit. To be sure, this does not mean that this critique is completely irrelevant today. Individuals are not entirely free to choose how and whether they engage with foreign cultures. Short of coercion, a globalized economy creates enormous pressures on non-English speaking groups to learn English, for example. Insofar as fluency in particular cultures translates into access to a host of important opportunities and goods, we can hardly say that individuals are fully free in deciding whether and to what extent they might engage with these cultures.[112]

More importantly, however, the "glocalization" argument fails to move the second critique at all. Deep imbalance in cultural flows, whereby Global North countries continue to dominate the global production and dissemination of cultural goods can be problematic for a second reason: namely, reinforcing the idea of a hierarchy of creator and consumer that emerged in the colonial era and that remains an important feature of racist ideology today.

To see this, let us take a step back. I argued in chapter 2 that individuals have an important interest in being recognized as social agents—broadly, agents with capacities to produce value.[113] The interest in equal recognition as social agents, I argued, lies in a more fundamental interest in social equality. As an ideal, social equality denotes relations between individuals that are governed by robust dispositions of mutual respect, reciprocity, and solidarity. Such relations are valuable because they enable individuals to experience freedom, maintain self-respect, and enjoy nonalienation with one another. Furthermore, I argued that social equality is important not only within societies, but also at the global level. I analyzed three forms of global hierarchies (i.e., authority, esteem, and moral standing) and argued that they are objectionable in themselves and that they constrain citizens' capacity to pursue domestic social equality.

If social equality is of such fundamental importance to individual freedom and well-being, such relations are also hard to attain. Groups privileged by objectionable hierarchies have vested material and psychological-cognitive interests in maintaining and justifying them. Over time, efforts to justify the unjustifiable tend to produce widespread, often nonconscious acceptance of distorted and/or misleading beliefs regarding subordinated groups and the way the world works. In Tommie Shelby's words, racist ideology contributes to "the stabilization of oppressive social relations" and "the promotion of the interests of a hegemonic group."[114]

Throughout modern history, a crucial piece of racist ideology has been the idea that nonwhite peoples are inferior social agents. As we saw in Césaire's analysis of colonial discourse, European colonialists, intellectuals, and writers developed claims about colonial subjects' inability to innovate, create, and, in short, contribute to human progress. Historically speaking, whenever members of a group have been seen as incapable or less capable of producing value, they also tend to be seen as dependent upon others' genius, and this helps justify their lack of relevant goods, rights, and opportunities within a particular social hierarchy. As Shelby argues, an integral part of anti-Black ideology is the idea that "so-called 'white culture' is the highest level of creative attainment so far achieved, while black cultural expression has lesser, or no, aesthetic worth."[115]

Importantly, ideas about a group's inferiority as social agents do not have to be explicitly or consciously held beliefs. More often, these ideas sediment as implicit biases and stereotypical associations that individuals who consciously subscribe to the moral equality of human beings may nonetheless act upon. Shelby characterizes ideology as a form of social consciousness—a "jungle of ideas" that "can at times be coherently articulated and defended by the individuals who hold then, [but] more often they cannot."[116] One reason why ideology critique and critical discourse analyses are so important is precisely because, as Shelby argues, individuals may not be completely aware that they are "in the grip of a particular picture of the world."[117] Instead, some forms of social consciousness may only be "implicit in the behavioral dispositions, utterances, conduct, and practices of social actors."[118]

Recent work in the psychology of implicit bias, prejudice, and stereotyping has lent further credence to the claim that racist ideology influences individuals subconsciously.[119] As philosophers of psychology Michael Brownstein and Jennifer Saul state, biases and associations are "evaluations of social groups that are largely outside conscious awareness of control."[120] Furthermore, when these attitudes are prevalent enough to erode egalitarian relations or reinforce objectionable hierarchies, it becomes even more difficult for members of the disadvantaged group to access the opportunities and resources needed for value-making. In other words, because ideas have material consequences, the myth of inferiority can be self-fulfilling. Historically, for example, women have been excluded from public life. One powerful justification was the idea that women are generally less capable than men in contributing to public life. This reinforced the exclusion of women, and the absence of women in public life, in turn, continued to feed the myth.

Finally, when others' objectionable attitudes toward oneself begin to take psychological hold, it becomes much harder to hold oneself up as an equal to others. As Césaire suggests, repeatedly being taught that one is inferior in value-making and lacking enough objective evidence in the world to suggest otherwise, it takes burdensome efforts for an individual in these positions to resist and overcome this barrier to asserting oneself as an equal to others.

Let us now return to the problem of asymmetric cultural flows between societies. What is the role of cultural production in this broader dynamic of racialized groups denied equal social agency? In principle, any production of value should compel others to recognize one as a social agent; not everyone has to be an artist. Historically, however, *cultural* production has been seen as an especially important external manifestation of a group's status as social agents. We can make sense of this in two ways. First, and more obviously, cultural production most often involves dispositions and traits associated with social agency, such as skill, hard work, critical reflection, and creativity. They are therefore some testament to their creators' agential capacities. Second, although cultural goods are created by artists, writers, filmmakers, and so on, their production does not occur in a vacuum. Instead, as discussed in the first section, titled "Culture and Colonialism," cultural producers tend to (explicitly or implicitly) draw on the social material—myths, collective memories, values, ways of life—available in their environment and that are collectively produced by members of a given group. In this way, cultural goods reflect not only the agential capacities of the producer but also of those with whom she shares a set of formative conditions. Apart from aesthetic value, then, cultural production also demonstrates that members of the group have exercised agential capacities in ways that create value.

Therefore, a group's capacity to produce and disseminate culture in relation to others takes on a particular political importance from the perspective of social equality, as it affects members of historically oppressed groups' standing as equal social agents. The political import of a group's perceived cultural achievements is one reason why Césaire emphasizes the colonizer's insistent erasure of culture from the colonized. As he writes sarcastically in *Discourse on Colonialism*,

> Before the arrival of the French in their country, the Vietnamese were people of an old culture, exquisite and refined. To recall the fact upsets the digestion of the Banque d'Indochine. Start the forgetting machine!
>
> These Madagascans who are being tortured today, less than a century ago were poets, artists, administrators? Shhhhh! Keep your lips buttoned! ...
>
> About the Sudanese empires? About the bronzes of Benin? Shango sculpture? ... The petty bourgeoisie doesn't want to hear any more.[121]

Taking the political import of cultural production seriously, the worry is that when contemporary global cultural production and dissemination remains deeply unequal, this can reinforce a persistent ideology of a hierarchy of creator and consumer inherited from the colonial era. Specifically, there are at least two ways in which this can happen.

Objectionable Cultural Representations

The first is perhaps more familiar: racist ideology can be reinforced as a result of the cultural content that individuals around the world are exposed to.[122] When marginalized societies are unable to export their cultural content to the rest of the world, their perspectives of the world also become underrepresented. Instead, the perspectives of the historically advantaged can continue to act as the authority to represent the developing world, as European powers did in the colonial era.[123] As Edward Said's classic work *Orientalism* argues, global relations of domination are maintained not only through military might, but also through the production of knowledge about, and therefore creation of, the dominated Other.[124] Many contemporary cultural representations of the Global South, for example, have been criticized for objectionable stereotypes, such as explicit or implicit portrayals of a permanently helpless, dependent, and uniform Africa.[125] These cultural representations not only help legitimize American and European political dominance and economic exploitation of Global South societies, but also shape reality as they become action-guiding.[126]

In other words, when members of historically marginalized groups lack the chance to shape others' perceptions of oneself as a rational agent capable of critical reflection and innovation, for example, others may come to see one's religious culture as static and necessarily oppressive toward women, and justify the use of coercion in this way. As Indira Gandhi stated in 1976, at the height of the NWICO debate, "We want to hear Africans on events in Africa. You should similarly be able to get an Indian explanation of events in India. It is astonishing that we know so little about leading poets, novelists, historians, and editors of various Asian, African, and Latin American countries while we are familiar with minor authors and columnists of Europe and America."[127]

Thus we might say that attitudes regarding a group *y*'s inferiority are likely to arise or be reinforced when a dominant group *x* has disproportionate power to produce representations of the world and when this group enjoys a position of political and economic advantage such that representations are likely to serve (explicitly or implicitly) to legitimize these advantages. As such, representations of the nondominant group are likely to be negative or otherwise objectionable.[128] Notice, however, that even if members of the nondominant group acquired more power to produce their own representations of the world, as long as the dominant group's position of political and economic advantage remains, the latter's power and wealth may still exert considerable influence on the content produced. The nondominant group may still rely on for-profit intermediaries to distribute their goods. As an example from the film and media industry, Anamik Saha's ethnographic study of British Asian filmmakers and media executives showed that these cultural producers tend to reproduce stereotypical representations due to pressures from increasing commercialization of media.[129] Their art must reproduce what is perceived as "mainstream" in order to be commissioned—and those who have power, of course, have historically determined what counts as mainstream.[130] Therefore, to fully address the problem of cultural representations, it is insufficient that marginalized groups are able to produce culture—rather, more fundamental changes to the corporate structure of cultural production and distribution, and changes to the distribution of political and economic power between groups, are needed.

Asymmetric Cultural Flows

Beyond problematic cultural content, however, within the context of a long history of colonial racism, real and perceived patterns of asymmetric cultural production and dissemination may *themselves* reinforce the colonial-era myth that one side—namely the (white) West—is the giver of culture, while the other side—the (nonwhite) postcolonial world—can only receive or, at best, react.[131] This seems especially likely when existing *political* and *economic* relations between these groups are structured in such a way that already lends power to the racial myth. As we saw in chapter 3, most postcolonies have had little choice but to rely on foreign investment, aid, technology, and expertise for their development. In such a context, the deep imbalance in who gets to make and send culture to others may reinforce the idea that postcolonial developing countries can only be dependent on the West—i.e., a racialized hierarchy of creator and consumer.

Therefore, again using x and y for shorthand here, a second way in which ideas about group y's inferiority may arise is when x has disproportionate power to produce and distribute cultural goods to y, and y has historically been seen as morally inferior to x, and/or y is in a relationship of political and economic dependency with x. In these cases, the fact that x can disproportionately produce and disseminate cultural goods to y may be seen as evidence to support x's unjustified attitudes about y's inferiority. Furthermore, while these conditions apply most obviously to postcolonial countries, we can remove the historical context of racial hierarchy and it is still possible that, by virtue of y's ongoing dependency on x, over time, the inequality in cultural production can be interpreted as evidence that y is inferior to x in the production of value. Therefore, even if two societies had no prior colonial relations, it is possible that imbalances in cultural production and distribution between them may become problematic over time. New hierarchies may emerge.

To be sure, anyone interpreting perceived imbalances in cultural flows as somehow an indication of a society's inferior capacities to produce value is obviously engaging in a distorted kind of reasoning. But such is the power of ideology that pointing out epistemic flaws is insufficient, not only because (as discussed above) most people do not consciously engage in such reasoning and instead hold implicit biases and stereotypes, but also because ideology can often appear to explain reality. As Vanessa Wills describes, racist ideology often "gets things 'right' at the level of appearance" but "mistakes that appearance for a 'deep' or essential truth."[132] The visible prevalence of Western cultural goods and dominance of Western science, on the surface, look like affirmations of the notion that some groups are inferior social agents. On the other hand, the reality of deeply unequal resources (stemming, of course, in no small part from past and ongoing global exploitation) combined with the practices of white appropriation and whitewashing remain invisible, inconvenient truths.

So far, I have argued that despite formal freedom for citizens of postcolonial states to engage in cultural production, the imbalance in global cultural flows continues to be problematic insofar as it reinforces a colonial-era racist hierarchy of social agency. Let me end this section with two concrete examples of objectionable attitudes toward one's own racialized group, which have persisted within postcolonial societies beyond formal colonialism.

First, an increasingly popular "rent-a-foreigner" industry has emerged in China. Firms hire out foreigners, with white foreigners the most expensive, to play roles ranging from wealthy investors to random city dwellers in order to make Chinese businesses and real estate look more prestigious, and therefore more valuable.[133] Second, the widespread practice of skin whitening in many postcolonial societies. According to a 2011 estimate from the World Health Organization, for example, 77 percent of women in Nigeria use skin-lightening and skin-bleaching products regularly, the highest in the world.[134] These products have been shown to lead to dangerous health conditions such as kidney failure and various kinds of cancers.[135] The governments of Rwanda, Ivory Coast, and Ghana have recently had to ban all skin-whitening products to protect their citizens from these health threats.

These cases of "colorism" should be read in the context of a global cultural environment that continues to be disproportionately made up of visible contributions from the "white West."[136] To be sure, the persistent myth of white superiority within former colonies cannot only be explained by the kinds of cultural goods that individuals are exposed to. But it also seems hard to deny that culture plays a role in individuals' formation of attitudes and beliefs about themselves and others.[137]

In other words, colonialism casts a long shadow. Its legacy of racism and cultural hierarchy continues to impact the ways in which people of color and postcolonial societies are perceived today. The idea of global social equality can seem strange in part because there does not seem to be a shared social environment and set of standards by which some are esteemed while others stigmatized. But, as the two examples above show, this could not be further from the truth.

For individuals living in societies deeply impacted by European colonialism and American cultural dominance today, the global ideology of "white is better" remains operative in everyday life, even as individuals no longer share political membership with those whom they are socialized to hold in higher esteem.

In chapter 3, I argued that citizens in postcolonial capital-poor countries have a claim to terms of global economic interaction that are regulated by the pursuit of social equality. This claim is grounded on a more basic claim that individuals have in relating to others as equals. The analysis developed thus far in this chapter suggests, I think, that realizing global social equality also requires enabling historically oppressed and racialized groups to exercise social agency in cultural production and dissemination and to be recognized for it.

In the next section, I argue that we can understand decolonizing cultural globalization as a process of restoring equal social agency. In this view, decolonizing cultural globalization entails institutional and extra-institutional efforts along two dimensions: empowerment and recovery of agency. Among other things, this justifies a host of measures that disproportionately favor opportunities for cultural producers from historically oppressed groups and which together aim to *democratize*—rather than liberalize—global cultural exchange; in short, to make cultural production and exchange much more egalitarian and participatory than it has been. Insofar as these initiatives help dismantle or at least destabilize a global racist ideology, historically privileged actors—from states to citizens— have a duty, grounded on a more fundamental duty to relate to others as equals, to endorse them. Following Ngũgĩ wa Thiong'o, we might think of this as a call to "decolonize the mind," although unlike Ngũgĩ, my emphasis is on historically advantaged agents' duty to do so, and hence it may be more aptly termed a duty to "decolonialize" the mind (i.e., to resist the biases and prejudices that individuals inevitably acquire in the context of unrectified historical injustice).

Until a more egalitarian cultural globalization is attained, however, I will also argue that postcolonial societies that remain marginalized from global cultural production have a pro tanto claim to engage in cultural protectionism. Importantly, as I discuss below, these cultural protectionist policies should aim to empower cultural producers to exercise their creative capacities—and therefore their social agency—rather than determine, from the outset, what kinds of cultural content ought to be preserved.

Decolonizing Cultural Globalization: Restoring Equal Social Agency

For decades the US government has pushed to liberalize global cultural exchange. After it rejoined UNESCO in 2003, the United States became one of only two states that voted against the Convention on the Protection and

Promotion of the Diversity of Cultural Expressions in 2005.[138] As mentioned in the introduction to this chapter, this continued push to liberalize global cultural exchange is purportedly grounded in the value of freedom of speech and information. Barriers to cross-border cultural flows are said to be unjustified infringements on sending parties' freedom of speech and on recipients' right to access information.

On the other hand, the decolonial demand, encapsulated in the NWICO and subsequent UNESCO initiatives, is to *democratize* global cultural exchange. This is grounded primarily on the value of equality. While not denying that individuals ought to have freedom of speech and access to information, this view emphasizes that, without reforming the infrastructures of global communication, the formal freedom to participate in cultural exchange translates into substantively unequal participation. Capital-poor postcolonial countries, and especially disadvantaged groups within these countries, lack an equal chance to produce and distribute cultural goods across the world.

In face of this, a guiding principle for decolonizing cultural globalization is to restore the social agency of members of previously marginalized groups. As we saw from the discussion above, the stifling and erasure of these groups' agency, especially in the areas of cultural (and knowledge) production, risk reinforcing a constitutive element of a global racist ideology inherited from the colonial era—the idea of a hierarchy of creator and consumer. This ideology is not only demeaning in itself but also contributes to the maintenance of neocolonial economic and political global relations by naturalizing dependency. Decolonizing cultural globalization as restoring equal social agency is therefore a project in challenging this ideology.

Before taking a closer look at the obligations and claims that follow from this imperative, it is important to stress that we ought not be deluded about the power of working for postcolonial global justice at the ideological level. Objectionable beliefs and the biases and stereotypical associations that embody them arise from specific relations of domination and exploitation. Without challenging the latter, the former is unlikely to be eradicated on its own. The path toward postcolonial global justice as global social equality cannot be only through cultural production. Still, it would be another extreme to claim that all efforts to engage in what Wills calls "conceptual interventions"— interventions at the level of ideas—are altogether futile. As Wills puts it, "Ideas are not merely epiphenomenal to the material conditions from which they emerge, but ideas themselves also have a causal impact on those conditions and partially determine them."[139] By increasing opportunities for citizens of postcolonial societies to engage in global cultural production and act as cultural and knowledge disseminators, the hope is to chip away at a central tenant of a global racist ideology and open a door to further political action.

Let us further break down the decolonial imperative of restoring equal social agency (in the cultural sphere) along two dimensions: first, empowering
individuals from historically oppressed and racialized groups to exercise creative agency by removing or addressing institutional and extra-institutional
constraints; and second, recovering the role of these groups in contributing to
shaping the world as we know it today. Together, these efforts aim to upend
the global hierarchy of creator and consumer.

Empowering Creative Agency

We can start by identifying some important constraints faced by cultural
producers from capital-poor, postcolonial societies. The most obvious is the
lack of resources and access to technology. Addressing this fully requires
large-scale reforms to global economic relations that determine the distribution of wealth (including a different kind of investment regime, as discussed
in chapter 3). But there are also measures more specific to cultural production. Here, we might revisit some of NWICO's proposed reforms aimed at
democratizing cultural production. Some continue to be supported by many
postcolonial countries in the Global South today. The proposed International
Program for the Development of Communication (IPDC) discussed at the
beginning of the chapter, for example, was meant to facilitate financial assistance and technology transfers for capital-poor postcolonial countries to
develop their media and cultural industries. As a matter of reparations for
cultural destruction in the colonial era, former colonial powers have an especially strong duty of justice (as opposed to charity) to support these initiatives, both to compensate for past wrongdoing but also, as I have argued, to
dismantle a racist ideology that they helped bring about.

Yet even with increased access to resources and technology, so long as the
market is dominated by a few players, it remains difficult for those with less
capital to participate in cultural production and dissemination. Moreover,
as mentioned in the previous section, cultural producers whose cultural expressions may challenge or deviate from the mainstream will also find it
difficult to get funding and/or opportunities for exhibition. As such, decolonial efforts to empower creative agency must also entail pushing back
against the trends of commercialization and monopolization in the media
and cultural industries and instead revitalize and support public and
independent cultural institutions such as public broadcasting, museums,
international festivals, and so on. As we saw, one of the main proposals of
the NWICO was for states to pursue antimonopoly practices to break up
transnational media conglomerates and to reverse privatization of media. To
the extent that these are important for enabling marginalized groups to

participate in global cultural production and dissemination, they can also be seen as decolonial initiatives.

Relatedly, a third constraint often faced by cultural producers whose creations may not fit neatly under existing cultural and epistemic frameworks is the lack of uptake. Shifting and pluralizing cultural and epistemic frameworks is a long-term project that is unlikely to occur simply because more artists and knowledge producers from historically marginalized groups have opportunities to create and disseminate their work. Again, it bears emphasizing that only when global political, economic, and social relations more closely resemble egalitarian relations should we expect genuine appreciation of cultural pluralism and the possibility of, as Césaire puts it, a "universal humanism" created by contributions from all groups across the world.[140]

Yet it would also be facile to think that nothing can be done to encourage more uptake than currently exists. If nothing else, this lets former colonial and neocolonial powers off the hook too easily. One long-standing demand from postcolonial countries, also featured in the NWICO, is for Global North countries to provide open and preferential access to their cultural markets.[141] The implication here is that former colonial powers such as France, which has historically taken up protectionist measures against foreign cultural influences, cannot justify imposing these costs and barriers when it comes to cultural flows from former colonies such as Algeria or Vietnam. We might go one step further and argue that countries like France should instead *prioritize* the import of cultural goods from former colonies and promote their visibility as well as the visibility of their producers. For example, this could be done through subsidizing domestic consumption of these goods—which may not be immediately appreciated by many—or providing commercial and public platforms with incentives to exhibit and promote these goods and their producers.

Finally, a fourth constraint faced by cultural producers from capital-poor, postcolonial countries is the inability of their governments to engage in cultural protectionist policies without encountering prohibitions under international trade agreements. Thus a much fought-over measure has been to exempt cultural goods from free trade to allow postcolonial states to nurture domestic cultural production. While the 2005 UNESCO Convention was a watershed moment in this fight as culture was, for the first time, recognized in international law as different from other kinds of goods, critics have pointed out that the convention remains subsumed under WTO rules and therefore has largely been toothless.[142] We will discuss cultural protectionism in greater detail shortly, but it is worth flagging here that it is a crucial piece of the decolonial effort at empowering marginalized groups to exercise their creative agency.

Recovering Creative Agency

Yet empowerment is insufficient. Time and again, even when members of historically oppressed groups have resisted or found ways to work within the many constraints on their creative agency and actually created much of what we now take to be valuable forms of culture and knowledge, this has remained largely invisible and unrecognized. As we saw previously, white appropriation and whitewashing are just two of the most common ways in which the role of racialized groups shaping and creating culture have been erased from the record, as it were. And yet, as I have argued, this adds to the perception that some groups have primarily been consumers of others' geniuses, thus reinforcing a demeaning and equality-undermining ideology.

Therefore, decolonizing cultural globalization as restoring equal social agency must also comprise efforts to *recover* marginalized social agency where it has been exercised. Broadly, this entails measures to revise historical narrative and vehicles of public memory, as well as protections against cultural and knowledge appropriation from dominant groups. As an important shaper of public memory, for example, museums should prioritize recovering the erased agency of former colonial subjects in creating and building many of the musical, literary, and artistic genres that we know today, as well as their roles in developing knowledge and innovations. School curriculum also needs to be significantly revised—especially in countries like the UK and France, where the role of the former colonies in building the metropole's wealth and culture continues to be almost completely elided—to reflect the fact that historically oppressed groups have always been creators as much as consumers.

Second, there have been efforts from postcolonial countries as well as Indigenous peoples to press for reforms to the intellectual property regime to give greater protections to "traditional" or Indigenous knowledge in order to prevent objectionable forms of appropriation.[143] This is a more radical claim than it might initially appear. The current IP regime, which emphasizes individual property rights, is ill fitted to recognize and protect Indigenous knowledge. Indigenous knowledge is collectively produced, and many knowledge holders do not want protections in the form of patents, but instead some legal mechanism by which the knowledge credited to its producers can still be shared for the common good.[144] In other words, the current IP regime, which has been criticized as a "means and mechanism of imperialism," would need to be significantly reformed.[145] To the extent that such reforms aim to empower members of historically oppressed groups to act as knowledge disseminators, they can be seen as furthering the broader project of cultural decolonization.

A contentious issue for which there has been little progress is the repatriation of stolen cultural objects from former metropoles to the postcolonial societies. While I cannot fully resolve this complex issue here, the guiding principle for decolonizing cultural globalization that I have proposed—restoring equal social agency—also has some implications for it. One argument for metropoles to hold on to these objects is that they have the resources and technology to maintain and keep them in the appropriate conditions. Yet at least one reason that counts in favor of returning these objects (aside from appeals to cultural property rights) is precisely that continued possession promotes a hierarchy in which former colonial powers act as global cultural caretakers and disseminators.[146] Historically, this was a role that colonizers often gave themselves—as Karuna Mantena has shown in her study of the late British empire, colonialists became convinced of the "irredeemable backwardness" of their subjects and moved from trying to assimilate colonial subjects to seeking to preserve what they thought of as "native culture."[147] The underlying assumption was that they knew the "native" better than anyone else did, including the "native." Instead of holding on to these objects, my argument suggests there is an egalitarian reason for former colonial powers (and their museums) to engage in resources and technology transfers and enable postcolonial societies to act as cultural disseminators and tell their own narratives about these cultural objects.

There are undoubtedly many more initiatives and measures that may contribute to decolonizing cultural globalization, understood as restoring the equal social agency of racialized and historically oppressed groups.[148] While we should not overstate the potential of these reforms without greater economic and political change—as I have argued throughout the book, the different aspects of postcolonial global justice are importantly linked—it would also be premature to dismiss changes to the infrastructure surrounding global cultural exchange as politically toothless. As Césaire observed, against a background of racial hierarchy, cultural production has critical political import: it enables oppressed groups to challenge the lie of inferiority and, at the same time, gives them an important basis for self-respect. Moreover, the underlying principle that guides cultural decolonization projects has radical implications. Recall that social agency denotes the broad set of capacities that enable human beings to "make a positive mark" on human history—whether that is making a piece of art, making an important scientific discovery, building a road, and so on. While it is beyond our scope to flesh this out here, we should note that taking seriously the moral significance of enabling individuals across the world to exercise and be recognized for their equal social agency has implications beyond the cultural sphere.

Finally, grounding a duty to "decolonialize the mind" on the importance of social equality means that this duty does not only implicate citizens of former colonial powers. Instead, wherever discourses regarding the inferiority of disadvantaged groups circulate, and this is accompanied by persistent imbalances in cross-border cultural flows, citizens have a duty to push back by (among other actions) supporting reforms to global cultural exchange. While we can expect such discourses to persist in former colonial powers that have not properly grappled with historical injustice, they are often also present or emergent in other societies, especially where one or both conditions discussed in the previous section obtain between two societies (that is, historical injustice and/or presently asymmetric relations of dependence).[149]

A Remedial Right to Cultural Protectionism

Yet there is a long way to go before substantive equality in cultural production and dissemination can be attained. Until then, I contend that postcolonial developing countries have a pro tanto claim to cultural protectionist rights as a *second-best remedial measure*, grounded on the interest in resisting objectionable hierarchies and their pernicious effects. Let us turn to this now.

By cultural protectionism, I mean a category of state measures that support domestic cultural production. There is extensive debate about the effectiveness of different kinds of protectionist policies in creating a successful cultural industry. Quotas on foreign content in the film industry, for example, have been criticized for ineffectiveness in promoting high-quality domestic cultural production.[150] There is also dispute regarding the effectiveness of direct subsidies from the state to cultural producers in fostering a dynamic culture, especially when states have political agendas of their own. In light of this, "indirect subsidies," such as financial and infrastructural assistance for marketing and exporting cultural goods, investment in communications technology and a skilled workforce, providing low-interest loans to cultural producers, setting up cultural production incubators, establishing artists' awards, and so on, may be more effective.[151] Seung-Ho Kwon and Joseph Kim argue, for example, that these strategies proved highly effective in the case of South Korea, which largely abandoned industry quotas since the 1990s, and whose global cultural exports have grown significantly in the past two decades.[152] In defending a remedial right to cultural protectionism, I am not defending a specific policy. Which cultural protectionist policy is all-things-considered justifiable will depend on the specific circumstances of a particular society, including its political system, model of economic development, and so on. For example, where a state has a track record of political censorship and violation of individual freedoms, protectionist policies that directly penalize foreign imports are less likely to be permissible due to the real risk of state abuse. My point is that postcolonial developing countries have a pro tanto claim to implement measures that broadly favor their own cultural production over foreign cultural goods.

Cultural protectionism goes some way to addressing the two ways in which unjustified attitudes tend to arise as a result of inequality in cultural production. On the one hand, we can expect cultural representations of postcolonial societies will become more diverse when members of these groups are able to produce and disseminate cultural goods, even if, as mentioned, privatization and commercialization of media continue to exert force in shaping cultural content. On the other hand, by nurturing and boosting domestic capacity for cultural production and distribution, cultural protectionism can help reverse the unreciprocated flow itself, thereby undermining the racialized "hierarchy of consumer and creator."

Nonetheless, several important concerns regarding cultural protectionism are worth considering here. First, we might worry that my argument lends support to the state deciding what productions represent the "national culture." Setting criteria for what counts as "Ghanaian culture" or "Guyanese culture" seems objectionably essentialist, not to mention self-defeating, if a vibrant culture is inherently dynamic. This worry can be addressed by going back to Césaire's argument regarding the political import of cultural production. Top-down definitions of "native culture," as Césaire argues, risk being detached from people's reality and thus fail to foster self-respect by embodying within cultural goods the agential capacities of the group. Unable to see their everyday demonstrations of innovation, creativity, critical thinking, and problem solving reflected in cultural goods handpicked by the state, these goods fall short as external manifestations of individuals' social agency. In my argument, what matters is that cultural producers in postcolonial societies are given the resources and freedom they need to make music, write novels, make films, and so on, so that their art is not prevented from connecting with people's lived experiences and perspectives. Grounding cultural protectionist rights on empowering and recovering individuals' agential capacities also places principled limits on the role of the state in promoting cultural production.

Relatedly, if states were to impose costs on cultural imports, the worry is that states become gatekeepers to what their citizens are exposed to. Notoriously, another politician who said that artists are "engineers of the soul" was Stalin.[153]

There are two responses available here. One is to condition the all-things-considered permissibility of protectionist measures on the political context of a specific society, as mentioned above. Another is to rule out certain kinds of protectionist policies altogether. Given the tendency of those in power to abuse it, this may be the safest route. Rather than having state authorities choose foreign films that are allowed to enter the market, for example, the state could tax streaming platforms such as Netflix for foreign cultural content and subsidize domestic film production with the revenue raised.[154] While some well-off regions of the world have already implemented such policies, my argument suggests that it is even more urgent that these instruments are made available for developing countries that lack the same power to fend off lawsuits from media corporations and obtain cultural exemptions in trade and investment agreements in the first place. Alternatively, cultural protectionism could focus on assisting domestic cultural producers to produce and distribute their goods via competitive business strategies rather than imposing penalties on foreign imports at all. Having a right to implement these policies would still be an important departure from the status quo, under which developing countries have had difficulty obtaining cultural exemptions that allow unequal treatment of domestic and foreign industry.[155]

Third, it is worth considering some implications of my view for *cultural producers*. If cultural protectionism for a group is justified on the grounds of undermining a racialized hierarchy of social and creative agency, do cultural producers have an obligation to produce certain kinds of content? We might worry that such an obligation runs the risk of censorship.

Insofar as one of the goals of contesting racist ideology is to restore a sense of self-respect and self-confidence for historically oppressed groups, cultural producers, in my view, *do* have a moral obligation not to produce content that is demeaning of the group. As Césaire argues, in the context of colonial oppression, an important responsibility of the cultural producer is to "counterbalance the inferiority complex" of her group—a goal that remains relevant in a neocolonial world—and cultural content that demeans and humiliates seems obviously contradictory to this end. At the same time, it seems plausible that the best way to enforce this obligation is not to give license to the state to engage in censorship due to associated risks. Instead, cultural producers' community self-monitoring may be best for sanctioning harmful content (e.g., public shaming/boycott).

Second, beyond this minimum moral demand that producers' art does not demean or humiliate the group, I submit that they have no further moral obligation—at least from the point of view of compelling recognition and fostering self-respect—to constrain the kinds of content they wish to produce. That is, cultural producers have no obligation to represent their group in the best possible light, or reproduce what is thought of as the group's "traditional repertoire" (although they can). Recall that one of Césaire's main worries regarding the lack of freedom to produce cultural goods was that colonial subjects would not be able to show that they are social agents that can generate change and respond to the problems of life—in a nutshell, make history by producing value. As such, cultural goods that express progressive social criticism rather than unreflective celebration of the group's traditions are likely to be better displays of social agency. As mentioned before, British colonialists recognized that colonized societies had social practices that resembled what they thought of as culture and, in a later phase of colonialism, colonialists even tried to preserve specific traditions.[156] Needless to say, this recognition did not result in treating colonial subjects as equals, *precisely* because the cultural elements that were ascribed to colonial subjects were seen as irrelevant to (and even obstacles for) modernity and human progress. Therefore, cultural goods that reflect (members of) the group's capacity to critique and adapt, respond to changing reality, and to put forth innovations, are likely to be most potent for challenging the idea that some groups are less capable social agents.

Most cultural content, however, will likely fall somewhere in the space between cultural content that is demeaning or humiliating, and content that amounts to progressive social commentary. Like cultural content produced by any other group, most cultural content is likely to contain a mix of more and less problematic representations. Yet recall Césaire's "hierarchy of creator and consumer" and its pernicious effects. His analysis suggests that even the most progressive, equality-promoting cultural content is insufficient for the purposes of overcoming objectionable notions of inferior and superior agency if it is still predominantly created by members of historically privileged groups. In the view that I have been defending, who is able to demonstrate and exercise their agency in the cultural sphere is at least as important as what is produced.

To sum up, in this section I have argued that we can understand decolonizing cultural globalization as the restoration of equal social agency to historically oppressed groups. This project is grounded on the more fundamental value of postcolonial global justice as social equality, which is undermined by a racist hierarchy of social agency that emerged in the colonial era and that persists today.

Rather than emphasizing the revival of any particular cultural content, this view emphasizes empowering members from these groups to be creative and innovative, as well as ensuring they receive the appropriate recognition for it. In the course of exercising this creativity, cultural producers might draw on a variety of sources, including "Western" and "non-Western," the foreign and the familiar. What matters is not so much the restoration of a coherent, authentic national culture, but instead, that individuals whose creativity has historically been suppressed or erased can freely and publicly exercise that creativity. This requires action at the state and nonstate levels from structural reforms in global communications to increased presence in cultural platforms. Moreover, until global communications is fully decolonized, I defended a right to cultural protectionism as a remedial, second-best measure for postcolonial developing states to combat the pernicious effects of inequality in global cultural production and dissemination. Yet grounding such rights on the importance of empowering individuals to exercise social agency also places moral limits on what postcolonial states can justifiably do in the name of protecting culture.

Before closing this section, it is worth considering a final worry. While I have argued for an account of cultural decolonizing that does not take a stance on what kinds of practices count as non-Western and indigenous, one might argue that creative agency *requires* the recovery of cultural and epistemic resources that have been destroyed or largely abandoned. Indeed, what if one constraint on cultural producers from postcolonial societies is precisely the lack of indigenous material to work with?

In response, we ought to make a distinction between recovering a cultural element (a practice, a tradition, a set of ideas, etc.) because it is non-Western/ indigenous and valuable for that reason, and doing so because creativity calls for it. The former invites fraught questions of authenticity and risks falling into the trappings of boundary-policing by the state or dominant groups within postcolonial societies. It also promotes a problematic valuation of culture that delegitimizes something just because it might be "tainted" by the foreign.[157] On the other hand, given the freedom and resources they need, cultural producers (including both individuals and organizations) may choose to recover neglected material that they find valuable for their art. The contemporary resurgence of the traditional Chinese dress, qipao, for example, was primarily initiated by designers in East Asia looking to blend this style of dress with Western fashion.[158] Again, going back to Césaire, rather than anyone drawing up an "a priori" plan for what "native culture" is, the goal is instead to dismantle the existing "hierarchy of creator and consumer" by empowering racialized and historically marginalized agents, and see what new cultural syntheses result. In this understanding of cultural decolonization, reclaiming the oppressor's culture as one's own—because one had an indispensable role in shaping it—is just as legitimate as turning to neglected cultures for creative inspiration.

Conclusion

This chapter has put forth a view of decolonizing cultural globalization as restoring equal status to historically oppressed groups as social agents. In this view, we ought to be concerned with patterns of asymmetric cultural flows between societies when those patterns obtain against a background of past and ongoing racial domination. Such patterns are likely to reinforce an ideology that portrays some groups as creators of value and others as consumers of the former's genius.

In face of this, I argued that decolonizing cultural globalization is a project in countering this hierarchy. This entails efforts along two dimensions: empowering historically oppressed groups to exercise agency in cultural production and dissemination, and recovering their forgotten roles in producing that which is socially valuable. Moreover, I suggested that this view of cultural decolonization contrasts with a view that takes cultural decolonization to be a matter of reviving particular kinds of content deemed authentically non-Western or indigenous.

As I have argued, while Césaire was deeply concerned about the destruction of Indigenous cultures, he located the central wrong of cultural imperialism in the suppression of indigenous agency in the cultural sphere, rather than particular cultural outcomes. If we accept, as I think we should, that individuals ought to be free to appropriate and integrate foreign cultural elements as they see fit, then while we should object when they lack that freedom, we should also find it unproblematic when changes in cultural content occur because they have that freedom.

As I have also argued, however, there is a distinct concern regarding cultural assimilation based on equality. This concern has to do with who gets to produce and disseminate culture to others, and goes back to Césaire's idea of a racialized hierarchy between consumer and producer. In this view, we ought to worry about patterns of cultural globalization that reproduce an objectionable hierarchy regarding particular groups' capacity to produce value. I argued that such a hierarchy can arise in two ways: when cultural content, disproportionately produced by powerful actors, represents the less powerful in problematic ways; and when there is a persistent and unreciprocated flow of cultural goods between unequally situated groups. When a racist ideology of unequal social agency threatens the possibility of egalitarian relations between groups, there is a need for measures (such as cultural protectionist policies) that help combat them by restoring recognition to individuals' status as equally capable producers of value. Cultural decolonization is therefore the broader project of which cultural protectionism as a remedial right is a part.

In this analysis, states (postcolonial and otherwise) also bear responsibility for cultural decolonization within their borders, a responsibility grounded on the principle of recognition as equal producers of value. Cultural decolonization at the domestic level calls for the restructuring of domestic media and cultural industries to make it possible for individuals from various subnational groups to have a fair and equal chance to participate in these forms of communication. In postcolonial countries, in building a national identity, states should not claim to represent one majority culture at the expense of all others. Rather, the same principle that demands states "democratize" global cultural production and exchange by making it more egalitarian and participatory also demands that postcolonial states do the same at the domestic level.

Importantly, our analysis has shown that domestic initiatives of cultural decolonization need to be complemented with corresponding rights and duties for global actors. In trying to implement egalitarian cultural policies, the constraints that states, especially developing countries, face are not only domestic in origin; rather, as we saw, pressure from developed countries like the

United States, backed by corporate interests, can significantly constrain domestic initiatives, as we saw in the demise of the NWICO. Hence, like the case of economic decolonization discussed in the previous chapter, the case of cultural decolonization shows that global and domestic institutions can interact in ways that produce and reinforce relations of inequality—in this case, inequality in recognition as producers of value.

Moreover, if cultural decolonization is grounded on the principle of restoring equal social agency, this gives us reason to rule out problematic forms of state-led cultural production and control. As discussed in "Decolonizing Cultural Globalization: Restoring Equal Social Agency," top-down cultural production is unlikely to do the moral work of compelling external and internal recognition of group members' social agency. If postcolonial cultural production became co-opted by the state to further its own political ends by upholding a particular view of national culture, then this kind of cultural production is, in my view, not worth protecting.[159] In focusing on protecting cultural producers, my view does not offer justification for the state to define the contours of the cultural content that is to be protected, and in fact counts against it.

In sum, I have argued that an important problem with cultural globalization today is that inequality in cultural production and distribution hinders the restoration of recognition to formerly colonized groups as equal producers of value. This generates all kinds of harms, including loss of self-respect, and reinforces inegalitarian relations. I defended a remedial right to cultural protectionism for postcolonial countries that remain at the margins of global cultural production, as well as a duty for former colonial powers and contemporary neocolonial powers to accept reforms to global communications.

In this analysis, cultural decolonization can be broadly thought of as a project in restoring individuals' status as equal value producers, thereby moving toward relations of social equality.[160] Rather than reviving particular kinds of cultural content, what matters more is that cultural producers from historically oppressed groups are empowered to produce and disseminate. Other means of restoring equal status as social agents might include re-centering groups' historical contributions as inventors, discoverers, producers, as well as giving substantive recognition to knowledge produced. Underlying these measures, including cultural protectionism in an age of continued inequality in cultural flows between the "West" and the "non-West," is the idea that individuals have equal capacities to produce value, and that recognition of this important fact is long overdue.

5

Decolonizing Global Governance

NEHRU AND THE PROBLEM
OF GLOBAL DEMOCRACY

IN 1946, under the leadership of Jawaharlal Nehru and his sister Vijaya Lakshmi Pandit, India filed a motion for the United Nations to condemn South Africa's apartheid regime and its treatment of Indians.[1] The case marked one of the first attempts to utilize an institution that embodied postwar hopes of a more democratic global governance. To observers, it was all the more surprising that an initiative to legitimize the UN's role in its members' "internal affairs" had come from a country that was just breaking from its colonial oppressors.[2] Despite Jan Smuts's fierce opposition, the motion passed, with Nehru hailing the UN as "a guardian of human rights."[3] In the decade immediately after World War II, newly independent postcolonial states shaped the UN General Assembly into a forum for the world's majority as they tabled motion after motion in support of decolonization, while the British foreign secretary lamented that the prevailing norm of the UN was the "misguided and false idea that the possession of Colonies is bad in itself."[4] If the disintegration of European empires marked an unprecedented wave of democratization in the former colonies, the creation of new states also democratized global governance like never before—by 1960, African and Asian countries held forty-six out of ninety-nine votes within the General Assembly.[5]

The rapid decline of the General Assembly is now a familiar story.[6] Having built special privileges for the powerful few into the very institution of the UN, dominant states easily sidelined the GA in favor of the Security Council. When the latter considered the issue of apartheid, Security Council members ignored the GA's resolution, and the United Kingdom and France refused to participate in a vote to condemn South Africa.[7] This foreshadowed how postwar global governance was to unfold: dominant states (and powerful corporate actors) determining the terms of global interaction while the majority of the world's population remain effectively disenfranchised.

Contemporary political theorists have considered this a problem of "democratic deficit"—a gap between global institutions that make the rules, and citizens across the world whose lives are constrained by them. Proposals to remedy this with some form of democracy at the global level, however, have been met with a plethora of objections. One persistent critique claims that democracy requires a shared culture, or at least a shared solidarity, to work.[8] This kind of solidarity comprises at least two components: trust and sympathetic identification, or mutual concern. David Miller, for example, argues that willing participants in democratic decision-making need some basis to believe that their interests will not be systemically and disproportionately disregarded even when their preferences lose out on a particular issue.[9] The basis of this solidarity is often construed as a common identity forged through shared history, norms, and beliefs.[10] At the global level, skeptics argue, it is difficult if not impossible for a "cosmopolitan solidarity" to emerge because of vast cultural pluralism. Yet without a shared identity, talk of global democracy is at best premature and at worst dangerous as it is likely to lead to greater distrust, conflict, and instability. Moreover, insofar as cultural pluralism is valuable and ought to be protected, our solution to this problem should not be to replace it with a universal global culture.[11] Instead, skeptics of global democracy tend to propose more conservative ways of improving global governance, such as relying on international law to constrain state behavior and improving accountability mechanisms within global institutions.[12] As Robert Dahl states, "We should openly recognize that international decision-making will not be democratic."[13]

Nehru, on the other hand, was a longtime believer of global democracy. As I reconstruct in the first section, titled "Nehru and Internationalism," this was driven by his socialist convictions. He believed that a democratic "World Union" capable of global redistribution and economic coordination was the only hope for addressing the root causes of imperialism. To this end, he also thought that cosmopolitan solidarity—or what he calls internationalism— was essential. But Nehru offered a different diagnosis of the difficulty in attaining such solidarity: the primary obstacle was not cultural pluralism but persistent subordination of historically oppressed populations within a global political hierarchy. Cultural pluralism, in his view, could be compatible with a democratic World Union if agents enjoyed substantive (as opposed to merely formal) political equality within that union. Although disagreement would always remain a fact of social life, agents who enjoyed equal standing could nonetheless develop shared trust and mutual concern on which to negotiate disagreement. But if international law and organizations remained instruments of the powerful for subordinating others, "narrow nationalism[s]" would only grow stronger and undermine the emergence of a cosmopolitan solidarity.[14]

These claims are grounded in Nehru's experiences in the Indian anticolonial struggle, during which he saw firsthand how oppression shapes people's moral psychology. For Nehru, the challenge of fostering cosmopolitan solidarity and building global democracy was not one of overcoming cultural pluralism but instead of cultivating an internationalist outlook among the very people who had good reason to retreat from global political integration and cooperation. Nehru's response was to foster cosmopolitan solidarity in the very process of contesting one's subordination. To this end, two strategies—internationalizing national politics and forging transnational coalitions—were particularly important. While he fought for national independence for India, he never lost sight of the broader socialist internationalist cause in which he thought India played an essential part, nor the enormous obstacles that had to be overcome for global democracy to be realized. As we will see, Nehru's thinking was not only characterized by what Michele Louro has called a "blend" of nationalism and internationalism, but also a mix of political realism and idealism.[15]

Drawing from Nehru's speeches and writings on internationalism and World Union, this chapter argues for a recharacterization of the problem of global democracy: from vertical deficit in democratic control between individual citizens and global institutions, to horizontal deficit in political equality between groups. This shift enables us to see that global democracy should be understood as a multifaceted project in resisting political marginalization. Instead of settling for modest reforms of accountability that skeptics of global democracy tend to propose, or aiming for idealistic proposals of world parliament, the path to global democracy depends on creating counterhegemonic power for marginalized state and nonstate actors.

In the following, I first reconstruct Nehru's views on global democracy and internationalism more broadly by tracing these themes in his writings, speeches, and political activism in the decades leading up to Indian independence. I argue that global democrats should take from Nehru two related lessons: first, the importance of attending to the moral-psychological obstacles that stem from conditions of subordination and that hinder cosmopolitan solidarity; second, the essential role of counterhegemonic power from marginalized state and nonstate actors in democratizing global governance. With these lessons in mind, in the second section, titled "Undemocratic Global Governance," I turn to the contemporary issue of undemocratic global governance and argue that both skeptics and proponents of global democracy must take more seriously the problem of global political inequality. Doing so entails a more ambitious and yet simultaneously more realist approach to democratizing global governance than prominent theorists have proposed. In the third section, titled "Decolonizing Global Governance as Counterhegemonic Political Empowerment," I look at what this approach implies for democratizing trade governance today by looking at an exemplary case of contemporary counterhegemonic power-building at the global level.

While the previous two chapters addressed two aspects of substantive change that postcolonial global justice as social equality demands—i.e., economic and cultural empowerment through a development-centered investment regime and a democratized global communications regime—this chapter addresses the question of decision-making at the global level. As such, it also indirectly considers the question of how the substantive changes to the international order defended throughout the book might be pursued through political contestation.

Nehru and Internationalism

To understand Nehru's commitments to global democracy, it is important to start from his socialist convictions, which he gradually acquired through participating in anticolonial transnational activism. In 1927, Nehru traveled to Brussels as the representative of the Indian National Congress to attend an international congress of anticolonial activists representing thirty-seven colonial territories.[16] There he met nationalists, socialists, and communists from Asia, Africa, and Latin America, as well as sympathetic leftist radicals from Europe. The Brussels congress set itself up explicitly against the League of Nations as a far more democratic and egalitarian global platform for tackling the world's most pressing problems at the time—imperialism and the wars that it brought about.[17] A significant theme of the congress was the relationship between global capitalism and imperialism. The organizers put forth a Leninist framework for understanding imperialism and emphasized the importance of connecting nationalist anticolonial struggles to a broader transnational workers' and peasants' struggle against capitalism. Lenin had famously argued that imperialism was the logical expansion of capitalism when the latter came up against falling rates of profit within domestic markets.[18] In this view, the fight against imperialism and capitalism were deeply intertwined. Unlike the Soviet Union's later stance of cutting ties with Third World nationalist movements altogether, the communists at the Brussels congress agreed that attaining national independence was the first step in freeing workers of the colonized world to join the struggle against global capital.[19] As such, delegates decided to establish the League Against Imperialism, a transnational organization that would bring together anticolonial activists to articulate a "shared condition of unfreedom."[20]

These exchanges and meetings amounted to an intellectual turning point for Nehru, who had previously not expressed any significant socialist inclinations.[21] In his autobiography, Nehru writes that upon returning from Europe to India after the Brussels congress, his "outlook was wider" and "nationalism seemed by itself to me definitely a narrow and insufficient creed."[22] While political freedom and independence were "no doubt essential," he states, "they were only steps in the right direction; without social freedom and a socialistic structure of society and the State, neither the country nor the individual could develop much."[23] As he explained to his colleagues in a report on the Brussels congress, "The whole basis of the League [Against Imperialism] is that imperialism and capitalism go hand in hand and back up each other and neither of them will disappear till both are put down."[24] Because of this relationship between imperialism and capitalism, the Indian anticolonial struggle must resist "nationalism of a narrow variety" and should instead adopt a "broader basis" by "deriv[ing] its strength from and work[ing] specifically for the masses, the peasants and the other workers."[25]

Although Nehru would break with the League by 1930, when it transformed from an ideologically diverse platform to a communist-led organization hostile to noncommunists, this socialist internationalist worldview would stay with him far beyond his participation in the organization. By the time Nehru was writing his magnum opus, *Discovery of India*, from prison in 1946, he had developed an analysis of the colonial situation that emphasized the injustices of capitalism. As we saw in chapter 1, Nehru saw colonial economics as essentially a project in breaking up communal forms of land ownership and artisanal practices in favor of private capital accumulation, a process that resulted in a dispossessed peasantry and urban proletariat.[26] Socialist democracy was, for him, essential for India to eradicate the structural inequalities of colonial capitalism.

Yet even more radically, Nehru thought that something similar was true at the global level. The root cause of war and imperial expansionism, Nehru argued in a series of speeches and essays on international politics and foreign policy, was economic inequality engendered by global capitalism.[27] Rather telegraphically, he suggests that the world needed a democratic "world union" that could engage in economic coordination and planning.[28] In this view, each nation would disarm their militaries and yield to decisions made by a democratic "Union Legislature" to which each nation would send their representatives, and the union would "work under a planned and socialized economy in order to end the conflicts of today."[29] As he wrote to his daughter from his first stint in prison in 1934, there was hope for "a World State, not a great empire, or universal sovereign, but a kind of World-Republic which would prevent the exploitation of one nation or people or class by another."[30]

To this end, an independent India should "agree to give up a measure of her freedom of action to an international body of which she is a member for the sake of world peace."[31] National independence should not be seen as the final goal. As he wrote on the brink of India's independence in 1946, "The end of colonialism and imperialism will not mean splitting up the world into a host of additional national states intent on their isolated independence."[32] Instead, when colonial populations were no longer subjugated, "a new grouping together or all nations" with a "new outlook" would result, one with "cooperation gradually replacing competition and conflict, to the utilization of the wonders of modern techniques and the vast sources of energy at the disposal of man for the advancement of the human race as a whole."[33] In language that can easily be seen as utopian, Nehru summarized that "it will lead to that one world of which wise statesmen have dreamed."[34]

This vision of global socialist democracy did not do away with cultural pluralism. Influenced by Rabindranath Tagore's internationalism, Nehru thought that nations would continue to exist as primarily cultural entities with limited sovereign powers.[35] As he writes in *Discovery*, "Real internationalism is not something in the air without roots or anchorage. It has to grow out of national cultures and can only flourish today on a basis of freedom and equality."[36] India, Nehru points out, already had a history of "welcoming and absorbing" other cultures, and Indians would continue to "play our part in this coming internationalism."[37] But this could only happen "if we are welcomed as equals and as comrades in a common quest."[38] Once freed from relations of domination and exploitation, Nehru states, "we [will] march to the one world of tomorrow where national cultures will be intermingled with the international culture of the human race. We shall therefore seek wisdom and knowledge and friendship and comradeship wherever we can find them, and co-operate with others in common tasks, but we are no suppliants for others' favours and patronage. Thus we shall remain true Indians and Asiatics, and become at the same time good internationalists and world citizens."[39] The end of racial and political subordination would allow a global multiculturalism to flourish on egalitarian terms.

As radical as this vision was, Nehru was no idle idealist and understood that the world was nowhere close to ready for such a union. The "greatest barrier," as it appeared to him, was overcoming the justified fear and suspicion that remained pervasive among populations who had long been oppressed under the guise of global political integration, whether it was the international law that legitimized European expansionism or global institutions like the League of Nations that, at the time, was the most innovative institution for global governance.[40] In a 1939 essay published in the *National Herald*, Nehru criticized the League for its democratic pretenses when in fact its "democracy was a cloak for the subjection of many peoples and nations."[41] By keeping most of the world under colonial subjugation and excluding their equal participation, the world association had betrayed the promise of democratic world union

and was merely a tool for "for the protection of [the imperialist powers']
vested interests in subject countries."[42] This was especially apparent in the fact
that the European powers refused to concede their sovereign powers to the
world's supposed new political authority. As Nehru lamented in "A Foreign
Policy for India," the great powers "[would] not even agree to compulsory
arbitration."[43] India could not submit to political inequality disguised as
democratic integration. Instead, Nehru warned, "[India] can only [give up a
measure of sovereignty] if other nations also agree to limit their sovereignty
in like measure."[44] In other words, only if "a real League of Nations arises working for peace," Nehru states, should India "gladly join."[45]

Still, Nehru thought that the justified suspicion that colonial subjects
had toward global institutions dominated by imperialist powers should not
preclude the possibility of transnational solidarity with *similarly situated*
populations. Yet even as their common predicament seemed clear enough to
him, Nehru was also astutely aware that transnational solidarity among the
oppressed would not come about naturally without deliberate (and often
strenuous) efforts to foster it through political education and organizing. The
dominating sentiment in his country, Nehru describes in his autobiography,
was nationalist.[46] His colleagues at the Indian National Congress "thought
largely in the narrowest nationalism."[47] This was a nationalism that "laid stress
on the glories of old times; the injuries, material and spiritual, caused by alien
rule; the sufferings of our people; the indignity of foreign domination over us
and our national honour demanding that we should be free; the necessity for
sacrifice at the altar of the motherland."[48] Nehru could see the pull of these
"familiar themes" as they "found an echo in every Indian heart," including his
own.[49] Yet he argues that these ideas, for all the truth they contained, were
"thin and thread-bare" and failed to capture the complexity of India's economic
and social predicament. "Their ceaseless repetition," he argues, "prevented the
consideration of other problems and vital aspects of our struggle. They only
fostered emotion and did not encourage thought."[50] As we will see, Nehru
observed that being under "a subject condition" cultivated what he would call
an "obsession" with one's own immediate plight that came into tension with
transnational solidarity.

In face of this dominant nationalist sentiment, in the interwar years Nehru
took it upon himself to promote a transnational solidarity through political
action. This consisted of efforts on two fronts: cross-border organizing to create a transnational political platform, and internationalizing domestic politics.
Regarding the former, Nehru took up an increasingly large role in the League
Against Imperialism, fundraising for its activities and helping to organize its
newsletter, as well as resisting communist efforts to undermine the League's
diverse membership across the anticolonial left.[51] Bringing together

anticolonial movements to develop a transnational diagnosis of empire and to coordinate resistance, the League was an important episode within a long history of oppressed groups across the world organizing to "expand the reach of political solidarity toward the transnational," as Inés Valdez puts it in her analysis of pan-Africanist organizing.[52]

Secondly, Nehru worked to internationalize the anticolonial struggle within India. Although the congress was still "a purely political and nationalistic body, unused to thinking on other lines,"[53] Nehru thought that "a beginning might be made," particularly in India's "labor circles."[54] To start, he advocated for the congress to become an associate member of the League Against Imperialism, arguing that this would enable the Indian anticolonial struggle to build relationships with "many Asiatic and other countries with problems not dissimilar to ours" and make use of the League's transnational network to disseminate anticolonial propaganda.[55] Listing out all the branches of the League being set up across Latin America, the Middle East, and Africa, Nehru beckoned his colleagues to not isolate India from this emerging transnational solidarity. For example, he argued, India's trade union movement could send representatives to the Trade Union Congress in China, and the Indian National Congress could also invite representatives from the Kuomintang to attend its sessions.[56] When the congress adopted Nehru's resolution to become an associate member of the League, he founded the Independence for India League as a bridgehead to connect the Indian National Congress with the League Against Imperialism.[57] Outside of the congress, Nehru persuaded grassroots organizations to affiliate with the League and managed to secure relationships with a range of important unions and peasants' organizations, including the All India Trade Union Congress (of which Nehru became president in 1929), the Workers and Peasants Party of Bombay, Bengal and Madras, the Sikh League, and others.[58] He also extended invitations to anticolonial activists across Asia to visit India, although obtaining visas from the colonial government was seldom successful.

Nehru's efforts to internationalize the Indian anticolonial struggle came to a head with his colleagues, including his own father, in the great debate on whether the Indian National Congress should demand complete independence from or dominion status within the British empire. Publicly opposing Motilal Nehru's proposal for the latter, Nehru argued for complete independence.[59] This was not only because he thought (as we saw from chapter 1) that national independence was necessary for the country to break away from colonial capitalism and authoritarianism, but also because only complete independence could enable India to play its proper role in the broader transnational struggle against imperialism and capitalism. First, Nehru argued that India had been conscripted into playing a crucial role in maintaining law and order within the

British empire. Under colonial rule, Indian troops and police were dispatched to various corners of the empire to quash rebellions and dissent. In a 1927 essay, "A Foreign Policy for India," Nehru argues that Indians had become "a hireling of the exploiters [who is] hated" around the oppressed world.[60] If the British empire is maintained by Indian force, Nehru argues, accepting dominion status instead of fighting for complete independence would amount to being complicit in the oppression of those with whom Indians should be allying instead. "Is India," Nehru asks, "to put herself in this group [of European imperial powers] which represents reaction and suppression of struggling peoples and nations?"[61]

Second, the British empire controlled India's borders and foreign contacts. This prevented activists and similarly oppressed groups from building cross-border relationships with one another, as the colonial government routinely denied visas to foreign anticolonial activists and censored incoming correspondence. This was impressed on Nehru as he tried multiple times to invite League Against Imperialism comrades to visit India and collaborate with the Indian National Congress. He also discovered that the information Indians had been receiving about other anticolonial struggles across the world was manipulated by the British. Thus Nehru argues that India must strive for nothing less than "the fullest freedom to develop as she will; she must control her finances, her military forces and her foreign relations."[62] That would enable India to stop supporting imperialist projects, contribute to world peace, and develop transnational alliances with those who shared a "common fate."[63]

Nehru thus spent much of the interwar years persuading his colleagues to adopt the goal of complete independence while also promoting a socialist and internationalist outlook in Indian anticolonial politics by building links to the global anticolonial movement. As World War II broke out, however, Nehru experienced the greatest challenge to internationalism in the anticolonial movement. This episode, on which he reflects extensively in the *Discovery of India*, reinforced in his mind the moral-psychological obstacles to fostering transnational solidarity in conditions of subordination. As we will see, this diagnosis of the "greatest barrier" to global democracy is particularly important for thinking about the democratic deficit in global governance today, and so is worth exploring in more detail.

After India's involvement in World War I, the Indian National Congress had declared in 1927 that Indian troops would not be involved in defending the British empire again.[64] But the subsequent rise of Hitler and Nazism created a difficult dilemma for Nehru and his colleagues. On the one hand, they were resolutely opposed to Nazism, which they saw as "the very embodiment and intensification of the imperialism and racialism against which the Congress was struggling."[65] On the other hand, to fight alongside the British would be to sacrifice Indian lives to defend the imperial status quo, especially when Churchill had repeatedly made his anti-Indian independence stance clear.[66] The "inconsistency of condemning fascism and Nazism and maintaining imperialist domination" in India made it nearly impossible for Indians to support the British empire's battle against Germany.[67]

Nehru frames this issue as a conflict between national and international solidarity. He observes that, "in a contest between nationalism and internationalism, nationalism was bound to win . . . in a country under foreign domination, with bitter memories of continuous struggle and suffering, that was an inevitable and unavoidable consequence."[68] It was both morally and politically difficult for the Indian National Congress to stand in solidarity with Europeans when India was still under the former's oppression. "Internationalism can indeed only develop in a free country," Nehru goes on to argue, because "all the thought and energy of a subject country are directed towards the achievement of its own freedom."[69] It was nearly impossible for those living under conditions of oppression to look beyond their immediate situation and work with their oppressor, even in the face of an evil like Nazism. He explains this with a powerful analogy to the body encountering illness:

> That subject condition is like a cancerous growth inside the body, which not only prevents any limb from becoming healthy but is a constant irritant to the mind and colors all thought and action. The history of a long succession of past conflicts and suffering becomes the inseparable companion of both the individual and the national mind. It becomes an obsession, a dominating passion, which cannot be exorcised except by removing its root cause. And even then, when the sense of subjection is gone, the cure is slow, *for the injuries of the mind take longer to heal than those of the body* [italics added].[70]

In other words, experiences of oppression gradually shape individuals' worldviews and compel them to focus exclusively on their own emancipation, which becomes the central anchor in people's actions. At an extreme, the "subject condition" can distort individuals' moral judgment and lead them to conclude that "every enemy of Britain should be treated as a friend," including Nazi Germany and imperialist Japan.[71] Subhas Chandra Bose, for example, a longtime socialist ally of Nehru's and two-term president of the Indian National Congress, publicly criticized Nehru for organizing aid for Chinese victims of Japanese aggression. Instead, Bose notoriously supported allying with the fascist powers to strengthen India's position vis-à-vis the British empire. Eventually the two parted ways as neither could tolerate the other's position on the war.[72]

To be sure, it is not in principle impossible for someone living under oppression to endorse both nationalism and internationalism. As Nehru points

out, Gandhi could do it: "[Gandhi's] nationalism . . . had a certain world outlook . . . Desiring the independence of India, he had come to believe that a
world federation of interdependent states was the only right goal, however
distant that might be."[73] Nehru describes how Gandhi influenced members of
the Indian National Congress to become much more "internationally
minded . . . in spite of our intense nationalism."[74] But if this was praiseworthy, it
was also a moral achievement above and beyond what can be reasonably expected of those fighting colonial oppression: "No other nationalist movement
of a subject country came anywhere near this," for the "general tendency in
such countries was to keep clear of international commitments."[75]

Instead, Nehru's point is that for most people who were not Gandhi, the
moral and psychological tension between fighting for one's freedom and cooperating in solidarity with one's oppressor is so great that it is impossible to
expect people to do so. "It seemed absurd and impossible," Nehru writes, "for
us to line up in defense of that very imperialism against which we had been
struggling for so long."[76] Moreover, the Indian National Congress as the
people's chosen leaders, would lose all credibility—as Nehru puts it, they
would be "stranded, isolated, and cut off"[77]—if they tried to persuade the
people to cooperate with the war effort while not receiving any concessions
for their own liberation. As Nehru argues, "Even if a few of us, in view of larger
considerations, considered [defending the British empire as] a lesser evil, it
was utterly beyond our capacity to carry our people."[78] Instead, he states, "only
freedom could release mass energy and convert bitterness into enthusiasm for
a cause. There was no other way."[79]

Trying to reconcile two competing values, the Indian National Congress
ended up pursuing a dual policy of conditioning Indian mobilization on the
British withdrawing from India after the war. They pressed the British on
the "absurdity of holding aloft the banner of democracy elsewhere and denying it to us in India."[80] This policy was still "no easy matter," Nehru describes,
because "most of our people had little appreciation of the international issues
involved and were expressing their resentment at recent British policy."[81] Most
people would have preferred the Congress to take advantage of Britain's
moment of vulnerability to strike at the empire. Nehru and other antifascist
Congress members thus had to walk the thin line between guiding the people
and losing their trust. Soon enough, however, the British dismissed the Congress's offer, and the Government of India began to dispatch Indian troops
without the Congress's consent. Nehru lambasted this decision. Once again,
he writes, the British had refused to treat them as "comrades and equals" and
instead saw them "as a slave people to do their bidding."[82]

This episode underscored for Nehru the difficulty of fostering concern for
and trust in others in a deeply hierarchical world. For the "hundreds of

millions of [people in] Asia and Africa," he argues in *The Discovery*, the experience of long decades of subjection meant that talk of internationalism and cooperation would always be viewed with suspicion.[83] Although "they welcome all attempts at world co-operation and the establishment of international order," he states, "they also wonder and suspect if this may not be another device for continuing the old domination."[84] For them, Nehru writes, the postwar global order that would emerge would be judged based on:

> Does it end the domination of one country over another? Will it enable us to live freely the life of our choice in co-operation with others? Does it bring equality and equal opportunity for nations as well as groups within each nation?[85]

In other words, the international order needed to secure freedom and equality for Asians and Africans to enjoy their willing endorsement. Global institutions needed to show that they prioritized rectifying long-standing unequal relations. Otherwise, they would be seen as yet another form of domination disguised as cosmopolitan integration. As Nehru argues, "Co-operation [between nations] can only be on a basis of equality and mutual welfare, on a pulling-up of the backward nations and peoples to a common level of well-being and cultural advancement, on an elimination of racialism and domination. No nation and no people are going to tolerate domination and exploitation by another, even though this is given some more pleasant name."[86]

After becoming the first prime minister of independent India, Nehru invested his hopes for a world government in the United Nations.[87] He warned against repeating the mistakes of the League of Nations by making the UN an exclusive club. When US President Herbert Hoover floated proposals in 1950 that the UN should be "reorganized without the communist countries in it," Nehru argued in a UN radio broadcast that this "seems to forget the very purpose and the very name of the United Nations . . . which offers a forum for all nations, even though they differ from each other."[88] He advocated for China's inclusion in the UN, again seeing political inclusion as an important way to encourage hostile countries to work with one another.[89] He believed that the United Nations, though deeply imperfect, was still the greatest chance there was for "One World" to be achieved. "The whole conception of One World," he stated in a radio speech, "however distant that One World may be, involves an organization like the United Nations."[90]

At the same time, Nehru utilized India's newfound independence to forge the kinds of counterhegemonic alliances that the British Raj had prevented. While he was critical of military alliances such as SEATO, or the Southeast Asia Treaty Organization, which he saw as a catalyst of conflict escalation and war, he was a leading proponent of nonmilitary associations that could foster a sense of transnational solidarity to counteract nationalist sentiment and an increasingly bipolar world. In 1947, for example, he organized the Asian Relations Conference, a historic event that centered the topics of development, gender equality, and antiracism, and brought together state and nonstate actors such as labor and feminist activists throughout colonial/postcolonial Asia.[91] Like the League Against Imperialism, Nehru thought of the conference as an attempt to instigate a "psychological revolution" that would take people out of national imaginaries of postcolonial emancipation.[92] While the ideal of "one world" and a "world federation" remained "essential," building pan-Asian solidarity was the first step along that long path. "In order to have 'one world,'" Nehru stated, "we must also, in Asia, think of the countries of Asia cooperating together for that larger ideal."[93] If the transition to a peaceful world union would not occur unless "human beings everywhere have freedom and security and opportunity," then it was essential to unite as countries facing the legacies of colonialism and to push for remaking "political, social and economic structures so that the burdens that have crushed [the common man] may be removed."[94] Therefore, the path to one world inevitably featured coalitions of the oppressed.

The Asian Relations Conference became the springboard from which later efforts such as the Bandung Conference and the Non-Aligned Movement grew. Nehru played an important leadership role in both. In face of an increasingly polarizing world in which the United States and the Soviet Union each put pressure on postcolonial states to abandon multilateralism and take sides in the Cold War, Nehru led and built counterhegemonic coalitions that strived toward peaceful and democratic cooperation. The Bandung Conference marked the first global gathering of postcolonial states and was, as Vijay Prashad has argued, a constitutional moment for the Third World.[95] Growing out of this, the Non-Aligned Movement was driven by Nehru's commitment to maintain multilateralism and global cooperation amid heightening distrust by uniting the Third World.[96]

It is important, however, not to romanticize or overstate the radical nature of these coalitions and movements. While the Asian Relations Conference (and the League Against Imperialism before it) did mark an important departure from statist decolonial politics, its offsprings were decreasingly radical. Historians have recently begun to correct for Richard Wright's myth-making account of Bandung by pointing to the ways in which the conference reinforced the primacy of the nation-state as the vehicle for postcolonial development.[97] Indeed, Michele Louro argues that, rather than an opening to anticolonial transnationalism, Bandung signified the closure of transnationalism for a Westphalian internationalism.[98] The Non-Aligned Movement was even more firmly rooted in the framework of the nation-state as it attempted to chart a neutral path out of the Cold War by affirming principles of nonintervention and national sovereignty. In this sense, each progeny of the League Against Imperialism was less able to break out of the nation-state. Still, it is important to recognize the real constraints on postcolonial states—including, among others, the tense climate of Cold War global politics in which proxy wars were carried out in former colonies.[99] Against this background as well as the internal turmoil of postcolonial India, for Nehru to try and forge a path of transnational solidarity and democratic cooperation is no small feat, even as, like so many decolonial aspirations, the vision was often constrained by political reality.[100]

To sum up this section, Nehru's global democratic commitments grew out of his socialism. Unlike many of his contemporaries, he was neither satisfied with greater autonomy as a dominion nor with Indian national independence. Instead, he was critical of the limits of the Indian National Congress as a nationalist organization dominated by the Indian middle class, and he tried in multiple ways to tether the Indian struggle to a broader anticolonial politics that took overthrowing global capitalism as its ultimate aim.

This led him to become a vocal proponent of democratic political integration at the global level. But the anticolonial struggle also gave him a deep understanding of how oppression and subordination can breed fear and resentment and alienate groups from one another, and he was also a realist that recognized that great powers would abuse and abandon multilateralism to suit their interests, thus driving a vicious cycle of distrust.

Against this background, Nehru's approach to global democracy consisted of a two-pronged approach that exemplified his signature blend of realism and idealism. First, to cultivate a transnational solidarity beyond one's own nation by forming counterhegemonic alliances with similarly situated peoples. This would instigate a "psychological revolution," whereby individuals are brought out of their nationalist outlook to identify with other oppressed nations. These alliances would do so by fighting for both procedural and substantive concessions within global politics, thus helping to democratize global governance. Second, when global institutions are suitably reformed as the result of the former's contestation, and more reliably track the interests and perspectives of oppressed populations, Nehru believed it would become possible to cultivate trust and solidarity between former oppressors and the oppressed, eventually making global democracy possible.

As the rest of the chapter shows, this approach to democratizing global governance holds important lessons for thinking about the democratic deficit in contemporary global institutions. Drawing from Nehru's diagnosis of the obstacles to global democracy and taking cue from his efforts to foster anticolonial transnational solidarity, I argue that we should understand the problem of undemocratic global governance as political inequality, and the project of global democracy as counterhegemonic political empowerment.

Undemocratic Global Governance

Contemporary global governance is rife with pervasive political inequality between states, and the citizens they represent. The changed political structure of the so-called postcolonial world has not eliminated the inequalities of power and status that Nehru argued would undermine the legitimacy of global political integration. As discussed in chapter 2, powerful states and transnational capitalists routinely dominate decision-making within global institutions.

Consider the case of trade governance, which the rest of this chapter will focus on as a quintessential example of undemocratic global governance. Global trade governance consists of one of the most developed forms of international law to date, and the impact of trade rules is felt every day by individuals across the world. Yet its governance, primarily carried out through the World Trade Organization, has historically been deeply undemocratic and laden with power imbalances. As a successor to the General Agreement on Tariffs and Trade (GATT), the WTO inherited the aims and decision-making procedures of the latter.[101] Many commentators have pointed out that this is highly problematic since the GATT was not designed as an inclusive and comprehensive global economic governance platform, but a narrower agreement among industrial countries to grant each other trading advantages.[102] Following the demise of the International Trade Organization, which the US Congress refused to ratify, the GATT took over as the de facto agreement for world trade, and consequently the WTO was founded with deep power asymmetries embedded in the organization's operations.[103]

For example, despite formal rules that grant each country one vote, most WTO agreements are negotiated in smaller, exclusionary "green room" meetings, a practice that originated from the GATT.[104] The resulting agreements are brought to the larger group and, through arm-twisting measures, imposed on everyone else.[105] Although consensus is required for agreements to come into effect, and in theory any member could halt the process by vetoing, in reality smaller and poorer countries have little power to push back against the powerful countries on which their economies depend. The international legal scholar Richard H. Steinberg finds, for example, that market size is a form of "invisible weighting" of votes in WTO decision-making, with large, affluent economies wielding significantly greater bargaining power over less affluent and/or small economies.[106]

Agenda setting happens in a similarly informal way that advantages powerful actors: small informal groups of members come up with proposals to bring to the larger membership in a process called "concentric circles."[107] Global South countries have struggled to get items of important economic interest to them included in the agenda, such as Global North countries' subsidies and quantitative restrictions for agriculture, textile, clothing, and raw material.[108] Global South countries' disadvantage in negotiations and agenda setting is compounded by the relative lack of resources and expertise in navigating the WTO system. Many smaller countries cannot afford a permanent delegation stationed in Geneva, which becomes an important obstacle to participating in the consensus decision-making in the WTO's everyday operations.[109] Similarly, they can often only send small delegations to trade conferences—at the Hong Kong ministerial conference, for example, the United States sent 356 delegates while Burundi had 3.[110] Even things like parallel meetings scheduled for the same time can become barriers for equal participation from these countries as their human resources are stretched to the limit.

Some commentators have hailed civil society actors' increasing role in trade governance as a democratizing force. Yet many of the prominent international NGOs are based in the Global North, and so their participation does not necessarily strengthen Global South countries' voices (although some have worked with Global South countries to amplify their demands—for example, NGOs helped West African countries get cotton on the agenda for the Hong Kong conference).[111] Furthermore, NGOs remain relatively sidelined at the WTO, where technocrats often view them with condescension and dismiss their concerns.[112] By contrast, corporate actors have often successfully advanced their agendas, such as lobbying for the TRIPS (Trade-Related Aspects of Intellectual Property Rights) agreement.[113]

The result has been persistent political marginalization of large swaths of the world's population who live in postcolonial Global South countries. Pro–Global North countries' biases in WTO rules and policies have been extensively studied, with one recent work arguing for a "Global New Deal" to replace a trade regime that has failed to live up to its promises of prosperity for all.[114] In the rest of the chapter, my focus is on the political injustice involved in undemocratic trade governance.

Political theorists have long criticized global governance for a "democratic deficit."[115] Existing debates commonly construe the problem as follows: with globalization, people's lives are increasingly intertwined. The global institutions that have emerged to deal with collective problems like trade, however, are primarily run by technocrats who are unaccountable to ordinary citizens around the world. Yet their decisions can significantly affect individuals' interests. Thus, there is a gap between so-called rule makers and rule takers where there would normally be electoral processes and/or other democratic decision-making mechanisms. Theorists troubled by this gap have proposed various forms of democratization: world federalism, a confederation of democratic states, democratization of nonstate actors (such as international NGOs), and proposals to enfranchise foreigners in domestic lawmaking.[116] While some believe that democracy at the global level is unlikely to resemble its domestic analog, others push for global political institutions that resemble domestic democracy. In particular, proponents of "cosmopolitan democracy" have argued that neither a confederation of democratic states nor greater civil society participation in international organizations are sufficient to address the democratic deficit—instead, as Daniele Archibugi puts it, "a cardinal institution of democratic governance is . . . a world parliament."[117] Through something like a world parliament, this view proposes, individuals would have a direct channel for political expression that is parallel to and independent of their state membership; each individual would enjoy a "world citizenship."[118]

On the other hand, skeptics have pushed back against the notion of global democracy. As mentioned previously, one recurring criticism is that there is no global public sharing a common set of norms and values regarding what issues are appropriate for collective determination and the normative framework under which to deliberate about them.[119] Absent these social conditions, democracy at the global level is not only infeasible but may create more conflict as minorities would have good reason to suspect that their rights and interests may not be protected. Another criticism presses on the relationship between global and domestic democracy. Since many states are not democratic themselves, a global democratic federation of states would not necessarily address the deficit for those living under undemocratic regimes.[120] Moreover, some argue that global democracy is unrealistically demanding on citizens—not only do they have to be informed decision-makers at the national level, but they would also have to participate regularly in global politics. Predictably, public participation would be low and technocrats would continue to run these institutions. Lastly, democracy is not only about voting procedures. If democratic institutions give people some measure of control over political decisions and secure important interests, it is not only because of the electoral process but also formal and informal institutions such as an independent judiciary, a free press, a vibrant civil society, and so on. Replicating that at the global level seems unrealistic. Instead, critics of global democracy argue that increasing accountability and transparency are the best we can hope for at present, and aiming for more is either dangerous, misguided, or simply utopian.[121]

To be sure, global democrats have also provided strong responses, including pointing out that skeptics tend to put forth unrealistically demanding requirements for democracy that are not even met within most liberal democracies, and that they confuse the present lack of global demos with the idea that creating such a demos is undesirable.[122] While there is truth in these responses, the skeptic may also reply that existing liberal democracies' failure to secure the conditions required for a healthy democratic political system is not a reason to dispense with those conditions, but a reason to refocus our efforts on creating them instead of shifting attention to the more nebulous global domain.[123] Moreover, although global democrats often claim that a demos can be created, they seldom engage in detailed theorization about how that might happen beyond gesturing at an emergent global civil society.

Drawing from Nehru's insights, I want to pursue a different line of response. These standard arguments against global democracy do not obviously address the problem of global political inequality. Put simply, the democratic deficit is uneven. Even if "citizens of the world" *as individuals* lack democratic control over global institutions, there is in fact significant political inequality among them by virtue of their membership in different *groups*. Some individuals, because of their membership in a dominant state and/or a powerful group (such as the capital-owning class or a racial group coded white) have their interests and views represented in global governance much more effectively than others.[124] Their interests and views tend to disproportionately drive the development of international law and policies.

This point becomes clearer if we shift our focus from seeing the problem of global democracy as a vertical deficit (that is, one between individual citizens of the world and global institutions) to a horizontal deficit (that is, one between groups across the world) in political equality. Instead of focusing almost exclusively—as much of the existing debate on global democracy has—on the question of whether "citizens of the world" in general can or should exercise popular control over global institutions, we might consider the problem from the perspective of citizens in the postcolonial Global South and their specific position within the history of international decision-making, where their voices and interests have long been marginalized.[125] For *these* citizens, regardless of whether a global demos exists and whether it might be feasible and/or desirable to create one, the fact is that some individuals, by virtue of membership in advantaged groups, have *already* been exercising greater influence over global governance than others, and *this* is the problem that urgently needs addressing. Another way to put the point is that, regardless of whether individuals need to exercise the same degree of authority over global decision-making as they do at the domestic level to be self-determining, there is a different question of whether *equal* authority is required if some groups are already wielding decision-making power.

To be sure, there is much variation within countries: many groups within even the most powerful countries remain politically marginalized by their own governments. My point is general and compatible with transnational understandings of global injustice[126]: citizens of affluent countries will *in general* find it easier to have their views and interests represented in global governance compared to citizens of most postcolonial countries. The latter lack a sufficiently powerful state that can effectively channel their views and interests, even if their governments are not driven exclusively by elite and/or dominant group interests.

Critics of global democracy do not suggest that the status quo is unproblematic. Yet they tend to propose alternatives to democratization that do little to address the issue of political inequality. Let us briefly review three such types of proposals.

First, David Miller argues that existing international law, treaties, and organizations, though imperfect, already regulate state behavior.[127] Stick-and-carrot mechanisms such as shaming and sanctions as well as membership conditions for organizations like the EU, Miller argues, can put pressure on states to act responsibly toward their own citizens as well as foreign societies.[128] NGOs can lobby states and shame them for failing to meet certain behavioral standards. The legitimacy of these actors and mechanisms, in his view, do not depend on their democratic credentials, and the goal of regulating state behavior (toward citizens and foreigners) does not require democratic institutions. Although decision outcomes may fall short of fairness, Miller concludes that there is no viable alternative, as global democracy requires a "sufficient convergence of interests and beliefs" that does not exist.[129]

Yet relying on these mechanisms does not address the problem of unequal regulation. Countries with large economies and powerful militaries have been able to sanction and/or incentivize others to behave in certain ways while the reverse has not generally been true. An obvious example is the UN Security Council's selective enforcement of international law. Another example is the International Criminal Court, which has almost exclusively only prosecuted or investigated citizens of African countries.[130] The court recently decided to set aside investigation of US crimes in Afghanistan, prompting further criticism of political bias.[131] Unequal enforcement of international law not only constitutes an objectionable hierarchy between states but also deepens distrust of global institutions among populations of those states.[132] As Nehru observed, perhaps more saliently than cultural difference, power asymmetries render global mechanisms for regulating state behavior illegitimate in the eyes of those for whom the mechanisms do not work. Even if these mechanisms can improve state and global governance, by themselves they cannot address the injustice of political inequality.

On the contrary, Sarah Song grapples directly with the problem of global political inequality. Yet she sees this as a reason to keep democracy bounded within the state. She argues that a crucial constitutive feature of democracy is substantive political equality.[133] That is, without addressing the background inequalities that undermine agents' ability to exercise an equal share of decision-making power, the resulting democracy would be hollow. But without a state that can address economic inequalities through redistribution, as well as a shared solidarity that would foster a willingness among agents to support such policies, Song argues that it is impossible to realize political equality at the global level.[134] Instead, she suggests modest proposals: states mutually self-limiting their own behavior via treaties; granting nonbinding external representation for affected foreigners (such as consultations); and setting up transnational deliberative (but not decision-making) forums.[135] In all of these options, it is worth noting that the relatively powerless remain at the will of the powerful—it is up to the latter to decide whether to practice restraint, listen to external concerns, and take into account the deliberations of transnational forums.

While Song is correct to identify the lack of substantive political equality as a major threat to any attempt to straightforwardly transplant domestic democratic institutions to the global level, it seems to me that the right lesson to take from this is to develop alternative ways of contesting global political inequality that do not require a world state instead of settling for the modest measures that do little to disturb existing power asymmetries. Moreover, if it is possible to foster cross-border solidarity in the very process of contesting political inequality, then the long-term project of building the conditions needed for global democracy may not be entirely utopian after all.

A slightly more ambitious proposal is put forth by Allen Buchanan and Robert Keohane, who develop what they call a "Complex Standard" for assessing the legitimacy of global institutions in the absence of prospects for global democracy.[136] The standard requires that global institutions make genuine accountability possible by increasing transparency toward external actors and revising their activities in light of contestation from the latter.[137] In this way, Buchanan and Keohane argue that global governance short of democracy can still promote equal consideration of interests as external actors can hold institutions accountable for excluding certain groups' interests. While improving accountability in the ways Buchanan and Keohane propose is undoubtedly an important part of promoting democratic global governance, this proposal still falls short of tackling *political inequality* between populations. International law and policymaking are still driven by powerful countries and advantaged groups within them, and the marginalized populations can only try to correct for unjust decision outcomes by monitoring and holding decision-makers accountable or potentially shaping decisions via consultation processes.

No doubt more variations of these proposals can be developed. But by now, the general worry should be clear: if we rely on relatively minor adjustments to global governance that skeptics of global democracy tend to propose, we can expect that those whose views and interests are currently marginalized from decision-making will largely remain so. And if we take on board Nehru's analysis of how relations of domination and subordination foster inward-looking sentiment and prevent the development of trust and solidarity, then what critics claim to be a precondition for global democracy that is not presently available will, in fact, likely never arise. In other words, the criticism that "there is no global demos because of lack of solidarity" becomes self-fulfilling.

Re-centering the problem of global political inequality and its role in continually undermining the possibility of global solidarity pushes us to go beyond the modest reforms to global governance that skeptics of global democracy propose. Instead, as I suggest in the next section, we should turn to measures that enable marginalized actors to build counterhegemonic power within and outside of global institutions. The project of global democracy is no longer a pie in the sky—as its opponents often portray it to be—if its main task is to figure out how to counter the unequal political power of hegemonic groups. On the contrary, democratizing global governance seen in this light is perhaps *the* most pressing topic of global justice since, regardless of what view of global justice one subscribes to, it amounts to who has the power to determine the terms of global interaction.[138]

But seeing the problem this way also takes us in a different—because more realist—direction to some proponents of global democracy. Specifically, in thinking about what is required for democratizing global governance, if global political inequality is at the forefront of our concern, then our emphasis ought to be targeted empowerment of disadvantaged groups rather than universal enfranchisement. The former requires institutional innovations and extra-institutional efforts that may not appear directly related to promoting "one person, one vote" or procedural equality more broadly, and may even contradict it. But without first countering immense global inequalities, even the most procedurally democratic proposals—such as a world citizens' assembly—would merely paper over persistent power asymmetries.[139]

Consider proposals for cosmopolitan democracy, as exemplified by David Held and Daniele Archibugi. Their proposals focus on institutional reforms that empower individuals qua world citizens in participating in global governance. For example, both argue for a world parliament that directly enfranchises individuals to establish a world citizenship. Responding to the Marxist critique that global democracy would only advance the interests of capital, Archibugi states that "cosmopolitan democracy proposes the creation of institutions and channels of representation for all citizens. The aim is [not] to do away with class distinctions but more modestly to ensure that the citizens' demands, whatever their class, are directly represented in global affairs."[140] Similarly, Held argues that the long-term aim of cosmopolitan democracy should be to entrench a charter of rights and obligations for all global actors.[141] On Held's list of short-term objectives for cosmopolitan democracy, only one—reform of the UN Security Council to give Global South countries a significant voice and effective decision-making capacity—is especially aimed at addressing political inequality across actors.[142] The rest, such as "establishing an effective, accountable, international, military force," "the use of transnational referenda," or the "foundation of a new economic agency," make no mention of how these institutions would avoid elite capture or address the existing inequalities that turn global institutions into the tools of dominant states and powerful nonstate actors. In short, the danger of aiming for cosmopolitan institutions without first focusing on the tricky task of politically empowering historically marginalized populations is that the resulting cosmopolitan democracy will be hollow, with the same patterns of power asymmetries driving much of global governance. Ironically, cosmopolitan democracy may end up in a very similar place to its fiercest critics: a global governance dominated by a few actors and that fosters further nationalist retreat among disillusioned populations.

To be sure, the problem of extra-procedural inequality rendering democratic procedures toothless is an old one that democratic theorists have spilled much ink over in the domestic context. One might wonder, then, why this should stop us from supporting universal enfranchisement. But this response fails to appreciate that the problem is far worse due to the distinctive nature of the global context. First, as Song argues, there's no global state to redistribute wealth and prevent, to a certain degree, wealth inequality from corrupting democratic procedures.[143] Economic inequality between states translates seamlessly into political inequality. Second, regime-shifting is a tried-and-true method for global actors to counter attempts at institutional reform: global actors subvert democratic and egalitarian reforms to global institutions by shifting to other forums to create alternative norms and laws. These norms and laws accumulatively destabilize existing regimes and create a de facto new regime that better promotes the interests of the powerful. Since, again, there is no global state that can enforce a given forum's monopoly on lawmaking, this strategy can effectively render global democratic reform moot.

The history of global governance is littered with examples of regime-shifting. Recall the case we started with—the UN General Assembly. Western powers began sidelining the UN General Assembly once postcolonial countries increasingly dominated the agenda by voting in majority blocs.[144] Another example more closely related to trade governance is the case of intellectual property law. Unlike the previous case, here it is primarily private actors—namely, foreign investors and transnational corporations—that employ regime-shifting to evade multilateral institutions.[145] When proposals for a treaty on intellectual property rights were first raised in the WTO, Global South countries worked to amend the agreement to allow more flexibility for the purposes of development and public health. Working with global civil society actors, they succeeded in obtaining important flexibilities in the resulting TRIPS agreement, including on patentability standards, data protection, and compulsory licensing. These flexibilities allowed India, for example, to maintain a relatively weaker regime of intellectual property rights and to become the world's generic drug manufacturer. Insofar as Global South countries' voices were effectively incorporated into the treaty and for once not brushed aside, this outcome can be seen as a nontrivial victory in democratizing trade governance. Since then, however, there has been a proliferation of bilateral investment treaties and regional trade agreements that contain more stringent protections for intellectual property, or what international legal scholars have called "TRIPS plus."[146] With these provisions in place, foreign investors can then litigate whenever countries' regulatory actions fail to uphold heightened protections for intellectual property.

In short, regime-shifting poses a significant threat to attempts to democratize global governance. Yet it is striking that global democratic theorists have said little about it. Instead, they have mainly drawn up lists of institutional reforms that seem desirable from a democrat's point of view. The pressing question, however, remains: What reason is there to think that dominant states would not simply abandon these platforms as soon as they are made more egalitarian? Far from a hypothetical, the United States has in recent years begun to withdraw from the WTO and frozen its operations by blocking the reappointment of appellate body members, as it is now seen as less advantageous to its national interests.[147]

To be sure, the problem of regime-shifting does not mean institutional reforms are altogether useless or irrelevant for democratizing global governance. But it does suggest that a theory of global democracy must put at its front-and-center the realities of unequal global political power. Thinking about global democracy this way means that the agenda for global democratic theorists shifts from asking questions about what cosmopolitan democratic institutions ought to look like, to questions about building, maintaining, and exercising counterhegemonic power at the global level. Doing so inevitably requires engaging with the insights and practices—the "political craft"[148]—of actors on the ground. I give an illustration of this exercise in the final section below.

Understanding the project of decolonizing global governance as forging counterhegemonic power marks an anticolonial approach to global democracy, one that breaks from the modest reforms that skeptics of global democracy put forth and the idealistic, utopian proposals that cosmopolitan democrats have defended.

Decolonizing Global Governance
as Counterhegemonic Political Empowerment

What does an approach to global democracy that centers the problem of political inequality entail? In this final section I defend measures that facilitate disadvantaged state and nonstate actors to build and maintain counterhegemonic power at the global level. Although I discuss institutional reforms that may empower disadvantaged states at the negotiation table, these reforms are ultimately limited in their potential to bring about greater global political equality.[149] As a result, I argue that prospects for global democracy depend crucially on whether locally organized but transnationally connected groups can mount credible threats to disrupt strategic points in the global economy.

The primary and immediate aim of building counterhegemonic power is to contest and correct for existing political inequalities in global governance— that is, enabling marginalized groups to press their views and interests upon dominant decision-makers. Yet there is also a secondary and longer-term aim. The hope is that transnational forms of political contestation can pave way for the *possible* emergence of a cosmopolitan solidarity. As I argued above, with Nehru, agents situated in relations of political subordination cannot reasonably be expected to trust or support the global institutions that perpetuate their marginalization. If counterhegemonic power can compel dominant actors to concede to egalitarian reforms within existing global institutions, Nehru's suggestion was that relations of equality would make it possible for historically oppressed groups to endorse global political integration. While disagreement and cultural pluralism would remain a fact of political life, this need not preclude collective decision-making.

To this end, Nehru saw transnational coalitions—between state actors as in the Asian Relations Conference, Bandung, Non-Alignment, etc., and between nonstate actors as in the League Against Imperialism—as playing a crucial role. By decentering nation-bounded forms of identifications, transnational forms of political contestation could instigate what he called a "psychological revolution" and plant the seeds of a more cosmopolitan outlook receptive to trust in and sympathetic identification with people who were not co-nationals.[150] Therefore, it is crucial that local organizing efforts do not merely entrench local identities but instead are accompanied by an awareness of global interconnectedness as well as a willingness to engage with similarly situated others in resisting political marginalization. As we saw from Nehru's efforts in the Indian anticolonial struggle, political leaders have an important role in fostering solidarity beyond national boundaries.

In other words, drawing from Nehru, we should think of the project of global democracy as a two-pronged process: first, build transnational (state and nonstate) coalitions that cultivate solidarity among the oppressed and that are essential for compelling dominant actors to concede to egalitarian institutional reforms (as well as substantive concessions). Second, when global institutions are suitably reformed to reliably track the views and interests of historically oppressed and marginalized groups, it becomes morally and psychologically possible for members of those groups to endorse these institutions and to embrace a cosmopolitan solidarity with formerly advantaged groups.

This is undoubtedly a very long-term process. But, as Nehru's analysis of the moral psychology of subordination reminds us, given centuries of colonial and imperial oppression often disguised as cosmopolitan political integration, it would be extremely naive to expect a functioning democratic global governance to emerge in any straightforward manner. Nonetheless, not all global institutions are equally resistant to democratic reforms, and we need not think of democratizing global governance as an all-or-nothing process. My point is that cosmopolitan democrats are misguided to short-circuit this process by recommending dramatic increases in universal global political integration without first building counterhegemonic power. Finally, we should not conceive of the process as linear and the attainment of global democracy as the attainment of perpetual peace. Given the non-ideal world we live in, there will always be new ways in which global institutions exclude or neglect some agents. Thus measures that make possible for similarly situated groups to organize transnationally and contest global political inequality should always be a feature of a democratic global governance.

Counterhegemonic Power-Building at the Global Level

Recall from chapter 2 that power consists of at least three dimensions: compelling behavioral change, agenda-setting, and shaping agents' perception of their own interests.[151] Counterhegemonic power in the context of global governance, then, is the capacity of disadvantaged actors to compel dominant actors (including states and corporations) to do what they would otherwise not do: accept tabling of issues that otherwise would be excluded from a given institution's agenda; concede to decision outcomes that reflect equal consideration of the views and interests of the marginalized; and work with new norms and discursive paradigms in which key issues are thought about in terms more amenable to the interests of marginalized groups.[152]

To start, the most obvious basis of global political power is coercive force in the form of militaries. So we might think that smaller states ought to form military alliances to build counterhegemonic power and increase their leverage. Yet Nehru was decidedly against military alliances, seeing these as destabilizing forces in the international order.[153] Having lived through two world wars and the Cold War arms race, Nehru saw how military alliances erode trust and drag actors into massive armed conflicts that might have been mitigated or contained had other actors stayed neutral, as the Non-Aligned Movement attempted during the Cold War. For Nehru, reciprocal disarmament between states is a necessary step in attaining lasting collective security.[154] Apart from these considerations, in the current state of technological warfare it also seems unrealistic to expect capital-poor states to match the military capacity of capital-rich states even when banded together. Finally, military force offers little promise for nonstate actors as a venue of power-building.

On the other end of the spectrum is something we might broadly call global public opinion. John Dryzek argues that "discursive power"—similar to Lukes's third type of power—is as important to democracy as voting and decision-making.[155] When agents engage in deliberation about matters that affect them, they can collectively create a public opinion that exerts political influence over international organizations, treaty and diplomatic negotiations, and so on.[156] Human rights activists, for example, can name and shame oppressive states; similarly, transnational activists can strive to create a global discourse that emphasizes the interests of postcolonial countries and marginalized groups across the world.[157] Discursive power can also be deployed against nonstate actors such as corporations. Through boycotts and protests, for example, consumers and workers have introduced fair trade, rather than mere efficiency or profit-making, as an alternative framework to think about global trade. Moreover, Dryzek sees greater promise in what he calls discursive democracy than cosmopolitan democracy, because there need not be a grand centralizing project susceptible to capture by vested interests, and it is also easier to maintain decentralized participation in opinion and idea shaping.[158]

Shaping the discursive frameworks under which global issues are negotiated and decisions are made is undoubtedly an important form of power. But we should also not exaggerate the ease with which this can be done. As we saw in the previous chapter, global communications remain deeply uneven, a problem largely tracing back to unequal capital. In other words, the capacity to participate in discourse production is still highly constrained by the availability of resources. Moreover, we should also be realistic about the extent to which public opinion can compel actors to do things they otherwise would not do. To start, global public opinion is diverse and, except in extraordinary cases when people mobilize across the world on a single issue, it is hard to say what the dominant sentiment regarding a specific issue or actor is. But even when powerful actors contravene a cohesive public opinion, as Kate Macdonald and Terry Macdonald's analysis suggests, it is often when public condemnation results in material loss (in this case, loss in profit) that it becomes a form of power.[159] Therefore, although counterhegemonic power will undoubtedly consist of a discursive aspect, this is by itself insufficient if not backed by material basis.

As discussed in chapter 3, neocolonial actors have historically weaponized asymmetric capital dependence to obtain terms of global interaction favorable to them. Yet neocolonial actors also depend on postcolonial countries for a supply of cheap labor and raw materials. They need the latter to willingly engage in trade and allow foreign investment. One way for marginalized actors to build global counterhegemonic power is to form interstate economic coalitions, which have historically played an important role in empowering postcolonial countries in global politics.[160] Though postcolonial countries have experimented with coalitions (and won important victories), these have not always been successful. A pressing task for an account of global democracy that centers the problem of political inequality, then, is to identify institutional reforms that make it easier for marginalized states to form interstate coalitions and exert influence.

As an illustration of this exercise, let us return to the WTO. The WTO currently has twenty-six coalitions, sixteen of which consist of only Global South countries.[161] Amrita Narlikar draws a distinction between bloc-type and issue-based coalitions: while the former tend to be founded on the basis of common values and/or interests that are more enduring, the latter tend to be more temporary and focused on single issues.[162] Analyzing the changing nature of coalitions within the WTO, she identifies a number of features that made Global South countries' coalitions at the Doha Development Round stronger than before, including collective internal agenda-setting; inclusion of each party's central demands/interests into the goals of the coalition; offering each other support such as side payments to most vulnerable parties (i.e., the "lowest-income" states) so they can forgo external offers to defect; an emphasis on the distinctiveness and specificity of common issues faced; and so on.[163] These strategies have helped create strong coalitions such as the African Group and the so-called Least Developed Countries (LDCs), which played important roles in pushing for TRIPS waivers in cases of public health emergencies.[164]

Democratizing trade governance can therefore take the form of institutional changes that facilitate counterhegemonic coalitions' political unity and agency. Some proposals that seem promising from this perspective are a moratorium on offers of bilateral deals to individual members of a coalition, or a coalition-specific most-favored-nation rule such that all members would benefit from any concessions offered by outsiders.[165] These rules would make it harder for dominant actors to undercut coalitions and regime-shift as they have little choice but to negotiate with the coalition if they are to trade with its members. To be sure, all things considered, the moral cost of rejecting bilateral deals may sometimes be too high—for example, if the economic situation is so dire that a country risks humanitarian disaster by refusing an offer—and the more vulnerable a country is, the higher the cost will be. It might be unreasonable for coalition partners to expect their more vulnerable counterparts to forgo opportunities to secure their citizens' most basic interests. Still, by practicing mutual aid in the ways Narlikar discusses above, coalition partners have an important role to play in preventing such dire situations. Mutual aid across countries is therefore crucial if counterhegemonic resistance is to succeed.

One might worry that focusing on state empowerment entrenches the nation-state system and creates further barriers to fostering a global demos. But transnational coalitions between similarly situated states can be a crucial intermediate step in promoting cosmopolitan solidarity in the long run. At their best, such coalitions can highlight common interests and tied fates, and foster transnational solidarity as members resist temptations to be "bought out" and practice mutual aid. As coalitions achieve victories that would otherwise not have been possible for each vulnerable party on its own, this highlights the importance of political mobilization beyond national borders.

A different worry here is that many of these states do not secure political equality for their citizens. If global democrats care about political equality, why should empowering these states be a democratic concern? To be sure, if empowering marginalized states can help correct for unjust decision outcomes, there is undoubtedly a straightforward way in which an undemocratic state's increased political authority at the global level still matters for its citizens. But beyond that, is there a further reason to think that greater political equality between states fulfills some important interest that individuals have?[166]

A version of this objection was considered in chapter 2. There, I argued that in circumstances where nationality has come to function as a social identity not dissimilar to race or ethnicity, political inequality between states can embody an objectionable form of unequal status between individual citizens, even if one or both states are not democracies. Here, I will add that empowering disadvantaged states is necessary even if not sufficient for attaining global political equality. Except for the most egregious cases of totalitarian rule, even in undemocratic states there is rarely a complete and comprehensive disconnect between citizens' views and interests and the domestic ruling elite's foreign policy pursuits. Individuals living under undemocratic regimes often still find ways to occasionally make themselves heard even if electoral processes are not available, especially in key issues involving basic interests. But even if they successfully overcome obstacles to exerting influence over their governments, the latter would still need to be able to channel their citizens' interests and views into global decision-making. To be sure, there are exceptions to these general claims. Those who are especially disempowered and marginalized within the state due to race, ethnicity, gender, and/or class may not be able to find any meaningful connection between the empowerment of their states in global forums and their own political equality.

This leads to a second and even more important requirement of global democracy beyond institutional reform: the existence of suitably organized groups with the capacity to disrupt the global economy. Like capital-poor states, many groups that are marginalized from domestic and global politics are also well placed to threaten the normal operations of global trade and investment. Factory workers in the Global South are an obvious example—when suitably organized and mobilized, they can and have disrupted the global value chain through general strikes, slow-downs, and so on. Indigenous peoples across the world have also halted investment projects through protest and withholding cooperation with multinational corporations. These political actions have attracted allies who respond to calls for solidarity and take their lead in engaging in protest.

To be sure, a threat is credible only to the extent that disruption can reliably be triggered when called for. This requires extensive on-the-ground local organizing and, crucially, a transnational architecture for sustained collaboration between groups.[167] Building this architecture is no small feat, since these are nonstate actors who also face marginalization (and often even repression) within their own states. Recall Nehru's League Against Imperialism as an example. The League provided a transnational platform for anticolonial activists to learn from each other's struggles and coordinate political actions together. Through circulations of anticolonial publications and funding activists to visit each other's unions and party congresses, the League also deepened the sense of global solidarity and facilitated a collective political education by showing colonial subjects how their struggles were interconnected.

An account of global democracy that addresses political inequality should therefore feature a theory of the transnational architecture needed for counterhegemonic power from below. This is a complex task that needs to be sensitive to context and will likely be successful only if developed in conjunction with the insights of practitioners on the ground.[168] While I cannot offer a full-blown account here, the rest of the chapter gives a brief illustration of this exercise. The history of Nehru's transnational organizing offers some inspiration for such an account—for example, the importance of political leaders bringing global connections to the forefront of domestic struggles—but the historical context in which he operated is also different from ours. Therefore, let us think about a transnational architecture for counterhegemonic power by looking at a contemporary case of contesting political inequality in trade governance: the world's largest peasant and farmer's movement, La Via Campesina.

La Via Campesina (LVC) is a transnational organization with 182 local affiliates in 81 countries.[169] It consists of peasants and farmers, including subsistence farmers, family farms, sharecroppers, agricultural wage laborers, and landless peasants.[170] Many are Indigenous persons, and a majority are women. These groups generally lack an effective voice and political representation within their own countries. Aside from racism and patriarchal oppression, these groups also experience harassment and violence from multinational agribusinesses looking to take over their land and/or forcing them to use their seeds.

LVC emerged as a response to the absence of farmers' and peasants' voices in global trade governance discussions. Dismissing the NGOs that claimed to speak on their behalf, one LVC leader stated in an interview, "In all global debates on agrarian policy, the peasant movement has been absent: we have not had a voice."[171] In contrast to NGOs, LVC sets itself up explicitly as grassroots movement, asserting that "[the peasants] are here and we can speak for ourselves."[172] For decades, peasants and farmers affiliated with LVC have mobilized against the WTO and their own governments to advance the principle of "food sovereignty": "the rights of local peoples to determine their own agricultural and food policy, organize production and consumption to meet local needs, and secure access to land, water, and seed."[173] Instead of pushing for further liberalization in agriculture, as their own governments have tended to do, the food sovereignty paradigm stipulates that agriculture should be kept out of free trade agreements altogether and that poverty cannot be addressed by foodstuff export–oriented growth. Accordingly, LVC advocates for domestic subsidies and antimonopoly policies that strengthen local agriculture and protect small and family farmers, as well as global trade regulations that prohibit overproduction and dumping from larger agroexport countries.[174] It emphasizes that food security can only be achieved when local communities, not corporations, control food production. Starting with interventions at the 1996 World Food Summit and culminating in the UNHCR Declaration on the Rights of Peasants, LVC has successfully popularized "food sovereignty" as an alternative paradigm for food production.[175] In this sense, they have gained considerable discursive power.

LVC is a good example of organizing to threaten dominant actors' economic interests. One of its key campaigns under the framework of food sovereignty, for example, is resisting the introduction of genetically modified seeds, which in their view would place farmers and peasants under the control of multinational corporations who owned the intellectual property rights to the seeds. As part of that campaign, LVC leaders and affiliates have engaged in direct actions such as uprooting Monsanto's genetically modified soya and occupying stores and labs distributing the seeds.[176] Moreover, the struggle over control of seeds is especially contentious in India, and their localized tactics even intentionally echo the anticolonial struggle. Every year on Gandhi's birthday, the regional coordinator of LVC organizes a massive farmers' rally to protest the liberalization of agriculture. In 1992, half a million Indian farmers participated in "Seed Satyagraha," a campaign calling on the government to reject the TRIPs agreement. They served "Quit India" notices to multinational companies, attacked Cargill Seeds offices, and burned Monsanto seeds and cotton crops.[177] As Desmarais's analysis suggests, Indian political leaders subsequently began to criticize the WTO more openly, and government negotiators pressed harder for concessions in the Doha Round.[178]

While La Via Campesina's campaign for food sovereignty makes demands of the state, the movement also maintains that the global and the national are intimately connected. Without the appropriate trade rules, their own governments could not enact the policies needed to protect local farmers even if they wanted to. Furthermore, LVC's organizing crosses boundaries of Global South and North. It sees the plight of farmers in both parts of the world as connected in a struggle against agricultural liberalization and the corporate food regime, and engages with local farmers' groups in countries like the United States, touting the slogan of "building unity within diversity."[179] Thus LVC emphasizes a blend of local and global activism with the long-term goal of promoting a "peasant internationalism" and a transnational "peasant identity."[180] To do this, they help organize cross-exchange schools for farmers to visit and learn from other farming communities; bring local leaders to international LVC conferences; employ rituals before every meeting—a performance surrounding seeds and soil, called *mistica*—to foster pride in a common peasant identity; and publish regular newsletters on issues to do with food sovereignty and peasant movements.[181] Moreover, when local affiliates engage in protest (as in the 2020 Indian farmers' protests), LVC issues calls for solidarity actions and helps publicize the peasants' plight.[182]

In organizing transnationally, however, LVC is also sensitive to power asymmetries within its membership—most obviously between Southern and Northern farmers, and between men and women. They therefore employ a "peer group" structure where no one local group is allowed to monopolize leadership, and they also practice leadership rotation and implement a gender quota so that male-female representation in the international leadership is equal. Moreover, for important decisions such as the details of the food sovereignty paradigm, the LVC emphasizes decision-making through a slow and gradual process of consensus-building that starts locally and moves upward to the international secretariat.[183]

From this brief discussion we can identify at least four features of the architecture needed to facilitate global counterhegemonic power from below: (1) a transnational platform for sustained collaboration; (2) sites for political education and discourse production and circulation; (3) practices aimed at fostering transnational solidarity and identity; (4) antihierarchy practices such as leadership rotation, gender quotas, and decision-making through consensus-building. While LVC is an exemplary case, many of these practices are not unique to LVC and have been employed by grassroots movements in the Global South.[184] To the extent that they succeed in making their members' voices heard in global governance, and in the process foster a transnational outlook, we can say that they are democratizing forces that serve to correct for global political inequality and leave open the possibility for a cosmopolitan solidarity.

Yet if transnational social movements like LVC are crucial for democratizing global governance, they are also not easy to sustain. One way to sustain them is for transnational social movements to be given an institutional role in global governance. Similar arguments have been put forth by international legal scholars regarding NGOs—that they should be given greater voice in global governance as a democratizing force.[185] Yet although it is essential for nonstate actors to work with global institutions to further their constituencies' interests and views, we should not take institutionalized representation of nonstate actors as the sole or even primary indicator of democratization, understood as moving toward political equality. To start, formal representation is often also given to corporations. The WTO Public Forum, for example, is an initiative to institutionalize a space for civil society actors within the WTO but has increasingly become hijacked by corporations and their lobbyists.[186] But even if these spaces are reserved only for nonprofit civil society actors, the worry is that once representatives gain institutionalized roles, they become targets of cooptation efforts and other forms of pressure that result in losing touch with their grassroots constituents. Kristin Hopewell's study of civil society at the WTO finds, for example, that post-Seattle, many NGOs changed their rhetoric and issue focus to gain the respect of WTO technocrats and access to key decision-makers. In the process, they weakened their advocacy on a range of issues such as labor protections and agriculture.[187] They also ended up employing the kinds of technocratic approaches that they had criticized the WTO for in the first place, in attempts to set themselves apart from the "radicals" protesting on the street. As a result, transparency and accountability toward their own constituents are traded off for donor support and legitimacy in the eyes of the WTO. On the other hand, grassroots NGOS— and especially those from the Global South with fewer resources and less social capital, and more radical agendas such as anti–free trade—tend to be sidelined as WTO technocrats embrace these "reformed" NGOS. For this reason, transnational grassroots movements like LVC practice cautious vetting before agreeing to participate in dialogues with international organizations.

LVC in particular is known to reject cooptation attempts, such as all-inclusive travel packages to fly leaders out for dialogue, or offers to help improve their online media presence in return for participation in public relations events.[188]

This suggests that, rather than increasing institutionalized representation for nonstate actors within international organizations, global democracy ultimately relies on the capacity of marginalized groups across the world to effectively trigger disruptive transnational political actions on the streets, in factories, at sites of environmental and/or cultural significance, and so on. While there are no easy fixes for the messy work of everyday organizing, we can nonetheless ask questions such as: What obstacles are there for marginalized groups across the world to engage in sustained communication and coordination with one another? What kinds of resources and infrastructure are needed to build and maintain a political identity with those whom regular interactions are scarce? Questions along these lines enable us to identify and subject certain international practices to a *democratic* critique: for example, border controls that prevent activists from engaging in regular face-to-face meetings or participating in political actions at global forums—a problem that Nehru and his fellow comrades regularly faced in their time and that remains a problem today.[189] Or the lack of secure access to communications infrastructure and technology as not only a problem for distributive justice but also a problem for *global democracy*, insofar as this hampers efforts to organize across borders and cultivate a transnational identity.

No doubt there are other institutional, discursive, and material hindrances to transnational political organizing. My point is that an account of global democracy should identify *these* as the main obstacles to narrowing the democratic deficit, construed as a horizontal deficit in political equality between groups. This emphasis comes from engaging with dilemmas and perspectives of transnational organizers. From anticolonial activists like Nehru's League Against Imperialism to today's La Via Campesina, transnational power-building from the marginalized offers insights into how promising forces for democratizing global governance might be built and what is needed for their emergence.

Before concluding, let us consider an objection. Like many postcolonial states, it might be objected that transnational social movements are not necessarily representative or democratic. Although LVC represents hundreds of millions of peasants and farmers, there are presumably also peasants and farmers who do not subscribe to the paradigm of food sovereignty and whose views are therefore not represented. Moreover, LVC is a rather exceptional case in terms of its care to build a transnational consensus around key issues before moving forward with external advocacy, even if it comes at a cost to efficiency.[190] One can imagine other transnational social movements that are less able or willing to do this. Therefore there are the dual problems of representativeness of a constituency and internal democracy within a transnational movement.

In response, we should distinguish between democratizing forces and democracy itself. The former is a means to the eventual attainment of the latter. It seems plausible that our criteria for what counts as a democratizing force should not be exactly the same as what democracy requires. Otherwise, this places unreasonable demands on actors for whom the clearest structures of democratic representation—i.e., authorization via free and fair voting—are not readily available. In the domestic setting, for example, democratic revolutions are not always instigated by groups that are internally democratic, and sometimes they consist of relatively decentralized networks of mass mobilization that do not have an obvious decision-making structure. Nonetheless, it would seem strange to not think of them as democratizing forces.

Still, this does not mean that anything goes. For an organized movement to count as a democratizing force, we might think about: first, whether it corrects for existing political inequality by upending power asymmetries. This means that pushing for a marginalized viewpoint may not in itself count as democratizing, if that viewpoint defends unjustified privileges of the advantaged. Instead, the group's aims must be read in the context of power asymmetries between social groups as well as between states. LVC, for example represents those whose primary means of subsistence and livelihood are under threat or have been taken away, and who face violence and silencing. They are thus empowering the relatively disempowered vis-à-vis corporations, domestic governments, and global institutions like the WTO.

Second, we might ask whether there are signs of popular support among the purported constituents for the movement/organization that would amount to what Terry Macdonald has called nonelectoral authorization of representatives.[191] While Macdonald's study focuses on NGOs, parts of her analysis are also relevant here. Macdonald puts forth a view of stakeholder democracy in which NGOs can be seen as legitimate representatives of their constituencies if they are authorized through what she calls delegation and empowerment.[192] Nonelectoral delegation can occur through stakeholders signaling their views and the putative representative publicly accepting responsibility for representing those views. Empowerment can take the form of conferring the resources needed for the representative to exercise political power. Additionally, nonelectoral accountability can occur through mechanisms of transparency and public disempowerment—ways for the constituents to know what is being done in their name, and to publicly express their disapproval or withdraw authorization if needed.[193]

Something similar might be expected of transnational social movements and organizations. Constituents might demonstrate their authorization of a movement to speak for their views and interests by enabling their operations through material support but also, perhaps more importantly, public showings of support when political mobilization is called for. Withdrawing these would be signals to outsiders that authorization has been withdrawn for a particular representative.

Third, to the extent that the primary goal is not undermined, we might ask whether the movement or organization is structured in ways that prevent internal political marginalization. This includes mechanisms and practices that foster accountability and open deliberation, as well as remedial measures that take into account power asymmetries within the organization. For example, they can consult members' views through regular assemblies, ensure that there is a transparent and fair process for channeling issues of concern and suggestions for reform, creating committees and other kinds of participatory spaces for bottom-up planning and strategizing, and, where possible, hold elections for local leadership or local referendums on important matters, such as the central demands to be brought to the WTO.

To conclude, counterhegemonic power-building for both marginalized states and nonstate actors should be seen as the first and most crucial task for democratizing global governance. Rather than accepting undemocratic global governance with increased accountability, or drawing up plans for a world constitution, we should instead think about the project of global democracy as a project in contesting the power asymmetries that render the status quo intolerable and utopianism hollow for the subordinated. To this end, organizing locally with an eye to fostering transnational links with similarly situated groups abroad offers the most promising strategy to contest global political inequality while planting seeds for a "psychological revolution" that paves way toward a democratic "one world."

Conclusion: Toward a Different Global Democratic Theory

This chapter has argued for a shift in understanding the problem of global democracy. Drawing on Nehru's analysis of the importance and difficulties of attaining democratic global governance, I argued that we should reframe the global "democratic deficit" as a problem of persistent political inequality between groups rather than a question of world citizens in general lacking control over global institutions. This shift is subtle, but it enables us to see that regardless of what the conditions for creating a "global demos" are and whether they have already been attained, democratizing global governance is an urgent issue that should not be dismissed as an idealist's exercise. Furthermore, drawing again on Nehru's internationalism from the interwar period to postindependence, I argued that the first step to contesting global political inequality is to empower disadvantaged states and nonstate actors to organize and build power transnationally. This has implications for both institutional design and extra-institutional measures that global democrats ought to investigate.

In broadening the agenda of global democratic theory—from asking whether the (idealized) conditions of democracy have been or can be obtained at the global level and what domestic institutions might be replicated for a cosmopolitan democracy, to grappling with the problem of existing global political inequality between groups—the most urgent questions that arise may appear as strategic ones about how to effectively build counterhegemonic power at the global level. One might wonder whether these are questions that normative theory is best placed to answer. To a certain extent, the emphasis on pragmatism is a useful corrective for utopian accounts of global democracy, and we ought not shy away from it. Yet, as we saw, engaging with the obstacles and dilemmas that political actors face on the ground also opens up questions beyond "what works." Global democratic theorists might defend, for example, the justifiability of various kinds of disobedience of global institutions and international law-breaking to disrupt the global economy and to democratize the overall international order more broadly; identify and critique features of the world order that hinder the emergence of democratizing forces; attend to moral questions such as what the oppressed owe each other in forming and sustaining transnational coalitions, and so on. Thinking about questions of global political action and resistance does not mean jettisoning ideals of justice (in our case, postcolonial global justice as social equality) that throw light on why political inequality at the global level is objectionable in the first place. But it does mean attending to topics such as prefigurative politics, means-ends, permissibility of disobedience, ethics of solidarity, and so on— topics that have primarily only been studied at the domestic level within analytic political philosophy/theory.

These normative concerns undoubtedly mark a different focus for global democratic theory than it has traditionally been conceived. Yet this focus is precisely what comes to light when taking up a postcolonial perspective on global justice. Ultimately, the prospect for realizing decolonization as egalitarian transformation depends on creating credible threats to power from organized political actors everywhere.

Conclusion

THIS BOOK has offered an account of global justice that takes decolonization as its guiding aim. To develop this account, I drew on the political thought of four influential anticolonial thinker-activists and put forth an interpretation of their normative aspirations for a decolonized world as centered around the value of equality. From this, I developed a view of postcolonial global justice grounded on an ideal of social equality. Equipped with this account, we investigated persistent colonial hierarchies in three different aspects of contemporary global justice and, drawing from the theoretical insights and political action of a different thinker for each topic, we developed distinct principles for decolonization in these areas. In the following, I review three central themes underlying the book.

Global Social Equality

Contra the long-standing neglect of social equality beyond shared societies among most social egalitarians, I have argued that reading anticolonial critiques of racial hierarchy, helps us see the moral relevance of equal status at the global level. The unequal status encapsulated in global hierarchies of power, esteem, and moral standing, I suggested, are objectionable both in themselves and for the consequences they have on individuals' lives. Chapter 2 put forth this point most explicitly by laying out an account of postcolonial global justice as social equality. In this view, individuals have a claim to relate to others across the world as social equals—that is, to relate as equally authoritative social agents whose interests deserve equal consideration. Such relations are important because they enable persons to live in freedom from domination and enjoy the valuable goods of solidarity and nonalienation with one another.

This view has important implications for diagnosing what has gone wrong with the ways our global relations are currently structured, and for thinking about what it might mean to change them. Specifically, the book explored three aspects of contemporary global politics.

First, we looked at global economic relations, focusing on international investment, and characterized such relations as neocolonial. I put forth a reading of Nkrumah's theory of neocolonialism that emphasizes (group-based) exploitation rather than mere foreign interference, which better enables us to capture the border-crossing nature of capital empowerments. In this view, neocolonialism occurs when a group is asymmetrically dependent on another group, and the latter offers the former terms of cooperation that enrich themselves at the expense of the dependent party's ability to escape persistent disadvantage. To illustrate, I argued that under the contemporary international investment regime, transnational capital-owners (i.e., corporations and investors) are empowered to undermine the ability of disadvantaged groups in capital-poor Global South countries (and sometimes even disadvantaged groups in Global North countries) to pursue measures that rectify global and domestic inequalities. Against this, I argued for changes to the practice of international investment that go beyond re-strengthening national sovereignty vis-à-vis foreign capital, but instead encompass targeted empowerments for the non-capital-owning class—such as working-class citizens and Indigenous peoples—to exercise greater control over foreign investment. Moreover, until such a regime is in place, I suggest that citizens in host states can justifiably press their governments to refuse to comply with investment arbitration when doing so would undermine or penalize the pursuit of social equality.

Second, we looked at patterns of global cultural production and transmission, focusing on the trade of cultural goods. Drawing on Césaire's critique of cultural imperialism, I argued that long-standing patterns of cultural trade, whereby Global North countries disproportionately export to the rest of the world, are problematic insofar as they reproduce racialized hierarchies of social agency. Such hierarchies have their roots in the colonial discourse of civilization and can reinforce global relations of domination and exploitation. Adding to the unequal flow of cultural goods are the two problems of whitewashing and appropriation, which together contribute to the persistent erasure of the social agency of racialized groups. Against this, I defended anticolonial demands to democratize global communications as encapsulated in the now largely forgotten New World Information and Communication Order. Moreover, until global cultural production and dissemination becomes more egalitarian, I argued for a remedial right to cultural protectionism for postcolonial societies that remain at the margins of the global cultural trade.

Finally, we turned to the problem of undemocratic global governance. Going back to the era of formal European colonialism, international lawmaking has always been a lopsided affair, but this chapter examines the persistent hierarchies of authority embedded in contemporary global institutions such as those that govern global trade. Drawing on Nehru's writings and speeches on the importance of democratic global integration, as well as his political efforts to push for a more egalitarian mode of global governance, I argued that we should recharacterize the problem of global democracy as persistent unequal political equality between groups rather than the lack of a global demos capable of exercising control over global institutions. Attaining the latter, if it is to be a goal at all, can only at best be seen as a distant, long-term end, but in the short and medium terms, the pressing task for global democrats is to evaluate and theorize institutional reforms and forms of global political action for their potential to counter global political inequality.

A Decolonial Politics beyond Nationalism

Postcolonial global justice as social equality is grounded in an egalitarian reading of anticolonial thought. Recovering equality as a central anticolonial value, I argued that we can read these thinkers' critiques of colonialism as a rejection of structural inequality, and their visions of decolonization as an egalitarian transformation, one that would replace global and domestic relations of hierarchy with relations of equality. The egalitarian face of decolonization, as I called it, focuses on attaining freedom by securing the institutional and social conditions that allow individuals to relate to one another as equals. In a particular historical juncture, the most appropriate institutions to do so may have been the nation-state, but even at the height of decolonization, anticolonial thinkers already saw and critiqued its limits, and many were open to transnational solutions and greater global political integration more broadly. By viewing anticolonial thought exclusively through a nationalist framework, we have missed facets of the tradition that ground a more cosmopolitan outlook that is based on relations of equality. This shapes not only our thinking about what a just postcolonial world should look like, but also concedes too much to postcolonial regimes that invoke anticolonialism and decolonization to justify strengthening national sovereignty at the expense of the equal freedom of their citizens and subjects. Instead, I suggested that a fuller understanding of the anticolonial tradition should include an account of its egalitarian aspirations.

This interpretive move has important implications for contemporary decolonial politics. As chapter 3 argued, for example, the charge of neocolonialism in the global economy should be read not only as a claim against foreign interference, but more substantively as a claim against the empowerment of (foreign and domestic) capital over postcolonial citizens' ability to enact measures antithetical to the former's material interests. Not only is this arrangement objectionable insofar as it undermines remedies for domestic and global inequalities, but the arrangement itself expresses a form of unequal moral standing by which persons' basic interests matter less in face of the self-enrichment of capital-owners, and therefore it is also objectionable for that reason. This way of understanding the concern about neocolonial economic relations enables us to critique both foreign and domestic agents that benefit from them, including postcolonial ruling elites.

Similarly, accusations of cultural imperialism need not rely on arguments about the protection of a specific form of national culture. Rather, a concern about persistent inequalities in global cultural production and dissemination can be grounded on an egalitarian concern about which groups are able to exercise social agency and are recognized for it. This account allows us to critique not only existing global arrangements surrounding media and communications more broadly, but also postcolonial states that elevate and promote a culture as *the* national culture, at the expense of minorities' opportunities to exercise their social agency. In doing so, the latter reproduces or creates new hierarchies of "creator and consumer," thus betraying anticolonial thinkers' egalitarian aspirations for a decolonized world.

Finally, we need not understand concerns about further global political integration as claims about the intrinsic incompatibility of cultural pluralism with global governance. Instead, if relations of equality formed a central ambition of anticolonial visions for a postcolonial world order, we should turn our focus to the persistent inequalities that turn ostensibly collaborative global governance institutions into sites of domination and exploitation. A global political integration that papers over the reality of global political inequality not only undermines the possibility of an emergent cosmopolitan solidarity, but also continues to provide fuel for regimes that reject the authority of global institutions, often when those institutions are their subjects' last hope for resisting injustice.

Cosmopolitanism without Imperialism

This leads to a third theme of the book. Thinking about global justice from a postcolonial perspective also serves as an important corrective to versions of liberal cosmopolitanism that dismiss too quickly the relevance of groups and collective rights. Focusing on the need to overcome objectionable global hierarchies helps us see why, even as we subscribe to normative individualism, there is nonetheless strong reason to support the empowerment of groups. If collective agency among the subordinated is central to political resistance, cosmopolitans committed to an ideal of global social equality can consistently defend collective rights for such groups including, as in the case of the European colonies from which our thinkers wrote, political self-determination through a new state. The moral basis of such a right need not lie in the claim that the group shares a particular form of ethnocultural identity distinct from their oppressors', even if such groups in practice often develop shared cultures across time. Instead, taking on the insight of the thinkers discussed in this book, common subjection to a set of objectionable hierarchies can ground rights to collective self-determination. Furthermore, such a view need not merely amount to an instrumental defense of collective self-determination.[1] A constitutive element of colonial oppression, as we saw, is the idea that some peoples are incapable of self-governance. For these groups to exercise collective self-determination is therefore itself a contestation of racial hierarchy.

Yet precisely because individuals are often subjected to multiple intersecting hierarchies, our view would not commit cosmopolitans to privileging collective political agency in the form of the nation-state. As I argued in the preceding chapters, subnational or transnational actors such as workers, peasants, and Indigenous peoples may often be better placed to contest global injustice. As I argued in the book, these agents can push their states to refuse compliance with exploitative terms of economic cooperation, play important roles in recovering the social agency of marginalized groups, and contest the undemocratic nature of global governance institutions. Their political agency, as Nkrumah put it, is ultimately what "make(s), maintain(s), or break(s) revolutions."[2] In short, taking individuals as the source and unit of moral concern need not commit cosmopolitans to abandoning the importance of collective political agency, and nor is such agency always best exercised through the nation-state.

Anticolonial Resistance and the Future of Postcolonial Global Justice

It is perhaps quickly becoming a cliché to say that the configuration of global power is undergoing dramatic changes today. The rise of China as a global hegemon will mark the first time in modern history that a postcolonial and majority nonwhite state has had the power to potentially redefine global relations. Already the Chinese regime has been offering capital and various forms of assistance to capital-poor countries, and explicitly portraying the relations that they aim to build with others across the world as a morally superior alternative to Western neo-imperialism. In 2019, for example, China became the single largest financier for infrastructure in Africa.[3] Nonetheless, there is increasing criticism and scrutiny of China's actions both abroad and at home. Some variants are undoubtedly driven by fears among right-wing elements in the West of no longer occupying the hegemonic position that they are used to.

Indeed, the rise of white nationalism in the United States is being fanned by hawkish and xenophobic politicians who use the threat of China as political currency. But criticism is also coming from those who find themselves at the worse end of these investment and trade deals, as well as internal minorities within China who have suffered the brunt of the regime's ethnocultural nationalist policies. On the former, an ambitious global infrastructure development plan known as the Belt and Road Initiative, launched under President Xi Jinping, has been criticized for loading developing countries with unsustainable debt.[4] On the latter, it has become increasingly apparent that the treatment of the Uighurs amounts to a form of Han Chinese colonization.[5] Having stood up against Western imperialism and neocolonialism for decades, China is now arguably on its path to becoming an imperialist power itself. Anticolonial thinkers' prescient warnings that new hegemons may arise if global and domestic hierarchies remain appear increasingly vindicated.

Amid these political developments, it is especially important to return to decolonization as a productive site of normative inquiry and moral imagination. An important set of questions that anticolonial thinkers spilled much ink over, and that this book could not fully address, pertains to resistance to injustice and transitions to justice. While I suggested in chapter 5 that the pursuit of postcolonial global justice ultimately depends on the organized efforts of oppressed and marginalized groups, there is undoubtedly much more to be said on the topic of global and transnational political resistance. Within political theory, there has been much philosophical work done on civil disobedience or the ethics of political action in the domestic setting, but until recently, relatively little attention has been paid to similar questions in the global context.[6] And yet the kinds of political organizing and political action required for resisting new and old hegemons and moving toward a postcolonial world are likely to be border-crossing in nature.

Theorizing global justice through sustained engagement with anticolonial thought brings these questions of global political action to the fore. What sorts of practices and structures need to be in place for disparate persons to form and exercise collective political agency outside of the state? What duties of solidarity might coalition members, whose interests can often diverge, owe each other? In the long-standing absence of an egalitarian and democratic process for lawmaking at the global level, what permissions might agents have to engage in international lawbreaking?[7] How might deep distrust and resentment fostered by persistent global inequalities be transformed in the process of resistance?

These questions about the ethics of global political resistance will only appear more pressing as the inegalitarian legacies of colonialism become more visible in new global challenges such as climate change and global health emergencies. As in developing an account of global justice, engaging with anticolonial thinker-activists in their situated struggles to shed light on enduring moral questions promises to be a fruitful mode of theorizing resistance to global injustice. I hope to have shown in this book that a normative political philosophy that engages with historically situated political actors offers a valuable perspective on the present. Ultimately, as Césaire suggests, a universal that is "rich from all of the particulars" is a universal "made to the measure of the world."[8]

NOTES

Introduction. Decolonization Unfinished: In Search of a Just Postcolonial World Order

1. Abrahm Lustgarten, "Barbados Resists Climate Colonialism in an Effort to Survive the Costs of Global Warming"; Nina Lakhani, "'A Continuation of Colonialism': Indigenous Activists Say Their Voices Are Missing at COP26"; BBC News, "Sri Lanka Protest over Chinese Investment Turns Ugly"; Jaysim Hanspaul, "Nigeria: Famous Benin Bronzes Will Finally Be Returned to Country."

2. Howard W. French, *China's Second Continent*.

3. To name two prominent examples from the postcolonial world: the Chinese Communist Party has historically portrayed itself as an agent of anti-imperialism and continues to claim leadership in today's battle against Western imperialism; India's Bharatiya Janata Party has invoked decolonization to strengthen Hindu nationalism.

4. Olúfẹ́mi Táíwò, *Against Decolonisation*, 66.

5. Katrina Forrester, "Reparations, History, and the Origins of Global Justice"; Jonathan Havercroft, "The Injustices of Global Justice Scholarship."

6. Bruce Robbins, Paulo Lemos Horta, Kwame Anthony Appiah, eds., *Cosmopolitanisms*.

7. Charles Beitz, *Political Theory and International Relations*; Thomas Nagel, "The Problem of Global Justice"; Michael Blake, "Distributive Justice, State Coercion, and Autonomy"; Simon Caney, *Justice beyond Borders*.

8. Charles Beitz, "Justice and International Relations"; Forrester, "Reparations, History, and the Origins of Global Justice," 47.

9. See Jeanne Morefield on the ahistorical nature of much of global justice scholarship, especially when it comes to grappling with colonial and imperial histories. Morefield, "Challenging Liberal Belief: Edward Said and the Critical Practice of History." For similar critiques also see Inder Marwah, "Contingency, History, Agency: On *Empire, Race and Global Justice*"; Robert Nichols, "Indigenous Peoples, Settler Colonialism, and Global Justice in Anglo-America."

10. John Rawls, *The Law of Peoples: With "The Idea of Public Reason Revisited,"* 108.

11. David Miller, *National Responsibility and Global Justice*, 16.

12. Miller, *National Responsibility and Global Justice*, 241–46.

13. It is worth noting that Miller argues it would be a "hard task" to show that the "overall impact" of colonialism on the development of postcolonial societies was "negative." As such, one is left to wonder how much his view of national responsibility for wrongdoing actually demands of advantaged societies. See Miller, *National Responsibility and Global Justice*, 251.

14. Turkuler Isiksel, "Cosmopolitanism and International Economic Institutions"; James Tully, *Public Philosophy in a New Key: Imperialism and Civic Freedom*, 2:151; Duncan Bell, "Introduction," in *Public Philosophy in a New Key: Imperialism and Civic Freedom*, 2:1–21.

15. Isiksel, "Cosmopolitanism and International Economic Institutions"; Samuel Moyn, *Not Enough: Human Rights in an Unequal World*, 146–72; Anne Philips, "Global Justice: Another Modernization Theory?"

16. Krushil Watene, "Transforming Global Justice Theorizing: Indigenous Philosophies"; Margaret Kohn, "Globalizing Global Justice."

17. Inés Valdez, "Association, Reciprocity, and Emancipation: A Transnational Account of the Politics of Global Justice"; Andrew Robinson and Simon Tormey, "Resisting 'Global Justice': Disrupting the Colonial Emancipatory Logic of the West."

18. Prominent scholars who have studied and debated this relationship include: Duncan Bell, Richard Tuck, James Tully, Sankar Muthu, Jennifer Pitts, Karuna Mantena, Jeanne Morefield, Barbara Arneil, and Uday Singh Mehta. For an overview, see Jennifer Pitts, "Political Theory of Empire and Imperialism."

19. Pitts, "Political Theory of Empire and Imperialism," 218.

20. Mills, "Race and Global Justice," 111.

21. See James Tully's analysis of Isaiah Berlin on Third World anticolonialism in Tully, "'Two Concepts of Liberty' in Context."

22. This term is coined by Gabriel Wollner in "The Third Wave of Theorizing Global Justice: A Review Essay."

23. Laura Valentini, *Justice in a Globalized World*.

24. Lea Ypi, *Global Justice and Avant-Garde Political Agency*.

25. Cécile Laborde, "Republicanism and Global Justice: A Sketch"; Cécile Laborde and Miriam Ronzoni, "What Is a Free State? Republican Internationalism and Globalisation"; Miriam Ronzoni, "Republicanism and Global Institutions: Three Desiderata in Tension."

26. Sarah Fine and Lea Ypi, eds., *Migration in Political Theory: The Ethics of Movement and Membership*; Aaron James, *Fairness in Practice: A Social Contract for A Global Economy*; Megan Blomfield, *Global Justice, Natural Resources, and Climate Change*; Lisa Herzog, "Global Currencies from the Perspective of Structural Global Justice: Distribution and Domination"; Peter Dietsch, *Catching Capital: The Ethics of Tax Competition*; Iris Marion Young, "Responsibility and Global Labor Justice."

27. James, *Fairness in Practice*.

28. Mathias Risse and Gabriel Wollner, *Trade Justice: A Philosophical Plea for a New Global Deal*.

29. With the exception of recent emergence of a reparations literature that increasingly frames reparative justice as a forward-looking project in transforming global structures. See Olúfẹ́mi O. Táíwò, *Reconsidering Reparations*, and Catherine Lu, *Justice and Reconciliation in World Politics*.

30. Charles Mills, "Revisionist Ontologies: Theorising White Supremacy," 108.

31. Táíwò, *Reconsidering Reparations*, 33.

32. Vincent Wong, "Racial Capitalism with Chinese Characteristics: Analyzing the Political Economy of Racialized Dispossession and Exploitation in Xinjiang."

33. B. S. Chimni, "International Institutions Today: An Imperial Global State in the Making," 1–2.

34. Adom Getachew and Olúfẹ́mi O. Táíwò both use this term; Getachew to describe anticolonial projects in the era of decolonization, and Táíwò to describe his forward-looking view of reparations. Getachew, *Worldmaking after Empire*; Táíwò, *Reconsidering Reparations*, 20.

35. See, for example, critiques of a prominent practice-dependent theorist Aaron James's approach to theorizing fairness in trade. Mathias Risse and Gabriel Wollner, "Critical Notice of Aaron James, Fairness in Practice: A Social Contract for a Global Economy."

36. Glen Coulthard, *Red Skin, White Masks: Rejecting the Colonial Politics of Recognition*, 41, also 32.

37. Aimé Césaire, "Man of Culture and His Responsibilities," 127.

38. Charles Mills, "White Ignorance," in *Black Rights/White Wrongs: The Critique of Racial Liberalism*, chap. 4.

39. Mills, "White Ignorance"; Fanon, *The Wretched of the Earth*, most obviously in his discussion of anticolonial violence (chap. 1), but also in postcolonial state-building, 140–44.

40. Simon Caney, "Responding to Global Injustice: On the Right of Resistance"; Caney, "The Right to Resist Global Injustice."

41. Makau W. Mutua, "What is TWAIL?"; Antony Anghie, *Imperialism, Sovereignty and the Making of International Law.*

42. For critical overviews of postcolonial theory and postcolonial studies, see Amia Loomba, *Colonialism/Postcolonialism* (Oxford: Routledge, 2015); Leela Gandhi, *Postcolonial Theory: A Critical Introduction: Second Edition.* Also see Anibal Quijano, "Coloniality of Power, Eurocentrism, and Latin America," *Nepantla: Views from South* 1, no. 3 (2000): 533–80; Water D. Mignolo, *The Darker Side of Western Modernity: Global Futures, Decolonial Options*; Mignolo, "Coloniality Is Far from Over, So Must Decoloniality."

43. Edward Said, *Orientalism*; Said, *Culture & Imperialism*; most famously, see Gayatri C. Spivak, "Can the Subaltern Speak?" For a helpful modification of Spivak's view, see Lata Mani, "Cultural Theory, Colonial Texts: Reading Eyewitness Accounts of Widow Burning." Also see Rosalind Morris, ed., *Can the Subaltern Speak? Reflections on the History of an Idea.*

44. See, for example, Sven Beckert, *Empire of Cotton: A Global History*; Stephanie E. Smallwood, *Saltwater Slavery: A Middle Passage from Africa to American Diaspora*; Jodi Melamed, "Racial Capitalism"; Robert Nichols, "Theft Is Property! The Recursive Logic of Dispossession."

45. Adom Getachew, *Worldmaking after Empire*; Manu Goswami, "Imaginary Futures and Colonial Internationalisms"; Gary Wilder, *Freedom Time: Negritude, Decolonization, and the Future of the World*; Frederick Cooper, *Citizenship between Empire and Nation*; Karuna Mantena, "Popular Sovereignty and Anti-colonialism."

46. A similar approach is Valdez's *Transnational Cosmopolitanism.* While Valdez focuses on developing accounts of transnational identity and activism, this book focuses on global institutional reform as informed by anticolonial perspectives. See Inés Valdez, *Transnational Cosmopolitanism: Kant, Du Bois, and Justice as a Political Craft.* Moreover, my approach shares some affinities with an emerging group of political theorists who call their approach "grounded normative theory," which, among other things, entails a commitment to include into normative theorizing the perspectives and voices of otherwise marginalized political actors. See Brooke Ackerly et al., "Unearthing Grounded Normative Theory: Practices and Commitments of Empirical Research in Political Theory."

47. B. S. Chimni defines insurgent cosmopolitanism as "a cosmopolitanism that embraces epistemological diversity and gives a serious hearing to non-European visions of a just world order." In Chimni, "Global Capitalism and Global Democracy: Subverting the Other?" 235. Getachew calls for a "postcolonial cosmopolitanism" in *Worldmaking after Empire*, 30–36. Also see Catherine Lu, *Justice and Reconciliation in World Politics*, 277.

48. Lu, "Decolonizing Borders, Self-Determination, and Global Justice," 252..

49. Stuart Hall, *The Fateful Triangle*, 101.

50. For an extended discussion of this point, see Táíwò, *Reconsidering Reparations*, chap. 2; also see Alasia Nuti, *Injustice and the Reproduction of History*, chap. 3.

51. Gandhi, *Postcolonial Theory*, 4.

52. Gandhi, *Postcolonial Theory*, 4.

53. Gyan Prakash, "Introduction," in Prakash, ed., *After Colonialism: Imperial Histories and Postcolonial Displacement*, 5.

54. Gandhi, *Postcolonial Theory*, 7. See also Morefield, "Challenging Liberal Belief."

55. Sandra Harding, ed., *The Feminist Standpoint Theory Reader: Intellectual and Political Controversies*, especially 1–16. Also see Táíwò's critique of standpoint theory in Táíwò, "'Being-in-the-Room Privilege': Elite Capture and Epistemic Deference," 108.

56. For an insightful discussion of how politics and morality can and often are "mutually constituting," see Lucia Rafanelli, "Political Craft as Moral Innovation."

57. Rafanelli, "Political Craft as Moral Innovation."

58. Nehru, *Discovery of India*. For a recent study on Indian anticolonial debates on this exact question, see Nazmul Sultan's *Waiting for the People*.

59. Mills, "White Ignorance," in *Black Rights/White Wrongs: The Critique of Racial Liberalism*, 18.

60. I say "apparent" because it's not clear that the group has morally valid "interests" of its own that are not reducible to the interests of individual members.

61. Indeed, situations such as these would seem to show that human rights *do* have important political value, even if exclusive reliance on such rights as ways to resist global inequalities is deeply inadequate.

62. Kevin Duong, "Universal Suffrage as Decolonization," 412.

63. Duong, "Universal Suffrage as Decolonization," 418.

64. Morefield, "Challenging Liberal Belief," 188–89.

65. Sundhya Pahuja, "Corporations, Universalism, and the Domestication of Race in International Law," 92.

66. Morefield, "Challenging Liberal Belief," 189.

67. Césaire, "Man of Culture and His Responsibilities," 131.

68. See epigraph to book.

69. Khader, *Decolonizing Universalisms*, 36–49.

70. Wilder writes, "Understandable fears of totalizing explanation and Eurocentric evaluation have led a generation of scholars to insist on the singularity of black, African, and non-Western forms of thought. But we now need to be less concerned with unmasking universalisms as covert European particularisms than with challenging the assumption that the universal is European property." *Freedom Time*, 10–11.

71. Wilder, *Freedom Time*, 10–11.

72. Adom Getachew, "Universalism after the Post-Colonial Turn: Interpreting the Haitian Revolution," 823.

73. Robert Nichols, "Indigenous Peoples, Settler Colonialism, and Global Justice in Anglo-America," 241.

74. These campaigns resulted in the United Nations Declaration on the Rights of Indigenous Peoples, adopted by the UN General Assembly on September 13, 2007. See UN Department of Social and Economic Affairs. "United Nations Declaration on the Rights of Indigenous Peoples."

75. Nichols, "Indigenous Peoples, Settler Colonialism, and Global Justice in Anglo-America," 231.

76. Lu, "Decolonizing Borders, Self-Determination, and Global Justice," 251–72.

77. Lu, "Decolonizing Borders, Self-Determination, and Global Justice," 271.

78. Most obviously, see the Standing Rock campaign in the United States. See National Museum of the American Indian, "Treaties Still Matter: The Dakota Access Pipeline." On cultural revival, see Coulthard, *Red Skin, White Masks*, especially chap. 5.

79. Nichols, "Indigenous Peoples, Settler Colonialism, and Global Justice in Anglo-America," 243.

80. Jodi A. Byrd and Michael Rothberg, "Between Subalternity and Indigeneity: Critical Categories for Postcolonial Studies." For more on this debate on the distinction and similarities between settler colonial and postcolonial contexts, see the recent special issue, "New Directions in Settler Colonial Studies," in *Postcolonial Studies* 23 (2020), especially Jane Carey and Ben Silverstein, "Thinking with and beyond Settler Colonialism: New Histories after the Postcolonial."

81. See David Temin, *Remapping Sovereignty*, for an account of what he calls "decolonization as earthmaking," which draws closely on Indigenous political thought.

82. Khader uses this to denote European ethnocentrism, but it is not hard to imagine how another kind of ethnocentrism may be possible when one claims to have *the* view of justice. See Serene J. Khader, *Decolonizing Universalisms: A Transnational Feminist Ethic*, 23.

83. Tully, "'Two Concepts of Liberty' in Context," 37.

84. Michael Walzer, "The Moral Standing of States: A Response to Four Critics," 227; David Miller, *On Nationality*, 88–90; Miller, *National Responsibility and Global Justice*, 68–75.

85. Getachew, *Worldmaking after Empire*.

86. Kwame Nkrumah, *Neocolonialism: The Last Stage of Imperialism*, 253.

87. Nehru, "World Union and Collective Security," 806–9.

88. Valdez, *Transnational Cosmopolitanism*.

89. Cooper, *Colonialism in Question: Theory, Knowledge, History*, 156.

90. Michele Louro, *Comrades against Imperialism: Nehru, India and Interwar Internationalism*.

91. Getachew, *Worldmaking after Empire*, 107–41.

92. C.L.R James, "Positive Action," in *Nkrumah and the Ghana Revolution*, chap. 7.

93. Fanon, "On Violence," in *The Wretched of the Earth*.

94. Mohandas Gandhi, *Gandhi: Hind Swaraj and Other Writings*.

95. Fanon, *The Wretched of the Earth*, 236.

96. See Frank Dikötter, *The Cultural Revolution: A People's History, 1962–1976*; also see Mao Zedong, *Collected Writings of Chairman Mao: Politics and Tactics*, vol. 2.

97. André Gorz, *Strategy for Labor: A Radical Proposal*.

98. Steven Metz, "In Lieu of Orthodoxy: The Socialist Theories of Nkrumah and Nyerere," 387.

99. Elizabeth Anderson, "What's the Point of Equality?"; Anderson, "Equality."

100. For example, Anne Philips, *Unconditional Equals*.

101. Anderson, "Equality," 52. T. M. Scanlon makes the argument that equal concern, for example, is inapplicable absent something like a domestic basic structure, in *Why Does Inequality Matter?* 11–13. In his recently published magnus opus on social hierarchy and inequality, Niko Kolodny does not mention social hierarchies at the global level, beyond a brief reference to colonialism (pp. 155–56). See Kolodny, *The Pecking Order: Social Hierarchy as a Philosophical Problem*.

102. David Miller makes this point in *National Responsibility and Global Justice*, 77–78.

103. Said, *Orientalism*; Ashis Nandy, *The Intimate Enemy*.

104. On the concept of global white supremacy, see Mills, "Race and Global Justice," 94–119; on the role of empire and slavery in the rise of global white supremacy, see Marilyn Lake and Henry Reynolds, *Drawing the Global Colour Line: White Men's Countries and the International Challenge of Racial Equality*; Eric Williams, *Capitalism and Slavery*.

105. See Mark Langan for a recent recovering of neocolonialism as foreign infringement. Langan, *Neo-colonialism and the Poverty of Development in Africa*, 1–33.

Chapter 1. Foundations of a Postcolonial Global Justice: The Egalitarian Face of Decolonization

1. On the interconnectedness of anticolonial leaders and movements, see Vijay Prashad, *The Darker Nations: A People's History of the Third World*; Reiland Rabaka, *The Negritude Movement: W.E.B. Du Bois, Leon Damas, Aime Césaire, Leopold Senghor, Frantz Fanon, and the Evolution of an Insurgent Idea* (London: Lexington Books, 2015); Michael Goebel, *Anti-Imperial Metropolis: Interwar Paris and the Seeds of Third-World Nationalism* (New York: Cambridge University Press, 2015). For different classifications of anticolonial movements, see Robert Young's survey in Young, *Postcolonialism: A Historical Introduction* (Oxford: Wiley-Blackwell, 2001), 161–66.

2. By nationalism, I mean the broad idea that groups sharing an imagined ethnic, cultural, or political identity ought to form independently governed territorial units. See John Breuilly ed., *The Oxford Handbook of The History of Nationalism*, especially chap. 1; Ernest Gellner, *Nations and Nationalism*; Benedict Anderson, *Imagined Communities: Reflections on the Origin and Spread of Nationalism*.

3. Two classic accounts are Rupert Emerson, *From Empire to Nation*, and John Plamenatz, *On Alien Rule and Self-Government*. Also see Elie Kedourie, *Nationalism*; Robert H. Jackson, *Quasi-States: Sovereignty, International Relations and the Third World*. Adria Lawrence, quoting Gary Wilder, calls this "the commonsensical view" of anticolonialism. Both challenge it in their work. See Lawrence, *Imperial Rule and the Politics of Nationalism*, 3; Wilder, *The French Imperial Nation-State: Negritude and Colonial Humanism Between the Two World Wars*, 127.

4. Michael Walzer, "The Moral Standing of States: A Response to Four Critics," 227; David Miller, *On Nationality*, 88–90; Miller, *National Responsibility and Global Justice*, 68–75; Miller, "Neo-Kantian Theories of Self-Determination: A Critique," 872.

5. Emerson, *From Empire to Nation*, 43. Similarly, Plamenatz's influential analysis of anticolonial arguments takes rejection of alien rule as their primary objective. Plamenatz, *On Alien Rule and Self-Government*, 1.

6. Emerson, *From Empire to Nation*, 43.

7. See Kwame Nkrumah, "On the Motion for Independence," delivered on July 10, 1953.

8. Gary Wilder, *Freedom Time: Negritude, Decolonization, and the Future of the World*; Frederick Cooper, *Citizenship between Empire and Nation*; Karuna Mantena, "Popular Sovereignty and Anti-colonialism."

9. Getachew, *Worldmaking after Empire*; Prashad, *The Darker Nations*; Lawrence, *Imperial Rule and the Politics of Nationalism*; Manu Goswami, "Imaginary Futures and Colonial Internationalisms"; Nils Gilman, "The New International Economic Order: A Reintroduction."

10. Mantena, "Popular Sovereignty and Anti-colonialism," 298–99; Frederick Cooper, *Africa Since the 1940s*, 20.

11. For a recent survey of the five main frameworks employed in historical scholarship on decolonization, see Jan C. Jansen and Jurgen Osterhammel, *Decolonization: A Short History*, 29–31. Jansen and Osterhammel list five explanatory models prevalent in the field of history: (i) transfer of power model: decolonization as a rational and purposeful transfer of power implemented by European powers; (ii) national liberation model: decolonization as the toppling of alien rule by nativist liberation movements; (iii) the neocolonialism model: decolonization as colonial powers' voluntary renunciation of coercive colonial structures, only to replace them with indirect domination via economic exploitation; (iv) unburdening model: decolonization as a planned effort to abandon overseas territories when their military and strategic value became increasingly doubtful; (v) world politics model: decolonization as the inevitable consequence of the new balance of power between the United States and the Soviet Union.

It is interesting to note that, in models (i) and (iii)–(v), it is Western agency that primarily drives decolonization, while the model (ii) is the standard nationalist narrative that I am concerned with in this chapter.

12. Plamenatz, *On Alien Rule*, 2.

13. Jessica Chapman, *Remaking the World: Decolonization and the Cold War*; also see Leslie James and Elisabeth Leake, eds., *Decolonization and the Cold War: Negotiating Independence*; and Odd Arne Westad, *The Global Cold War*.

14. The assassination of anticolonial leader and the first prime minister of the Democratic Republic of Congo, Patrice Lumumba, sent shockwaves across postcolonial Africa. Many at the time believed what was later proven to be correct—that the United States and Belgium were heavily involved in his assassination. Lumumba's contemporaries, such as Kwame Nkrumah, grew increasingly suspicious of similar conspiracies against them. These suspicions proved to be true for Nkrumah, as he was later deposed in a CIA-sponsored coup d'état. See Ama Biney, "The Development of Kwame Nkrumah's Political Thought in Exile, 1966–1972," 84.

15. Chapman, *Remaking the World*, 40–73.

16. Corrie Decker and Elisabeth McMahon, *The Idea of Development in Africa: A History* (Cambridge University Press, 2020), 143–63.

17. Isaiah Berlin and Ian Harris, "Two Concepts of Liberty," 203.

18. Berlin and Harris, "Two Concepts of Liberty," 201.

19. Berlin and Harris, "Two Concepts of Liberty," 204.

20. Nigel C. Gibson, "Fanon and Marx Revisited"; William W. Hansen, "Another Side of Frantz Fanon: Reflections on Socialism and Democracy."

21. Césaire was a member of the French Communist Party until he resigned in 1956; Nkrumah was influenced by Lenin's treatise on imperialism and Marxism more broadly; Nehru was a self-declared socialist. See Césaire, "Letter to Maurice Thorez"; Jeffrey S. Ahlman, *Living with Nkrumahism: Nation, State, and Pan-Africanism in Ghana*, 37–39; Bal Ram Nanda, *Jawaharlal Nehru: Rebel and Statesman*, 185–94. Also see Westad's classic historical study of anticolonial movements during the Cold War, in which he argues that there were at least "two main ideological directions of the anticolonial resistance—Communism and nativism." Westad, *The Global Cold War*, 80–81.

22. Lea Ypi makes a similar argument regarding colonial injustice as unequal terms of political association. Unlike Ypi, however, nothing in my view implies that colonized populations lacked claims to particular territory. See Ypi, "What's Wrong with Colonialism."

23. Nkrumah, *Africa Must Unite*, 2–11; Nehru, *The Discovery of India*, 318–20; Fanon, *The Wretched of the Earth*, 3–8; Césaire, *Discourse On Colonialism*, 42–43. Partha Chatterjee refers to this as "the rule of colonial difference." See Chatterjee, *The Nation and its Fragments: Colonial and Postcolonial Histories*, 18.

24. Nkrumah, *Africa Must Unite*, 11.

25. Nkrumah, *Africa Must Unite*, 11.

26. For a classic account of the long-term impact of this colonial strategy, see Mahmood Mamdani, *Citizen and Subject: Contemporary Africa and the Legacy of Late Colonialism.*

27. Nehru, *The Discovery of India*, 334–35.

28. Nehru, *The Discovery of India*, 334–35.

29. Nehru, *The Discovery of India*, 334–35.

30. Césaire, *Discourse On Colonialism*, 43–44; Nkrumah, *Africa Must Unite*, 22–31.

31. Nehru, *The Discovery of India*, 330–33.

32. Nehru, *The Discovery of India*, 330.

33. Nehru, *The Discovery of India*, 330.

34. Nehru, *The Discovery of India*, 330.

35. Nehru, *The Discovery of India*, 331.

36. Unlike Gandhi, who defended village economies as a superior alternative to industrialization. See Gandhi, *Hind Swaraj*, especially 109–10.

37. Nehru, *The Discovery of India*, 446.

38. Nehru, *The Discovery of India*, 330–31. Also see Fanon's famous depiction of the "two worlds" within French Algeria, which illustrates the stark economic inequality between the colonizer's sector and the people's "slums." Fanon, *The Wretched of the Earth*, 114.

39. Césaire, *Discourse on Colonialism*, 42.

40. Césaire, *Discourse on Colonialism*, 44.

41. Césaire, *Discourse on Colonialism*, 44.

42. Césaire, *Discourse on Colonialism*, 44.

43. Nehru, *The Discovery of India*, 444. Nkrumah, *Africa Must Unite*, 26–27. For an extended analysis of colonial underdevelopment, see Walter Rodney, *How Europe Underdeveloped Africa.*

44. Nehru, *The Discovery of India*, 444.

45. Nehru, *The Discovery of India*, 332.

46. Nehru, *The Discovery of India*, 329.

47. Nkrumah, *Africa Must Unite*, 26–27.

48. Nkrumah, *Neocolonialism*.

49. Nkrumah, *Neocolonialism*, 239.

50. Nehru, *The Discovery of India*, 356.

51. Nehru, *The Discovery of India*, 356.

52. Nkrumah, *Africa Must Unite*, 1. Similarly, Fanon argues that "it is clear that what divides this world is first and foremost what species, what race one belongs to. In the colonies the economic infrastructure is also a superstructure. The cause is effect: You are rich because you are white, and you are white because you are rich." Fanon, *The Wretched*, 5.

53. Nkrumah, *Africa Must Unite*, xii.

54. Nkrumah, *Africa Must Unite*, xii.

55. Nkrumah, *Africa Must Unite*, 1.

56. Nkrumah, *Africa Must Unite*, 1.

57. Césaire, *Discourse on Colonialism*, 43.

58. Getachew and Mantena, "Anticolonialism and the Decolonization of Political Theory," 373.

59. Césaire, "Man of Culture and His Responsibilities," 127.

60. Nehru, *The Discovery of India*, 146. See also Sunil Khilnani, "Introduction," xxi.

61. Nehru, *The Discovery of India*, 69.

62. Nehru, *The Discovery of India*, 55.

63. Nehru, *The Discovery of India*, 629.

64. Nehru, *The Discovery of India*, 157.

65. Nehru, *The Discovery of India*, 262.

66. Nehru, *The Discovery of India*, 328–29.

67. Nehru, *The Discovery of India*, 328–29.

68. Nehru, *The Discovery of India*, 328–29.

69. Nehru, *The Discovery of India*, 328–29.

70. Manjeet Ramgotra, "India's Republican Moment," 196.

71. Césaire, *Discourse on Colonialism*, 33.

72. On Césaire's conception of culture, see "Culture and Colonisation," 194–96. I call this a democratic conception of culture and discuss it in more detail in chapter 4.

73. Césaire, *Discourse on Colonialism*, 33.

74. Césaire, *Discourse on Colonialism*, 42.

75. Césaire, *Discourse on Colonialism*, 42.

76. Césaire, "Culture and Colonisation," 195.

77. Fanon's essay on the radio in French Algeria provides an important analysis of how the colonial settler's status as a culturally distinct and superior alien requires deliberate maintenance. He writes, "On the farms, the radio reminds the settler of the reality of colonial power and, by its very existence, dispenses safety, serenity . . . The Paris music, extracts from the metropolitan press, the French government crises, constitute a coherent background from which colonial society draws its density and its justification. Radio-Alger sustains the occupant's culture, marks it off from the non-culture, from the nature of the occupied. Radio-Alger, the voice of France in Algeria, constitutes the sole center of reference at the level of news. Radio-Alger, for the settler, is a daily invitation not to 'go native,' not to forget the rightfulness of his culture." Fanon, "This is the Voice of Algeria," in *A Dying Colonialism*, 71.

78. Fanon, "The Algerian Family," in *A Dying Colonialism*, 119.

79. Fanon, "The Algerian Family," in *A Dying Colonialism*, 119.

80. Fanon, *The Wretched of the Earth*, 83.

81. Fanon, *The Wretched of the Earth*, 83–84.

82. As Fanon argues, in the first stage of the anticolonial struggle the colonizers try to "defuse" the people's demands by promising reform, but ultimately both parties come to realize that colonialism is inherently "incapable of achieving a program of socio-economic reforms that would satisfy the aspirations of the colonized masses." Fanon, *The Wretched of the Earth*, 146.

83. Nehru, *The Discovery of India*, 417.

84. Nehru, *The Discovery of India*, 417.

85. Nehru, *The Discovery of India*, 417..

86. Nehru, *The Discovery of India*, 417.

87. Nehru, *The Discovery of India*, 439–41. Also see 581–82.

88. Nehru, *The Discovery of India*, 441.

89. Nehru, *The Discovery of India*, 435–36.

90. Nehru, *The Discovery of India*, 436.

91. Quoted in Wilder, *Freedom Time*, 110.

92. Quoted in Wilder, *Freedom Time*, 124–25.

93. Quoted in Wilder, *Freedom Time*, 124.

94. Nkrumah, *Africa Must Unite*, 51.

95. Fanon, *The Wretched of the Earth*, 42.

96. Nkrumah, *I Speak of Freedom*, 82.

97. Quoted in Ahlman, *Living with Nkrumahism*, 29.

98. Fanon, *The Wretched of the Earth*, 93.

99. Fanon, *The Wretched of the Earth*, 93.

100. Fanon, *The Wretched of the Earth*, 144.

101. Nehru, *The Discovery of India*, 334–35; Fanon, *The Wretched of the Earth*, 93–95; 152.

102. Fanon, *The Wretched of the Earth*, 113–14.

103. Fanon, *The Wretched of the Earth*, 100.

104. Nehru, "Social Fabric of a Nation," in *Essential Writings of Jawaharlal Nehru*, 2:5–7. See Wilder on Césaire's support for departmentalization as a way of attaining economic redistribution from France, in *Freedom Time*.

105. Nehru, *The Discovery of India*, 566.

106. Nkrumah, *Neocolonialism: The Last Stage of Imperialism*, 11. Getachew, *Worldmaking after Empire*, 107–41.

107. Nehru, "World Union and Collective Security," 809; Nehru, *The Discovery of India*, 583.

108. Fanon, *The Wretched of the Earth*, 2.

109. This vision of decolonization as egalitarian transformation extended to gender relations. Many anticolonial thinkers were strong advocates for gender equality and the emancipation of women. They argued that the equal and active political participation of women, both in the anticolonial struggle and in a just postcolonial society, was essential. Fanon, "Algeria Unveiled," in *A Dying Colonialism*, 35–68; Nehru, "The Role of Women," in *Essential Writings of Jawaharlal Nehru*, 2:21–23; Nkrumah, *I Speak of Freedom*, 7.

110. Nehru, *The Discovery of India*, 580.

111. As Kevin Duong argues, postcolonial states' pursuit of democratic reforms became the most significant episode of democratization in world history (though, for Duong, the revolutionary potential of democracy was blunted by its individualized form). Duong, "Universal Suffrage as Decolonization."

112. Nkrumah, *Africa Must Unite*, 11.

113. Nkrumah, *Africa Must Unite*, 11.

114. Nkrumah, *I Speak of Freedom*, 76.

115. Nkrumah, *I Speak of Freedom*, 273. Elsewhere, Nkrumah states, "We welcome men of goodwill everywhere to join us, irrespective of their race, religion or nationality. When I speak of Africa for Africans this should be interpreted in the light of my emphatic declaration, that I do not believe in racialism and colonialism. The concept 'Africa for Africans' does not mean that other races are excluded from it. No. It only means that Africans, who naturally are in the majority in Africa, shall and must govern themselves in their own countries. The fight is for the future of humanity, and that is the most important fight." Nkrumah, *I Speak of Freedom*, 220.

116. Nehru, "World Union and Collective Security," 805–9; Nehru, "A World Federation," *Essential Writings of Jawaharlal Nehru*, 2:216–17. For a historical account of how Nehru's idea of "One World," advocated through the diplomacy and leadership of Nehru's sister "Madame" Vijaya Lakshmi Pandit, played an important role in the formation of the United Nations, see Manu Bhagavan, *India and the Quest for One World*.

117. Nehru, "A Real Commonwealth," in *Essential Writings of Jawaharlal Nehru*, 2:218. Nkrumah makes a similar point in *I Speak of Freedom*, x.

118. Nehru, *The Discovery of India*, 465.

119. Nkrumah, *Africa Must Unite*, 103. Later, he also states, "An essential element in our industrial development must be the building up of our store of technical and managerial knowledge. We are encouraging foreign investment, but to accept it merely for the purpose of widening our industrial base without strengthening our own skills and techniques will leave us as economically impoverished as we were under colonialism. Unless our nationals are given the opportunity of learning the job on the spot, side by side with foreign 'experts,' we shall be as ignorantly backward as ever." *Africa Must Unite*, 111.

120. Nkrumah, *Africa Must Unite*, 112.

121. Fanon, *The Wretched of the Earth*, 58–60.

122. Fanon, *The Wretched of the Earth*, 53.

123. Fanon, *The Wretched of the Earth*, 58.

124. Fanon, *The Wretched of the Earth*, 59.

125. Fanon, *The Wretched of the Earth*, 59.

126. Nkrumah, *Neocolonialism*, xix–xx.

127. Nkrumah, *Neocolonialism*, 9.

128. Nkrumah, *Neocolonialism*, 253.

129. Fanon, *The Wretched of the Earth*, 55.

130. Fanon, *The Wretched of the Earth*, 56. Nkrumah, "African Socialism Revisited," reprinted in Nkruma, *Revolutionary Path*. Also see Priya Lal's analysis of Julius Nyerere's form of African socialism, based on the ujamaa, in Lal, *African Socialism in Postcolonial Tanzania: Between the Village and the World*. For a survey of African socialism, see Kelly Askew, "African Socialism." For a comparative survey of postcolonial socialist land reform, see D. A. Low, *The Egalitarian Moment: Asia and Africa, 1950–1980*.

131. Fanon, *The Wretched of the Earth*, 135.

132. Léopold Sédar Senghor, *On African Socialism*, 45–46.

133. Fanon on popular control of the tertiary sectors, see *The Wretched of the Earth*, 123–24; Senghor, *On African Socialism*, 46.

134. This, arguably, is what ended up happening in the latter half of the twentieth century. I take up the question of decolonizing the global economy in chapter 3. See Quinn Slobodian for a historical account of the neoliberal response to decolonization and how it has shaped international trade and investment today. Slobodian, *Globalists: The End of Empire and the Birth of Neoliberalism*.

135. Mark Mazower, *Governing the World: The History of an Idea*. I take up the question of decolonizing global governance in chapter 5.

136. Fanon uses the phrase "history-making" to describe the process of decolonization. *The Wretched of the Earth*, 2.

137. Césaire, "Man of Culture and His Responsibilities," 24–25, 127.

138. Césaire, "Man of Culture and His Responsibilities," 24–25, 127.

139. Césaire, "Man of Culture and His Responsibilities," 24–25, 127.

140. Césaire, "Man of Culture and His Responsibilities," 24–25, 127.

141. Césaire, "Man of Culture and His Responsibilities," 127.

142. Césaire, *Discourse on Colonialism*, 45.

143. Césaire, "Culture and Colonisation," 206.

144. Césaire, "Culture and Colonisation," 206–7.

145. Nkrumah, *Neocolonialism*, 255–59; Nehru, *The Discovery of India*, 602; Nehru, "The Root Causes of Wars"; Césaire, *Discourse On Colonialism*, 74–78.

146. Nehru, *The Discovery of India*, 583.

147. Nehru, *The Discovery of India*, 463.

148. Nehru, *The Discovery of India*, 583.

149. Nehru, "World Union and Collective Security," 809.

150. Priya Chacko calls this a "post-sovereign internationalist ethic." Chacko, "The Internationalist Nationalist: Pursuing an ethical modernity with Jawaharlal Nehru," 195.

151. Nehru, *The Discovery of India*, 631.

152. Fanon, *The Wretched of the Earth*, 316.

153. Fanon, *The Wretched of the Earth*, 314.

154. Fanon, *The Wretched of the Earth*, 314.

155. Fanon, *The Wretched of the Earth*, 314.

156. Fanon, *The Wretched of the Earth*, 315.

Chapter 2. Postcolonial Global Justice as Social Equality

1. With a few exceptions, contemporary social egalitarians have not theorized social equality at the global level. For notable exceptions, see Kevin Ip, *Egalitarianism and Global Justice*; Rekha Nath, "Equal Standing in the Global Community"; Désirée Lim uses a social equality framework to discuss the politics of immigration in Lim, *Immigration and Social Equality: The Ethics of Skill-Selective Immigration Policy*. See especially her helpful discussion of a "universal entitlement to social equality" in chapter 2.

2. Samuel Scheffler, "The Practice of Equality"; Elizabeth Anderson, "What Is the Point of Equality?"; Jonathan Wolff, "Social Equality and Social Inequality"; Carina Fourie, "What Is Social Equality?"

3. One might object that it is possible to re-construe relational equality in distributive terms, by saying that we need equal distributions of status, authority, recognition, respect, and so on. Sam Scheffler responds to this objection compellingly, in my view, by pointing out that a relational view of equality is fundamentally concerned about the nature of interactions between equals, which *is* affected by distributions of status, authority, etc., but not reducible to them. The practice of mutual justifiability, which I mention in the next section, for example, is a practice between moral equals and yet is not something that can be "distributed." See Scheffler, "The Practice of Equality," 23.

4. Fanon, *The Wretched of the Earth*, 3.

5. Fanon, *The Wretched of the Earth*, 4.

6. Fanon, *The Wretched of the Earth*, 4.

7. Fanon, *The Wretched of the Earth*, 4.

8. Fanon, *The Wretched of the Earth*, 14.

9. Thus, as Fanon says, the colonialist *fabricates* the colonized.

10. Fanon, *The Wretched of the Earth*, 2–3.

11. Fanon, *The Wretched of the Earth*, 2.

12. Fanon, *The Wretched of the Earth*, 238. Fanon, *Black Skin, White Masks*, final chapter.

13. In fact, Michael Blake makes a similar argument without using the language of distributive and relational equality, in Blake, "Coercion and Egalitarian Justice." I agree with Blake that the focus should be on eliminating objectionable kinds of relations, but I disagree with Blake that this means global and domestic justice are different. In my view, social equality is also an ideal for domestic social justice. Furthermore, I disagree with Blake that the point of reforming global

relations is only so that people can be self-determining within their own states, because, in my view, more than one kind of hierarchy exists globally (i.e., not just political coercion, but also exploitation and status hierarchy).

14. Laura Valentini, *Justice in a Globalized World: A Normative Framework.*

15. Cécile Laborde and Miriam Ronzoni, "What Is a Free State? Republican Internationalism and Globalisation."

16. See the introduction for a discussion of what a postcolonial perspective entails.

17. Niall Ferguson, *Empire: How Britain Made the Modern World.*

18. Walter Rodney, *How Europe Underdeveloped Africa*; Nehru, *The Discovery of India*, esp. 450–55; Nkrumah, *Africa Must Unite*, 26–31.

19. I say "essential economic development" because it is questionable how much of the development that European colonialism imposed on the colonies was actually essential for the welfare of its subjects as *they themselves* understand it. Opium production, for example, is obviously nonessential. But other things like railways and industrial factories may also not have been essential, if we take up a Gandhian perspective on well-being. See Gandhi, *Hind Swaraj.*

20. To be sure, one might object that, under non-ideal circumstances where political opposition to egalitarian development is strong, a society still ought to prioritize antipoverty measures over egalitarian development. This objection, however, cannot be made by the imperialists themselves insofar as they constitute (part of) the opposition. Moreover, even if an economic model compatible with relational equality is not possible at a certain historical juncture, those subjected to relational inequality retain a complaint, which at the minimum would demand that the possibility for a different kind of economic development is regularly revisited in a process that included them. Finally, the complaint may ground further compensatory claims down the line. I thank Jim Wilson for pressing me to clarify this point.

21. Fanon, *The Wretched of the Earth*, 56.

22. Fanon, *The Wretched of the Earth*, 237.

23. Relational and social equality are often used interchangeably in the contemporary philosophical literature. In the rest of the book, I use "social equality" to refer to the robust ideal of global justice that I defend.

24. Fanon, "Medicine and Colonialism," in *A Dying Colonialism*, 121.

25. Fanon, "Medicine and Colonialism," in *A Dying Colonialism*, 126.

26. Fanon, "Medicine and Colonialism," in *A Dying Colonialism*, 123.

27. Fanon, "Medicine and Colonialism," in *A Dying Colonialism*, 121.

28. Fanon, "Medicine and Colonialism," in *A Dying Colonialism*, 122.

29. Fanon, "Medicine and Colonialism," in *A Dying Colonialism*, 125–26.

30. Though not in the exact same ways, social egalitarians have characterized social equality in similar terms. See Elizabeth Anderson, "Equality"; Wilson, *Democratic Equality*; Scheffler, "The Practice of Equality"; Fourie, "What Is Social Equality."

31. Stephen Darwall, "Two Kinds of Respect."

32. Scanlon calls this "mutual justifiability"—that is, our moral obligation to regulate our actions by principles that would not be reasonably rejected by other individuals who similarly accept such an obligation. Scanlon, *What We Owe to Each Other*. Other social/relational egalitarians defend a similar obligation: see Anderson, and Scheffler (although Scheffler's "egalitarian deliberative constraint" is not exactly the same—he says that treating someone as an equal requires that their comparatively weighty interests are similarly weighty in my deliberation. This seems like one specific way in which mutual justifiability is fulfilled. Scheffler's formulation is more or less the principle of equal standing that I defend in the third section, "Global Hierarchies and Global Social Equality.")

33. Some thinkers define solidarity much more narrowly. For Iris Marion Young, solidarity is a "sense of commitment and justice owed to people" that is not based on "fellow feeling" but rather on "being affected by and relating to the [social structure]" in which agents live, and the

consequences of that structure. I do not deny that solidarity can be shared among agents without "fellow feeling." Iris M. Young, *Inclusion and Democracy*.

34. This is perhaps one reason why intimate or personal relations may not always require equal distribution of the kinds of goods that may be necessary for socially egalitarian relations with other people. Individuals can point to their deep and intimate knowledge of how a friend or partner is disposed to behave and interact with them, as evidence for their reasonable confidence. Such "data," so to speak, is generally not available beyond these kinds of relationships.

35. Because of this requirement of robustness, social egalitarian relations are not compatible with utilitarian political morality. As James Wilson argues, we should differentiate between "merely basic" egalitarianism and "substantive" egalitarianism. While the former recognizes the equality of persons in some sense, substantial inequalities are compatible with "merely basic" egalitarianism. Under merely basic egalitarianism, of which utilitarianism is a kind, individuals cannot experience robust social equality, since the conditions required to maintain social equality are always at risk of erosion. On the other hand, "substantive egalitarianism" sees equality as "[manifesting] ... regularly and visibly ... the ideal of equal status is not merely derivative ... but actually generates the content of the requirements of equality, through its connection to the ideal of relationships among equals." Wilson, *Democratic Equality*, 30–31.

36. Waheed Hussain, "Pitting People against Each Other."

37. Thomas W. Simpson, "Freedom and Trust: A Rejoinder to Lovett and Pettit"; Kolodny, "Being under the Power of Others."

38. See Fanon, *The Wretched of the Earth*; Césaire, *Discourse on Colonialism*; W.E. B. Du Bois, *The Souls of Black Folk*, esp. chap. 1.

39. Fanon, *The Wretched of the Earth*; Césaire, *Discourse on Colonialism*.

40. Fanon, *A Dying Colonialism*,1; 23.

41. Elizabeth Anderson, "Equality."

42. This language of "social positions" is borrowed from Iris Young, *Inclusion and Democracy*, chap. 5.

43. This tripartite model of social hierarchies is drawn from Elizabeth Anderson, "Equality."

44. Lukes calls these the three faces of power: decision-making power, non-decision-making power, and ideological power. Steven Lukes, *Power: A Radical View*.

45. Niko Kolodny, *The Pecking Order*, 97–100; 125–26.

46. Jennifer E. Sessions, *By Sword and Plow: France and the Conquest of Algeria*, 320–21.

47. Darwall, "Two Kinds of Respect."

48. Fanon, *The Wretched of the Earth*, 7.

49. Fanon, *The Wretched of the Earth*, 7.

50. Fanon, *The Wretched of the Earth*, 7–8.

51. Scanlon, *Why Does Inequality Matter?* 11–26.

52. Wilson, *Democratic Equality*, 19.

53. With an exception being Rekha Nath, who argues that social equality also applies transnationally. See Nath, "On the Scope and Grounds of Social Equality."

54. Anderson, "What's the Point of Equality?" 316.

55. Kolodny, *The Pecking Order*.

56. Laborde and Ronzoni, "What Is a Free State? Republican Internationalism and Globalisation."

57. David Miller, *National Responsibility and Global Justice*, 77–78.

58. I do not mean to suggest this problem is unique to thinking about social equality at the global level. Within the domestic context, one can also question the relationship between measures that empower, say, women as a gender grouping, and social equality for *individuals* who may or may not identify as women. But the individual-collective question is certainly more acute at the global level, if only because of the scale involved. For a classic discussion on the

individual-group question, see Iris M. Young, "Gender as Seriality: Thinking about Women as a Social Collective," and Alcoff, *Visible Identities: Race, Gender, and the Self.*

59. Alcoff, *Visible Identities.*

60. IMF, "IMF Members' Quotas and Voting Power."

61. Shefali Sharma, "WTO Decision-Making: A Broken Process."

62. Consider, for example, Taiwan's reliance on the United States for protection against China.

63. Competition for foreign investment among developing countries, for example, has driven countries to sign bilateral investment treaties. See Zachary Elkins, Andrew Guzman, and Beth Simmons, "Competing for Capital: The Diffusion of Bilateral Investment Treaties, 1960–2000."

64. A 2017 UNCTAD report stated that nine more developing economies became dependent on commodity exports between 2010 and 2015. Around two-thirds of all 135 developing countries are commodity dependent. A country is commodity dependent when its commodity exports account for more than 60 percent of its total merchandise exports in value terms. See UNCTAD, "Commodity Dependence Worsens for Developing Countries."

65. UNDP, "Towards Human Resilience: Sustaining MDG Progress in an Age of Economic Uncertainty," chap. 2.

66. Kolodny, *The Pecking Order.*

67. As in the case of Israel's annexation of the West Bank, supported by the United States.

68. James Petras and Henry Veltmeyer, *Multinationals on Trial: Foreign Investment Matters,* 118–19.

69. Philip Pettit, *Republicanism: A Theory of Freedom and Government.*

70. I don't mean to suggest that these are the only interests that these agents have. But it seems reasonable to say that these are primary interests that guide their actions.

71. One example of a transnational corporation doing so is Wal-Mart paying bribes to government officials in Mexico and China. See Debter, "Wal-Mart Will Cough Up $282 Million to Put Years-Long Bribery Investigation Behind It."

72. Fanon, *The Wretched of the Earth,* 100–1.

73. See Anuja Bose on Fanon's account of Third World solidarity, for example. Bose, "Frantz Fanon and the Politicization and the Third World as Collective Subject."

74. Fanon, *The Wretched of the Earth,* 112–13.

75. For example, the Universal Negro Improvement Association and African Communities League, founded by Marcus Garvey, was an attempt to build for the global African diaspora an alternative platform for legal and political representation. See Desmond Jagmohan, "Between Race and Nation: Marcus Garvey and the Politics of Self-Determination."

To be clear, my point is not that empowering these groups adequately makes up for the shortfall in global equal authority. So long as units that have power to coerce do not secure individuals' equal authority, there remains an important shortfall from realizing global equal authority.

76. In other words, what Du Bois famously coined the global color line.

77. For a classic account of the structure of contemporary racism (in the US context), see Eduardo Bonilla-Silva, *Racism without Racists: Color-Blind Racism and the Persistence of Racial Inequality in the US.*

78. There is a huge critical race literature on each of these areas. For an important volume on the topic of racism in the study and practice of international relations, see Alexander Anievas, Nivi Manchanda, and Robbie Shilliam, eds., *Race and Racism in International Relations: Confronting the Global Colour Line.* For an account of racism in the field of international development, see Kalpana Wilson, *Race and Racism in International Development: Interrogating History, Discourse, and Practice.*

79. For example, Tarak Barkawi and Keith Stanski argue that the public discourse surrounding the "War on Terror" relies on orientalist understandings of the world. The "East" continues to be represented as the threatening and inferior other that is juxtaposed against the "West." Barkawi and Stanski, eds., *Orientalism and War*, 2–16.

80. Think about the stereotypes surrounding the working class, individuals without homes, and individuals who receive social welfare.

81. Scanlon, *Why Does Inequality Matter?* 29, 31.

82. Charles Beitz, "Does Global Inequality Matter?" 105.

83. Rawls, *A Theory of Justice*, 388 and 470.

84. Consider the historical role that jeans (especially Levi's 501s) played in the "cultural Cold War" between the United States and the USSR.

85. Maybe members of society B shouldn't be so vulnerable to advertising. But this reply misses the point. If status inequality between jeans-owning members and jeans-lacking members of society A is objectionable, why is it not objectionable now between members of A and B?

86. Nils Gilman, *Mandarins of the Future: Modernization Theory in Cold War America*.

87. Gilman, *Mandarins of the Future*, 6.

88. Rupert Emerson, *Political Modernization: The Single-Party System*, 4–5.

89. There is much written on this topic within postcolonial studies. For a classic statement of this critique, see Arturo Escobar, *Encountering Development: The Making and Unmaking of the Third World*.

90. Scanlon, *Why Does Inequality Matter?* 28.

91. People who are denied epistemic equality experience epistemic injustice. See Miranda Fricker, *Epistemic Injustice: Power and the Ethics of Knowing*.

92. Emma Crewe and Elizabeth Harrison, *Whose Development? An Ethnography of Aid*, 76.

93. Crewe and Harrison, *Whose Development?* 82–83.

94. Crewe and Harrison, *Whose Development?* 76.

95. Fanon, *The Wretched of the Earth*; Fanon, *Black Skin, White Masks*; Césaire, "Culture and Colonisation"; Nehru, *The Discovery of India*; Nehru, *Glimpses of World History*.

96. Two prominent examples being Karl Marx and Friedrich Engels, *The Communist Manifesto* (London: Penguin Books, 2002); and G.W.F. Hegel, *Lectures on the Philosophy of World History* (Cambridge: Cambridge University Press, 1975).

97. This idea is further discussed in chapter 4 and draws from Césaire, "Culture and Colonisation."

98. I do not mean that the value of these activities only comes from being a form of problem solving. Some of these activities are valuable in themselves; some of them are instrumentally valuable in ways I haven't listed. I mean that, whatever other function and sources of value they might have, they are also forms of problem solving, and they are valuable because they improve human life in some way.

99. Obviously individuals can leave terrible marks on history, too. That alone does not exclude them from the status of a social agent. Social agency is not an all-things-considered judgment about an individual; rather, it's a capacity that everyone has, even if some choose to exercise it more than others.

100. Césaire ends his essay on "Culture and Colonisation" with the demand, "Let the black peoples take their place upon the great stage of history!" (207) This also suggests at least one wrong in appropriating value generated by others, as in cultural appropriation. If a members of a marginalized group produced x, which is valuable, but members of a dominant group take credit for x, this reinforces a status hierarchy in which the former is seen as lacking social agency.

101. Thus recognition as social agents is distinct from the kind of "asymmetrical and nonreciprocal" recognition that has (rightly, in my view) come under criticism from Indigenous political thinkers. While the latter form of "recognition" consists of the settler state and society imposing

a uniform legal status of citizen onto Indigenous peoples, thus furthering their forced assimilation, the former kind of recognition demands, at a minimum, that agents have access to the conditions that enable their free exercise of social agency. For example, to recognize Indigenous peoples as social agents would plausibly require respecting rights over land that have historically been essential to their exercise of social agency. For a critique of the colonial politics of recognition, see Glen Coulthard, *Red Skin, White Masks: Rejecting the Colonial Politics of Recognition*.

102. Scanlon, *Why Does Inequality Matter?* 11–13.

103. Although Scanlon refrains from giving a full account of the kind(s) of collective agent/institution that might bear a duty of equal concern, he does suggest this way of grounding the duty near the end of the discussion: "But what agents have such an obligation [of equal concern], and to whom? I do not have a general answer to this question. . . . This argument by appeal to examples can be given some support by a sketch of why governments should be under such a requirement. If the powers that governments exercise, to make and enforce laws, and to require citizens to pay taxes, rest on the benefits that they provide for their citizens, these must be benefits for *all* of their citizens (all who are required to obey the law and to pay taxes). Otherwise the others would have no reason to accept this justification for these powers" (22).

104. Julius, "Nagel's Atlas."

105. Oxfam estimated in 2003 that Mexico's corn prices had fallen by 70 percent since NAFTA was enacted. Since then, the United States has continued to insist on making agricultural goods an exemption to antidumping rules at the WTO. See Oxfam Policy & Practice, "Dumping without borders: How US Agricultural Policies Are Destroying the Livelihoods of Mexican Corn Famers."

106. A notorious example of this is a WTO lawsuit in 1999: at the height of the AIDS epidemic, forty-one US drug companies sued South Africa for a law that would enable local drug companies to produce affordable generic versions of patented drugs (at 50 percent to 90 percent of the initial cost of $10,000 per patient) to treat HIV positive patients. The lawsuit was eventually suspended in face of the huge public controversy that it generated (*The Observer*, "How Drug Giants Let Millions Die of Aids").

107. A lottery, for example, at least recognizes that no participant is more entitled than the others to have their basic interests secured. Scheffler suggests a range of alternative procedures in the context of interpersonal relations. See Scheffler, "The Practice of Equality," 25–26.

108. Fanon, *The Wretched of the Earth*, 11.

109. Fanon, *The Wretched of the Earth*, 11–12.

110. See his discussion of women's equality in his essay on the "Algerian family," for example. See Fanon, "Algeria Unveiled," in *A Dying Colonialism*, chap. 1.

Chapter 3. Decolonizing the Global Economy: Nkrumah, International Investment, and the Problem of Neocolonialism

1. Paulo Prada, "Bolivia Nationalizes the Oil and Gas Sector." This involved levying a new tax, requiring foreign energy companies to renegotiate contracts, and state repurchasing of majority shares in previously privatized companies.

2. Ricardo M. Simarro and María José Paz Antolín, "Development Strategy of the MAS in Bolivia: Characterization and an Early Assessment."

3. See Investment Dispute Settlement Navigator, "AEI v. Bolivia," and Investment Dispute Settlement Navigator, "Pan American v. Bolivia."

4. In the case of AEI, $121 million, and in the case of Pan American Energy, $357 million.

5. South African Government, "Broad-Based Black Economic Empowerment Act."

6. Turkuler Isiksel, "The Rights of Man and the Rights of the Man-made: Corporations and Human Rights," *Human Rights Quarterly* 38, no. 2 (2016): 294–349.

7. Isiksel, "The Rights of Man and the Rights of the Man-made."

8. Kwame Nkrumah, *Neocolonialism: The Last Stage of Imperialism*, 239.

9. Quinn Slobodian, *Globalists*, 141.

10. Nkrumah, *Neocolonialism*, x.

11. UN General Assembly, "Permanent Sovereignty over Natural Resources General Assembly Resolution 1803 (XVII)."

12. Mohammed Bedjaoui, *Towards a New International Economic Order*; Nils Gilman, "The New International Economic Order: A Reintroduction," *Humanity* 6.1 (2015): 1–16. See entire special issue for more on the NIEO. Also see Getachew, *Worldmaking after Empire*, chap. 5.

13. Burns H. Weston, "The Charter of Economic Rights and Duties of States and the Deprivation of Foreign Owned Wealth."

14. Slobodian calls this the "bilateral fix." Slobodian, *Globalists*, 143.

15. Getachew, *Worldmaking after Empire*, 180.

16. See Mark Langan for a recent recovering of neocolonialism as foreign infringement. Langan, *Neo-colonialism and the Poverty of "Development" in Africa*, 1–33.

17. Nkrumah, *Neocolonialism*, 47.

18. Nkrumah, *Africa Must Unite*, 118–31.

19. See James Mahoney and Diana Rodríguez-Franco, "Dependency Theory." Some classic works in dependency theory include: Fernando Henrique Cardoso and Enzo Faletto, *Dependency and Development in Latin America*; Theotonio dos Santos, "The Structure of Dependence"; Samir Amin, "Underdevelopment and Dependence in Black Africa: Origins and Contemporary Forms"; Andre Gunder Frank, *Capitalism and Underdevelopment in Latin America: Historical Studies of Chile and Brazil*; Peter Evans, *Dependent Development*.

20. See Robert A. Packenham for an overview of these criticisms. Packenham, *The Dependency Movement: Scholarship and Politics in Development*. To be sure, not all these criticisms are fair—indeed, some reassessments of dependency theory point out it was never meant to be a set of empirical hypotheses to be tested directly but rather a theoretical framework meant to act as a corrective to the discourse of modernization theory prevalent in developmental economics at the time. See Mahoney and Rodriguez-Franco, "Dependency Theory," 24–25; Peter Evans, "Review: After Dependency: Recent Studies of Class, State, and Industrialization"; Paul James, "Postdependency? The Third World in an Era of Globalism and Late-Capitalism."

21. Langan, *Neo-colonialism and the Poverty of "Development" in Africa*, 15.

22. Nkrumah, *Africa Must Unite*.

23. See Organization of African Unity, "OAU Charter."

24. Nkrumah, *Neocolonialism*.

25. Nkrumah, *Neocolonialism*, ix–x.

26. Nkrumah, *Neocolonialism*, ix–x.

27. Nkrumah, *Africa Must Unite*, xiii.

28. Nkrumah, *Africa Must Unite*, xiv.

29. Nkrumah, *Neocolonialism*, 33.

30. Nkrumah, *Neocolonialism*, x.

31. Nkrumah, *Neocolonialism*, 22.

32. Nkrumah, *Neocolonialism*, x.

33. Nkrumah, *Neocolonialism*, 26.

34. Nkrumah, *Neocolonialism*, 35.

35. Nkrumah, *Neocolonialism*, 30.

36. Nkrumah, *Neocolonialism*, 256–57.

37. Nkrumah, *Neocolonialism*, xv.

38. Nkrumah, *Neocolonialism*.

39. Nkrumah, *Neocolonialism*, 86.

40. Nkrumah, *Neocolonialism*, 109.

41. Nkrumah, *Neocolonialism*, xi.

42. Nkrumah, *Neocolonialism*, xi.

43. See Kelly Askew, "African Socialism."

44. Léopold Senghor, *On African Socialism*, 72–75.

45. Senghor, *On African Socialism*, 9.

46. Nkrumah, "African Socialism Revisited," in *Revolutionary Path*, 444.

47. Steven Metz, "In Lieu of Orthodoxy: The Socialist Theories of Nkrumah and Nyerere," 382. Indeed, Nkrumah spared no nostalgia for precolonial African society and argued that "all available evidence from the history of Africa, up to the eve of the European colonization, shows that African society was neither classless nor devoid of a social hierarchy. Feudalism existed in some parts of Africa . . . slavery existed . . . A return to the pre-colonial African society is evidently not worthy of the ingenuity and efforts of our people." *Revolutionary Path*, 440–41.

48. Metz, "In Lieu of Orthodoxy," 382.

49. Nkrumah, *Revolutionary Path*, 440–41.

50. Nkrumah, *Revolutionary Path*, 440–41.

51. Nkrumah, *Revolutionary Path*, 441–42.

52. Nkrumah, *Revolutionary Path*, 444.

53. Nkrumah, *Revolutionary Path*, 444.

54. Nkrumah, *Neocolonialism*, 55.

55. Nkrumah, *Neocolonialism*, xx.

56. Nkrumah, *Neocolonialism*, x.

57. Nkrumah, *Neocolonialism*, x.

58. Vicky Randall, "Using and Abusing the Concept of the Third World: Geopolitics and the Comparative Political Study of Development and Underdevelopment."

59. Nkrumah, *Neocolonialism*, 255.

60. Nkrumah, *Neocolonialism*, xiii and 255.

61. Nkrumah, *Neocolonialism*, 256.

62. For an extended analysis of this point, see Inés Valdez, *Transnational Cosmopolitanism*.

63. Valdez, *Transnational Cosmopolitanism*, 254.

64. Nkrumah, *Neocolonialism*, xv.

65. Nkrumah, *Neocolonialism*, 256.

66. Nkrumah, *Neocolonialism*, 257.

67. Nkrumah, *Neocolonialism*, 257–58.

68. Branko Milanovic, *Global Inequality: A New Approach for the Age of Globalization*.

69. Milanovic, *Global Inequality*, 131. Also see Dani Rodrik, *The Globalization Paradox*, 149–56.

70. Nkrumah, *Neocolonialism*, x.

71. Nkrumah, *Neocolonialism*, x.

72. Anuja Bose, "Delinking from the Global Economy: The Regionalisms of Samir Amin and Walter Rodney," unpublished manuscript.

73. Bose, "Delinking from the Global Economy," 254.

74. Nkrumah, *Neocolonialism*, p. xiv.

75. Bose, "Delinking from the Global Economy," 253.

76. Getachew, *Worldmaking after Empire*, 107–41.

77. See Gabriel Wollner and Mathias Risse's helpful overview of competing theories of exploitation, in *Trade Justice: A Philosophical Plea for a New Global Deal*, 81–85. Also see Ben Ferguson and Hillel Steiner, "Exploitation."

78. Nicholas Vrousalis, "The Capitalist Cage: Structural Domination and Collective Agency in the Market."

79. Vrousalis, "The Capitalist Cage," 42.

80. Vrousalis, "The Capitalist Cage," 46–47.

81. Kate Miles, *The Origins of International Investment Law: Empire, Environment and the Safeguarding of Capital*; M. Sornarajah, "The Battle Continues: Rebuilding Empire through

Internationalization of State Contracts," 175–77; Jeffery A. Frieden, "International Investment and Colonial Control: A New Interpretation."

82. Ciaran Cross and Christian Schliemann-Radbruch, "When Investment Arbitration Curbs Domestic Regulatory Space," 5.

83. I follow Jonathan Bonnichta et al. in calling "the >3,000 investment treaties and >700 known treaty arbitrations" a "regime." Since tribunals regularly refer to precedents in deciding cases, arbitrators do not merely decide on particular cases, but together, they create a body of rules and norms that can be said to constitute a legal regime. See Jonathan Bonnitcha, Lauge N. Skovgaard Poulsen, and Michael Waibel, *The Political Economy of the Investment Treaty Regime*, 2–3.

84. Quinn Slobodian writes that, faced with the rise of mass democracies as newly independent nation-states were created in the postwar era, classical liberal thinkers advocated for global economic institutions that would "inoculate capitalism against the threat of democracy," one of which included the international investment law that exists today. Slobodian, *Globalists: The End of Empire and the Birth of Neoliberalism.*

85. Slobodian, *Globalists*, 139–40. Also see Sornarajah, "The Battle Continues," 186.

86. Sornarajah, "The Battle Continues."

87. Only a handful of recent papers by political theorists/philosophers exist on this topic. See Banai, "Is Investor-State Arbitration Unfair?"; Kniess; James.

88. Helen V. Milner, "Introduction: The Global Economy, FDI, and the Regime for Investment," 2.

89. Pierre Kohler and Francis Cripps, "Do Trade and Investment (Agreements) Foster Development or Inequality?" 6; Tim Büthe and Helen V. Milner, "Foreign Direct Investment and Institutional Diversity in Trade Agreements: Credibility, Commitment, and Economic Flows in the Developing World, 1971–2007."

90. See D. A. Low, *The Egalitarian Movement: Asia and Africa, 1950–1980.*

91. Todd Allee and Clint Peinhardt, "Evaluating Three Explanations for the Design of Bilateral Investment Treaties," 49.

92. Beth Simmons, "Bargaining over BITs, Arbitrating Awards: The Regime for Protection and Promotion of International Investment."

93. Alex Grabowski, "The Definition of Investment under the ICSID Convention: A Defense of Salini Comments," 295.

94. Lukas Vanhonnaeker, *Intellectual Property Rights as Foreign Direct Investments: From Collision to Collaboration*, 37–101; Sornarajah, *The International Law on Foreign Investment*, 11–13.

95. Vanhonnaeker, *Intellectual Property Rights as Foreign Direct Investments*, 241.

96. See Técnicas Medioambientales Tecmed, S. A v. Mexico.

97. Jurisdiction-shopping refers to the practice where corporations set up subsidiaries in a third country for the purpose of utilizing an investment treaty.

98. Sornarajah, *International Law on Foreign Investment*, 241 and 385.

99. Sornarajah, *International Law on Foreign Investment*, 242.

100. As will be discussed later, the South African government removed this clause in its new model BIT because of worries that they would not have enough law enforcement resources to deal with labor unrest and service delivery protests, which are common in South Africa, and that this would "open the floodgates of litigation," as Malebakeng Forere describes. See Forere, "The New South African Protection of Investment Act," 271.

101. Barton Legum, "Defining Investment and Investor: Who is Entitled to Claim?" *Arbitration International* 22 (2006): 521–24, 524.

102. Haley S. Edwards, *Shadow Courts: The Tribunals that Rule Global Trade*, 69. The estimated average cost of litigation to the investor was $4 million in 2015. Award amounts sought are usually confidential, but about half of the cases brought in 2018 were disclosed, with amounts ranging from $3 million to $15 billion.

103. Brooke Guven and Lise Johnson, "The Policy Impacts of Third-Party Funding in Investor-State Dispute Settlement"; Frank J. Garcia, "Third-Party Funding as Exploitation of the Investment Treaty System."

104. Simmons, "Bargaining over BITs," 17.

105. See UNCTAD, "Fact Sheet on Investor-State Dispute Settlement Cases in 2018."

106. UNCTAD, "Fact Sheet on Investor-State Dispute Settlement Cases in 2018," 4.

107. Gus Van Harten, "Who Has Benefited Financially from Investment Treaty Arbitration? An Evaluation of the Size and Wealth of Claimants," 1–18.

108. Simmons, "Bargaining over BITs," 19.

109. Pia Eberhardt and Cecilia Olivet, *Profiting from Injustice: How Law Firms, Arbitrators and Financiers are Fuelling an Investment Arbitration Boom*, 14.

110. For example, see Edwards, *Shadow Courts*.

111. Elizabeth Anderson, "What Is the Point of Equality?"

112. Scanlon, *Why Does Inequality Matter?*

113. Jacob Blumenfeld, "Expropriation of the Expropriators." See, for example, Parliament of the Republic of South Africa, "The Expropriation Bill [B23–2020]."

114. South Africa is often seen as the leading example in this regard. See Christopher Colvin, "Overview of the Reparations Program in South Africa."

115. Virginia Held, *Justice and Care: Essential Readings in Feminist Ethics*.

116. Elizabeth Anderson, *Private Government: How Employers Rule Our Lives*.

117. Ama Biney, *The Political and Social Thought of Kwame Nkrumah*, 125–26.

118. See Jodi Melamed, "Racial Capitalism."

119. John Rawls famously ruled out both laissez-fare and welfare capitalism as incompatible with a free and equal society. In his essay "Why Not Socialism?" G. A. Cohen suggests that capitalism necessitates and promotes dispositions that are antithetical to relating to each other in a spirit of equality and community. Rawls, *A Theory of Justice*; Cohen, *Why Not Socialism?*

120. UNCTAD, "Commodity Dependence Worsens for Developing Countries." For a critique of constraints on developmental strategy, see Ha-Joon Chang, *Kicking away the Ladder: Development Strategy in Historical Perspective*.

121. Dani Rodrik argues that the developmental strategies available to China, for example, played a large part in its economic "miracle." Foreign investors are required to undertake joint ventures with domestic firms in key industries such as mobile phone and computer production; similarly, foreign auto manufacturers had to achieve 70 percent of Chinese content within three years, forcing companies to work with local suppliers. Rodrik, *The Globalization Paradox*, 149–56.

122. The need to attract investors has been regularly offered as justification for incorporating these terms into investment agreements. See Nicolás M. Perrone, "UNCTAD's World Investment Reports 1991–2015: 25 Years of Narratives Justifying and Balancing Foreign Investor Rights."

123. See Perrone on the constraints that investment treaties impose on sustainable and egalitarian forms of economic development, "The ISDS Reform Process: The Missing Development Agenda."

124. Gus Van Harten, "Investment Treaty Arbitration: Procedural Fairness, and the Rule of Law."

125. Simarro and Antolín, "Development Strategy of the MAS in Bolivia: Characterization and an Early Assessment," 533–34.

126. Andres Arauz, Mark Weisbrot, Andrew Bunker, and Jake Johnson, "Bolivia's Economic Transformation: Macroeconomic Policies, Institutional Changes, and Results."

127. Arauz et al., "Bolivia's Economic Transformation," 12–13.

128. Ethan Lou, "TransCanada's $15 Billion U.S. Keystone XL NAFTA Suit Suspended."

129. See Glamis Gold, Ltd. v. The United States of America.

130. Fabio Morosini and Michelle Badin, eds., "Introduction," in *Reconceptualizing International Investment Law from the Global South*, 11.

131. Lise Johnson and Lisa Sachs, "Investment Treaties, Investor-State Dispute Settlement, and Inequality: How International Rules and Institutions Can Exacerbate Domestic Disparities." Although the hypothesis that investment treaties are *direct* drivers of domestic inequality remains to be tested, these papers find that investment treaties obstruct regulatory interventions aimed at reducing inequality, and impose severe fiscal costs. On this point, see Manuel Montes, "The Impact of Foreign Investor Protections on Domestic Inequality," especially at 105.

132. See chapter 2 for a discussion of these harms.

133. Rawls, *Law of Peoples*, 108.

134. Alan Patten, "Should We Stop Thinking about Poverty in Terms of Helping the Poor?" 23.

135. Lauge Poulsen and Emma Aisbett, "When the Claim Hits: Bilateral Investment Treaties and Bounded Rational Learning."

136. Poulsen, "Bounded Rationality and the Diffusion of Modern Investment Treaties."

137. Ayelet Banai, "Is Investor Arbitration Fair? A Freedom-Based Perspective," especially 74–78.

138. Poulsen, "Bounded Rationality."

139. BBC News, "Vietnam Detains 100 after Anti-China Economic Zone Protests Turn Violent."

140. Dilip Hiro, "Protests in Kazakhstan Rattle China and Russia."

141. This parallels Kristi Olson's critique of Aaron James's account of fairness in trade, which takes autarky—lack of trade—as the moral baseline against which to calculate the gains of trade to be distributed fairly. As Olson argues, using autarky as a moral baseline (as opposed to some other moralized baseline, such as an egalitarian one) to determine what justice requires compounds existing inequalities. Kristi Olson, "Autarky as a Moral Naseline."

142. Joseph Stiglitz, *Globalization and Its Discontents*, 23–54.

143. See Maria Abi-Habib, "How China Got Sri Lanka to Cough Up a Port."

144. For a critique of the existing international IP regime, see Allen Buchanan, Tony Cole, and Robert O. Keohane, "Justice in the Diffusion of Innovation."

145. Some people argue that human rights is a "trump card" in that human rights can never be outweighed by other considerations. Unlike human rights, a regulative ideal *regulates* decision-making by giving significant, though not indefeasible, weight to the values that constitute the ideal.

146. Morosini and Badin, eds., *Reconceptualizing International Investment Law from the Global South*.

147. Forere, "The New South African Protection of Investment Act," 251–23.

148. Morosini and Badin, *Reconceptualizing*, 37.

149. Morosini and Badin, *Reconceptualizing*, 39.

150. Forere, "The New South African Protection of Investment Act," 274–76.

151. Sergio Puig and Gregory Shaffer, "Imperfect Alternatives: Institutional Choice and the Reform of Investment Law."

152. Sornarajah, *International Law on Foreign Investment*, 13.

153. Gorz, *Strategy for Labor*; also see Amna Akbar on nonreformist reforms, in "Demands for a Democratic Political Economy."

154. Turkuler Isiksel, "The Rights of Man and the Rights of the Man-Made: Corporations and Human Rights," 300–1.

155. Richard Meeran, "Access to Remedy: The United Kingdom Experience of Multinational Corporation Tort Litigation for Human Rights Violations."

156. Richard Meeran, "Multinational Human Rights Litigation in the UK: A Retrospective," 259.

157. See Matthew C. Porterfield, "Reforming the International Investment Regime through a Framework Convention on Investment and Sustainable Development." Also see a helpful summary of proposed reforms (both substantive and procedural) submitted to UNCITRAL by Lorenzo Cotula et al., *UNCITRAL Working Group III on ISDS Reform: How Cross-Cutting Issues Reform Options.*

158. Morosini and Badin, "Introduction: Reconceptualizing International Investment Law," 31.

159. Forere, "The New South African Protection of Investment Act," 268.

160. I develop a fuller account of justified expropriation (albeit for reparative justice purposes) in Shuk Ying Chan, "Expropriation as Reparation."

161. Sornarajah, *Resistance and Change in International Law*, 196.

162. Sornarajah, *Resistance and Change in International Law*, 196.

163. See Anahí Wiedenbrüg for a compelling argument regarding refusing to pay sovereign debt that parallels the case of investment. Wiedenbrüg, "What Citizens Owe: Two Grounds for Challenging Debt Repayment."

164. See Robert Goodin, "Toward an International Rule of Law: Distinguishing International Law-Breakers from Would-Be Law-Makers," for an analysis of international lawbreaking as lawmaking.

165. Bonnitcha, Poulsen, and Waibel, *The Political Economy of the Investment Treaty Regime*, chap. 6.

166. Vivienne Bath, "The South and Alternative Models of Trade and Investment Regulation: Chinese Investment and Approaches to International Investment Agreements," 47–94.

167. Nkrumah, *Neo-colonialism*, xix.

168. Nkrumah, *Neocolonialism*, 246–54.

169. Nkrumah, *Neocolonialism*, 246.

Chapter 4. Decolonizing Cultural Globalization: Césaire and the Hierarchy of Creator and Consumer

1. Sean MacBride et al., *Many Voices, One World.*

2. Communications scholar and one of the NWICO's main proponents Kaarle Nordenstreng calls the report and the NWICO part of the 1970s "decolonization offensive." Nordenstreng, "The New World Information and Communication Order: An Idea that Refuses to Die," 478.

3. "Groundbreaking" because it marked the first international statement on the relationship between an emerging global media and its consequences on human rights, racism, and war. Its full title is telling: "Declaration on Fundamental Principles concerning the Contribution of the Mass Media to Strengthening Peace and International Understanding, to the Promotion of Human Rights and to Countering Racialism, Apartheid and Incitement to War." See UNESCO, "Declaration on Fundamental Principles . . ."

4. Macbride et al., *Many Voices*, 268.

5. A resolution on the NWICO adopted at the twenty-first session of the UNESCO General Conference lists some considerations on which the new order should be based, including (to select a few): elimination of imbalances and inequalities in present global communications; elimination of negative effects of monopolies and excessive concentrations in media and cultural production; the need for plurality of sources and channels of information; capacity of developing countries to develop infrastructures for information and communication and train personnel; the "sincere will" of developed countries to assist in these objectives; the right of each nation to "inform the world about its interests, its aspirations and its social and cultural values," and so on. See "UNESCO Resolution 4/19," Belgrade 1980, http://ulis2.unesco.org/images/0011/001140/114029EO.pdf.

6. Sean MacBride and Colleen Roach, "The New International Information Order," 10.

7. See UNESCO, "Declaration on Fundamental Principles . . . ," Section 3, Article II.

8. Wolfgang Kleinwachter, "Three Waves of the Debate," 16–19. For a recent and detailed historical account of the clashes between the United States and the Global South on the issue of liberalizing global communications, see Diana Lemberg, *Barriers Down: How American Power and Free-Flow Policies Shaped Global Media*, especially 178–202.

9. Kleinwachter, "Three Waves of the Debate," 16.

10. At the time, the United States' financial contributions to UNESCO accounted for 25 percent of the organization's budget. Joanne Omang, "UNESCO Withdrawal Announced."

11. The Venezuelan government, for example, proposed in 1974 a set of national communications policies that included decentralization and regulatory measures aimed at improving the quality and variety of media content, with special measures to encourage the expression of the country's popular culture. Despite having strong support from journalists' associations and media professionals, the policies were met with a hostile press campaign and were quietly dropped in the end. See Robert A. White, "The New Order and the Third World," 30.

12. Richard C. Vincent, "Justice and Communication: Looking Beyond WSIS," 201–3.

13. See, in particular, the global debate surrounding UNESCO's efforts to address the effects of American global cultural dominance. Eireann Brooks, "Cultural Imperialism vs. Cultural Protectionism: Hollywood's Response to UNESCO Efforts to Promote Cultural Diversity." For an analysis of cultural imperialism as a critique and theory, see John Tomlinson, *Cultural Imperialism: A Critical Introduction*.

14. See Márton Demeter for a critical analysis of inequality in global knowledge production, in *Academic Knowledge Production and the Global South: Questioning Inequality and Under-Representation*.

15. Two exceptions include Kok-Chor Tan and James Christensen, whose works on global justice include brief discussions of cultural trade and self-determination. Kok-Chor Tan, *Justice without Borders*, 115–20; James Christensen, *Trade Justice*, 63–90. For a recent intervention in postcolonial studies, see Boaventura de Sousa Santos, *The End of the Cognitive Empire: The Coming of Age of Epistemologies of the South*. For some classic studies on this topic in media and cultural studies, see Herbert Schiller, *Mass Communications and American Empire*, and Jeremy Tunstall, *The Media Are American: Anglo-American Media the World*.

16. Will Kymlicka, *Multicultural Citizenship: A Liberal Theory of Minority Rights*; Iris M. Young, *Justice and the Politics of Difference*; Brian Barry, *Culture and Equality*; Alan Patten, *Equal Recognition: The Moral Foundations of Minority Rights*.

17. See Barry, *Culture and Equality*; Kymlicka, *Multicultural Citizenship*; Iris Young, *Justice and the Politics of Difference*; Patten, *Equal Recognition*.

18. David Miller, *Strangers in Our Midst*; David Miller, *On Nationality*.

19. Olúfẹ́mi Táíwò makes this critique most forcefully in his recent book *Against Decolonization: Taking African Agency Seriously*.

20. Uma Narayan, "Essence of Culture and a Sense of History: A Feminist Critique of Cultural Essentialism."

21. Táíwò, *Against Decolonization*, 15.

22. David Scott, *Conscripts of Modernity: The Tragedy of Colonial Enlightenment*.

23. Adom Getachew and Karuna Mantena, "Anticolonialism and the Decolonization of Political Theory," 374. They put the point even more sharply when it comes to Black political thought: "The paradigmatic instance of a layered, conscripted, and creative tradition is the tradition of Black political thought, which, formed against the dislocations of transatlantic slavery, was never articulated as entirely outside the West but rather was co-constituted with Western political thought" (371).

24. Rajeev Bhargava, "Overcoming the Epistemic Injustice of Colonialism," 417.

25. Kwame Anthony Appiah, *Cosmopolitanism: Ethics in a World of Strangers*, 113.

26. For an extended discussion of social agency, see chapter 2.

27. See Colin Sparks, "Media and Cultural Imperialism Reconsidered." For a compelling critique of the idea that globalization is creating a homogenous global culture, see Stuart Hall, *Fateful Triangle*, 111–24. For an overview of the debate, see Rodrigo Gómez Garcia and Ben Birkinbine, "Cultural Imperialism Theories."

28. Césaire, "Culture and Colonisation," 194.

29. See Patten, *Equal Recognition*, 38–69.

30. Césaire, "Culture and Colonisation," 195.

31. Jane Hiddleston, *Aimé Césaire: Inventors of Souls*, chap. 1.

32. Hiddleston, *Aimé Césaire: Inventors of Souls*, chap. 1.

33. Sociologist of culture Wendy Griswold states that humans need meaning, as transmitted via cultural objects, because unlike nonhuman animals, humans cannot survive solely based on the genetic information encoded at a biological level. Instead, humans must also *learn* how to live, and learning for humans is inherently a "social process of interaction and socialization whereby cultural is transmitted." Griswold, *Cultures and Society in a Changing World*, 21.

34. Césaire, "Culture and Colonisation," 196.

35. Césaire, "Culture and Colonisation," 196.

36. Césaire, *Discourse on Colonialism*, 44.

37. Césaire, "Culture and Colonisation," 198.

38. Césaire, "Culture and Colonisation," 197.

39. Césaire, *Discourse on Colonialism*, 33.

40. Césaire, *Discourse on Colonialism*, 203.

41. Césaire, *Discourse on Colonialism*, 203.

42. Césaire, *Discourse on Colonialism*, 204.

43. See Rahel Jaeggi, *Alienation*.

44. Césaire, "Culture and Colonisation," 203.

45. Césaire, "Culture and Colonisation," 203.

46. Alistair Horne, *A Savage War of Peace: Algeria 1954–1962*, 60.

47. Even as colonial rule gradually shifted from a civilizing mission that forced subjects to "convert" to European culture, to greater emphasis on preserving "traditional cultures" under indirect forms of rule, colonial subjects were still denied the freedom to redefine their cultures through dynamic appropriations of cultural elements old and new. Rather, the culture that came to be preserved consisted of practices and institutions handpicked by colonial academics and local authorities empowered by colonialists. See Karuna Mantena, *Alibis of Empire: Henry Maine and the Ends of Liberal Imperialism*, for an account of this shift.

48. Césaire, "Man of Culture and His Responsibilities," 127.

49. Césaire, "Man of Culture and His Responsibilities," 130.

50. Césaire, "Man of Culture and His Responsibilities," 130.

51. Césaire, "Man of Culture and His Responsibilities," 130.

52. Césaire, "Culture and Colonisation," 205.

53. Coulthard, *Red Skin, White Masks*, chap. 5.

54. Getachew and Mantena, "Anticolonialism and the Decolonization of Political Theory," 373.

55. Interview with René Depestre, in Césaire, *Discourse on Colonialism*, 88–94. Also see Wilder, *Freedom Time*.

56. Césaire, "Man of Culture and His Responsibilities," 130.

57. Césaire, "Man of Culture and His Responsibilities," 130.

58. Césaire, "Man of Culture and His Responsibilities," 130.

59. For example, see Césaire's adaptation of Shakespeare's *The Tempest*, in which he uses Shakespeare's characters but brings to the foreground the race of the main characters and the enslavement of Black characters by a white man, thereby exploring the power dynamics between them. Césaire, *A Tempest*.

60. As Gary Wilder has argued, Césaire was a proponent of reappropriating the French culture as weapons against the hypocrisy of the French empire. See Wilder, *Freedom Time*, 17–48.

61. Edward Said, *Culture and Imperialism*, 275.

62. Interview with René Depestre, collected in *Discourse on Colonialism*, 83.

63. Césaire, "Man of Culture and His Responsibilities," 127.

64. Césaire, "Man of Culture and His Responsibilities," 127.

65. Césaire, "Man of Culture and His Responsibilities," 127.

66. Césaire, "Man of Culture and His Responsibilities," 127.

67. For a discussion of vigilance in the anticolonial and postcolonial tradition, see Anuja Bose, *Frantz Fanon and the Politics of a Global Anti-imperialism*, unpublished manuscript.

68. See Fanon on the importance of political education in decolonization in *The Wretched of the Earth*, especially 138–39. He echoes Césaire at one point: "Political education means opening up the mind, awakening the mind, and introducing it to the world. It is as Césaire said: 'To invent the souls of men.' To politicize the masses is not and cannot be to make a political speech. It means driving home to the masses that everything depends on them, that if we stagnate the fault is theirs, and that if we progress, they too are responsible, that there is no demiurge, no illustrious man taking responsibility for everything, but that the demiurge is the people and the magic lies in their hands and their hands alone." Fanon, *The Wretched of the Earth*, 138.

69. Césaire, "Man of Culture and His Responsibilities," 129.

70. Fanon, for example, argues in *The Wretched of the Earth* that postcolonial economic development should involve citizens in ways that give them a sense of empowerment—for example, by training them to become active makers of the country's infrastructure rather than passive takers of foreign expertise and technology. This sense of empowerment, for Fanon, could sometimes be more important than the practical benefits of economic development itself. See, for example, Fanon on empowering citizens to learn how to build bridges, *The Wretched of the Earth*, 141.

71. Césaire, "Man of Culture and His Responsibilities," 127.

72. Césaire, "Man of Culture and His Responsibilities," 127.

73. Said, *Culture and Imperialism*, 276.

74. Jane Hiddleston, *Aimé Césaire*, chap. 1.

75. Hiddleston, *Aimé Césaire*, chap. 1.

76. Césaire, "Culture and Colonisation," 207.

77. Césaire, "Man of Culture and His Responsibilities," 132.

78. Césaire, "Man of Culture and His Responsibilities," 126.

79. Césaire, "Man of Culture and His Responsibilities," 126.

80. Césaire, "Man of Culture and His Responsibilities," 126.

81. Jeremy Waldron, "Minority Cultures and the Cosmopolitan Alternative."

82. David Held and Anthony McGrew, *Globalization/Anti-Globalization: Beyond the Great Divide*, 40.

83. Waldron, "Minority Cultures," 787–88.

84. I put these in quotation marks to indicate and acknowledge the problematic connotations of these terms. Nonetheless, I use them in the ensuing discussion for the sake of clarity because the data is largely based on UNESCO reports, which use the official country classification system of the United Nations. The reader can therefore easily look at which countries these categories refer to.

85. See UNESCO, "International Flows of Selected Cultural Goods and Services, 1994–2003."

86. UNESCO, "International Flows."

87. On "contra-flows," see Daya Thussu, "Mapping Global Media Flow and Contra-flow." Thussu states that, with the exception of Japanese animation, the "revenues of non-Western

media organizations . . . are relatively small and their global impact is restricted to geo-cultural markets or at best to small pockets of regional transnational consumers" (234).

88. UNESCO, "Reshaping Cultural Policies: Advancing Creativity for Development."

89. UNESCO, "Reshaping Cultural Policies."

90. UNESCO, "The Globalisation of Cultural Trade: A Shift in Consumption."

91. UNESCO, "Reshaping Policies for Creativity: Addressing Culture as a Global Public Good," 164.

92. UNESCO, "Reshaping Policies for Creativity: Addressing Culture as a Global Public Good," 172.

93. Tanner Mirrlees, *Hearts and Mines: The US Empire's Cultural Industry*, 108. Also see Dal Yong Jin, "The Construction of Platform Imperialism in the Globalization Era."

94. Dongchul Kwak and Minjung Kim, "Trade Negotiations in the Digital Era: The Case of OTT Video Streaming Services," 19.

95. Verónica Amarante et al., "Underrepresentation of Developing Country Researchers in Development Research." Findings are summarized in Laya Liverpool, "Researchers from Global South Under-Represented in Development Research."

96. Malgorzata Blicharska et al., "Steps to Overcome the North–South Divide in Research Relevant to Climate Change Policy and Practice."

97. Janet Wasko, "Can Hollywood Still Rule the World?" 191.

98. Mirrlees, *Hearts and Mines*, 112.

99. For example, by promoting intellectual property rights and free trade of cultural goods, as well as pushing for privatization of media and cultural industries in other countries, thus enabling US media firms to invest and acquire those businesses. Wasko, "Can Hollywood Still Rule the World?" 191. See also Mirrlees, *Hearts and Mines*, 119–26.

100. Ikechi Mgbeoji, *Global Biopiracy: Patents, Plants, and Indigenous Knowledge*, 13.

101. Elisabeth Pain, "French Institute Agrees to Share Patent Benefits after Biopiracy Accusations."

102. See Hochan Kim, "Cultural Appropriation and Social Recognition."

103. BBC News, "Isabel Marant: Designer Apologises for Mexican Appropriation."

104. Andrew Chow, "Black Artists Helped Build Country Music."

105. Stephen Howe, *The New Imperial Histories Reader*. On the making of English identity in the British empire, see Catherine Hall, *Civilising Subjects: Metropole and Colony in the English Imagination*.

106. Maria Abi-Habib, "The Forgotten Colonial Forces of WWII."

107. Lauren Collins, "The Haitian Revolution and the Hole in French High-School History."

108. Getachew and Mantena, "Anticolonialism and the Decolonization of Political Theory," 373.

109. Miranda Fricker, *Epistemic Injustice*, chap. 7.

110. Getachew and Mantena, "Anticolonialism and Decolonization of Political Theory," 372.

111. Paul Hopper, *Understanding Cultural Globalization*, 104–5.

112. The solution to this problem can go different ways: one solution is to delink access to *important* opportunities and goods from mastery of a specific language and culture; another is to ensure in some way that individuals have a fair chance to master that language and culture. While the former may seem impractical if not impossible at this stage of globalization, it's important to note that, unlike the latter, delinking is able to take into account the interest in appropriative agency, as well as an interest in self-respect, which may be threatened by being compelled to adopt a language and culture that has historically been part and parcel of one's own oppression. For reasons of space I cannot delve into this issue further but thought this worth noting.

113. As I discussed in chapter 2, social agency is an alternative way of thinking about the notion of historical agency, one that decouples agency from teleological notions of progress. In this alternative, social agency just is the capacity to create value. Value is understood here in a very broad sense and can encompass most (morally permissible) conceptions of the good.

Examples of producing value may include discovering a cure for a disease, writing a good book of philosophy, helping to build a bridge, raising and nurturing children, and so on. In general, by producing value I just mean doing something that contributes to the good of others (even as it may also benefit oneself). To be sure, these activities have different levels of social prestige attached to them, even as they all produce some social value.

114. Tommie Shelby, "Ideology, Racism, and Critical Social Theory," 164.

115. Shelby, "Ideology, Racism, and Critical Social Theory," 169.

116. Shelby, "Ideology, Racism, and Critical Social Theory," 161.

117. Shelby, "Ideology, Racism, and Critical Social Theory," 161.

118. Shelby, "Ideology, Racism, and Critical Social Theory," 161.

119. For a comprehensive overview of recent research on these topics, see Todd Nelson, ed., *Handbook of Prejudice, Stereotyping, and Discrimination*. For a study specifically on the relationship between culture and implicit bias, see Perry Hinton, "Implicit Stereotypes and the Predictive Brain: Cognition and Culture in 'Biased' Person Perception." Hinton argues that the implicit stereotypical associations that individuals make reflect the associations prevalent in their culture, instead of individual prejudice.

120. Michael Brownstein and Jennifer Saul, eds., *Implicit Bias and Philosophy*, 1:1.

121. Césaire, *Discourse on Colonialism*, 52–53.

122. Many empirical studies have found correlations between exposure to stereotyping in popular media and racial prejudice, bias, and stereotyping. For a recent review of these studies, see Tara Ross, "Media and Stereotypes." Also see the Society for the Psychological Study of Social Issues' special issue on "Media Representations of Race and Ethnicity: implications for Identity, Intergroup Relations, and Public Policy," especially Dana Mastro, "Why the Media's Role in Issues of Race and Ethnicity Should be in the Spotlight.".

123. See Edward Said's classic statement of this in *Orientalism*. A 2013 World Bank study on Hollywood film representations of development found that there is a general tendency to focus on individual rather than structural causes of war and poverty in developing countries, as well as a privileging of Western engagement with developing countries at the expense of local voices. David Lewis, Dennis Rodgers and Michael Woolcock, "The Project of Development: Cinematic Representation as An(other) Source of Authoritative Knowledge?"

It is important to note that within developed countries there are also significant imbalances in who gets to produce culture—in Hollywood, for example, five white film-writers are employed for every one film-writer of color. See Hunt et al., *Hollywood Diversity Report*.

124. Said, *Orientalism*.

125. For example, a 2002 study found that 80 percent of the British public believed that the developing world was in a "permanent state of disaster." See Claire Cozens, "Charity Blames Media for Perpetuating Stereotypes."

For a discussion of racial stereotyping in US media and its consequences, see Dana Mastro, "Race and Ethnicity in US Media Content and Effects."

126. See Oliver Kearns's analysis of the role that cultural and racial stereotyping played in US intelligence failures leading up to the Iraq War. Kearns, *The Covert Colour Line: The Racialized Politics of Western State Intelligence*. Also see Tanner Mirrlees's *Hearts and Mines*, which explores the close relationship between the US Department of Defense and the film and computer/video games industry in creating cultural goods that portray the US military and the CIA in a heroic fashion, and their methods—such as drone strikes or torture—as necessary and effective tools against terrorism. See Mirrlees, *Hearts and Mines*, 181–82.

127. Quoted in MacBride and Roach, "The New International Information Order," 6.

128. Not all objectionable stereotypes are negative in a straightforward sense. Consider the stereotype that emerged in the United States in the 1800s, when Chinese migrant labor was used on large scale, that Chinese men tend to be single-mindedly focused on labor and unusually productive. See Marilyn Lake and Henry Reynolds, *Drawing the Global Colour Line*.

129. Anamik Saha, "'Beards, Scarves, Halal Meat, Terrorists, Forced Marriage': Television Industries and the Production of 'Race.'"

130. Saha, "'Beards, Scarves, Halal Meat, Terrorists, Forced Marriage': Television Industries and the Production of 'Race,'" 429.

131. Consider, for example, *US News and World Report*'s 2020 rankings for "international cultural influence." Based on a survey of twenty thousand people, Brazil is the only developing country in the top ten, while the top five consist of former European colonial powers (Italy, France, Spain, and the UK) plus the United States. To be sure, given the sample size, the survey can at best serve as anecdotal evidence. See *US News and World Report*, "Cultural Influence."

132. Vanessa Wills, "'And He Ate Jim Crow': Racist Ideology as False Consciousness," 36.

133. Lara Farrar, "Chinese Companies 'Rent' White Foreigners."

134. Ola Brown, "Banning Bleaching Products in Africa Won't Work as Long as Fair Skin is Linked with Beauty and Success," CNN, January 15, 2019, https://www.cnn.com/2019/01/15/health/banning-bleaching-products-in-africa/index.html.

135. Mohammed Adow, "Nigeria's Dangerous Skin Whitening Obsession."

136. For more on "colorism," especially in countries with historical legacies of racism, see the volume edited by Evelyn Nakano Glenn, *Shades of Difference: Why Skin Color Matters*.

137. In the context of US media, Ramasubramanian, Doshi, and Saleem found that exposure to mainstream media led to a decrease in self-esteem among racialized "ethnic" groups in the United States, while exposure to "ethnic" media had the opposite effect. See Srividya Ramasubramanian, Marissa J. Doshi, and Muniba Saleem, "Mainstream Versus Ethnic Media: How They Shape Ethnic Pride and Self-Esteem among Ethnic Minority Audiences." Similarly, see Adolfo Mora and Seok Kang, "English-Language Latino Themed Programming and Social Identity: The Relationship between Viewing and Self-Esteem among Latina/Os."

138. Alan Riding, "US All But Alone in Opposing Unesco Cultural Pact," *New York Times*, October 20, 2005, https://www.nytimes.com/2005/10/20/world/americas/us-all-but-alone-in-opposing-unesco-cultural-pact.html.

139. Wills, "'And He Ate Jim Crow': Racist Ideology as False Consciousness," 35.

140. Césaire, "Man of Culture and His Responsibilities," 132. Or, as Léopold Senghor calls it, the creation of a "Civilization of the Universal." For a disaggregation of this concept, see Mabana, "Léopold Sédar Senghor and the Civilization of the Universal."

141. In 2014, developing countries had on average thirty-six destination countries for exports of visual arts goods, while developed countries had ninety destination countries. Similarly, the number of export destinations for developing countries' audiovisual and music goods *decreased* by 66 percent from 2005 to 2014, while the number of export destinations for *developed* countries increased by 55 percent over the same period. Therefore, while developed countries are gaining increasing access to the cultural markets of developing countries, the reverse has not been true. See UNESCO, "Reshaping Cultural Policies: Advancing Creativity for Development," 132–33. To be sure, the majority of cultural exports from developed countries tend to go to other developed countries—for example, the UK's largest cultural goods trading partner in 2013 was the United States. However, they do also export to developing countries, while the reverse is generally not true. This means that (1) for any developing country and developed country, there is a much higher chance of the latter exporting to the former rather than the reverse; (2) developing countries' overall level of cultural exports is disproportionately low. See UNESCO, "The Globalization of Cultural Trade."

142. See Tania Voon, *Cultural Products and the World Trade Organization*.

143. Haidy Geismar, *Treasured Possessions: Indigenous Interventions into Cultural and Intellectual Property*; Helen Tilley, "Traditional Medicine Goes Global: Pan-African Precedents, Cultural Decolonization, and Cold War Rights/Properties."

144. Leanne R. Simpson, "Anticolonial Strategies for the Recovery and Maintenance of Indigenous Knowledge," *American Indian Quarterly* 28, no. 3/4 (2004): 373–84.

145. Darrell A. Posey and Graham Dutfield, *Beyond Intellectual Property: Toward Traditional Resource Rights for Indigenous Peoples and Local Communities.*

146. Repatriation of stolen cultural objects is indeed a tricky issue, in part because one might think that the continued display of such objects in former metropoles could work to counter the notion that former colonial subjects lacked creative capacities. But this would be an erroneous assumption. Objects themselves—especially when displayed out of context—do not necessarily reflect cultural dynamism, and in fact valuing these objects has historically been compatible with portrayals of their creators as having static cultures. Thus the opportunity to tell a narrative about one's culture may be just as important as the opportunity to create specific cultural objects. For a different account of restitution, see Daniel Butt, *Rectifying International Injustice: Principles of Compensation and Restitution Between Nations.*

147. Mantena, *Alibis of Empire.*

148. For example, see Hochan Kim's discussion of cultural ambassadorship as an alternative mode of cultural collaboration between dominant and marginalized groups, in contrast to cultural appropriation. Kim, "Cultural Appropriation and Social Recognition."

149. Think of anti-Black racism in China, which has gained increasing public attention in recent years. It is perhaps no accident that Chinese economic ties (in the form of loans and investment) with African countries have increased substantially in these years.

150. Young Il Kim, Shi Young Lee, Eun-mee Kim, "The Effect of the Korean Screen Quota System on Box Office Performance."

151. Jimmyn Parc, "The Effects of Protection in Cultural Industries: The Case of the Korean Film Policies," 628; Seung-Ho Kwon and Joseph Kim, "The Cultural Industry Policies of the Korean Government and the Korean Wave."

152. Kwon and Kim, "The Cultural Industry Policies of the Korean Government and the Korean Wave," 423.

153. Frank Westerman, *Engineers of the Soul: In the Footsteps of Stalin's Writers.*

154. The European Union's most recent (2018) Audiovisual and Media Services Directive does this. See European Commission, "Audiovisual and Media Services." Similarly, Australia has introduced a "Netflix tax" of this sort, partly for distributive justice reasons and partly for cultural protectionist reasons. See Kali Sanyal, "Applying GST to Digital Products and Services Imported by Customers."

155. See Diana Crane, "Cultural Globalization and the Dominance of the American Film Industry: Cultural Policies, National Film Industries, and Transnational Film," 372.

156. Mantena, *Alibis of Empire.*

157. Táíwò makes this point forcefully when discussing the politics of linguistic decolonization in *Against Decolonization,* 68–69.

158. Matthew Chew, "Contemporary Re-Emergence of the Qipao: Political Nationalism, Cultural Production and Popular Consumption of a Traditional Chinese Dress."

159. As is arguably the case in contemporary China, where cultural goods that critique the ruling party are heavily sanctioned, if not outright prohibited. In the latest effort to censor cultural production, for example, Chinese President Xi Jinping put the Communist Party's propaganda office in charge of regulating the film industry. See Lee and Hong, "China Is Stifling Its Own Movie Business."

160. One argument for "decolonizing public spaces" like university campuses, I think, relies not only on the subjective experience of individuals, who may feel injured by certain kinds of campus décor—although that is an important argument—but appeals to the idea that our social environment should be arranged in a way that encourages us to see and relate to each other as equals, and that certain kinds of décor (such as statues that celebrate well-known colonialists like Rhodes at the University of Cape Town, or, until recently, the lack of commemorative representations of women alumni and alumni of color at Princeton University) may hinder that. When and whether certain cultural objects hinder egalitarian relations will often be

context-dependent, and rightly so (I think). The history of colonial racism is one important context, but there are undoubtedly others.

Chapter 5. Decolonizing Global Governance:
Nehru and the Problem of Global Democracy

1. Mark Mazower, *No Enchanted Palace: The End of Empire and the Ideological Origins of the United Nations*, 149–190.
2. Mazower, *No Enchanted Palace*, 176.
3. Quoted in Mazower, *No Enchanted Palace*, 179.
4. Quoted in Mazower, *No Enchanted Palace*, 185.
5. Quoted in Mazower, *No Enchanted Palace*, 185.
6. Mark Mazower, *Governing the World: The History of an Idea, 1815 to the Present*, 212.
7. Mazower, *No Enchanted Palace*, 186.
8. Robert A. Dahl, "Can International Organizations Be Democratic? A Skeptic's View," 26 and 31–32; David Miller, "Against Global Democracy"; Sarah Song, "The Boundary Problem in Democratic Theory: Why the Demos Should Be Bounded by the State"; Richard Bellamy, "Globalization and Representative Democracy: Normative Challenges," 661.
9. Miller, "Against Global Democracy."
10. Miller, "Against Global Democracy"; Dahl, "Can International Organizations Be Democratic?"
11. Song, "The Boundary Problem in Democratic Theory," 61; Carol Gould, despite being a global democrat herself, makes a similar criticism of cosmopolitan democrats such as David Held for not being attentive enough to this problem. Gould, *Globalizing Democracy and Human Rights*, 170.
12. Song, "The Boundary Problem in Democratic Theory," 64–65.
13. Dahl, "Can International Organizations Be Democratic?" 23.
14. Nehru, *The Discovery of India*, 609.
15. Michele Louro, *Comrades against Imperialism: Nehru, India and Interwar Internationalism*.
16. Louro, *Comrades against Imperialism*, 34.
17. Michele Louro et al., "The League Against Imperialism: Lives and Afterlives."
18. V.I. Lenin, *Imperialism: The Highest Stage of Capitalism*.
19. Louro, *Comrades against Imperialism*, 22. Nehru, "Report on Brussels Congress."
20. For an account of the League's different iterations of this shared condition, see Disha Karnad Jani, "Unfreedom and Its Opposite: Towards an Intellectual History of the League Against Imperialism, 1927–1929."
21. Jani, "Unfreedom and Its Opposite," 25; Benjamin Zachariah, *Nehru*, 58–61.
22. Nehru, *Autobiography*, 166.
23. Nehru, *Autobiography*, 166.
24. Nehru, *Autobiography*, 166.
25. Nehru, *Autobiography*, 287.
26. Nehru, *The Discovery of India*, 330–33.
27. Nehru, "Ends and Means," see 428–29; Nehru, "World Union and Collective Security," 806–9.
28. Nehru, "World Union and Collective Security." Though, as Mark Mazower notes, Nehru was far from an idealist and realized that it was more practical to argue for an egalitarian commonwealth of nations in the more immediate term. Mazower, *No Enchanted Palace*, 168.
29. Nehru, "World Union and Collective Security," 807.
30. Nehru, *Glimpses of World History*, 95–96. See Chacko's discussion of this particular theme in Nehru's thought in Chacko, "The Internationalist Nationalist: Pursuing an Ethical Modernity with Jawaharlal Nehru."

31. Nehru, "World Union and Collective Security," 807.

32. Nehru, "Colonialism Must Go," 224.

33. Nehru, "Colonialism Must Go," 224.

34. Nehru, "Colonialism Must Go," 224.

35. Chacko, "The Internationalist Nationalist."

36. Nehru, *The Discovery of India*, 631.

37. Nehru, *The Discovery of India*, 630–31.

38. Nehru, *The Discovery of India*, 630–31.

39. Nehru, *The Discovery of India*, 631.

40. Nehru, "A World Government Must Come Sometime or Other," 812; also see Nehru, "A Real Commonwealth," 219.

41. Nehru, "World Union and Collective Security," 807.

42. Nehru, "World Union and Collective Security," 809.

43. Nehru, "World Union and Collective Security," 809.

44. Nehru, "A Foreign Policy for India," 354–55.

45. Nehru, "A Foreign Policy for India," 354–55.

46. Nehru, *An Autobiography*, 365.

47. Nehru, *An Autobiography*, 182.

48. Nehru, *An Autobiography*, 182.

49. Nehru, *An Autobiography*, 182.

50. Nehru, *An Autobiography*, 182.

51. Louro, *Comrades against Imperialism*, chap. 3.

52. As Valdez discusses, the Pan-African Congress spearheaded by Du Bois (also in response to Versailles) is another good example. Valdez, *Transnational Cosmopolitanism*, chap. 3.

53. Nehru, *An Autobiography*, 166.

54. Nehru, *An Autobiography*, 166.

55. Nehru, "Report on Brussels Congress," 286.

56. Nehru, "Report on Brussels Congress," 295.

57. Louro, *Comrades against Imperialism*, 120.

58. Louro, *Comrades against Imperialism*, 115.

59. Louro, *Comrades against Imperialism*, 90–91.

60. Nehru, "A Foreign Policy for India," 353.

61. Nehru, "A Foreign Policy for India," 356.

62. Nehru, "A Foreign Policy for India," 354.

63. Nehru, "A Foreign Policy for India," 354.

64. Nehru, *The Discovery of India*, 461.

65. Nehru, *The Discovery of India*, 461.

66. Nehru, *The Discovery of India*, 484–85. Also see Nanda, *Nehru: Rebel and Statesman*, 142.

67. Nehru, *The Discovery of India*, 467.

68. Nehru, *The Discovery of India*, 462.

69. Nehru, *The Discovery of India*, 463.

70. Nehru, *The Discovery of India*, 463.

71. Nehru, *The Discovery of India*, 465.

72. Nehru, *The Discovery of India*, 466; Louro, *Comrades against Imperialism*, 252–53.

73. Nehru, *The Discovery of India*, 463–64.

74. Nehru, *The Discovery of India*, 465.

75. Nehru, *The Discovery of India*, 465.

76. Nehru, *The Discovery of India*, 466.

77. Nehru, *The Discovery of India*, 475.

78. Nehru, *The Discovery of India*, 466–67.

79. Nehru, *The Discovery of India*, 467.

80. Nehru, *The Discovery of India*, 467.

81. Nehru, *The Discovery of India*, 474.

82. Nehru, *The Discovery of India*, 475.

83. Nehru, *The Discovery of India*, 609.

84. Nehru, *The Discovery of India*, 609.

85. Nehru, *The Discovery of India*, 609.

86. Quoted in Nazeem Jabbar, *Historiography and Writing in Postcolonial India* (London: Routledge, 2009), 90.

87. See Manu Bhagavan, *India and the Quest for One World: The Peacemakers* (New York: Palgrave Macmillan, 2013); Bhagavan, "A New Hope: India, the United Nations and the Making of the Universal Declaration of Human Rights"; Klaus Schlichtmann, "India and the Quest for an Effective United Nations."

88. Nehru, "Message for the UN Radio Department Broadcast in a UN Programme."

89. Chacko, "The Internationalist Nationalist."

90. Nehru, "Message for the UN Radio Department Broadcast in a UN Programme."

91. The ground-breaking nature of the event is captured partly by the response from former colonial powers such as Great Britain. They were concerned that Nehru wanted to build an Asian communist bloc, which could not be further from the truth. Vineet Thakur, "An Asian Drama: The Asian Relations Conference, 1947."

92. Speech at the Bombay Branch of the Indian Council of World Affairs, 1946. Quoted in Thakur, "An Asian Drama," 677.

93. Nehru, "A United Asia," 232.

94. Nehru, "A United Asia," 231.

95. Vijay Prashad, *The Darker Nations*, 31–50.

96. Chacko, "The Internationalist Nationalist," 190–94.

97. Richard Wright, *The Color Curtain: A Report on the Bandung Conference*. See recent critical essays in Luis Eslava et al., *Bandung, Global History, and International Law: Critical Pasts and Pending Futures*.

98. Louro, *Comrades against Imperialism*, 256–83.

99. Odd Arne Westad, *The Global Cold War: Third World Interventions and the Making of Our Times*, especially chaps. 1–3.

100. As Nehru's biographer B. R. Nanda states, "After the attainment of independence . . . Nehru had to reckon with other, and, in some ways, more serious constraints. The communal fanaticism and violence which followed the partition of the subcontinent, the mass migration of refugees across the new borders with Pakistan, the virtual breakdown of an administration whose cadres had been reshuffled on a religious basis, the reorganization of the armed forces, the scarcity of food and necessities of life, the accentuation of inflationary pressures inherited from the war period, the problem of integrating 500-odd princely states in the Indian Union, the crisis in Hyderabad and the armed conflict with Pakistan over Kashmir, together made up a formidable agenda for Nehru's government during the first years of independence. And as if this was not enough, the international situation was bedevilled by the cold war between the United States and the Soviet Union." *Jawaharlal Nehru: Rebel and Statesman*, chap. 9.

101. Rorden Wilkinson, *The WTO: Crisis and the Governance of Global Trade*.

102. Amrita Narlikar, "Who Makes the Rules? The Politics of Developing Country Participation and Influence in the WTO"; also see Narlikar, *The World Trade Organization: A Very Short Introduction*.

103. Soo Yeon Kim, *Power and the Governance of Global Trade: From the GATT to the WTO*, 23–55.

104. Wilkinson, *The WTO*, 8.

105. Ilan Kapoor, "Deliberative Democracy and the WTO," 533; Fatoumata Jawara and Aileen Kwa, *Behind the Scenes at the WTO: The Real World of International Trade Negotiations*, xxxviii–xli.

106. Richard H. Steinberg, "In the Shadow of Law or Power? Consensus-Based Bargaining and Outcomes in the GATT/WTO," 347–48.

107. Bernard Hoekman, "Global Trade Governance," 609.

108. Wilkinson, *The WTO*, 75–100.

109. Narlikar, "Who Makes the Rules?" 86.

110. Sarah Joseph, *Blame It on the WTO? A Human Rights Critique*, 62.

111. James Scott, Erin Hannah, Amy Janzwood, and Rorden Wilkinson, "What Kind of Civil Society? The Changing Complexion of Public Engagement at the WTO."

112. Kristen Hopewell, "Invisible Barricades: Civil Society and the Discourse of the WTO."

113. Joseph, *Blame It on the WTO?* 58.

114. Mathias Risse and Gabriel Wollner, *Trade Justice: A Philosophical Plea for a Global New Deal*.

115. See, for example, David Held, *Democracy and the Global Order: From the Modern State to Cosmopolitan Governance*, and Held, *Global Covenant*; Daniele Archibugi, *The Global Commonwealth of Citizens*; Carol Gould, *Globalizing Democracy and Human Rights*.

116. Archibugi et al., "Mapping Global Democracy"; Terry Macdonald, *Global Stakeholder Democracy: Power and Representation Beyond Liberal States*; Mathias Koenig-Archibugi, "Fuzzy Citizenship in Global Society."

117. Daniele Archibugi, "Cosmopolitan Democracy and Its Critics: A Review," 451.

118. Archibugi, *Global Commonwealth*, 114–19.

119. Miller, "Against Global Democracy"; Song, "The Boundary Problem in Democratic Theory"; Thomas Christiano, "Is Democratic Legitimacy Possible for International Institutions?"; Charles Beitz, "Global Political Justice and the Democratic Deficit."

120. Buchanan and Keohane, "The Legitimacy of Global Governance Institutions."

121. Buchanan and Keohane, "The Legitimacy of Global Governance Institutions."

122. Adrian Little and Kate Macdonald, "Pathways to Global Democracy? Escaping the Statist Imaginary"; Laura Valentini, "No Global Demos, No Global Democracy? A Systematization and Critique."

123. Miller does not make this response entirely, but he does motivate his critique of global democracy with the concern that democrats ought to prioritize saving domestic democracy from backsliding. Miller, "Against Global Democracy," 159.

124. Valdez makes a similar point in her critique of Habermas's view of democratizing global governance (and of neo-Kantians in general). Valdez, *Transnational Cosmopolitanism*, 61.

125. John Glenn, "Global Governance the Democratic Deficit: Stifling Voices of the Global South.".

126. See Valdez, *Transnational Cosmopolitanism*, for a compelling account of transnational global injustice.

127. Miller, "Against Global Democracy," 156–59.

128. Miller, "Against Global Democracy," 158.

129. Miller, "Against Global Democracy," 158.

130. To be sure, the critique is also driven by heads of state desiring immunity from prosecution, and the ICC as an important last resort for justice among many African civil society organizations. Many ICC cases are also self-referred by African governments. But there is nonetheless a problem of unequal enforcement when Western heads of state are almost never prosecuted for war crimes. For a critique of the anti-Africa narrative, see Brendon J. Cannon, Dominic R. Pkalya, and Bosire Maragia, "The International Criminal Court and Africa: Contextualizing the Anti-ICC Narrative."

131. Federica Marsi, "Can the ICC Deliver Justice in Afghanistan?"

132. See the African Union's criticism of the ICC. African Union, "Withdrawal Strategy Document."

133. Song, "The Boundary Problem in Democratic Theory."

134. Song, "The Boundary Problem in Democratic Theory," 62.

135. Song, "The Boundary Problem in Democratic Theory," 62–65.

136. Buchanan and Keohane, "The Legitimacy of Global Governance Institutions."

137. Buchanan and Keohane, "The Legitimacy of Global Governance Institutions," 432–33.

138. James Bohman makes a similar point regarding the importance of transnational democracy for nondomination in *Democracy across Borders: From Dêmos to Dêmoi*, 6–11.

139. B. S. Chimni makes a similar critique in Chimni, "Global Capitalism and Global Democracy: Subverting the Other?" in *Global Democracy*, 233–54. Also see Klaus Dingwerth, "Global Democracy and the Democratic Minimum: Why a Procedural Account Alone Is Insufficient."

140. Chimni, "Global Capitalism and Global Democracy: Subverting the Other?" in *Global Democracy*, 133.

141. Held, *Democracy and the Global Order*, 279–80.

142. Held, *Democracy and the Global Order*, 279–80.

143. Song, "The Boundary Problem in Democratic Theory."

144. Mazower, *Governing the World*, 305–42.

145. Laurence R. Helfer, "Regime Shifting in the International Intellectual Property System."

146. Susan K. Sell, "TRIPS Was Never Enough: Vertical Forum Shifting, FTAS, ACTA, and TPP."

147. Keith Johnson, "US Effort to Depart WTO Gathers Momentum," *Foreign Policy*, May 27, 2020, https://foreignpolicy.com/2020/05/27/world-trade-organization-united-states-departure-china/.

148. Valdez, *Transnational Cosmopolitanism*.

149. Richard Miller also warns against the "fatal lure" of global institutional reform and instead advocates placing hope on global social movements. Miller, "Global Institutional Reform and Global Social Movements: From False Promise to Realistic Hope," especially 511–14.

150. Thakur, "An Asian Drama," 81.

151. Steven Lukes, *Power: A Radical View*.

152. Although my focus is counterhegemonic power in global governance, that is, marginalized actors influencing decision-making at the global level, one way of compelling dominant states to act more justly in general is to intervene in their domestic politics. For a compelling account of counterhegemonic reform intervention—i.e., interventions that promote justice within (hegemonic) foreign societies, see Lucia Rafanelli, *Promoting Justice across Borders: The Ethics of Reform Intervention*.

153. A. M. Rosenthal, "Nehru Denounces West's Alliances; Calls Them Threat to Peace—Cites Matters on Which US and India Differ."

154. Nehru, "World Union and Collective Security."

155. John Dryzek, *Deliberative Global Politics, Discourse and Democracy in a Divided World*.

156. Dryzek, *Deliberative Global Politics*, 22–28.

157. As in the case of making public health an important part of the discursive framework surrounding intellectual property.

158. Dryzek, *Deliberative Global Politics*, 159–60.

159. Kate Macdonald and Terry Macdonald, "Non-Electoral Accountability in Global Politics: Strengthening Democratic Control within the Global Garment Industry."

160. OPEC is a classic example. See Christopher Dietrich, *Oil Revolution: Anticolonial Elites, Sovereign Rights, and the Economic Culture of Decolonization*.

161. World Trade Organization, "Groups in the Negotiations."

162. Amrita Narlikar, "Collective Agency, Systemic Consequences: Bargaining Coalitions in the WTO," 185–92.

163. Narlikar, "Collective Agency," 192–94.

164. Narlikar, "Collective Agency," 195.

165. Narlikar, "Collective Agency," 198–200.

166. Charles Beitz expresses skepticism about the importance of global political equality in realizing individuals' interest in being recognized by others as equals. Beitz, "Global Political Justice and the Democratic Deficit," 244.

167. On the importance of institutionalizing transnational social movements, see Sidney Tarrow, *The New Transnational Activism*, 176.

168. On such an approach to normative theorizing, see Brooke Acklery et al., "Unearthing Grounded Normative Theory: Practices and Commitments of Empirical Research in Political Theory."

169. La Via Campesina, "La Via Campesina Members."

170. M. Jahi Chappell, "Global Movements for Food Justice," 720.

171. María Elena Martínez-Torres and Peter M. Rosset, "La Vía Campesina: The Birth and Evolution of a Transnational Social Movement," 158.

172. Martínez-Torres and Peter M. Rosset, "La Vía Campesina," 158.

173. Hannah Wittman, "Reconnecting Agriculture and the Environment: Food Sovereignty and the Agrarian Basis of Ecological Citizenship," 91–105.

174. La Via Campesina, "About La Via Campesina: Via Campesina." On the "food sovereignty" movement, see Raj Patel, "Food Sovereignty."

175. UNHCR, "UN Declaration on the Rights of Peasants and Other People Working in Rural Areas," UNHCR Resolution 39/12 (2018), https://digitallibrary.un.org/record/1650694?ln=en#record-files-collapse-header.

176. Annette A. Desmarais, *La Via Campesina: Globalization and the Power of Peasants*, 128.

177. Desmarais, *La Via Campesina: Globalization and the Power of Peasants*, 129.

178. Desmarais, *La Via Campesina*, 130.

179. Desmarais, *La Via Campesina*, 130.

180. Martínez-Torres and Rosset, "La Vía Campesina"; Chappell, "Global Movements for Food Justice," 720.

181. La Via Campesina, "Mistica Is One of the Principles Uniting La Via Campesina."

182. La Via Campesina, "Salute to India's Farmers! Global Social Movements Issue Solidarity as Protest Completes a Year."

183. Chappell, "Global Movements for Food Justice," 725.

184. See the case of the Zapatistas and the Movimento Sem Terra. Amory Starr, María Elena Martínez-Torres, and Peter Rosset, "Participatory Democracy in Action. Practices of the Zapatistas and the Movimento Sem Terra," *Latin American Perspectives* (2011) 30(1): 102–119.

185. Jonas Tallberg et al., "NGO Influence in International Organizations: Information, Access and Exchange."

186. Erin Hannah, James Scott, and Rorden Wilkinson, "Reforming WTO-Civil Society Engagement," 432. As one LVC leader states in Annette A. Desmarais's study, "Multilateral institutions tend to slot us all into one space—a space that we must also share with agribusiness. This multi-stakeholder process is the bureaucratization of participation. It smells rotten and effectively serves to distance the base." Desmarais, *Globalization and the Power of Peasants*, 133.

187. Kristen Hopewell, "Multilateral Trade Governance as Social Field: Global Civil Society and the WTO."

188. Martínez-Torres and Rosset, "La Vía Campesina," 162. Desmarais, *Globalization and the Power of Peasants*, 132–33.

189. See the case of hundreds of African activists denied entry into Canada to protest at the 2022 International AIDS conference. See Cullinan, "AIDS Conference Activists Protest 'Systemic Racism' behind Canadian Visa Denials to African Delegates."

190. Desmarais, *Globalization and the Power of Peasants*, 133.

191. Terry Macdonald, *Global Stakeholder Democracy: Power and Representation Beyond Liberal States*.

192. Macdonald, *Global Stakeholder Democracy*, 163–92.

193. Macdonald, *Global Stakeholder Democracy*, 172–91 and 211–18.

Conclusion

1. See Anna Stilz for a compelling critique of instrumentalist justifications of self-determination. Stilz, "Decolonization and Self-Determination," 6.

2. Nkrumah, *Neocolonialism*, 254.

3. David Herbling and Dandan Li, "China's Belt and Road Leaves Kenya with a Railroad to Nowhere."

4. Herbling and Li, "China's Belt and Road."

5. Uighurs have always had second-class citizenship within China, and they now face forced assimilation, forced sterilization, arbitrary detention, and other human rights abuses. See Amnesty International, "China: Draconian Repression of Muslims in Xinjiang Amounts to Crimes against Humanity."

6. There is now an emerging philosophical literature on global and transnational resistance after a long period of neglect by theorists of global justice. See Lea Ypi, *Global Justice and Avant-Garde Political Agency*, especially 154–74; Simon Caney, "Responding to Global Injustice: On the Right of Resistance"; Inés Valdez, *Transnational Cosmopolitanism: Kant, Du Bois, and Justice as Political Craft*; Monique Deveaux, *Poverty, Solidarity, and Poor-Led Social Movements*; Lucia Rafanelli, "Not Just War by Other Means: Cross-Border Engagement as Political Struggle."

7. See Burke Hendrix on the idea of normative permissions in the context of Indigenous political resistance. Hendrix, *Strategies of Justice: Aboriginal Peoples, Persistent Injustice, and the Ethics of Political Action*.

8. Césaire, *Letter to Maurice Thorez*, 152; Césaire, *Discourse on Colonialism*, 73.

REFERENCES

Abi-Habib, Maria. "The Forgotten Colonial Forces of World War II." *New York Times Magazine*, September 1, 2020. https://www.nytimes.com/2020/09/01/magazine/the-forgotten -colonial-forces-of-world-war-ii.html.

———. "How China Got Sri Lanka to Cough Up a Port." *New York Times*, June 25, 2018. https://www.nytimes.com/2018/06/25/world/asia/china-sri-lanka-port.html.

Ackerly, Brooke, Luis Cabrera, Fonna Forman, Genevieve Fuji Johnson, Chris Tenove, and Antje Wiener. "Unearthing Grounded Normative Theory: Practices and Commitments of Empirical Research in Political Theory." *Critical Review of International Social and Political Philosophy* 27, no. 2 (February 2024): 156–82. https://doi.org/10.1080/13698230.2021 .1894020.

Adow, Mohammed. "Nigeria's Dangerous Skin Whitening Obsession." *Al Jazeera*, April 6, 2013. https://www.aljazeera.com/features/2013/4/6/nigerias-dangerous-skin-whitening -obsession.

African Union. "Withdrawal Strategy Document." January 12, 2017. Posted on Human Rights Watch website. https://www.hrw.org/sites/default/files/supporting_resources/icc _withdrawal_strategy_jan._2017.pdf.

Ahlman, Jeffrey S. *Living with Nkrumahism: Nation, State, and Pan-Africanism in Ghana*. Athens: Ohio University Press, 2017.

Akbar, Amna A. "Demands for a Democratic Political Economy." *Harvard Law Review* 132, no. 1 (November 2020): 90–118.

Alcoff, Linda Martín. *Visible Identities: Race, Gender, and the Self*. Oxford: Oxford University Press, 2005.

Allee, Todd, and Clint Peinhardt. "Evaluating Three Explanations for the Design of Bilateral Investment Treaties." *World Politics* 66, no. 1 (January 2014): 47–87. https://doi.org/10.1017 /S0043887113000324.

Amarante, Verónica, Ronelle Burger, Grieve Chelwa, John Cockburn, Ana Kassouf, Andrew McKay, and Julieta Zurbrigg. "Underrepresentation of Developing Country Researchers in Development Research." *Applied Economics Letters* 29, no. 17 (October 2022): 1659–64. https://doi.org/10.1080/13504851.2021.1965528.

Amin, Samir. "Underdevelopment and Dependence in Black Africa—Origins and Contemporary Forms." *Journal of Modern African Studies* 10, no. 4 (December 1972): 503–24. https://doi.org/10.1017/S0022278X00022801.

Amnesty International. "China: Draconian Repression of Muslims in Xinjiang Amounts to Crimes against Humanity." June 10, 2021. https://www.amnesty.org/en/latest/news/2021/06 /china-draconian-repression-of-muslims-in-xinjiang-amounts-to-crimes-against-humanity/.

Anderson, Benedict. *Imagined Communities: Reflections on the Origin and Spread of Nationalism*. Brooklyn, NY: Verso, 2006.

Anderson, Elizabeth. "Equality." In *The Oxford Handbook of Political Philosophy*, edited by David Estlund, 40–57. Oxford: Oxford University Press, 2012.

Anderson, Elizabeth. *Private Government: How Employers Rule Our Lives (and Why We Don't Talk about It)*. Princeton, NJ: Princeton University Press, 2019.

———. "What Is the Point of Equality?" *Ethics* 109, no. 2 (January 1999): 287–337. https://doi.org/10.1086/233897.

Anghie, Antony. *Imperialism, Sovereignty and the Making of International Law*. Cambridge: Cambridge University Press, 2007.

Anievas, Alexander, Nivi Manchanda, and Robbie Shilliam, eds. *Race and Racism in International Relations: Confronting the Global Colour Line*. London: Routledge, 2014.

Appiah, Kwame Anthony. *Cosmopolitanism: Ethics in a World of Strangers*. London: Penguin UK, 2015.

Arauz, Andres, Mark Weisbrot, Andrew Bunker, and Jake Johnson. "Bolivia's Economic Transformation: Macroeconomic Policies, Institutional Changes, and Results." Center for Economic and Policy Research, October 2019. http://cepr.net/images/stories/reports/bolivia-macro-2019-10.pdf.

Archibugi, Daniele. "Cosmopolitan Democracy and Its Critics: A Review." *European Journal of International Relations* 10, no. 3 (September 2004): 437–73. https://doi.org/10.1177/1354066104045543.

———. *The Global Commonwealth of Citizens: Toward Cosmopolitan Democracy*. Princeton, NJ: Princeton University Press, 2008.

Archibugi, Daniele, Mathias Koenig-Archibugi, and Raffaele Marchetti, eds. "Mapping Global Democracy." In *Global Democracy: Normative and Empirical Perspectives*, 1–21. Cambridge University Press, 2011.

Askew, Kelly. "African Socialism." Entry in Oxford Bibliographies. Last modified February 22, 2018. https://www.oxfordbibliographies.com/display/document/obo-9780199846733/obo-9780199846733-0200.xml.

Banai, Ayelet. "Is Investor-State Arbitration Unfair? A Freedom-Based Perspective." *Global Justice: Theory Practice Rhetoric* 10, no. 1 (December 2017). https://doi.org/10.21248/gjn.10.1.112.

Barkawi, Tarak, and Keith Stanski, eds. *Orientalism and War*. New York: Columbia University Press, 2012.

Barry, Brian. *Culture and Equality: An Egalitarian Critique of Multiculturalism*. Cambridge, MA: Harvard University Press, 2002.

Bath, Vivienne. "The South and Alternative Models of Trade and Investment Regulation: Chinese Investment and Approaches to International Investment Agreements." In *Reconceptualizing International Investment Law from the Global South*, edited by Fabio Morosini and Michelle Ratton Sanchez Badin, 47–94. Cambridge: Cambridge University Press, 2017.

BBC News. "Isabel Marant: Designer Apologises for Mexican Appropriation." November 17, 2020. https://www.bbc.com/news/world-latin-america-54971582.

———. "Sri Lanka Protest over Chinese Investment Turns Ugly." January 7, 2017. https://www.bbc.com/news/world-asia-38541673.

———. "Vietnam Detains 100 after Anti-China Economic Zone Protests Turn Violent." June 11, 2018. https://www.bbc.com/news/world-asia-44436019.

Beckert, Sven. *Empire of Cotton: A Global History*. New York: Knopf Doubleday Publishing Group, 2014.

Bedjaoui, Mohammed. *Towards a New International Economic Order*. Teaneck, NJ: Holmes & Meier, 1979.

Beitz, Charles R. "Does Global Inequality Matter?" *Metaphilosophy* 32, no. 1–2 (2001): 95–112. https://doi.org/10.1111/1467-9973.00177.

———. "Global Political Justice and the Democratic Deficit." In *Reasons and Recognition: Essays on the Philosophy of T. M. Scanlon*, edited by R. Jay Wallace, Rahul Kumar, and Samuel Freeman, 232–50. Oxford: Oxford University Press, 2011.

———. "Justice and International Relations." *Philosophy & Public Affairs* 4, no. 4 (1975): 360–89.

———. *Political Theory and International Relations: Revised Edition.* Princeton, NJ: Princeton University Press, 1999.

Bell, Duncan, ed. *Empire, Race and Global Justice.* Cambridge: Cambridge University Press, 2019.

Bellamy, Richard. "Globalization and Representative Democracy: Normative Challenges." In *The Oxford Handbook of Political Representation in Liberal Democracies,* edited by Robert Rohrschneider and Jacques Thomassen, 655–72. Oxford: Oxford University Press, 2020.

Berlin, Isaiah, and Ian Harris. "Two Concepts of Liberty." In *Liberty,* edited by Henry Hardy. Oxford: Oxford University Press, 2016.

Bernstorff, Jochen von, and Philipp Dann. *The Battle for International Law: South-North Perspectives on the Decolonization Era.* Oxford: Oxford University Press, 2019.

Bhagavan, Manu. *India and the Quest for One World: The Peacemakers.* New York: Springer, 2013.

———. "A New Hope: India, the United Nations and the Making of the Universal Declaration of Human Rights." *Modern Asian Studies* 44, no. 2 (March 2010): 311–47. https://doi.org/10.1017/S0026749X08003600.

Bhargava, Rajeev. "Overcoming the Epistemic Injustice of Colonialism." *Global Policy* 4, no. 4 (2013): 413–17. https://doi.org/10.1111/1758-5899.12093.

Bhatia, Udit. *The Indian Constituent Assembly: Deliberations on Democracy.* UK: Taylor & Francis, 2017.

Biney, Ama. "The Development of Kwame Nkrumah's Political Thought in Exile, 1966–1972." *Journal of African History* 50, no. 1 (March 2009): 81–100. https://doi.org/10.1017/S0021853709004216.

———. *The Political and Social Thought of Kwame Nkrumah.* New York: Springer, 2011.

Blake, Michael. "Distributive Justice, State Coercion, and Autonomy." *Philosophy & Public Affairs* 30, no. 3 (2001): 257–96. https://doi.org/10.1111/j.1088-4963.2001.00257.x.

Blicharska, Malgorzata, Richard J. Smithers, Magdalena Kuchler, Ganesh K. Agrawal, José M. Gutiérrez, Ahmed Hassanali, Saleemul Huq, et al. "Steps to Overcome the North–South Divide in Research Relevant to Climate Change Policy and Practice." *Nature Climate Change* 7, no. 1 (January 2017): 21–27. https://doi.org/10.1038/nclimate3163.

Blomfield, Megan. *Global Justice, Natural Resources, and Climate Change.* Oxford: Oxford University Press, 2019.

Blumenfeld, Jacob. "Expropriation of the Expropriators." *Philosophy & Social Criticism* 49, no. 4 (May 2023): 431–47. https://doi.org/10.1177/01914537211059513.

Bohman, James. *Democracy across Borders: From Dêmos to Dêmoi.* Cambridge, MA: MIT Press, 2010.

Bonilla-Silva, Eduardo. *Racism without Racists: Color-Blind Racism and the Persistence of Racial Inequality in America.* Lanham, MD: Rowman & Littlefield, 2021.

Bonnitcha, Jonathan, Lauge N. Skovgaard Poulsen, and Michael Waibel. *The Political Economy of the Investment Treaty Regime.* Oxford: Oxford University Press, 2018.

Bose, Anuja. "Frantz Fanon and the Politicization of the Third World as a Collective Subject." *Interventions* 21, no. 5 (4 July 2019): 671–89. https://doi.org/10.1080/1369801X.2019.1585925.

———. "Frantz Fanon and the Politics of a Global Anti-Imperialism," n.d.

Breuilly, John. *The Oxford Handbook of the History of Nationalism.* Oxford: Oxford University Press, 2013.

Brooks, Eireann. "Cultural Imperialism vs. Cultural Protectionism: Hollywood's Response to UNESCO Efforts to Promote Cultural Diversity Note." *Journal of International Business and Law* 5 (2006): 112–36.

Brooks, Thom. *The Oxford Handbook of Global Justice.* Oxford: Oxford University Press, 2020.

Brown, Ola. "The Health Dangers of Linking Fair Skin with Beauty and Success." CNN, January 15, 2019. https://www.cnn.com/2019/01/15/health/banning-bleaching-products-in-africa/index.html.

Brownstein, Michael S., and Jennifer Mather Saul, eds. *Implicit Bias and Philosophy: Metaphysics and Epistemology*. Oxford: Oxford University Press, 2016.

Buchanan, Allen, and Robert O. Keohane. "The Legitimacy of Global Governance Institutions." *Ethics & International Affairs* 20, no. 4 (December 2006): 405–37. https://doi.org/10.1111/j.1747-7093.2006.00043.x.

Buchanan, Allen, Tony Cole, and Robert O. Keohane. "Justice in the Diffusion of Innovation." In *Political Theory Without Borders*, edited by Robert E. Goodin and James S. Fishkin, 133–61. Hoboken, NJ: John Wiley & Sons, 2015.

Büthe, Tim, and Helen V. Milner. "Foreign Direct Investment and Institutional Diversity in Trade Agreements: Credibility, Commitment, and Economic Flows in the Developing World, 1971–2007." *World Politics* 66, no. 1 (January 2014): 88–122. https://doi.org/10.1017/S0043887113000336.

Butt, Daniel. *Rectifying International Injustice: Principles of Compensation and Restitution between Nations*. Oxford: Oxford University Press 2009.

Byrd, Jodi A., and Michael Rothberg. "Between Subalternity and Indigeneity: Critical Categories for Postcolonial Studies." *Interventions* 13, no. 1 (1 March 2011): 1–12. https://doi.org/10.1080/1369801X.2011.545574.

Caney, Simon. *Justice beyond Borders: A Global Political Theory*. Oxford: Oxford University Press, 2006.

———. "Responding to Global Injustice: On the Right of Resistance." *Social Philosophy and Policy* 32, no. 1 (October 2015): 51–73. https://doi.org/10.1017/S0265052515000072.

———. "The Right to Resist Global Injustice." In *The Oxford Handbook of Global Justice*, edited by Thom Brooks, 511–35. Oxford: Oxford University Press, 2020.

Cannon, Brendon J., Dominic R. Pkalya, and Bosire Maragia. "The International Criminal Court and Africa: Contextualizing the Anti-ICC Narrative." *African Journal of International Criminal Justice* 2, no. 1/2 (2016): 6–28.

Cardoso, Fernando Henrique, and Enzo Faletto. *Dependency and Development in Latin America*. Translated by Marjory Mattingly Urquidi. Oakland: University of California Press, 1979.

Carey, Jane, and Ben Silverstein. "Thinking with and beyond Settler Colonial Studies: New Histories after the Postcolonial." *Postcolonial Studies* 23, no. 1 (2 January 2020): 1–20. https://doi.org/10.1080/13688790.2020.1719569.

Césaire, Aimé. *A Tempest: Based on Shakespeare's The Tempest, Adaptation for a Black Theatre*. Translated by Richard Miller. 1st TCG ed. New York: TCG Translations, 2002.

———. "Culture and Colonisation." *Présence Africaine*, 1956, 193–207.

———. *Discourse on Colonialism*. New York: NYU Press, 2001.

———. "Letter to Maurice Thorez." *Social Text* 28, no. 2 (2010): 145–52. https://doi.org/10.1215/01642472-2009-072.

———. "Man of Culture and His Responsibilities." *Présence Africaine*, no. 24/25 (1959): 125–32.

Chacko, Priya. "The Internationalist Nationalist: Pursuing an Ethical Modernity with Jawaharlal Nehru." In *International Relations and Non-Western Thought: Imperialism, Colonialism and Investigations of Global Modernity*, edited by Robbie Shilliam, 178–96. London: Routledge, 2010.

Chan, Shuk Ying. "Expropriation as Reparation." *American Journal of Political Science* (August 2024). https://doi.org/10.1111/ajps.12891.

Chang, Ha-Joon. *Kicking away the Ladder: Development Strategy in Historical Perspective*. London: Anthem Press, 2002.

Chapman, Jessica M. *Remaking the World: Decolonization and the Cold War*. Lexington: University Press of Kentucky, 2023.

Chappell, M. Jahi. "Global Movements for Food Justice." In *The Oxford Handbook of Food, Politics, and Society*, edited by Ronald J. Herring, 717–38. Oxford: Oxford University Press, 2014.

Chatterjee, Partha. *The Nation and Its Fragments: Colonial and Postcolonial Histories.* Princeton, NJ: Princeton University Press, 2020.

Chew, Matthew. "Contemporary Re-Emergence of the Qipao: Political Nationalism, Cultural Production and Popular Consumption of a Traditional Chinese Dress." *China Quarterly* 189 (March 2007): 144–61. https://doi.org/10.1017/S0305741006000841.

Chimni, B. S. "Global Capitalism and Global Democracy: Subverting the Other?" In *Global Democracy: Normative and Empirical Perspectives,* edited by Daniele Archibugi, Mathias Koenig-Archibugi, and Raffaele Marchetti, 233–54. Cambridge: Cambridge University Press, 2011.

———. "International Institutions Today: An Imperial Global State in the Making." *European Journal of International Law* 15, no. 1 (February 2004): 1–37. https://doi.org/10.1093/ejil/15.1.1.

Chow, Andrew R. "Black Artists Built Country Music—And Then It Left Them Behind." *TIME,* September 11, 2019. https://time.com/5673476/ken-burns-country-music-black-artists/.

Christensen, James. *Trade Justice.* Oxford: Oxford University Press, 2017.

Christiano, Thomas. "Is Democratic Legitimacy Possible for International Institutions?" In *Global Democracy: Normative and Empirical Perspectives,* edited by Daniele Archibugi, Mathias Koenig-Archibugi, and Raffaele Marchetti, 69–95. Cambridge: Cambridge University Press, 2011.

Cohen, Gerald A. *Why Not Socialism?* Princeton, NJ: Princeton University Press, 2009.

Collins, Lauren. "The Haitian Revolution and the Hole in French High-School History." *New Yorker,* December 3, 2020. https://www.newyorker.com/culture/culture-desk/the-haitian-revolution-and-the-hole-in-french-high-school-history.

Colvin, Christopher. "Overview of the Reparations Program in South Africa." In *The Handbook of Reparations,* edited by Pablo De Greiff, 176–214. Oxford: Oxford University Press, 2008.

Cooper, Frederick. *Africa since 1940: The Past of the Present.* Cambridge: Cambridge University Press, 2002.

———. *Citizenship between Empire and Nation: Remaking France and French Africa, 1945–1960.* Princeton, NJ: Princeton University Press, 2014.

———. *Colonialism in Question: Theory, Knowledge, History.* Oakland: University of California Press, 2005.

Cotula, Lorenzo, Thierry Berger, Lise Johnson, Guven Brooke, and Jesse Coleman. *UNCITRAL Working Group III on ISDS Reform: How Cross-Cutting Issues Reshape Reform Options.* New York: Columbia Center on Sustainable Investment, July 2019. https://scholarship.law.columbia.edu/sustainable_investment_staffpubs/148.

Coulthard, Glen Sean. *Red Skin, White Masks: Rejecting the Colonial Politics of Recognition.* Minneapolis: University of Minnesota Press, 2014.

Cozens, Claire. "Charity Blames Media for Perpetuating Stereotypes." *The Guardian,* January 7, 2002. https://www.theguardian.com/society/2002/jan/07/charities.

Crane, Diana. "Cultural Globalization and the Dominance of the American Film Industry: Cultural Policies, National Film Industries, and Transnational Film." *International Journal of Cultural Policy* 20, no. 4 (August 2014): 365–82. https://doi.org/10.1080/10286632.2013.832233.

Crewe, Emma, and Elizabeth Harrison. *Whose Development?: An Ethnography of Aid.* London: Bloomsbury Academic, 1998.

Cross, Ciaran, and Christian Schliemann-Radbruch. "When Investment Arbitration Curbs Domestic Regulatory Space: Consistent Solutions through Amicus Curiae Submissions by Regional Organisations." *Law and Development Review* 6, no. 2 (January 2013). https://doi.org/10.1515/ldr-2013-0021.

Cullinan, Kerry. "AIDS Conference Activists Protest 'Systemic Racism' behind Canadian Visa Denials too African Delegates." Health Policy Watch, July 29, 2022. https://healthpolicy-watch.news/aids-conference-protests-systemic-racism/.

Dahl, Robert A. "Can International Organizations Be Democratic? A Skeptic's View." In *Democracy's Edges*, edited by Ian Shapiro and Casiano Hacker-Cordón, 19–36. Cambridge: Cambridge University Press, 1999.

Darwall, Stephen L. "Two Kinds of Respect." *Ethics* 88, no. 1 (October 1977): 36–49. https://doi.org/10.1086/292054.

Debter, Lauren. "Walmart Will Cough Up $282 Million to Put Years-Long Bribery Investigation Behind It." *Forbes*, June 20, 2019. https://www.forbes.com/sites/laurendebter/2019/06/20/walmart-will-cough-up-282-million-to-put-years-long-bribery-investigation-behind-it/#4e386edd4ac5.

Demeter, Márton. *Academic Knowledge Production and the Global South: Questioning Inequality and Under-Representation.* New York: Springer Nature, 2020.

Desmarais, Annette Aurélie. *La Via Campesina: Globalization and the Power of Peasants.* Chicago: Pluto Press, 2007.

Deveaux, Monique. *Poverty, Solidarity, and Poor-Led Social Movements.* Oxford: Oxford University Press, 2021.

Dietrich, Christopher R. W. *Oil Revolution: Anticolonial Elites, Sovereign Rights, and the Economic Culture of Decolonization.* Cambridge: Cambridge University Press, 2017.

Dietsch, Peter. *Catching Capital: The Ethics of Tax Competition.* Oxford: Oxford University Press, 2015.

Dikötter, Frank. *The Cultural Revolution: A People's History, 1962–1976.* London: Bloomsbury Publishing, 2016.

Dingwerth, Klaus. "Global Democracy and the Democratic Minimum: Why a Procedural Account Alone Is Insufficient." *European Journal of International Relations* 20, no. 4 (December 2014): 1124–47. https://doi.org/10.1177/1354066113509116.

Dos Santos, Theotonio. "The Structure of Dependence." *American Economic Review* 60, no. 2 (1970): 231–36.

Dryzek, John S. *Deliberative Global Politics: Discourse and Democracy in a Divided World.* Hoboken, NJ: Wiley, 2006.

Du Bois, W.E.B. *The Souls of Black Folk by W.E.B. Du Bois Illustrated Edition.* 2020.

Duong, Kevin. "Universal Suffrage as Decolonization." *American Political Science Review* 115, no. 2 (May 2021): 412–28. https://doi.org/10.1017/S0003055420000994.

Eberhardt, Pia, and Cecilia Olivet. *Profiting from Injustice: How Law Firms, Arbitrators and Financiers Are Fuelling an Investment Arbitration Boom.* Brussels: Corporate Europe Observatory, 2012.

Edwards, Haley Sweetland. *Shadow Courts: The Tribunals That Rule Global Trade.* New York: Columbia Global Reports, 2016.

Elkins, Zachary, Andrew T. Guzman, and Beth A. Simmons. "Competing for Capital: The Diffusion of Bilateral Investment Treaties, 1960–2000." *International Organization* 60, no. 4 (October 2006). https://doi.org/10.1017/S0020818306060279.

Emerson, Rupert. *From Empire to Nation: The Rise to Self-Assertion of Asian and African Peoples.* Cambridge, MA: Harvard University Press, 1960.

———. *Political Modernization: The Single-Party System.* Denver, CO: Social Science Foundation at the University of Denver, 1963.

Escobar, Arturo. *Encountering Development: The Making and Unmaking of the Third World.* Princeton, NJ: Princeton University Press, 2011.

Eslava, Luis, Michael Fakhri, and Vasuki Nesiah. *Bandung, Global History, and International Law: Critical Pasts and Pending Futures.* Cambridge: Cambridge University Press, 2017.

European Commission. "Audiovisual and Media Services: Shaping Europe's Digital Future." August 28, 2024. https://digital-strategy.ec.europa.eu/en/policies/audiovisual-and-media-services.

Evans, Peter. "Review: After Dependency: Recent Studies of Class, State, and Industrialization." *Latin American Research Review* 20, no. 2 (1985): 149–60.

———. *Dependent Development: The Alliance of Multinational, State, and Local Capital in Brazil.* Princeton, NJ: Princeton University Press, 2018.

Fanon, Frantz. *A Dying Colonialism.* New York: Grove Atlantic, 2022.

———. *Black Skin, White Masks.* Chicago: Pluto Press, 2017.

———. *The Wretched of the Earth.* New York: Grove Atlantic, 2007.

Farrar, Lara. "Chinese Companies 'Rent' Foreigners." CNN, June 29, 2017. http://www.cnn.com/2010/BUSINESS/06/29/china.rent.white.people/index.html.

Ferguson, Ben, and Hillel Steiner. "Exploitation." In *The Oxford Handbook of Distributive Justice*, edited by Serena Olsaretti, 533–54. Oxford: Oxford University Press, 2018.

Ferguson, Niall. *Empire: How Britain Made the Modern World.* London: Penguin UK, 2012.

Fine, Sarah, and Lea Ypi, eds. *Migration in Political Theory: The Ethics of Movement and Membership.* Oxford: Oxford University Press, 2016.

Forere, Malebakeng. "The New South African Protection of Investment Act." In *Reconceptualizing International Investment Law from the Global South*, edited by Fabio Morosini and Michelle Ratton Sanchez Badin, 218–50. Cambridge: Cambridge University Press, 2017.

Forrester, Katrina. "Reparations, History, and the Origins of Global Justice." In *Empire, Race and Global Justice*, edited by Duncan Bell, 22–51. Cambridge: Cambridge University Press, 2019.

Fourie, Carina. "What Is Social Equality? An Analysis of Status Equality as a Strongly Egalitarian Ideal." *Res Publica* 18, no. 2 (May 2012): 107–26. https://doi.org/10.1007/s11158-011-9162-2.

Fourie, Carina, Fabian Schuppert, and Ivo Wallimann-Helmer, eds. *Social Equality: On What It Means to Be Equals.* Oxford: Oxford University Press, 2014.

Frank, Andre Gunder. *Capitalism and Underdevelopment in Latin America: Historical Studies of Chile and Brazil.* New York: Monthly Review Press, 1969.

French, Howard W. *China's Second Continent: How a Million Migrants Are Building a New Empire in Africa.* New York: Alfred A. Knopf, 2014.

Fricker, Miranda. *Epistemic Injustice: Power and the Ethics of Knowing.* Oxford: Clarendon Press, 2007.

Frieden, Jeffry A. "International Investment and Colonial Control: A New Interpretation." *International Organization* 48, no. 4 (1994): 559–93. https://doi.org/10.1017/S0020818300028319.

Gandhi, Leela. *Postcolonial Theory: A Critical Introduction.* New York: Columbia University Press, 2019.

Gandhi, Mohandas. *Gandhi: "Hind Swaraj" and Other Writings.* Cambridge: Cambridge University Press, 2009.

Garcia, Frank J. "Third-Party Funding as Exploitation of the Investment Treaty System Essays: Third-Party Funding and Investor-State Dispute Settlements." *Boston College Law Review* 59, no. 8 (2018): 2911–34.

Garcia, Rodrigo Gómez, and Ben Birkinbine. "Cultural Imperialism Theories." Entry in Oxford Bibliographies. https://www.oxfordbibliographies.com/display/document/obo-9780199756841/obo-9780199756841-0209.xml.

Geismar, Haidy. *Treasured Possessions: Indigenous Interventions into Cultural and Intellectual Property.* Durham, NC: Duke University Press, 2013.

Gellner, Ernest. *Nations and Nationalism.* Ithaca, NY: Cornell University Press, 2008.

Gerbner, George, Sean MacBride, and Colleen Roach. "The New International Information Order." In *The Global Media Debate: Its Rise, Fall and Renewal*, edited by Hamid Mowlana, Kaarle Nordenstreng, and George Gerbner, 3–12. London: Bloomsbury Academic, 1993.

Getachew, Adom. "Universalism after the Post-Colonial Turn: Interpreting the Haitian Revolution." *Political Theory* 44, no. 6 (December 2016): 821–45. https://doi.org/10.1177/0090591 716661018.

———. *Worldmaking after Empire: The Rise and Fall of Self-Determination*. Princeton, NJ: Princeton University Press, 2019. https://doi.org/10.1515/9780691184340.

Getachew, Adom, and Karuna Mantena. "Anticolonialism and the Decolonization of Political Theory." *Critical Times* 4, no. 3 (December 2021): 359–88. https://doi.org/10.1215/26410478 -9355193.

Gibson, Nigel C. "Fanon and Marx Revisited." *Journal of the British Society for Phenomenology* 51, no. 4 (October 2020): 320–36. https://doi.org/10.1080/00071773.2020.1732570.

Gilman, Nils. *Mandarins of the Future: Modernization Theory in Cold War America*. Baltimore, MD: Johns Hopkins University Press, 2007.

Glamis Gold, Ltd. v. The United States of America. 1976. https://www.italaw.com/cases/487.

Glenn, Evelyn Nakano. *Shades of Difference: Why Skin Color Matters*. Stanford, CA: Stanford University Press, 2009.

Glenn, John. "Global Governance and the Democratic Deficit: Stifling the Voice of the South." *Third World Quarterly* 29, no. 2 (February 2008): 217–38. https://doi.org/10.1080/014365 90701806798.

Goodin, Robert E. "Toward an International Rule of Law: Distinguishing International Law-Breakers from Would-Be Law-Makers." In *Current Debates in Global Justice*, edited by Gillian Brock and Darrel Moellendorf, 2:225–46. Berlin/Heidelberg: Springer-Verlag, 2005. https://doi.org/10.1007/1-4020-3847-X_11.

Gorz, André. *Strategy for Labor: A Radical Proposal*. Boston, MA: Beacon Press, 1967.

Goswami, Manu. "Imaginary Futures and Colonial Internationalisms." *American Historical Review* 117, no. 5 (December 2012): 1461–85. https://doi.org/10.1093/ahr/117.5.1461.

Gould, Carol C. *Globalizing Democracy and Human Rights*. Cambridge: Cambridge University Press, 2004.

Grabowski, Alex. "The Definition of Investment under the ICSID Convention: A Defense of Salini Comments." *Chicago Journal of International Law* 15, no. 1 (2015 2014): 287–309.

Griswold, Wendy. *Cultures and Societies in a Changing World*. Los Angeles: SAGE Publications, 2012.

Guven, Brooke, and Lise Johnson. "The Policy Implications of Third-Party Funding in Investor-State Dispute Settlement." *SSRN Electronic Journal*, 2019. https://doi.org/10.2139/ssrn .3661129.

Hall, Catherine. *Civilising Subjects: Colony and Metropole in the English Imagination, 1830–1867*. Chicago: University of Chicago Press, 2002.

Hall, Stuart. *The Fateful Triangle: Race, Ethnicity, Nation*. Cambridge, MA: Harvard University Press, 2017.

Hannah, Erin, James Scott, and Rorden Wilkinson. "Reforming WTO-Civil Society Engagement." *World Trade Review* 16, no. 3 (July 2017): 427–48. https://doi.org/10.1017/S14747456 16000446.

Hansen, William W. "Another Side of Frantz Fanon: Reflections on Socialism and Democracy." *New Political Science* 19, no. 3 (September 1997): 89–111. https://doi.org/10.1080/073931497 08429805.

Hanspal, Jaysim. "Nigeria: Famous Benin Bronzes Will Finally Be Returned to Country." *The Africa Report*, August 8, 2022. https://www.theafricareport.com/229882/nigeria-famous -benin-bronzes-will-finally-be-returned-to-country/.

Harding, Sandra G. *The Feminist Standpoint Theory Reader: Intellectual and Political Controversies*. London: Psychology Press, 2004.

Havercroft, Jonathan. "The Injustices of Global Justice Scholarship." *European Journal of Political Theory* 22, no. 1 (January 2023): 161–70. https://doi.org/10.1177/14748851211000604.

Held, David. *Democracy and the Global Order: From the Modern State to Cosmopolitan Governance*. Hoboken, NJ: John Wiley & Sons, 2013.

———. *Global Covenant: The Social Democratic Alternative to the Washington Consensus*. Hoboken, NJ: John Wiley & Sons, 2013.

Held, David, and Anthony McGrew. *Globalization/Anti-Globalization: Beyond the Great Divide*. Cambridge, UK: Polity, 2007.

Held, Virginia. *Justice and Care: Essential Readings in Feminist Ethics*. London: Routledge, 1995.

Helfer, Laurence R. "Regime Shifting in the International Intellectual Property System." *Perspectives on Politics* 7, no. 1 (March 2009): 39–44. https://doi.org/10.1017/S1537592709090069.

Hendrix, Burke A. *Strategies of Justice: Aboriginal Peoples, Persistent Injustice, and the Ethics of Political Action*. Oxford: Oxford University Press, 2019.

Herbling, David, and Dandan Li. "China's Belt and Road Leaves Kenya with a Railroad to Nowhere." Bloomberg, July 19, 2019. https://www.bloomberg.com/news/features/2019-07-19/china-s-belt-and-road-leaves-kenya-with-a-railroad-to-nowhere.

Herzog, Lisa. "Global Reserve Currencies from the Perspective of Structural Global Justice: Distribution and Domination." *Critical Review of International Social and Political Philosophy* 24, no. 7 (November 2021): 931–53. https://doi.org/10.1080/13698230.2019.1616441.

Hiddleston, Jane. *Aimé Césaire: Inventor of Souls*. Cambridge, UK: Polity, 2025.

Hinton, Perry. "Implicit Stereotypes and the Predictive Brain: Cognition and Culture in 'Biased' Person Perception." *Palgrave Communications* 3, no. 1 (September 2017): 17086. https://doi.org/10.1057/palcomms.2017.86.

Hiro, Dilip. "Protests in Kazakhstan Rattle Russia and China." *The Nation*, February 4, 2022. https://www.thenation.com/article/world/kazakhstan-protest-russia-china/.

Hoekman, Bernard. "Global Trade Governance." In *International Organization and Global Governance*, edited by Thomas G. Weiss and Rorden Wilkinson, 603–15. London: Routledge, 2013.

Hopewell, Kristen. "Invisible Barricades: Civil Society and the Discourse of the WTO." *Globalizations* 14, no. 1 (January 2017): 51–65. https://doi.org/10.1080/14747731.2016.1162984.

———. "Multilateral Trade Governance as Social Field: Global Civil Society and the WTO." *Review of International Political Economy* 22, no. 6 (November 2015): 1128–58. https://doi.org/10.1080/09692290.2015.1066696.

Hopper, Paul. *Understanding Cultural Globalization*. Cambridge, UK: Polity, 2007.

Horne, Alistair. *A Savage War of Peace: Algeria 1954–1962*. London: Pan Macmillan, 2012.

Howe, Stephen. *The New Imperial Histories Reader*. London: Routledge, 2020.

Hunt, Darnell, Ana-Christian Ramón, Michael Tran, Debanjan Roychoudhury, Christina Chica, and Alexandria Brown. *Hollywood Diversity Report 2019: Old Story, New Beginning*. UCLA Social Sciences, 2019. https://socialsciences.ucla.edu/wp-content/uploads/2024/06/UCLA-Hollywood-Diversity-Report-2019-2-21-2019.pdf.

Hussain, Waheed. "Pitting People against Each Other." *Philosophy & Public Affairs* 48, no. 1 (2020): 79–113.

Il Kim, Young, Shi-Young Lee, and Eun–mee Kim. "The Effect of the Korean Screen Quota System on Box Office Performance." *Journal of World Trade* 42, no. 2 (April 2008): 335–46. https://doi.org/10.54648/TRAD2008015.

IMF. "IMF Members' Quotas and Voting Power, and IMF Board of Governors." Accessed October 9, 2024. https://www.imf.org/en/About/executive-board/members-quotas.

Investment Dispute Settlement Navigator. "AEI v. Bolivia." Database accessed October 9, 2024. https://investmentpolicy.unctad.org/investment-dispute-settlement/cases/295/aei-v-bolivia.

———. "Pan American v. Bolivia." Database accessed October 9, 2024. https://investmentpolicy.unctad.org/investment-dispute-settlement/cases/385/pan-american-v-bolivia.

Ip, Kevin K. W. *Egalitarianism and Global Justice: From a Relational Perspective*. New York: Springer, 2016.

Isiksel, Turkuler. "Cosmopolitanism and International Economic Institutions." *Journal of Politics* 82, no. 1 (January 2020): 211–24. https://doi.org/10.1086/705743.

Jabbar, Naheem. *Historiography and Writing Postcolonial India*. London: Routledge, 2009.

Jackson, Robert H. *Quasi-States: Sovereignty, International Relations and the Third World*. Cambridge: Cambridge University Press, 1990.

Jagmohan, Desmond. "Between Race and Nation: Marcus Garvey and the Politics of Self-Determination." *Political Theory* 48, no. 3 (June 2020): 271–302. https://doi.org/10.1177/0090591719897569.

James, Aaron. *Fairness in Practice: A Social Contract for a Global Economy*. Oxford: Oxford University Press, 2012.

James, C.L.R. *Nkrumah and the Ghana Revolution*. Durham, NC: Duke University Press, 2022.

Jaeggi, Rahel. *Alienation*. Translated by Frederick Neuhouser and Alan E. Smith. New York: Columbia University Press, 2016.

James, Leslie, and Elisabeth Leake. *Decolonization and the Cold War: Negotiating Independence*. London: Bloomsbury Publishing, 2015.

James, Paul. "Postdependency? The Third World in an Era of Globalism and Late-Capitalism." *Alternatives* 22, no. 2 (April 1997): 205–26. https://doi.org/10.1177/030437549702200204.

Jani, Disha Karnad. "Unfreedom and Its Opposite: Towards an Intellectual History of the League Against Imperialism." In *The League Against Imperialism: Lives and Afterlives*, edited by Michele L. Louro, Carolien Stolte, Heather Streets-Salter, and Sana Tannoury-Karam, 237–56. Amsterdam: Amsterdam University Press, 2020.

Jansen, Jan C., and Jürgen Osterhammel. *Decolonization: A Short History*. Translated by Jeremiah Riemer. Princeton, NJ: Princeton University Press, 2019.

Jawara, Fatoumata, and Aileen Kwa. *Behind the Scenes at the WTO: The Real World of International Trade Negotiations*. London: Zed Books, 2004.

Jin, Dal Yong. "The Construction of Platform Imperialism in the Globalization Era." *tripleC: Communication, Capitalism & Critique. Open Access Journal for a Global Sustainable Information Society* 11, no. 1 (January 2013): 145–72. https://doi.org/10.31269/triplec.v11i1.458.

Johnson, Keith. "US Frustration at WTO Boils Over, but Departure Would Be Self-Defeating." *Foreign Policy*, May 27, 2020. https://foreignpolicy.com/2020/05/27/world-trade-organization-united-states-departure-china/.

Johnson, Lise, and Lisa Sachs. "Investment Treaties, Investor-State Dispute Settlement, and Inequality: How International Rules and Institutions Can Exacerbate Domestic Disparities." In *International Policy Rules and Inequality: Implications for Global Economic Governance*, edited by José Antonio Ocampo, 112–42. New York: Columbia University Press, 2019.

Joseph, Sarah. *Blame It on the WTO?: A Human Rights Critique*. Oxford: Oxford University Press, 2013.

Julius, A. J. "Nagel's Atlas." *Philosophy and Public Affairs* 34, no. 2 (2006): 176–92.

Kapoor, Ilan. "Deliberative Democracy and the WTO." *Review of International Political Economy* 11, no. 3 (June 2004): 522–41. https://doi.org/10.1080/0969229042000252882.

Kearns, Oliver. *The Covert Colour Line: The Racialised Politics of Western State Intelligence*. Chicago: Pluto Press, 2023.

Kedourie, Elie. *Nationalism*. London: Hutchinson & Co, 1960.

Khader, Serene J. *Decolonizing Universalism: A Transnational Feminist Ethic*. Oxford: Oxford University Press, 2018.

Khilnani, Sunil. "Introduction." In *The Discovery of India*, by Jawaharlal Nehru. New Delhi: Penguin Books India, 2004.

Kim, Hochan. "Cultural Appropriation and Social Recognition." *Philosophy & Public Affairs* 52, no. 3 (2024): 254–88. https://doi.org/10.1111/papa.12261.

Kim, Soo Yeon. *Power and the Governance of Global Trade: From the GATT to the WTO*. Ithaca, NY: Cornell University Press, 2011.

Kleinwachter, Wolfgang. "Three Waves of the Debate." In *The Global Media Debate: Its Rise, Fall and Renewal*, edited by Hamid Mowlana, Kaarle Nordenstreng, and George Gerbner, 13–20. London: Bloomsbury Academic, 1993.

Koenig-Archibugi, Mathias. "Fuzzy Citizenship in Global Society." *Journal of Political Philosophy* 20, no. 4 (2012): 456–80. https://doi.org/10.1111/j.1467-9760.2011.00405.x.

Kohler, Pierre, and Francis Cripps. "Do Trade and Investment (Agreements) Foster Development or Inequality?" GDAE-UNCTAD Working Paper, no. 18 (2018): 3–44.

Kohn, Margaret. "Globalizing Global Justice." In *Empire, Race and Global Justice*, edited by Duncan Bell, 163–83. Cambridge: Cambridge University Press, 2019.

Kolodny, Niko. "Being under the Power of Others." In *Republicanism and the Future of Democracy*, edited by Geneviève Rousselière and Yiftah Elazar, 99–114. Cambridge: Cambridge University Press, 2019.

———. *The Pecking Order: Social Hierarchy as a Philosophical Problem.* Cambridge, MA: Harvard University Press, 2023.

Kwak, Dongchul, and Minjung Kim. "Trade Negotiations in the Digital Era: The Case of OTT Video Streaming Services." *Global Policy* 11, no. S2 (2020): 14–22. https://doi.org/10.1111/1758-5899.12819.

Kwon, Seung-Ho, and Joseph Kim. "The Cultural Industry Policies of the Korean Government and the Korean Wave." *International Journal of Cultural Policy* 20, no. 4 (August 2014): 422–39. https://doi.org/10.1080/10286632.2013.829052.

Kymlicka, Will. *Multicultural Citizenship: A Liberal Theory of Minority Rights.* Oxford: Clarendon Press, 1996.

La Via Campesina. "About La Via Campesina: Via Campesina." Accessed October 10, 2024. https://viacampesina.org/en/international-peasants-voice/.

———. "La Via Campesina Members." 2018. https://viacampesina.org/en/wp-content/uploads/sites/2/2018/03/List-of-members.pdf.

———. "Mistica Is One of the Principles Uniting La Via Campesina." January 10, 2022. https://viacampesina.org/en/mistica-is-one-of-the-principles-uniting-la-via-campesina/.

———. "Salute to India's Farmers! Global Social Movements Issue Solidarity as Protest Completes a Year." November 26, 2021. https://viacampesina.org/en/salute-to-indias-farmers-global-social-movements-issue-solidarity-as-protest-completes-a-year/.

Laborde, Cécile. "Republicanism and Global Justice: A Sketch." *European Journal of Political Theory* 9, no. 1 (January 2010): 48–69. https://doi.org/10.1177/1474885109349404.

Laborde, Cécile, and Miriam Ronzoni. "What Is a Free State? Republican Internationalism and Globalisation." *Political Studies* 64, no. 2 (June 2016): 279–96. https://doi.org/10.1111/1467-9248.12190.

Lake, Marilyn, and Henry Reynolds. *Drawing the Global Colour Line: White Men's Countries and the International Challenge of Racial Equality.* Cambridge: Cambridge University Press, 2008.

Lakhani, Nina. "'A Continuation of Colonialism': Indigenous Activists Say Their Voices Are Missing at Cop26." *The Guardian*, November 3, 2021. https://www.theguardian.com/environment/2021/nov/02/cop26-indigenous-activists-climate-crisis.

Lal, Priya. *African Socialism in Postcolonial Tanzania: Between the Village and the World.* Cambridge: Cambridge University Press, 2015.

Lancaster, Carol, and Nicolas van de Walle. *The Oxford Handbook of the Politics of Development.* Oxford: Oxford University Press, 2018.

Langan, Mark. *Neo-Colonialism and the Poverty of "Development" in Africa.* New York: Springer, 2017.

Lawrence, Adria K. *Imperial Rule and the Politics of Nationalism: Anti-Colonial Protest in the French Empire.* Cambridge: Cambridge University Press, 2013.

Lee, Sheryl, and Jinshan Hong. "China Is Stifling Its Own Movie Business." Bloomberg, July 10, 2019. https://www.bloomberg.com/news/articles/2019-07-10/china-s-movie-business-is-taking-a-hit-from-its-own-government.

Legum, B. "Defining Investment and Investor: Who Is Entitled to Claim?" *Arbitration International* 22, no. 4 (December 2006): 521–26. https://doi.org/10.1093/arbitration/22.4.521.

Lemberg, Diana. *Barriers Down: How American Power and Free-Flow Policies Shaped Global Media*. New York: Columbia University Press, 2019.

Lenin, V. I. *Imperialism: The Highest Stage of Capitalism*. Chicago: Pluto Press, 1996.

Lewis, David, Dennis Rodgers, and Michael Woolcock. "The Project of Development: Cinematic Representation as An(Other) Source of Authoritative Knowledge?" Policy Research Working Paper 6491. World Bank, 2013. https://documents1.worldbank.org/curated/en/199351468158997763/pdf/WPS6491.pdf.

Lim, Désirée. *Immigration and Social Equality: The Ethics of Skill-Selective Immigration Policy*. Oxford: Oxford University Press, 2023.

Little, Adrian, and Kate Macdonald. "Pathways to Global Democracy? Escaping the Statist Imaginary." *Review of International Studies* 39, no. 4 (October 2013): 789–813. https://doi.org/10.1017/S0260210512000551.

Liverpool, Layal. "Researchers from Global South Under-Represented in Development Research." *Nature*, September 17, 2021. https://doi.org/10.1038/d41586-021-02549-9.

Lou, Ethan. "TransCanada's $15 Billion U.S. Keystone XL NAFTA Suit Suspended." Reuters, February 28, 2017. https://www.reuters.com/article/business/transcanadas-15-billion-us-keystone-xl-nafta-suit-suspended-idUSKBN1671W0/.

Louro, Michele L. *Comrades against Imperialism: Nehru, India, and Interwar Internationalism*. Cambridge: Cambridge University Press, 2018.

Louro, Michele L., Carolien Stolte, Heather Streets-Salter, and Sana Tannoury-Karam. *The League Against Imperialism: Lives and Afterlives*. Amsterdam: Amsterdam University Press, 2020.

Low, D. A. *The Egalitarian Movement: Asia and Africa, 1950–1980*. Cambridge: Cambridge University Press, 1996.

Lu, Catherine. "Decolonizing Borders, Self-Determination, and Global Justice." In *Empire, Race and Global Justice*, edited by Duncan Bell, 251–72. Cambridge: Cambridge University Press, 2019.

———. *Justice and Reconciliation in World Politics*. Cambridge: Cambridge University Press, 2017.

Lukes, Steven. *Power: A Radical View*. London: Bloomsbury Academic, 2021.

Lustgarten, Abrahm. "Barbados Resists Climate Colonialism in an Effort to Survive the Costs of Global Warming." ProPublica, July 27, 2022. https://www.propublica.org/article/mia-mottley-barbados-imf-climate-change.

Mabana, Kahiudi C. "Léopold Sédar Senghor and the Civilization of the Universal." *Diogenes* 59, no. 3–4 (2012): 4–12. https://doi.org/10.1177/0392192113493741.

MacBride, Sean. *Many Voices, One World*. New York: UNESCO, 1984.

Macdonald, Terry. *Global Stakeholder Democracy: Power and Representation beyond Liberal States*. Oxford: Oxford University Press, 2008.

Macdonald, Terry, and Kate Macdonald. "Non-Electoral Accountability in Global Politics: Strengthening Democratic Control within the Global Garment Industry." *European Journal of International Law* 17, no. 1 (February 2006): 89–119. https://doi.org/10.1093/ejil/chi160.

Mahoney, James, and Diana Rodriguez-Franco. "Dependency Theory." In *The Oxford Handbook of the Politics of Development*, edited by Carol Lancaster and Nicolas van de Walle, 23–49. Oxford: Oxford University Press, 2018.

Mamdani, Mahmood. *Citizen and Subject: Contemporary Africa and the Legacy of Late Colonialism*. Princeton, NJ: Princeton University Press, 2018.

Mani, Lata. "Cultural Theory, Colonial Texts: Reading Eyewitness Accounts of Widow Burning." In *Cultural Studies*, edited by Lawrence Grossberg, Cary Nelson, and Paula Treichler, 392–404. New York: Routledge, 2013.

Mantena, Karuna. *Alibis of Empire: Henry Maine and the Ends of Liberal Imperialism*. Princeton, NJ: Princeton University Press, 2010.

———. "Popular Sovereignty and Anti-Colonialism." In *Popular Sovereignty in Historical Perspective*, edited by Richard Bourke and Quentin Skinner, 297–319. Cambridge: Cambridge University Press, 2016.

Marsi, Federica. "Analysis: Can the ICC Deliver Justice in Afghanistan?" *Al Jazeera*, November 4, 2021. https://www.aljazeera.com/news/2021/11/4/analysis-can-the-icc-deliver-justice-in-afghanistan.

Martínez-Torres, María Elena, and Peter M. Rosset. "La Vía Campesina: The Birth and Evolution of a Transnational Social Movement." *Journal of Peasant Studies* 37, no. 1 (January 2010): 149–75. https://doi.org/10.1080/03066150903498804.

Marwah, Inder S. "Contingency, History, Agency: On *Empire, Race and Global Justice*." *Cambridge Review of International Affairs* 34, no. 6 (November 2021): 840–45. https://doi.org/10.1080/09557571.2021.1994302.

Mastro, Dana. "Why the Media's Role in Issues of Race and Ethnicity Should Be in the Spotlight." *Journal of Social Issues* 71, no. 1 (2015): 1–16. https://doi.org/10.1111/josi.12093.

Matthes, Erich Hatala. "Cultural Appropriation and Oppression." *Philosophical Studies: An International Journal for Philosophy in the Analytic Tradition* 176, no. 4 (2019): 1003–13.

Mazower, Mark. *Governing the World: The History of an Idea*. London: Penguin UK, 2012.

———. *No Enchanted Palace: The End of Empire and the Ideological Origins of the United Nations*. Princeton, NJ: Princeton University Press, 2013.

Meeran, Richard. "Access to Remedy: The United Kingdom Experience of Multinational Corporation Tort Litigation for Human Rights Violations." In *Human Rights Obligations of Business: Beyond the Corporate Responsibility to Respect?*, edited by Surya Deva and David Bilchitz, 378–402. Cambridge: Cambridge University Press, 2013.

———. "Multinational Human Rights Litigation in the UK: A Retrospective." *Business and Human Rights Journal* 6, no. 2 (June 2021): 255–69. https://doi.org/10.1017/bhj.2021.15.

Melamed, Jodi. "Racial Capitalism." *Critical Ethnic Studies* 1, no. 1 (2015): 76–85. https://doi.org/10.5749/jcritethnstud.1.1.0076.

Metz, Steven. "In Lieu of Orthodoxy: The Socialist Theories of Nkrumah and Nyerere." *Journal of Modern African Studies* 20, no. 3 (September 1982): 377–92. https://doi.org/10.1017/S0022278X00056883.

Mgbeoji, Ikechi. *Global Biopiracy: Patents, Plants, and Indigenous Knowledge*. Ithaca, NY: UBC Press, 2007.

Mignolo, Walter. "Coloniality Is Far from Over, and So Must Be Decoloniality." *Afterall: A Journal of Art, Context and Enquiry* 43 (March 2017): 38–45. https://doi.org/10.1086/692552.

———. *The Darker Side of Western Modernity: Global Futures, Decolonial Options*. Durham, NC: Duke University Press, 2011.

Milanovic, Branko. *Global Inequality: A New Approach for the Age of Globalization*. Cambridge, MA: Harvard University Press, 2016.

Miles, Kate. *The Origins of International Investment Law: Empire, Environment and the Safeguarding of Capital*. Cambridge: Cambridge University Press, 2013.

Miller, David. "Against Global Democracy." In *After the Nation?: Critical Reflections on Nationalism and Postnationalism*, edited by K. Breen and S. O'Neill, 141–60. Springer, 2010.

———. *National Responsibility and Global Justice*. Oxford: Oxford University Press, 2007.

———. "Neo-Kantian Theories of Self-Determination: A Critique." *Review of International Studies* 42, no. 5 (December 2016): 858–75. https://doi.org/10.1017/S0260210516000115.

———. *On Nationality*. Oxford: Clarendon Press, 1995.

———. *Strangers in Our Midst: The Political Philosophy of Immigration*. Cambridge, MA: Harvard University Press, 2016.

Miller, Richard W. "Global Institutional Reform and Global Social Movements: From False Promise to Realistic Hope Symposium: Global Justice: Poverty, Human Rights, and Responsibilities: Panel 1: Human Rights and Global Responsibilities." *Cornell International Law Journal* 39, no. 3 (2006): 501–14.

Mills, Charles. *Black Rights/White Wrongs: The Critique of Racial Liberalism.* Oxford: Oxford University Press, 2017.

———. "Race and Global Justice." In *Empire, Race and Global Justice*, edited by Duncan Bell, 94–119. Cambridge: Cambridge University Press, 2019.

———. "Revisionist Ontologies: Theorizing White Supremacy." *Social and Economic Studies* 43, no. 3 (1994): 105–34.

Milner, Helen V. "Introduction: The Global Economy, FDI, and the Regime for Investment." *World Politics* 66, no. 1 (January 2014): 1–11. https://doi.org/10.1017/S0043887113000300.

Mirrlees, Tanner. *Hearts and Mines: The US Empire's Culture Industry.* Ithaca, NY: UBC Press, 2016.

Montes, Manuel F. "The Impact of Foreign Investor Protections on Domestic Inequality." In *International Policy Rules and Inequality: Implications for Global Economic Governance*, edited by José Antonio Ocampo, 82–111. New York: Columbia University Press, 2019.

Mora, Adolfo R., and Seok Kang. "English-Language Latino Themed Programming and Social Identity: The Relationship between Viewing and Self-Esteem among Latina/Os." *Howard Journal of Communications* 27, no. 1 (January 2016): 16–37. https://doi.org/10.1080/10646175.2015.1080635.

Morefield, Jeanne. "Challenging Liberal Belief: Edward Said and the Critical Practice of History." In *Empire, Race and Global Justice*, edited by Duncan Bell, 184–210. Cambridge: Cambridge University Press, 2019.

Morosini, Fabio, and Michelle Ratton Sanchez Badin, eds. *Reconceptualizing International Investment Law from the Global South.* Cambridge: Cambridge University Press, 2017.

Morris, Rosalind, ed. *Can the Subaltern Speak?: Reflections on the History of an Idea.* New York: Columbia University Press, 2010.

Moyn, Samuel. *Not Enough: Human Rights in an Unequal World.* Cambridge, MA: Harvard University Press, 2018.

Mutua, Makau. "What Is TWAIL?" *Proceedings of the ASIL Annual Meeting* 94 (January 2000): 31–38. https://doi.org/10.1017/S0272503700054896.

Nagel, Thomas. "The Problem of Global Justice." *Philosophy & Public Affairs* 33, no. 2 (2005): 113–47. https://doi.org/10.1111/j.1088-4963.2005.00027.x.

Nanda, Bal Ram. *Jawaharlal Nehru: Rebel and Statesman.* Oxford: Oxford University Press, 1995.

Nandy, Ashis. *The Intimate Enemy: Loss and Recovery of Self under Colonialism.* Oxford: Oxford University Press, 2009.

Narayan, Uma. "Essence of Culture and a Sense of History: A Feminist Critique of Cultural Essentialism." *Hypatia* 13, no. 2 (1998): 86–106. https://doi.org/10.1111/j.1527-2001.1998.tb01227.x.

Narlikar, Amrita. "Collective Agency, Systemic Consequences: Bargaining Coalitions in the WTO." In *The Oxford Handbook on The World Trade Organization*, edited by Amrita Narlikar, Martin Daunton, and Robert M. Stern, 184–200. Oxford: Oxford University Press, 2012.

———. "Who Makes the Rules? The Politics of Developing Country Participation and Influence in the WTO." In *Making the International: Economic Interdependence and Political Order*, edited by Simon Bromley, Maureen Mackintosh, and William Arthur Brown, 75–80. London: Pluto, 2004.

———. *The World Trade Organization: A Very Short Introduction.* Oxford: Oxford University Press, 2005.

Nath, Rekha. "Equal Standing in the Global Community." *The Monist* 94, no. 4 (2011): 593–614.

―――. "On the Scope and Grounds of Social Equality." In *Social Equality: On What It Means to Be Equals*, edited by Carina Fourie, Fabian Schuppert, and Ivo Wallimann-Helmer, 186–208. Oxford: Oxford University Press, 2014.

National Museum of the American Indian. "Treaties Still Matter: The Dakota Access Pipeline" Accessed October 9, 2024. http://nmai.si.edu/nk360/plains-treaties/dapl.cshtml.

Nehru, Jawaharlal. "A Foreign Policy for India." In *Selected Works of Jawaharlal Nehru: Second Series*, 2:348–64. Jawaharlal Nehru Memorial Fund, 1984.

―――. "A Real Commonwealth." In *The Essential Writings of Jawaharlal Nehru*, 219. Oxford: Oxford University Press, 2003.

―――. "A United Asia." In *The Essential Writings of Jawaharlal Nehru*, 229–32. Oxford: Oxford University Press, 2003.

―――. "A World Government Must Come Sometime or Other." In *Documents on Political Thought in Modern India*, edited by Angadipuram Appadorai, 812–13. Oxford: Oxford University Press, 1976.

―――. "Colonialism Must Go." In *The Essential Writings of Jawaharlal Nehru*, 222–24. Oxford: Oxford University Press, 2003.

―――. "Ends and Means." In *The Essential Writings of Jawaharlal Nehru*, 428–29. Oxford: Oxford University Press, 2003.

―――. "Exclusion of Some Countries from the UN." In *The Essential Writings of Jawaharlal Nehru*, 263. Oxford: Oxford University Press, 2003.

―――. *Glimpses of World History*. Penguin Random House India Private Limited, 2004.

―――. "Message for the UN Radio Department Broadcast in a UN Programme." In *The Essential Writings of Jawaharlal Nehru*, 265. Oxford: Oxford University Press, 2003.

―――. "Report on Brussels Congress." In *Selected Works of Jawaharlal Nehru: Second Series*. Vol. 2. Jawaharlal Nehru Memorial Fund, 1984.

―――. *The Discovery of India*. New Delhi: Penguin Books India, 2004.

―――. *The Essential Writings of Jawaharlal Nehru*. Oxford: Oxford University Press, 2003.

―――. "The Root Causes of Wars." In *Documents on Political Thought in Modern India*, edited by Angadipuram Appadorai, 728–29. Oxford: Oxford University Press, 1976.

―――. "World Union and Collective Security." In *Documents on Political Thought in Modern India*, edited by Angadipuram Appadorai, 806–9. Oxford: Oxford University Press, 1976.

Nelson, Todd D., ed. *Handbook of Prejudice, Stereotyping, and Discrimination*. New York London: Psychology Press, 2016.

Nichols, Robert. "Indigenous Peoples, Settler Colonialism, and Global Justice in Anglo-America." In *Empire, Race and Global Justice*, edited by Duncan Bell, 228–50. Cambridge: Cambridge University Press, 2019.

―――. "Theft Is Property! The Recursive Logic of Dispossession." *Political Theory* 46, no. 1 (February 2018): 3–28. https://doi.org/10.1177/0090591717701709.

Nkrumah, Kwame. *Africa Must Unite*. International Publishers, 1970.

―――. *I Speak of Freedom*. 1961.

―――. *Neo-Colonialism: The Last Stage of Imperialism*. Panaf, 2009.

―――. "On the Motion for Independence." In *Pan-Africanism Or Communism*, by George Padmore, 386–87. New York: Doubleday, 1971.

―――. *Revolutionary Path*. International Publishers, 1973.

Nordenstreng, Kaarle. "The New World Information and Communication Order: An Idea That Refuses to Die." In *The International Encyclopedia of Media Studies: Media History and the Foundations of Media Studies*, edited by Angharad N. Valdivia, John C. Nerone, Vicki Mayer, Sharon R. Mazzarella, Radhika E. Parameswaran, Erica Scharrer, Fabienne Darling-Wolf, and Kelly Gates. Hoboken, NJ: Wiley-Blackwell, 2013.

Nuti, Alasia. *Injustice and the Reproduction of History: Structural Inequalities, Gender and Redress*. Cambridge: Cambridge University Press, 2019.

The Observer. "How Drug Giants Let Millions Die of Aids." December 18, 1999. https://www
.theguardian.com/uk/1999/dec/19/theobserver.uknews6.

Ocampo, José Antonio. *International Policy Rules and Inequality: Implications for Global Economic Governance*. New York: Columbia University Press, 2019.

Olson, Kristi A. "Autarky as a Moral Baseline." *Canadian Journal of Philosophy* 44, no. 2 (2014): 264–85.

Omang, Joanne. "UNESCO Withdrawal Announced." *Washington Post*, December 20, 1984. https://www.washingtonpost.com/archive/politics/1984/12/20/unesco-withdrawal -announced/b9c6dc92-a31f-443a-977b-f3468faf44fe/.

Organization of African Unity. "OAU Charter." N.d. https://au.int/sites/default/files/treaties /7759-file-oau_charter_1963.pdf.

Oxfam Policy & Practice. "Dumping without Borders: How US Agricultural Policies Are De- stroying the Livelihoods of Mexican Corn Farmers." October 9, 2024. https://policy -practice.oxfam.org/resources/dumping-without-borders-how-us-agricultural-policies-are -destroying-the-livelih-114471/.

Packenham, Robert A. *The Dependency Movement: Scholarship and Politics in Development Stud- ies*. Cambridge, MA: Harvard University Press, 1992.

Padmore, George. *Pan-Africanism Or Communism*. New York: Doubleday, 1971.

Pahuja, Sundhya. "Corporations, Universalism, and the Domestication of Race in International Law." In *Empire, Race and Global Justice*, edited by Duncan Bell, 74–93. Cambridge: Cam- bridge University Press, 2019.

Pain, Elisabeth. "French Institute Agrees to Share Patent Benefits after Biopiracy Accusations." *Science*, February 10, 2016. https://www.science.org/content/article/french-institute-agrees -share-patent-benefits-after-biopiracy-accusations.

Parc, Jimmyn. "The Effects of Protection in Cultural Industries: The Case of the Korean Film Policies." *International Journal of Cultural Policy* 23, no. 5 (September 2017): 618–33. https:// doi.org/10.1080/10286632.2015.1116526.

Parliament of the Republic of South Africa. "The Expropriation Bill [B23–2020]." Accessed October 9, 2024. https://www.parliament.gov.za/project-event-details/1670.

Patel, Raj. "Food Sovereignty." *Journal of Peasant Studies* 36, no. 3 (July 2009): 663–706. https:// doi.org/10.1080/03066150903143079.

Patten, Alan. *Equal Recognition: The Moral Foundations of Minority Rights*. Princeton, NJ: Prince- ton University Press, 2016.

———. "Should We Stop Thinking about Poverty in Terms of Helping the Poor?" *Ethics & International Affairs* 19, no. 1 (March 2005): 19–27. https://doi.org/10.1111/j.1747-7093.2005 .tb00486.x.

Perrone, Nicolás M. "The ISDS Reform Process: The Missing Development Agenda." *Investment Policy Brief* 19 (March 2020): 1–5.

———. "UNCTAD's World Investment Reports 1991–2015: 25 Years of Narratives Justifying and Balancing Foreign Investor Rights." *Journal of World Investment & Trade* 19, no. 1 (2018): 7–40.

Petras, James, and Henry Veltmeyer. *Multinationals on Trial: Foreign Investment Matters*. New York: Routledge, 2016.

Pettit, Philip. *Republicanism: A Theory of Freedom and Government*. Oxford: Clarendon Press, 1997.

Philips, Anne. "Global Justice: Another Modernization Theory?" In *Empire, Race and Global Justice*, edited by Duncan Bell, 145–62. Cambridge: Cambridge University Press, 2019.

———. *Unconditional Equals*. Princeton, NJ: Princeton University Press, 2021.

Pitts, Jennifer. "Political Theory of Empire and Imperialism." *Annual Review of Political Science* 13, no. 13, 2010 (June 2010): 211–35. https://doi.org/10.1146/annurev.polisci.051508.214538.

Plamenatz, John. *On Alien Rule and Self-Government*. London: Longmans, 1960.

Porterfield, Matthew C. "Reforming the International Investment Regime through a Framework Convention on Investment and Sustainable Development." New York: Columbia Center on Sustainable Investment, October 2020.

Posey, Darrell Addison, and Graham Dutfield. *Beyond Intellectual Property: Toward Traditional Resource Rights for Indigenous Peoples and Local Communities*. Ottawa: International Development Research Centre (IDRC), 1996.

Poulsen, Lauge N. Skovgaard. "Bounded Rationality and the Diffusion of Modern Investment Treaties." *International Studies Quarterly* 58, no. 1 (March 2014): 1–14. https://doi.org/10.1111/isqu.12051.

Poulsen, Lauge N. Skovgaard, and Emma Aisbett. "When the Claim Hits: Bilateral Investment Treaties and Bounded Rational Learning." *World Politics* 65, no. 2 (April 2013): 273–313. https://doi.org/10.1017/S0043887113000063.

Prada, Paulo. "Bolivia Nationalizes the Oil and Gas Sector." *New York Times*, May 2, 2006. https://www.nytimes.com/2006/05/02/world/americas/02bolivia.html.

Prakash, Gyan. *After Colonialism: Imperial Histories and Postcolonial Displacements*. Princeton, NJ: Princeton University Press, 1995.

Prashad, Vijay. *The Darker Nations: A People's History of the Third World*. New York: New Press, 2007.

Puig, Sergio, and Gregory Shaffer. "Imperfect Alternatives: Institutional Choice and the Reform of Investment Law." *American Journal of International Law* 112, no. 3 (July 2018): 361–409. https://doi.org/10.1017/ajil.2018.70.

Quijano, Aníbal. "Coloniality of Power and Eurocentrism in Latin America." *International Sociology* 15, no. 2 (June 2000): 215–32. https://doi.org/10.1177/0268580900015002005.

Rafanelli, Lucia M. "Not Just War by Other Means: Cross-border Engagement as Political Struggle." *Constellations* (October 2023). https://doi.org/10.1111/1467-8675.12719.

———. "Political Craft as Moral Innovation." *Philosophy and Global Affairs* 4, no. 1 (August 2024): 189–94. https://doi.org/10.5840/pga2024416.

———. *Promoting Justice across Borders: The Ethics of Reform Intervention*. Oxford: Oxford University Press, 2021.

Ramasubramanian, Srividya, Marissa Joanna Doshi, and Muniba Saleem. "Mainstream Versus Ethnic Media: How They Shape Ethnic Pride and Self-Esteem among Ethnic Minority Audiences." *International Journal of Communication* 11 (2017): 21.

Ramgotra, Manjeet. "India's Republican Moment." In *The Indian Constituent Assembly: Deliberations on Democracy*, edited by Udit Bhatia, 196–221. UK: Taylor & Francis, 2017.

Randall, Vicky. "Using and Abusing the Concept of the Third World: Geopolitics and the Comparative Political Study of Development and Underdevelopment." *Third World Quarterly* 25, no. 1 (February 2004): 41–53. https://doi.org/10.1080/0143659042000185327.

Rawls, John. *A Theory of Justice*. Cambridge, MA: Harvard University Press, 2009.

———. *The Law of Peoples: With "The Idea of Public Reason Revisited."* Cambridge, MA: Harvard University Press, 1999.

Risse, Mathias, and Gabriel Wollner. "Critical Notice of Aaron James, Fairness in Practice: A Social Contract for a Global Economy." *Canadian Journal of Philosophy* 43, no. 3 (January 2013): 382–401. https://doi.org/10.1080/00455091.2013.847351.

———. *On Trade Justice: A Philosophical Plea for a New Global Deal*. Oxford: Oxford University Press, 2019.

Robbins, Bruce, Paulo Lemos Horta, and Kwame Anthony Appiah, eds. *Cosmopolitanisms*. New York: NYU Press, 2017.

Robinson, Andrew, and Simon Tormey. "Resisting 'Global Justice': Disrupting the Colonial Emancipatory Logic of the West." In *Social Justice, Global Dynamics: Theoretical and*

Empirical Perspectives, edited by Ayelet Banai, Miriam Ronzoni, and Christian Schemmel, 61–74. New York: Routledge, 2011.

Rodney, Walter. *How Europe Underdeveloped Africa*. Brooklyn, NY: Verso, 2018.

Rodrik, Dani. *The Globalization Paradox: Why Global Markets, States, and Democracy Can't Coexist*. Oxford: Oxford University Press, 2012.

Ronzoni, Miriam. "Republicanism and Global Institutions: Three Desiderata in Tension." *Social Philosophy and Policy* 34, no. 1 (July 2017): 186–208. https://doi.org/10.1017/S0265052517000097.

Rosenthal, A. M. "Nehru Denounces West's Alliances; Calls Them Threat to Peace—Cites Matters on Which US and India Differ." *New York Times*, March 21, 1956. https://www.nytimes.com/1956/03/21/archives/nehru-denounces-wests-alliances-calls-them-threat-to-peace-cites.html.

Ross, Tara. "Media and Stereotypes." In *The Palgrave Handbook of Ethnicity*, edited by Steven Ratuva, 1–17. Singapore: Springer Singapore, 2019.

Saha, Anamik. "'Beards, Scarves, Halal Meat, Terrorists, Forced Marriage': Television Industries and the Production of 'Race.'" *Media, Culture & Society* 34, no. 4 (May 2012): 424–38. https://doi.org/10.1177/0163443711436356.

Said, Edward W. *Culture and Imperialism*. New York: Random House, 2014.

———. *Orientalism*. London: Penguin Books, 2019.

Santos, Boaventura de Sousa. *The End of the Cognitive Empire: The Coming of Age of Epistemologies of the South*. Durham, NC: Duke University Press, 2018.

Sanyal, Kali. "Applying GST to Digital Products and Services Imported by Customers." Parliament of Australia, 2017. https://www.aph.gov.au/About_Parliament/Parliamentary_Departments/Parliamentary_Library/pubs/rp/BudgetReview201516/Digital.

Scanlon, T. M. *What We Owe to Each Other*. Cambridge, MA: Harvard University Press, 2000.

———. *Why Does Inequality Matter?* Oxford: Oxford University Press, 2018.

Scheffler, Samuel. "The Practice of Equality." In *Social Equality: On What It Means to Be Equals*, edited by Carina Fourie, Fabian Schuppert, and Ivo Wallimann-Helmer, 21–44. Oxford: Oxford University Press, 2014.

Schiller, Herbert I. *Mass Communications and American Empire*. Boulder, CO: Westview Press, 1992.

Schlichtmann, Klaus. "India and the Quest for an Effective United Nations." *Peace Research* 35, no. 2 (November 2003): 27–49.

Scott, David. *Conscripts of Modernity: The Tragedy of Colonial Enlightenment*. Durham, NC: Duke University Press, 2004.

Scott, James, Erin Norma Hannah, and Amy Janzwood. "What Kind of Civil Society? The Changing Complexion of Public Engagement at the WTO." *Journal of World Trade* 52, no. 1 (February 2018): 113–41. https://doi.org/10.54648/TRAD2018006.

Sell, Susan K. "TRIPS Was Never Enough: Vertical Forum Shifting, FTAS, ACTA, and TPP." *Journal of Intellectual Property Law* 18, no. 2 (2011 2010): 447–78.

Senghor, Léopold Sédar. *African Socialism: A Report to the Constitutive Congress of the Party of African Federation*. American Society of African Culture, 1959.

Sessions, Jennifer E. *By Sword and Plow: France and the Conquest of Algeria*. Ithaca, NY: Cornell University Press, 2017.

Sharma, Shefali. "WTO Decision Making: A Broken Process." WTO Cancun Series Paper, no. 4. Institute for Agriculture and Trade Policy. 2003.

Shelby, Tommie. "Ideology, Racism, and Critical Social Theory." *Philosophical Forum* 34, no. 2 (2003): 153–88. https://doi.org/10.1111/1467-9191.00132.

Shilliam, Robbie. *International Relations and Non-Western Thought: Imperialism, Colonialism and Investigations of Global Modernity*. London: Routledge, 2010.

Simarro, Ricardo Molero, and María José Paz Antolín. "Development Strategy of the MAS in Bolivia: Characterization and an Early Assessment." *Development and Change* 43, no. 2 (2012): 531–56. https://doi.org/10.1111/j.1467-7660.2012.01766.x.

Simmons, Beth A. "Bargaining over BITs, Arbitrating Awards: The Regime for Protection and Promotion of International Investment." *World Politics* 66, no. 1 (January 2014): 12–46. https://doi.org/10.1017/S0043887113000312.

Simpson, Thomas W. "Freedom and Trust: A Rejoinder to Lovett and Pettit." *Philosophy and Public Affairs* 47, no. 4 (2019): 412–24.

Slobodian, Quinn. *Globalists: The End of Empire and the Birth of Neoliberalism*. Cambridge, MA: Harvard University Press, 2020.

Smallwood, Stephanie E. *Saltwater Slavery: A Middle Passage from Africa to American Diaspora*. Cambridge, MA: Harvard University Press, 2009.

Song, Sarah. "The Boundary Problem in Democratic Theory: Why the Demos Should Be Bounded by the State." *International Theory* 4, no. 1 (2012): 39–68.

Sornarajah, Muthucumaraswamy. "The Battle Continues: Rebuilding Empire through Internationalization of State Contracts." In *The Battle for International Law: South-North Perspectives on the Decolonization Era*, edited by Jochen von Bernstorff and Philipp Dann, 175–77. Oxford: Oxford University Press, 2019.

———. *The International Law on Foreign Investment*. Cambridge: Cambridge University Press, 2017.

———. *Resistance and Change in the International Law on Foreign Investment*. Cambridge: Cambridge University Press, 2015.

South African Government. "Broad-Based Black Economic Empowerment Act 53 of 2003: South African Government." https://www.gov.za/documents/broad-based-black-economic-empowerment-act.

Sparks, Colin. "Media and Cultural Imperialism Reconsidered." *Chinese Journal of Communication* 5, no. 3 (September 2012): 281–99. https://doi.org/10.1080/17544750.2012.701417.

Starr, Amory, María Elena Martínez-Torres, and Peter Rosset. "Participatory Democracy in Action: Practices of the Zapatistas and the Movimento Sem Terra." *Latin American Perspectives* 38, no. 1 (January 2011): 102–19. https://doi.org/10.1177/0094582X10384214.

Steinberg, Richard H. "In the Shadow of Law or Power? Consensus-Based Bargaining and Outcomes in the GATT/WTO." *International Organization* 56, no. 2 (2002): 339–74. https://doi.org/10.1162/002081802320005504.

Stiglitz, Joseph. *Globalization and Its Discontents*. London: Penguin UK, 2015.

Stilz, Anna. "Decolonization and Self-Determination." *Social Philosophy and Policy* 32, no. 1 (2015): 1–24. https://doi.org/10.1017/S0265052515000059.

Sultan, Nazmul. *Waiting for the People: The Idea of Democracy in Indian Anticolonial Thought*. Cambridge, MA: Harvard University Press, 2024.

Táíwò, Olúfẹ́mi. *Against Decolonisation: Taking African Agency Seriously*. London: Hurst Publishers, 2022.

Táíwò, Olúfẹ́mi O. "'Being-in-the-Room Privilege': Elite Capture and Epistemic Deference." *The Philosopher*, November 20, 2021. https://www.thephilosopher1923.org/post/being-in-the-room-privilege-elite-capture-and-epistemic-deference.

———. *Reconsidering Reparations*. Oxford: Oxford University Press, 2022.

Tallberg, Jonas, Lisa M. Dellmuth, Hans Agné, and Andreas Duit. "NGO Influence in International Organizations: Information, Access and Exchange." *British Journal of Political Science* 48, no. 1 (January 2018): 213–38. https://doi.org/10.1017/S000712341500037X.

Tan, Kok-Chor. *Justice without Borders: Cosmopolitanism, Nationalism, and Patriotism*. Cambridge: Cambridge University Press, 2004.

Tarrow, Sidney. *The New Transnational Activism*. Cambridge: Cambridge University Press, 2005.

Técnicas Medioambientales Tecmed, S. A v. Mexico. Accessed via British Institute of International and Comparative Law. https://www.biicl.org/files/3917_2003_tecmed_v_mexico.pdf.

Temin, David. *Remapping Sovereignty: Decolonization and Self-Determination in North American Indigenous Political Thought*. Chicago: University of Chicago Press, 2023.

Thakur, Vineet. "An Asian Drama: The Asian Relations Conference, 1947." *International History Review* 41, no. 3 (May 2019): 673–95. https://doi.org/10.1080/07075332.2018.1434809.

Thussu, Daya Kishan. "Mapping Global Media Flow and Contra-Flow." In *International Communication: Continuity and Change*, edited by Daya Kishan Thussu, 221–38. London: Bloomsbury Academic, 2010.

Tilley, Helen. "Traditional Medicine Goes Global: Pan-African Precedents, Cultural Decolonization, and Cold War Rights/Properties." *Osiris* 36 (2021). https://doi.org/10.1086/714329.

Tomlinson, John. *Cultural Imperialism: A Critical Introduction*. London: A&C Black, 2001.

Tully, James. *Public Philosophy in a New Key: Imperialism and Civic Freedom*. Vol. 2. Cambridge: Cambridge University Press, 2008.

———. "'Two Concepts of Liberty' in Context." In *Isaiah Berlin and the Politics of Freedom: "Two Concepts of Liberty" 50 Years Later*, edited by Bruce Baum and Robert Nichols, 23–68. London: Routledge, 2013.

Tunstall, Jeremy. *The Media Are American: Anglo-American Media in the World*. London: Constable, 1994.

UN Conference on Trade and Development (UNCTD). "Commodity Dependence Worsens For Developing Countries." UN Trade and Development, October 13, 2017. https://unctad.org/press-material/commodity-dependence-worsens-developing-countries.

———. "Fact Sheet on Investor-State Dispute Settlement Cases in 2018." 2019. https://unctad.org/system/files/official-document/diaepcbinf2019d4_en.pdf.

UN Department of Social and Economic Affairs (UNDESA). "United Nations Declaration on the Rights of Indigenous Peoples." https://social.desa.un.org/issues/indigenous-peoples/united-nations-declaration-on-the-rights-of-indigenous-peoples.

UN Development Program (UNDP). "Towards Human Resilience: Sustaining MDG Progress in an Age of Economic Uncertainty." https://www.undp.org/publications/towards-human-resilience-sustaining-mdg-progress-age-economic-uncertainty.

UN Educational, Scientific, and Cultural Organization (UNESCO). "Declaration on Fundamental Principles Concerning the Contribution of the Mass Media to Strengthening Peace and International Understanding, to the Promotion of Human Rights and to Countering Racialism, Apartheid and Incitement to War." November 28, 1978. https://www.unesco.org/en/legal-affairs/declaration-fundamental-principles-concerning-contribution-mass-media-strengthening-peace-and.

———. "The Globalisation of Cultural Trade: A Shift in Consumption." 2013. https://uis.unesco.org/sites/default/files/documents/the-globalisation-of-cultural-trade-a-shift-in-consumption-international-flows-of-cultural-goods-services-2004-2013-en_0.pdf.

———. "International Flows of Selected Cultural Goods and Services, 1994–2003." 2005. https://uis.unesco.org/sites/default/files/documents/international-flows-of-selected-cultural-goods-and-services-1994-2003-en_1.pdf.

———. "Records of the General Conference, 21st Session, Belgrade, 23 September to 28 October 1980." Accessed August 2, 2022. https://doi.org/10.58337/OILN3726.

———. "Reshaping Cultural Policies: Advancing Creativity for Development." 2018. https://uis.unesco.org/sites/default/files/documents/reshaping-cultural-policies-2018-en.pdf.

———. "Reshaping Policies for Creativity: Addressing Culture as a Global Public Good." August 2, 2022. https://doi.org/10.58337/OILN3726.

UN General Assembly. "Permanent Sovereignty over Natural Resources, General Assembly Resolution 1803 (XVII)." Accessed via Audiovisual Library of International Law, October 9, 2024. https://legal.un.org/avl/ha/ga_1803/ga_1803.html.

US News and World Report. "Cultural Influence." Accessed October 10, 2024. https://www
.usnews.com/news/best-countries/rankings/influence.

Valdez, Inés. "Association, Reciprocity, and Emancipation: A Transnational Account of the
Politics of Global Justice." In *Empire, Race and Global Justice,* edited by Duncan Bell, 120–44.
Cambridge: Cambridge University Press, 2019.

———. *Transnational Cosmopolitanism: Kant, Du Bois, and Justice as a Political Craft.* Cambridge: Cambridge University Press, 2019.

Valentini, Laura. *Justice in a Globalized World: A Normative Framework.* Oxford: Oxford University Press, 2011.

———. "No Global Demos, No Global Democracy? A Systematization and Critique." *Perspectives on Politics* 12, no. 4 (December 2014): 789–807. https://doi.org/10.1017/S15375927
14002138.

Van Harten, Gus. "Investment Treaty Arbitration: Procedural Fairness, and the Rule of Law."
In *International Investment Law and Comparative Public Law,* edited by Stephan W. Schill,
627–58. Oxford: Oxford University Press, 2010.

———. "Who Has Benefited Financially from Investment Treaty Arbitration? An Evaluation
of the Size and Wealth of Claimants." In *Osgood Legal Studies Research Paper Series* 135 (2016).
https://digitalcommons.osgoode.yorku.ca/cgi/viewcontent.cgi?article=1136&context
=olsrps.

Vanhonnaeker, Lukas. *Intellectual Property Rights as Foreign Direct Investments: From Collision to
Collaboration.* UK: Edward Elgar Publishing, 2015.

Vincent, Richard C. "Justice and Communication: Looking beyond WSIS." In *Towards Equity
in Global Communication: MacBride Update,* edited by Richard C. Vincent, Kaarle Nordenstreng, and Michael Traber. New York: Hampton Press, 1999.

Voon, Tania. *Cultural Products and the World Trade Organization.* Cambridge: Cambridge University Press, 2007.

Vrousalis, Nicholas. "The Capitalist Cage: Structural Domination and Collective Agency in the
Market." *Journal of Applied Philosophy* 38, no. 1 (2021): 40–54. https://doi.org/10.1111/japp
.12414.

Waldron, Jeremy. "Minority Cultures and the Cosmopolitan Alternative." *University of Michigan
Journal of Law Reform* 25, nos. 3/4 (1992/1991): 751–94.

Walzer, Michael. "The Moral Standing of States: A Response to Four Critics." *Philosophy &
Public Affairs* 9, no. 3 (1980): 209–29.

Wasko, Janet. "Can Hollywood Still Rule the World?" In *Cultural Politics in a Global Age: Uncertainty, Solidarity and Innovation,* edited by Henrietta L. Moore, David Held, and Kevin
Young. Ipswich, MA: Ebsco Publishing, 2007.

Watene, Krushil. "Transforming Global Justice Theorizing: Indigenous Philosophies." In *The
Oxford Handbook of Global Justice,* edited by Thom Brooks, 163–80. Oxford: Oxford University Press, 2023.

Westad, Odd Arne. *The Global Cold War: Third World Interventions and the Making of Our Times.*
Cambridge: Cambridge University Press, 2005.

Westerman, Frank. *Engineers of the Soul: In the Footsteps of Stalin's Writers.* New York: Random
House, 2011.

Weston, Burns H. "The Charter of Economic Rights and Duties of States and the Deprivation
of Foreign-Owned Wealth." *American Journal of International Law* 75, no. 3 (July 1981):
437–75. https://doi.org/10.2307/2200684.

White, Robert A. "The New Order and the Third World." In *The Global Media Debate: Its Rise,
Fall and Renewal,* edited by Hamid Mowlana, Kaarle Nordenstreng, and George Gerbner,
21–34. London: Bloomsbury Academic, 1993.

Wiedenbrüg, Anahí. "What Citizens Owe: Two Grounds for Challenging Debt Repayment."
Journal of Political Philosophy 26, no. 3 (2018): 368–87. https://doi.org/10.1111/jopp.12163.

Wilder, Gary. *Freedom Time: Negritude, Decolonization, and the Future of the World*. Durham, NC: Duke University Press, 2015.

———. *The French Imperial Nation-State: Negritude and Colonial Humanism between the Two World Wars*. Chicago: University of Chicago Press, 2020.

Wilkinson, Rorden. *The WTO: Crisis and the Governance of Global Trade*. London: Routledge, 2013.

Williams, Eric. *Capitalism and Slavery*. New York: Penguin Books, Limited, 2022.

Wills, Vanessa. "'And He Ate Jim Crow': Racist Ideology as False Consciousness." In *The Movement for Black Lives: Philosophical Perspectives*, edited by Brandon Hogan, Michael Cholbi, Alex Madva, and Benjamin S. Yost, 35–58. Oxford: Oxford University Press, 2021.

Wilson, James Lindley. *Democratic Equality*. Princeton, NJ: Princeton University Press, 2019.

Wilson, Kalpana. *Race, Racism and Development: Interrogating History, Discourse and Practice*. London: Zed Books, 2012.

Wittman, Hannah. "Reconnecting Agriculture and the Environment: Food Sovereignty and the Agrarian Basis of Ecological Citizenship." In *Food Sovereignty: Reconnecting Food, Nature and Community*, edited by Annette Aurélie Desmarais, Nettie Wiebe, and Hannah Wittman, 91–105. Oxford: Pambazuka Press, 2011.

Wolff, Jonathan. "Social Equality and Social Inequality." In *Social Equality: On What It Means to Be Equals*, edited by Carina Fourie, Fabian Schuppert, and Ivo Wallimann-Helmer, 209–26. Oxford: Oxford University Press, 2014.

Wollner, Gabriel. "The Third Wave of Theorizing Global Justice. A Review Essay." *Global Justice: Theory Practice Rhetoric* 6 (2013). https://doi.org/10.21248/gjn.6.0.37.

Wong, Vincent. "Racial Capitalism with Chinese Characteristics: Analyzing the Political Economy of Racialized Dispossession and Exploitation in Xinjiang." *African Journal of International Economic Law* 3 (2022): 7–39.

World Trade Organization. "Groups in the Negotiations." April 12, 2021. https://www.wto.org/english/tratop_e/dda_e/negotiating_groups_e.htm.

Wright, Richard. *The Color Curtain: A Report on the Bandung Conference*. Jackson: University Press of Mississippi, 1995.

Young, Iris Marion. "Gender as Seriality: Thinking about Women as a Social Collective." *Signs: Journal of Women in Culture and Society* 19, no. 3 (April 1994): 713–38. https://doi.org/10.1086/494918.

———. *Inclusion and Democracy*. Oxford: Oxford University Press, 2002.

———. *Justice and the Politics of Difference*. Princeton, NJ: Princeton University Press, 2022.

———. "Responsibility and Global Labor Justice." *Journal of Political Philosophy* 12, no. 4 (2004): 365–88. https://doi.org/10.1111/j.1467-9760.2004.00205.x.

Ypi, Lea. *Global Justice and Avant-Garde Political Agency*. Oxford: Oxford University Press, 2012.

———. "What's Wrong with Colonialism." *Philosophy & Public Affairs* 41, no. 2 (2013): 158–91. https://doi.org/10.1111/papa.12014.

Zachariah, Benjamin. *Nehru*. London: Routledge, 2004.

Zedong, Mao. *Collected Writings of Chairman Mao: Guerrilla Warfare*. Vol. 2. El Paso, TX: El Paso Norte Press, 2009.

INDEX

Abs, Hermann Joseph, 101
Africa Must Unite (Nkrumah), 34, 90
African Group, 184
African socialism, 93–95. *See also* Nkrumah, Kwame
Alcoff, Linda, 65
All-African People's Conference, 90
All India Trade Union Congress, 165
Anderson, Elizabeth, 24, 64
anticolonial thought: characterization of colonialism in, 37–38; on decolonization, 17, 44–50; on economic sovereignty, 86; egalitarianism and, 29, 33–34, 207n21, 209n109; inequality and, 29–33; moral discourse and, 13–14; nationalism and, 20–22, 29–33, 40–44; on national sovereignty, 39–44; nation-state and, 19; neocolonialism and, 31; status and, 32–33. *See also* Césaire, Aimé; Fanon, Frantz; Nehru, Jawaharlal; Nkrumah, Kwame
Appiah, Kwame Anthony, 124
"Aquaculture for Local Community" (ALCOM), 76
Archibugi, Daniele, 174
Asian Relations Conference, 170, 232n91
asymmetric dependence, 66–67, 90, 110. *See also* global social equality
Azikiwe, Nnamdi, 21

Badin, Michelle, 108
Bandung Conference, 170
Beitz, Charles, 3, 73, 235n166
Bell, Duncan, 5
Belt and Road Initiative, 199
Berlin, Isaiah, 20, 32–33
Bhargava, Rajeev, 124
Black Economic Empowerment Act, 85, 113, 116
Black Skin, White Masks (Fanon), 54–55

Bose, Subhas Chandra, 167
Brownstein, Michael, 140
Buchanan, Allen, 177
Byrd, Jodi, 19

Calvo doctrine, 102
capital flight, 118–19
capitalism, 99, 106
Césaire, Aimé: as an anticolonial thinker, 22–24, 29; on colonial capitalism, 35; cultural inferiority complex and, 37; on cultural production, 8, 130–33, 150, 195, 224n59; on culture and colonialism, 39, 127–30, 140–41, 152–56, 215n100; definition of culture, 126–27; on economic reforms, 41; inferiority complex and, 8; on nationalism, 43; on normative theory, 17; on social agency, 15, 78; on universal humanism, 148. *See also* anticolonial thought
Chapman, Jessica, 32
Charter of the Economic Rights and Duties of States (CERD), 87
Chimni, B. S., 7, 203n47
Churchill, Winston, 167
Cold War, 20–21, 32, 170–71
collective action: colonialism and, 39; global governance and, 44–45; political collective, 40
colonialism: alienation and, 37, 128; culture and, 127–30; examples of economic impact, 85; inequalities that characterize, 34–37, 54; inferiority complex as a result of, 129–30; political and economic reform attempts within, 40–41; shared identity and, 37, 39–40. *See also* anticolonial thought; collective action; egalitarianism
commodity dependence, 106–7

Convention on the Protection and
Promotion of the Diversity of Cultural
Expression, 145–46
Convention People's Party, 41, 87
Cooper, Frederick, 21
cosmopolitan democracy, 174, 178–79.
See also global governance
cosmopolitan solidarity, 159–60, 181. See also
solidarity
Coulthard, Glen, 8, 129
counterhegemonic legal entrepreneurship, 118
Crewe, Emma, 76
Cripps, Francis, 102
Cross, Ciaran, 101
Cultural Congress of Havana 1967, 131
cultural globalization: asymmetric culture
flows and, 122–23, 134–38, 143–45, 228n131,
228n137; conclusions about, 155–57;
creative agency and, 147–51, 228n141,
229n146, 229n149, 229n159; glocalization
of, 138–39, 226n112; imperialism and,
122–23; social agency and, 146. See also
cultural protectionism
cultural imperialism: cultural globalization
and, 122–23; liberalism and, 5; problems
with, 127–30, 224n47; social agency and,
138–41, 197–98
cultural pluralism, 159, 163
cultural protectionism, 134, 151–55, 229n154
culture: appropriation of, 137, 149; cultural
diversity within colonized countries,
37–39; cultural goods definition, 127,
224n33; cultural inferiority, 37; cultural
production, 37, 140–41, 153; decolonization and, 46–47; definition of, 126–27;
intellectual property regime, 149–50;
objectionable cultural representations,
142–43; oppressed groups as cultural
producers, 136–37; shared identity, 159.
See also cultural globalization; race
"Culture and Colonialism" (Césaire), 39,
127, 215n100

Dahl, Robert, 159
Declaration on the Rights of Peasants
(UNHCR), 187
decolonization: conclusions about, 196–97;
cultural, 123–24, 223n23; of cultural
globalization, 145–47, 229n160; cultural
production and, 130–33; democratization

and, 44; economic decolonization, 45–46,
210n134; global governance and, 44–45;
internationalism and, 48–50; nationalism
and, 20–22, 31, 48–50, 196–97, 206n11;
relations and, 54–55; social agency and,
124–25; sociocultural, 46–47; Third
World, 49; unrealized goals of, 50–51.
See also egalitarianism
de Gaulle, Charles, 63
democratic deficit, 159
dependency theory, 88, 95–97, 136,
217n20
Desmarais, Annette A., 188
Discourse on Colonialism (Césaire), 35,
39, 141
Discovery of India (Nehru), 37–38, 43, 48,
162–63, 169
discursive power, 183
Doha Development Round, 184
Dryzek, John, 183
Duong, Kevin, 15

egalitarianism: anticolonial thought and, 29,
33–34; decolonization and, 28, 44–50,
209n109; economic policies, 104–7, 113;
social egalitarian relations, 60–61. See also
equality
Emerson, Rupert, 30, 74
equality: distributive, 53, 55, 211n13; epistemic,
75–76; relational, 53, 55–56, 211n3, 211n13,
212n19–20; social, 56–65, 100, 213n34–35.
See also global social equality; hierarchies;
inequality

Fanon, Frantz: as an anticolonial thinker,
22–24, 29; on collective action, 39–40,
83–84, 208n77, 208n82; on colonialism, 8,
16, 54; on colonial racial hierarchies, 42,
63, 82, 208n52; on cultural inferiority, 129;
on decolonization, 44, 54–55, 210n136,
225n68, 225n70; on economic decolonization, 45–46; internationalism and,
49; Marxism and, 33; on nationalism,
42–43; on political equality, 71; on social
equality, 57–58, 61. See also anticolonial
thought
food sovereignty, 187–88
"A Foreign Policy for India" (Nehru), 166
Foresti, 85
Forrester, Katrina, 5

Gandhi, Indira, 142
Gandhi, Leela, 10
Gandhi, Mahatma, 22–23, 129, 168, 188
General Agreement on Tariffs and Trade
    (GATT), 172
General Assembly, 66
Getachew, Adom, 18, 21, 37, 124, 138
global communication: censorship, 153,
    229n154; global digital platform market,
    135; inequities in film industry, 135–36,
    226n99; initiatives to democratize, 121–22
global democracy: alternate proposals from
    critics of, 176–79; conclusions drawn
    about, 192–93; criticism of, 174–76,
    233n123; global democratic theory and,
    193; institutional reform and, 184–86;
    organized groups to disrupt the global
    economy for, 186; proponents of, 174;
    transnational architecture for, 186.
    See also global governance
global governance: case of contesting
    political inequality in, 186–89; cosmo-
    politan democracy, 178–79; counterhege-
    monic power and, 182–86, 188–89, 234n149,
    234n152; decolonization through coun-
    terhegemonic political empowerment,
    181–82; democratic deficit within, 173–75;
    democratizing, 178, 184–86; intellectual
    property law and, 179–80; regime-shifting
    and, 179–80; transnational social move-
    ments and, 186–92; undemocratic global
    trade governance, 172–73. See also global
    democracy
global justice: conclusions about, 194–200;
    future of, 198–200; liberalism and, 5;
    postcolonial perspective of, 10–12; rela-
    tional focus and, 56–57; social equality
    and, 24–28, 64–65; theories on cultural
    globalization, 123; theory about, 3–8;
    unrealized goals of decolonization,
    50–51. See also equality; global social
    equality
global social equality: capitalism and, 106;
    conclusions drawn about, 194–95; defense
    of global justice as, 24–28; empowerment
    and, 65, 213n58; equalizing global political
    power, 70–72, 214n75; equalizing global
    standing, 81–82, 216n107; equal recogni-
    tion of social agency, 77–78, 215n98–101;
    global hierarchies of esteem, 72–77,

215n84–85; global hierarchies of political
    power, 65–70, 214n63–64; global hierar-
    chies of standing, 79–81; theories about,
    211n1. See also asymmetric dependence;
    global justice; hierarchies; legal
    empowerment
Gold Coast Legislative Assembly, 42
Gorz, André, 23

Harrison, Elizabeth, 76
Held, David, 134
hierarchies: definition of, 61; of esteem,
    62–63; global hierarchies of esteem, 72–78;
    global hierarchies of political power,
    65–72; global hierarchies of standing,
    79–82; global level, 64–66, 89–90; of
    moral standing, 63; policies that prevent
    state, 106; power/authority, 61–62; status
    and, 63–64. See also equality; global social
    equality; inequality; power
historical agency, 77
Hitler, Adolph, 166
Hoover, Herbert, 169
Hopewell, Kristin, 189
Hussain, Waheed, 60

Independence for India League, 165
Indian National Congress, 161, 164, 171
individualism, 14–16
inequality: anticolonial thought and,
    29, 40–44; within colonialism, 54; in
    cultural production and dissemination,
    137–38; domestic, 109; global political,
    176–78; kinds of, 25. See also culture;
    equality; hierarchies; race
intellectual property regime, 149–50.
    See also culture
Inter-American Association of the
    Press, 122
International Congress of Black Writers and
    Artists, 130
International Criminal Court, 176, 233n130
international investment regime: bilateralism
    and, 102–3; connections between neoco-
    lonialism and, 101–2, 119–20, 219n83–84;
    egalitarian policies and the, 107–9,
    220n121–22, 221n131; investor-state
    arbitration and, 104, 219n102; neocolonial-
    ism and the, 111, 221n141; reforms needed
    to, 113–17, 221n145; regime-shifting,

international investment regime (*continued*) 117–19; strong investor protections and, 103, 219n100; vagueness of treaty provisions within, 103, 109–10

internationalism: decolonization and, 48–50; Fanon's view of, 49; nationalism and, 159–60, 167–68; Nehru's vision of, 27, 45, 48–49, 165–71

International Monetary Fund (IMF), 66, 108, 111

International Program for the Development of Communication (IPDC), 121–22, 147

Jaeggi, Rahel, 128

Jeans: A Cultural History of an American Icon (Sullivan), 78

Keohane, Robert, 177

Keystone XL Pipeline, 108

Khader, Serene, 17, 20, 204n82

Kim, Joseph, 151

Kohler, Pierre, 102

Kolodny, Niko, 25, 61, 64

Kwon, Seung-Ho, 151

Laborde, Cécile, 6, 55

laissez-faire capitalism, 94

La Via Campesina, 186–89, 191, 235n186

League Against Imperialism, 161–62, 164–66, 186

League of Nations, 161, 163–64, 169

Least Developed Countries (LDCs), 184

legal empowerment, 114–17

Louro, Michele, 21, 160, 170

Lu, Catherine, 19

Lukes, Steven, 61, 183

Lumumba, Patrice, 32, 206n14

MacBride, Sean, 121

Macdonald, Kate, 183

Macdonald, Terry, 183, 191

"Man of Culture and His Responsibilities" (Césaire), 47

Mantena, Karuna, 31, 37, 124, 138, 150

Many Voices, One World (UNESCO), 121, 222n3, 222n5

Marant, Isabel, 137

"Mass Media Declaration" (UNESCO), 121–22

McGrew, Anthony, 134

"Medicine and Colonialism" (Fanon), 57

Metz, Steven, 23, 94

Miller, David, 4, 64, 72, 159, 176, 201n13, 233n123

Mills, Charles, 5–6, 8, 14

Mirrlees, Tanner, 135

modernization theory, 74

Morales, Evo, 85

Morefield, Jeanne, 17

Morosini, Fabio, 108

Motion Pictures Association of America, 136

Moyn, Samuel, 14

Nardal, Paulette, 132

Narlikar, Amrita, 184–85

National Herald, 163

nationalism: anticolonial thinkers and, 20–22, 29–33, 40–44; Césaire on, 43; decolonization and, 20–22, 31, 48–50, 196–97, 206n11; definition of, 205n2; Fanon on, 42–43; in India, 164; internationalism and, 159–60, 167–68; limitations of, 42–44; Nehru on, 43; Nkrumah on, 30–31; in response to inequality, 32; Third World and, 101, 161

nationality, 68–69

Nature, 135

Nazism, 166

Negritude movement, 130, 132

Nehru, Jawaharlal: as an anticolonial thinker, 21–24, 29; on cultural diversity within colonized India, 37–38; on decolonization, 44; on economic inequality of colonialism, 35; on economic reforms in India, 40–41; efforts to promote transnational solidarity, 164–65, 186; global democracy and, 158–60, 171, 181–82, 192, 195–96, 232n100; on global political domination, 69; on Indian princes, 34–35; internationalism and, 27, 45, 48, 165–71; military alliances and, 182–83; on nationalism, 43; on political equality in India, 40; on power asymmetries, 176; on racial hierarchies, 36; socialism and, 161–63, 171. *See also* anticolonial thought

Nehru, Motilal, 165

neocolonialism: agents of, 91–93; anticolonial thought and, 31; cosmopolitans and, 4–5; debt traps as, 111; definition of, 7;

international intellectual property law as, 112; Nkrumah on, 87–88, 90–99; social equality and, 100; socialism in conflict with, 94–95; solutions to, 98–99; structural adjustment loans as, 111. *See also* international investment regime; Nkrumah, Kwame

Neocolonialism (Nkrumah), 32, 90, 96

New International Economic Order (NIEO), 14, 87, 121, 142

New World Information and Communication Order (NWICO), 121–22, 146–47, 223n11

Ngũgĩ wa Thiong'o, 145

Nichols, Robert, 19

Nkrumah, Kwame: African socialism and, 93–95, 106, 218n47; as an anticolonial thinker, 21–24, 29; on asymmetric dependence, 66, 110; capitalism and, 106; on colonial political rule, 34; on economic inequality of colonialism, 36, 45–46, 210n119; on films, 120; nationalism and, 30–31; *Neocolonialism*, 32, 90, 96; neocolonialism and, 18, 26, 87–88, 90–99, 114, 119–20, 195; on postcolonialism, 86; on racial inferiority, 36–37; on self-government, 41–44, 209n115. *See also* anticolonial thought; neocolonialism

Non-Aligned Movement, 122, 170

non-governmental organization (NGO), 173, 176

normative theory: individualism *vs.* collectivism within, 14–16; moral philosophy and, 13; universalism *vs.* particularism within, 16–20

Not Enough (Moyn), 14

On African Socialism (Senghor), 93

Organization for African Unity Charter, 90

Orientalism (Said), 142

Pahuja, Sundhya, 17

Pandit, Vijaya Lakshmi, 158

Patten, Alan, 126

Permanent Sovereignty over Natural Resources, 86

Pitts, Jennifer, 5

Plamenatz, John, 31

postcolonial perspective, 11–12

Poulsen, Lauge, 110

power: counterhegemonic, 182, 184–86, 188–89; discursive, 183; global political power, 182–83. *See also* global governance; hierarchies

Prakash, Gyan, 11

Prashad, Vijay, 170

Protection of Investment Bill, 113

race: global justice theory and, 5–7; hierarchy of esteem and, 62–63; ideology of racial hierarchy as a colonial structural inequality, 36–37, 46–47, 208n52; racial inferiority, 8, 129–30, 140–41; racist ideology, 140, 142–45, 205n104, 227n19, 227n122–23, 227n126, 227n128; self-government as a response to inequality in, 41–44; social equality and, 58–59; social identities and, 68–69. *See also* culture

Ramgotra, Manjeet, 39

Rawls, John, 3–4, 73, 220n119

Reagan, Ronald, 122

reciprocity, 58

respect, 58

Revue du monde noir (Nardal), 132

Rodney, Walter, 56

Ronzoni, Miriam, 6, 55

Rostow, Walt, 74

Rothberg, Michael, 19

Saha, Anamik, 142

Said, Edward, 130, 132, 142

Saul, Jennifer, 140

Scanlon, Thomas M., 25, 72, 75, 79, 205n101, 212n32, 216n103

Schliemann-Radbruch, Christian, 101

Senghor, Léopold Sédar, 15, 46, 93–94, 130

Shelby, Tommie, 139–40

skin whitening, 144

Smuts, Jan, 158

social agency: cultural imperialism and, 138–41; decolonizing cultural globalization and, 124–25, 144–47, 149–57, 195–98; global social equality and, 77–78, 226–27n113

solidarity: definition of, 212n33; global democracy and, 27, 159–60; hierarchies and, 63; social egalitarian relations and, 61; social equality and, 58–59; transnational, 164–67, 170–71, 181–82, 185–86

Song, Sarah, 176–77, 179
Sornarajah, Muthucumaraswamy, 102, 114
Southeast Asia Treaty Organization
  (SEATO), 169–70
sovereignty, 41–44
state-centric reforms, 113–14
Steinberg, Richard H., 172
structural domination, 99
Sullivan, James, 78

Tagore, Rabindranath, 163
Táíwò, Olúfẹ́mi, 2, 124
Táíwò, Olúfẹ́mi O., 7
Third World: anticolonial thought, 18–20,
  124; asymmetric dependence and, 71,
  95–97; Bandung conference and the, 170;
  decolonization, 49; nationalism and, 101,
  161; neocolonialism and, 87
Third World Approaches to International
  Law (TWAIL), 7, 9, 101
Trade-Related Aspects of Intellectual
  Property Rights (TRIPS), 112, 173, 180,
  184, 188
"Two Concepts of Liberty" (Berlin), 32

United International Pictures, 136
United Nations Educational, Scientific, and
  Cultural Organization (UNESCO), 121,
  135, 145, 148
United Nations Food and Agriculture
  Organization (FAO), 76
United Nations General Assembly, 158
United Nations General Assembly
  Resolution 1803, 86

United Nations Security Council, 66, 176
United Nations Trade and Development
  (UNCTAD), 106
universalism, 16–20

Valdez, Inés, 21, 165, 203n46
Valentini, Laura, 5, 55
Vrousalis, Nicholas, 99

Waldron, Jeremy, 134
"What's the Point of Equality?," 24
whitewashing, 137, 149
Wilder, Gary, 18, 203n70
Wills, Vanessa, 144, 146
Wilson, James, 64
World Health Organization (WHO), 144
worldmaking, 7, 202n34
World Trade Organization (WTO): culture
  under international law by, 148; decision-
  making power of, 66; example of contesting political inequality of, 187–89;
  global communication and, 122; global
  governance and, 172–73; hierarchies of
  standing and, 79, 216n106; interstate
  coalitions and, 184; regime-shifting
  and, 180
World War II, 166–68
The Wretched of the Earth (Fanon), 44, 49,
  54–55
Wright, Richard, 170

Xi Jinping, 199

Ypi, Lea, 6, 207n22